PUBLIC POLICY ANALY

Peter Knoepfel, Corinne Larrue, Frédéric Michael Hill

First published in Great Britain in 2007 by

The Policy Press
University of Bristol
Fourth Floor
Beacon House
Queen's Road
Bristol BS8 1QU
UK

Tel +44 (0)117 331 4054
Fax +44 (0)117 331 4093
e-mail tpp-info@bristol.ac.uk
www.policypress.co.uk

North American office:
The Policy Press
c/o International Specialized Books Services (ISBS)
920 NE 58th Avenue, Suite 300
Portland, OR 97213-3786, USA
Tel +1 503 287 3093
Fax +1 503 280 8832
e-mail info@isbs.com

© Peter Knoepfel, Corinne Larrue, Frédéric Varone and Michael Hill 2007

Transferred to Digital Print 2010

British Library Cataloguing in Publication Data
A catalogue record for this book is available from the British Library.

Library of Congress Cataloging-in-Publication Data
A catalog record for this book has been requested.

ISBN 978 1 86134 907 1 hardcover

Peter Knoepfel is a professor at the Swiss Graduate School of Public Administration at the University of Lausanne, Corinne Larrue is a professor at the University of Tours, France, Frédéric Varone is a professor at the University of Geneva, Switzerland, and Michael Hill is Emeritus Professor of the University of Newcastle and a visiting professor at Queen Mary, University of London and at the University of Brighton.

The right of Peter Knoepfel, Corinne Larrue, Frédéric Varone and Michael Hill to be identified as the authors of this work has been asserted by them in accordance with the 1988 Copyright, Designs and Patents Act.

All rights reserved: no part of this publication may be reproduced, stored in a retrieval system, or transmitted in any form or by any means, electronic, mechanical, photocopying, recording, or otherwise without the prior permission of The Policy Press.

The statements and opinions contained within this publication are solely those of the editors and contributors and not of The University of Bristol or The Policy Press. The University of Bristol and The Policy Press disclaim responsibility for any injury to persons or property resulting from any material published in this publication.

The Policy Press works to counter discrimination on grounds of gender, race, disability, age and sexuality.

Cover design by Qube Design Associates, Bristol
Printed and bound in Great Britain by Marston Book Services, Oxford

Contents

List of tables and figures		v
Preface to the English edition		vii
Introduction		ix

Part I	**Theoretical framework**	**1**
one	Theoretical perspectives on policy analysis	3

Part II	**Keys to the analysis**	**17**
two	Public policy	21
three	Policy actors	39
four	Policy resources	63
five	Institutional rules	91

Part III	**Analysis model**	**111**
six	Analysis model	113
seven	Political agenda setting	125
eight	Policy programming	151
nine	Policy implementation	187
ten	Evaluating policy effects	221
eleven	Research and working hypotheses	251
twelve	Conclusion	273

References	289

List of tables and figures

Tables

2.1	The different sequences of a public policy	31
2.2	Similarities between the policy cycle and the stages of problem solving	35
5.1	Synopsis of neo-institutionalist schools	93
7.1	The relationships between the structuring of a problem and political strategies	138
7.2	Variables for the political agenda setting of public problems	146
8.1	Actors, resources and institutional rules involved in the decision-making process (programming)	183
9.1	Differences between the 'top-down' and 'bottom-up' visions of policy implementation	196
9.2	Qualification of the products PAP, action plan and formal implementation acts according to the type of legal dimension	199
11.1	Utility of the model on the basis of the level and ambition of the proposed empirical research	252
11.2	Summary of the operational elements for the analysis of the six products of a public policy	254

Figures

1	Key elements of public policy analysis	18
2.1	The different constituent elements of a public policy	30
2.2	The policy cycle	32
2.3	The public policy process and filtering mechanisms	34
3.1	The basic triangle of policy actors	57
4.1	Overview of the different public policy resources	65
5.1	The hierarchy of institutional rules	103
6.1	Policy stages and products (postulate no 1)	114
6.2	The direct and indirect influence of the triangle of actors on the first two stages of a public policy (postulate no 2)	117
6.3	Theoretical model for the analysis of a public policy	120
7.1	Definition process for public problems and possible pitfalls	131
8.1	The constituent elements of a political-administrative programme	154

8.2	Detailed and framework political-administrative systems compared	169
8.3	Political-administrative arrangement – substantive, institutional or mixed	170
8.4	Heterogeneous administrative contexts	180
8.5	Homogeneous administrative contexts	181
9.1	Links needed between political-administrative programme objectives, planning priorities and outputs (scope for implementation deficits)	201
9.2	Actors and substantive results of implementation	213
10.1	Objectives and criteria of evaluation	236
11.1	Direct and indirect games based on the substantive and institutional content of policy products	261
11.2	Causal sequences formalised in the research hypotheses	263
11.3	Possible combinations of variables for the formulation of working hypotheses	266

Preface to the English edition

This book is a manual on public policy analysis; it makes no claim to present a new theory of the state. It is aimed at students and practitioners of public administration. It is based upon a book originally written in French titled *Analyse et pilotage des politiques publiques*.

The manual is structured and written in a way that is comprehensible to readers who may not have an academic background in the social sciences, but introduces and explains key ideas from law, sociology, political science and administrative science. It presents an analytical framework that can be used to carry out empirical studies on different public policies. It can also be used as an aid in the formulation, implementation and/or evaluation of new public policies.

Based on analysis and research carried out by the authors and applied to different domains of public action, this manual presents a model for the analysis of public policy as well as examples of the application of this model in everyday political-administrative situations. The original examples were mostly drawn from Switzerland and France. Most of these have been retained; others have been added from the UK. There is a substantial British literature from which it has only been practical to draw on to a limited extent, using examples that illustrate the model used in the book. For wider material readers could usefully refer to Dorey's *Policy making in Britain* (2005) or to Richards and Smith's *Governance and public policy in the UK* (2002).

France and Switzerland basically represent two extremes in terms of their modes of government: Switzerland is a federal state with direct democratic procedures based on consensus between the political parties while at the same time displaying a high level of linguistic, confessional and regional diversity; and France is a centralised state that is primarily founded on a system of representative democracy, organised on the basis of political bipartisanship and rooted in a shared republican history that aims (for at least the past two centuries) to homogenise local situations in terms of language, mode of political representation and support for one and the same conception of the public interest. The UK is (notwithstanding recent devolution) another centralised state, but with a rather different set of institutions to France.

In referring to these contrasting types of government, we shall illustrate the public policy analysis model presented in this manual and identify both the common elements and specific features of the different modes of public action.

The book was translated by Susan Cox. This translation included the rendering of quotations from other languages into English. It also included the putting back into English of some quotations that had originally been in that language. Checks have been made to try to ensure that they have returned to their original English but it is possible that errors may have crept in.

The English author has confined his changes to the text to the minimum necessary to make it an appropriate book for use by readers from the UK, other English-speaking countries and countries where English is very widely used as a teaching medium. This has particularly involved the introduction of new illustrations and examples, and the deletion of some less appropriate ones. However, most of the original references have been retained, enabling readers able to read French or German to go to key sources in those languages. The book reflects the influence of leading German and French scholars who have made important contributions to the study of the policy process that are not widely recognised among English-speaking scholars.

Some modifications of the original argument in the French edition have been introduced after discussion with the original authors. As is clearly acknowledged in the concluding chapter, this book is based on practical experience in research and teaching in relation to a diverse and changing policy world. Some emerging difficulties with the approach adopted are explored in those conclusions. The development of an edition for use in another country has contributed to some new solutions to those difficulties, particularly the elaboration of the notion of policy target groups to recognise their diversity and complexity.

We are grateful to Verlag Rügger of Zurich for permission to produce an English version of *Analyse et pilotage des politiques publiques*, and to Erika Blank of IDHEAP for her assistance with the compilation of figures and other material. Thanks are due to Philip de Bary, Jo Morton, Emily Watt and Dave Worth at The Policy Press for all their assistance with the preparation of this book, to Dawn Rushen for the copy editing and to Marie Doherty for the typesetting.

Introduction

The recent evolution of western democracies is characterised by the myriad challenges currently facing public sector actors. These include:

- the reduction of budget deficits and structural debt;
- the maintenance of political control over the economy in the face of the increasing influence of globalisation processes;
- the fulfilment of increased public expectations with respect to the levels of services provided;
- the increasing competition between public authorities at local, regional and international level;
- the management of the redistribution conflicts associated with the long-term exclusion of certain social groups;
- the need for the more professional management of (increasingly) scarce public resources;
- the democratic imperative of a systematic evaluation of the effects of laws and regulations;
- the political integration of minorities and the consensual management of the conflicts that result in their opposition to the majority.

Various institutional responses to these problems are currently being tested in the majority of western democratic regimes. Governmental and parliamentary agendas at all levels (local, regional, national and European) currently feature numerous pilot projects involving New Public Management or the reinvention/modernisation of the state, various accompanying processes involving liberalisation, deregulation and privatisation of certain public sectors and companies and alternative proposals for the reform of legislative and executive bodies. In this context of growing uncertainty, political-administrative actors are seeking credible and consensual solutions and, hence also, expertise on the different possible solutions for the modernisation of the political-administrative system and its interventions.

Policy analysis as presented in this manual aims to provide an understanding of, or response to, these basic questions concerning the legitimacy, efficacy and durability of public action.

Characteristics of the proposed method of policy analysis

The proposed method of policy analysis rests on three definitive analytical areas – the interaction between public and private actors, public problems and comparative analysis.

Analysis of the interaction between public and private actors

Policy analysis proposes to interpret the state[1] and, more generally, the political-administrative system using the yardstick of its influence on the economy and society. Without denying or obscuring the power relationships inherent in all political-administrative processes, policy analysis concentrates on existing or emerging administrative organisations and the actual services they provide to the public.

Thus, with the emphasis on the comprehension of the complex workings of public action, the political institutions – previously the focus of research interest – are analysed from the perspective of the constraints and opportunities they offer to policy actors. What is involved, therefore, is the reaching of an understanding of the state 'in action', starting with the public and private actors involved in a particular sector, their resources and the institutions that govern their actions. These three basic elements make it possible to understand collective and individual behaviour and the results they achieve in terms of their influence on civil society and in institutional terms, that is, with respect to the organisation of the political-administrative system.

Thus, the approach presented here attempts to describe and understand the action logic of these (para) state bodies from the perspective of their contributions to the resolution of the defined collective problems. In this sense, it 'sticks' to social, economic and political reality: the starting point for all empirical analysis is, therefore, the daily practice of public administrations and the study of their services that makes it possible to locate the public actors in time and space and to analyse public action in situ. In fact, it is a question of identifying the interfaces between the state (or public actors) and civil society; that is, where the mediation takes place between public actors, whose job it is to defend the long-term public interest, and private actors, who often defend individual short-term interests.

This kind of analysis enables the demystification of the approach, according to which the state, its institutions and its policies are constantly changing entities that should be interpreted on the basis of purely utilitarian ends. In reconstructing the analytical discourse on the state, policy analysis also tries to identify certain recurring phenomena in the interaction between public and private actors.

One of the consequences of the adoption of this pragmatic approach is that policy analysts find themselves being commissioned to carry out expert evaluations of policies by legislative and/or executive bodies. The analytical framework proposed in this book has proved directly applicable for the execution of such mandates.

In view of the increasing inclusion of evaluation clauses in legislation passed in different countries, the demand for practitioners to carry out this kind of work is on the increase. Thus, the approach presented here aims to make a contribution to the training and professional qualification of policy analysts who will be qualified to work as researchers in government departments, universities and private consultancies.

Analysis of public problems

The second definitive area of policy analysis involves the interpretation of structures and bureaucratic procedures from the perspective of the overall management of policies, and not only in terms of their internal coherence and efficiency.

Needless to say, the professional management of public administrations and the resources at their disposal (particularly with respect to personnel, finance and organisation) is essential; the improvement of the intrinsic functioning of the public sector is not, however, an end in itself but one of the prerequisites of quality public service. However, the approach proposed here differs from strictly managerial approaches that treat administrative services as autonomous entities whose products will not be subject to an explicit evaluation from the perspective of their contribution to the resolution of public problems.

By analysing an administrative body from the perspective of its products, their coordination with other public activities (internal coordination and coordination between policies) and their effects on the social groups affected by the problem to be resolved, policy analysis registers all organisational reform from the perspective of an improvement of the efficacy of public action and, by extension, its legitimacy.

In this context, the 'management' of public resources proposed in this book is aimed at the concerted management of the different resources that may be combined to improve the results and effects achieved by policies rather than a 'resource by resource' optimisation (for example, the reduction of costs, modification of personnel status, reduction of deadlines for the production of administrative services).

Comparative analysis

The analysis model presented here has been developed in such a way that it can also be used in comparative studies. The reason for this is that the quality of policies increasingly needs to be considered on the basis of their actual implementation by different public authorities.

The benchmarking principle, which was created as a substitute for the application of market prices for non-market public services, is frequently adopted as a guide in the evaluation of administrative products and policies. This makes it possible to improve the ability to evaluate the efficiency of public administrations offering similar services. Benchmarking also leads to greater transparency with respect to the costs and advantages of public action. Thus, it also gives rise to indirect competition between the different public authorities responsible for the implementation of policies. Both analysts and practitioners should also take into account this recent development in political-administrative practice.

The approach proposed here benefits from a research tradition that is extensive in both synchronic (spatial) and diachronic (temporal) terms. Thus, the analytical framework presented in this book has already been applied on several occasions. These empirical studies have made it possible, inter alia, to identify the main factors behind the success and failure of policies. Furthermore, highlighting differences and similarities with respect to the implementation and effects of one and the same policy by different public authorities makes it possible to guarantee the transfer of knowledge and, indeed, learning processes between public administrations. This improvement in the status of comparative studies proves particularly interesting for federal systems that are, in themselves, veritable 'policy laboratories'.

Research and practical objectives

From a research perspective, policy analysis draws on several of the social science disciplines. Part I of this book presents a general survey of the theoretical basis of this approach and suggests that policy analysis aims to interpret 'politics' and the state in the light of (the results) of its 'policies', and not on the basis of strategic power games. Nevertheless, this analytical model does not lose sight of the institutional structures and processes on which the state bases and supports its democratic legitimacy.

Although it deconstructs the state into multiple tangible policies, which are, in turn, subdivided into several clearly distinct constituent elements (see Part III), the approach used here also presents a view of all of the individualised and sometimes complementary and contradictory actions of the different political-administrative actors. In order to make sense of a multitude of individual and concrete acts, which are dispersed through time and space but concretely observable in reality, the analyst must engage in an interpretive process involving the reconstruction (or designation) of a policy as a group of decisions and activities taken and implemented by private and public actors and aimed at the resolution of a clearly delineated public problem. For the researcher or the practitioner, the objective of this analytical redefinition process is to be able to judge the relevance, efficacy and efficiency of these state interventions with respect to a social situation that is judged as politically problematic and unacceptable. Thus, it is a question of identifying an action logic and discussing its coherence and implementation with the main aim of attributing responsibility to the public and private actors involved in the different state arenas (in particular legislative, executive and judicial bodies; local, regional, national and supranational levels).

Furthermore, policy analysis can also help political actors and public agents in their efforts to estimate the chances of success of modernisation projects undertaken by the state and, more generally, the political-administrative institutions[2].

Through the accumulation of the results of their research and expert mandates, policy analysts are able to demonstrate certain empirical consistencies (or, indeed, laws) specific to the functioning of public authorities and policies. By taking such information into account, political-administrative actors are better placed to judge the level of innovation and scope of various reforms in the course of being implemented (in particular with respect to previous experience with approaches such as the Planning, Programming and Budgeting System [PPBS], management by objectives and zero-base budgeting). This will facilitate the improved management of changes in administrative services and policies that are sometimes perceived as unfolding too quickly. In this sense, the approach proposed in this manual offers a useful framework for the re-examination of certain hypotheses with respect to the inefficacy and shortcomings of the public sector as compared to the private sector. In summary, the ideas presented in this book subscribe to the viewpoint that supports the professionalisation of practitioners who deal with policy; this professionalisation is necessary for the improvement of the art of government and modes of managing public action.

An original analysis model

To conclude this introduction, we need to locate this book in the context of other publications on the subject.

First, this manual is part of the work being carried out by a growing community of researchers working on the subject of policy in many countries. As such, it does not see itself as an academic treatise that will revolutionise the current status of knowledge and concepts in this area, nor does it see itself as providing a simple bibliographical account of the subject; rather it aims to achieve a middle ground between these two extremes that exist in the literature.

Second, our approach may be deemed original for at least five reasons:

- *It concerns analysis with operational objections:* the authors teach undergraduate and postgraduate students who must apply the presented theoretical concepts in their coursework and theses. In view of this, the authors have made a considerable effort to produce an operational analysis of policy. This concern with concrete and operational dimensions is demonstrated in both our teaching practice and in this manual through the use of numerous examples.
- *It is a comparative analysis:* we have refrained from providing a chapter explicitly dedicated to the methods and techniques of comparative analysis in political science as these are very well represented in several specialised textbooks. However, the concepts and analysis dimensions proposed here are based on a comparative rationale. Almost all of them were actually developed in the context of comparative, theoretical or applied national and international research. Thus, the dimensions used in this manual to describe, classify and relate empirical observations and research hypotheses facilitate the comparison of actors, the resources used, the acting institutions and policy products either throughout the different phases of one and the same policy (diachronic analysis) or during the decision-making processes implemented in different zones or countries relating to one or more policies (synchronic analysis).
- *The concrete applications are drawn from countries with particularly diverse systems:* the examples given in the original book were

taken almost exclusively from the French and Swiss contexts. This choice was not solely based on the authors' nationality and place of residence. In effect, in compliance with the typologies currently used in the comparison of systems of government (Lijphart, 1999) and with respect to most of the dimensions explored in this literature, these two countries represent the two extremes of these typologies. This is particularly true with respect to the degree of centralisation (France is one of Europe's most centralised countries and Switzerland is the most decentralised of European federal states), the system of government (in France the semi-presidential system is linked with a parliamentary majority; in Switzerland there is a consensual system whereby the government does not depend on a parliamentary majority, that is, a semi-direct democratic system), cultural and linguistic diversity (France has a relatively homogeneous culture; Switzerland has extremely heterogeneous cultures and languages) and membership of the European Union (France has been a member since the foundation of the European Economic Community [EEC]; Switzerland is a non-member state). Thus, the two countries present extremes among European countries. It is highly likely that the policies adopted in all European countries can be found in some shape or form within these two types. The examples introduced to this edition from the UK come from another very centralised state with much in common with France, but with a parliamentary system increasingly dominated by the executive.

- *The analysis is based on a distinction between the substantive and institutional aspects:* whether at the level of explanatory variables (interplay of actors who operate resources governed by institutional rules), or at the level of the different policy products (ranging from the definition of public problems to the implementation acts and evaluative statements), the approach presented here places greater emphasis on institutional aspects than other textbooks on the same subject. Thus, we explicitly stress the institutional content of political decisions. This desire is reflected in the dedication of an entire chapter to the institutional rules that are considered as a determining factor in terms of actor interplay and in the identification of institutional dimensions in each of the chapters dedicated to the different policy products. The conceptualisation of these rules in terms of analysis dimensions underlines the sometimes major institutional political stakes involved in policies that can be equivalent to the

stakes involved in the substantive content of the decisions taken. Furthermore, this makes it possible to identify more effectively the purely institutional dimensions of the actors' strategies. In reality, these institutional dimensions are frequently characterised (at least in certain phases) by major uncertainties. Thus, they clearly dominate actors' preoccupations.
- *The proposed analysis facilitates policy management:* the model proposed in this book for the empirical analysis of different policies is not merely applicable in the comparative explanation of policy content; it can also facilitate the anticipation of the intermediate results of future policy phases. The proposed public action logic, which is based on the interplay of actors, their resources and the relevant institutional rules, should enable public and private actors to calculate better their strategy and the expected results. Thus, throughout this manual we undertake to provide our readers with milestones in the form of working hypotheses to enable them to improve their co-management of public decision-making processes on the basis of their interests, beliefs and political views. In doing this, we are continuing a venerable North American tradition initiated by Eugène Bardach's (1977) *The implementation game,* by introducing – cautiously and voluntarily – recommendations targeted at public sector decision makers.

This manual is divided into three parts. Part I presents the theoretical framework of policy analysis. It also provides a quick review of the literature from the traditional schools of policy analysis and then presents the specific theoretic framework adopted here.

Part II presents the keys to policy analysis. These focus on the individual and collective behaviour of the actors involved in the different stages of a policy. In this section, we present the theory that the substantive and institutional content of public action (variable to be explained) is the result of interactions between the political-administrative authorities, on the one hand, and the social groups that cause and/or support the negative effects of the collective problem that the public action aims to remedy (explanatory variables), on the other. In themselves, these actors' interactions depend on the resources that they manage to mobilise to defend their positions and also on the constraints and opportunities engendered by the institutional rules in force.

Thus, Part II comprises four major chapters. Chapter Two defines the constituent elements of a policy. Chapter Three defines policy actors. Having explained the implications of the actor concept, we then examine the different types of policy actors: political-administrative actors, social actors, target groups, beneficiaries and so on. Chapter Four tackles the questions of the resources at the disposal of the different types of actors and their management: 10 resources are identified and analysed in this chapter. This is followed by an exploration of their management. Chapter Five deals with the institutional rules behind the decisions and activities of policy actors. The different influences that the institutions exert on policies are also presented. We also identify the different types of institutions involved and this leads to the operationalisation of the institution concept.

The proposed analytical model is presented in Part III of the manual. The constituent elements of policies that are subjected to the analysis are explored. Resuming the analysis in terms of the policy cycle, the processes involved in the adopting of public problems on the agenda, the implementation of these actions and finally the processes involved in policy evaluation are analysed successively. This section is divided into six chapters. Chapter Six presents a general survey of the different policy stages and products and the analysis logic of different policy segments. Chapter Seven presents different phases and questions concerning policy agenda setting. Chapter Eight analyses the process involving policy programming from the perspective of both the constituent elements of a policy programme and that of the actor arrangements involved. Chapter Nine presents the process of policy implementation from both a theoretical and practical perspective. Chapter Ten defines the effects of policies and the ways in which they are evaluated. Chapter Eleven formulates hypotheses that underlie all of the processes involved in policy analysis, irrespective of whether its purpose is explanatory, evaluative or predicative.

Chapter Twelve provides some overall conclusions, including reflections on the strengths and weaknesses of the approach used.

Notes

[1] In this context, the term 'state' refers to all of the public institutions comprising what is referred to as the political-administrative system.

[2] Note that the use of 'political-administrative system' in this text takes into account the complexity of contemporary policy systems that is often described in the English literature as the shift from 'government' to 'governance' (see, for example, Richards and Smith, 2002).

Part I
Theoretical framework

In the first part of the manual, we provide a clear and detailed presentation of the theoretical framework on which our policy analysis model is based.

ONE

Theoretical perspectives on policy analysis

Policy analysis consists in the "study of the action of public authorities within society" (Mény and Thoenig, 1989, p 9). In terms of disciplines, a number of academic sectors have been and are associated with it. It was adopted as early as 1979 by Wildavsky (1979, p 15) in his plea for the development of this approach: "Policy analysis is an applied subfield whose contents cannot be determined by disciplinary boundaries but by whatever appears appropriate to the circumstances of the time and the nature of the problem". Similarly, Muller (1990, p 3) mentions that "policy analysis is located at the junction of previously established knowledge from which it borrows its principal concepts".

We start by presenting a quick review of the literature from the traditional policy analysis schools[1] and then go on to examine the specific theoretical framework adopted in this book.

1.1 Various currents in policy analysis

The main disciplines that can be observed within the different schools define themselves in accordance with the theoretical and normative perspectives, on which the positions of the different authors are based and/or towards which they tend. Thus, after Mény and Thoenig (1989) and Muller (1990, p 3), it is possible to identify three major currents in policy analysis that reflect different aims without, however, being mutually exclusive. These currents differ mainly in terms of their focuses on specific fields of analysis.

Thus, we make distinctions between a first school of thought that associates policy analysis and the theory of state, a second that explains the way in which public action works and, finally, a third that focuses on the evaluation of the results and effects of the latter.

1.1.1 Policy analysis based on the theories of state

For the first group of authors, policy analysis is a means of explaining the actual essence of public action because policies are interpreted as revealing its nature. This current, which the political sciences dominates and lays claim to, in France in particular, attempts to link the policy approach with political philosophy and major questions concerning the theory of state. Thus, Mény and Thoenig (1989) define their approach in terms of a contribution to questions concerning 'the emergence and nature of the state' or to 'the essence of politics'. Similarly, Jobert and Muller locate their work on *The state in action* (*L'etat en action*) in the context of "bridging the gap that today still separates research on policies and the more general reflections on the state in contemporary society" (Jobert and Muller 1987, p 9). It is subdivided into different approaches that Mény and Thoenig (1989, p 67) classify on the basis of three 'theoretical models':

- The first model is part of a *pluralist* approach that conceives the state as a 'service hatch' whose purpose is to respond to social demands. From this perspective, public policies are conceived as responses to social demands and their analysis is in turn located in a perspective based on the optimisation of collective choices, the rationality of the decision-making processes and the behaviour of 'bureaucrats' ('public choice' school[2], theory of limited rationality[3]). According to this concept, the lack of policies in the area of sport, for example, is a reflection of the fact that there is no public problem to be resolved. However, this absence could also be interpreted as the result of corporate or private actions that are aimed at controlling this sector despite the existence of significant public problems (in particular drug use, corruption etc).
- The second interpretative model places the emphasis on the state as an instrument at the service of either a social class (*neo-Marxist* approach[4]) or specific groups (*neo-managerial* approach[5]). In this context, the analysis of public action makes it possible to demonstrate the weak autonomy of the state with respect to capitalist interests and/or with respect to the private actors and organisations of which it consists. Seen in this way, a social problem can only become a public problem if its resolution serves the interests of the (economically) dominant classes. The neo-managerial approach starts from a similar standpoint in that it replaces the class concept with the concept of elites.
- Finally, the third model stresses the distribution of power and interaction among and between actors, either through the representation and organisation of different sector-based or category-based interests (*neo-corporatist*[6] approach), or through the organisations and institutional rules that frame these

interactions (*neo-institutionalist*[7] approach). Seen from the neo-corporatist perspective, public sector employees are for the most part 'captured' by the interest groups ('clients'), with which they maintain privileged and exclusive relationships in the exercising of public power. In the UK a related approach involves emphasis on the roles of policy networks and policy communities[8]. The influence of agricultural interests has been analysed in this way in various countries. In France, this analysis results in the emphasising of the role of large state bodies and their privileged relationships with their colleagues who work in the private sector as a factor that explains the way the central administration works.

In these theoretical models policy analysis is treated as a way of verifying the hypotheses underlying the favoured model. In summary, the main characteristic of the first school is that it does not focus on policies in themselves but as a way of understanding the role of the public sector in society and its evolution in time, which results in the introduction 'of policy' into the empirical analysis of public action and organisations and in the focusing of the analysis on this interface.

The status of the thinking, trends and claims of this school is reflected in French work such as the fourth volume of the *Traité de science politique* (Grawitz and Leca, 1985) and in Mény and Thoenig's (1989) book on policy. More recent and more informal references can be found in the debates organised by the 'policy' group of the French Association of the Political Sciences, whose findings are published in the *Revue Française de Sciences Politiques* (see, in particular, Majone, 1996; Muller et al, 1996). Hill explores the Anglo-American literature of a similar kind in *The public policy process* (2005, chapters 2 to 5).

Our own approach is partly rooted in this perspective, because many of the authors who inspired it belong to this school and also because the work we have done in this area facilitates, in part, a real interpretation of the role of the state in society without making this the primary aim. However, our approach borrows more strongly from the second and third schools.

1.1.2 Explaining how public action functions

The second school aims to explain the way public action works. Thus, in this context, the function of policy analysis is not to explain the general functioning of the political system but to act as a way of understanding the operational modes and logic of public action (see

Dente, 1985, 1989; Dente and Fareri, 1993; Gomà and Subirats, 1998, pp 21-36).

This approach does not exclude the adoption of a viewpoint based on the above-presented theories, which explains why several authors from this second group actually have a foot in both camps. Here, however, the focus is not on the justification of a theory, but on the demonstration of continuities, general rules of functioning that are specific to public actions. In this context, policy analysis makes it possible to understand how the state and, more broadly, public authorities work.

This second approach actually constitutes the initial set of issues tackled by policy analysts. Historically, the latter were strongly influenced by North American political scientists, whose initial considerations in this area emerged between 1950 and 1960 and were linked with a context of the 'rationalisation' of public decision making with a view to improving its efficacy. Lerner and Lasswell published *The policy sciences* in the United States as early as 1951, thereby laying the foundations for this approach.

However, this "unified approach to the study of public problems and policy ... soon settled into two main approaches" (Parsons, 1995, pp 18-19), one that endeavours to develop a better knowledge of the policy formation and implementation processes (the analysis *of* policy), while the other concentrates on developing knowledge that is usable in and for the policy formation and implementation processes (analysis *in* and *for* policy). It should be stressed, however, that the analyses carried out by one school feed into the experiences of the other, and vice versa. Thus, in their critique of this approach, Mény and Thoenig (1989, p 65) make a distinction between the function of the scientist who is interested in the progress of knowledge and learning and that of the professional whose aim is to apply the sciences for the purpose of action.

The second approach adopts its theoretical thrust from several different scientific approaches: administrative science, the sciences of complexity (particularly systems analysis), the sociology of (public) decision making and, more generally, the sociology of collective action, the economic sciences and the information sciences.

The emergence of this approach was dominated by four major figures (Mény and Thoenig, 1989; Parsons, 1995). The first is the North American political scientist Lasswell (1951) who was the movement's main source of inspiration and who adopted a completely 'managerial' approach: his work deliberately attempted to construct a dialogue between social scientific researchers, economic circles and public decision makers so as to improve the efficacy of public action. The second is Simon (1957), whose work on human decision-making processes directed this type of approach towards the analysis of public decision-making processes (using the concept of 'bounded rationality'). Lindblom (1959) also impacted on the development of policy analysis by concentrating the analysis on the limited room for manoeuvre at the disposal of public decision makers (using the concept of 'incrementalism'). Finally, there was Easton (1965), who was one of the first political scientists to apply the science of systems analysis to the policy world as a whole, and who made a significant contribution to the development of the main concepts of contemporary policy analysis.

All of these authors, who belonged to sometimes radically diverging schools of thought, had an impact on the emergence of this approach, and on the definition of the concepts used in this type of analysis and discussed in this book. For them the state is no longer considered as a single actor but as a complex and often heterogeneous *political-administrative system* whose workings need to be understood to enable the formulation of 'predictions' or 'recommendations'. Nevertheless, here again there are several different perspectives.

- Certain authors focused their analyses on the decision-making process and actor strategies. This type of analysis is related on the one hand to the work of *sociologists of public organisations*, whose main representatives in France are Crozier and Friedberg (1977). It is also connected with the application of systems analysis to human decision making in the tradition of the work of Simon (1957), Morin (1977, 1980) and Le Moigne (1990), and with endeavours to engage in *the analysis of systems actors* or concrete action systems. The professional consequence of this approach was the emergence of 'public management' that was promoted, in particular, by the work carried out by the Organisation for Economic Co-operation and Development (OECD). Thus, the OECD's Public Management Service (PUMA) regularly publishes literature on the role of 'managers' in public organisations. This approach is, however, not very sensitive for the analysis of the specific policies implemented by the analysed administrations.
- Other works in this area are based on the tools and instruments of public intervention. Economic approaches and, in particular, research on the *political economy* predominate here. This work analyses the modes of public action in terms of their efficacy

from either a macro-economic point of view (in the tradition of Pareto, and Keynes (1936) and Musgrave (1959) or from a micro-economic point of view (in particular, the approach adopted by the clientele of public services at the centre of what is known as 'New Public Management'[9]).

- Other works again focus on the structures, procedures and institutional forms of public administration. This approach constitutes the essence of the administrative sciences and administrative law. It describes the way *administrative institutions* work and, more generally, studies institutional policies as defined by Quermonne[10]. In France, this approach mainly refers to administrative reforms and, in particular, to the policies for the decentralisation of power. This approach is of little interest for the concrete policies implemented by the administrations studied. However, some of the work that forms part of policy analysis is published in the *Revue Française d'Administration Publique*[11]. In Switzerland, the term 'institutional policies' generally refers to the modes of control employed by the different types of public administration, the questions of representativeness in the composition of ministries (languages, sexes, age, political parties etc), the civil servants' statute, the (in)formal relationships between the federal authorities and the cantons etc. In terms of policy, the work carried out by the political scientist Germann (1996) is closest to these analyses.

- Finally, a specific public policy approach has been emerging for some years now. It is known as the cognitive approach, "which attempts to understand public policies as cognitive and normative matrices constituting systems of interpretation of reality, within which the different public and private actors can register their actions" (Muller and Surel, 1998, p 47). This approach stresses the role of ideas and representations in the formation (and, in particular, the definition of problems subject to public action) and alteration of public policies. The distinctive element of this approach is the emphasis it places on general principles, the argumentation and values that define 'a global vision' that reflects and/or produces the public policy.

In summary, the characteristic feature of this second school is the concern to understand the complexity of the public decision making processes by dividing the object of the analysis into different variables (for example, actor rationality, internal decision-making processes in organisations and so on). This approach was perpetuated, inter alia, in the public management and decision aid methods; however it differs strongly from them in terms of its lack of direct operationalisation.

Our own approach is based on both a scientific *and* operational perspective. As Friedberg (1993, p 22) reminds us, the analyst "now has two interdependent tasks: on the one hand to produce a concrete knowledge of the human reality underlying the context of action analysed and, on the other, to help the interested parties to both position themselves with respect to this knowledge and to draw consequences from it and integrate these into their practices by modifying them".

1.1.3 Evaluation of the effects of public action

The third school of thought tries to explain the results of public action and its effect on society from the viewpoint of the objectives pursued and/or in terms of indirect or undesirable effects. Compared with the previous one, this approach is more evaluative than explanatory. For the past 10 years or so, this approach has become particularly fashionable in France and Switzerland where initiatives, symposiums and publications on policy analysis are thriving[12]. In the UK the related concern has been with 'evidence' for policy[13].

It is possible to identify two main concerns in the context of evaluation:

- The first of these involves the development of a *methodological approach* and an evaluation 'tool box': thus, numerous studies have undertaken to define evaluation methods that can be applied to the non-market activities of the public sector. This work is based on the statistical processing of quantitative data, multi-criteria analysis (Maystre et al, 1994); (quasi) experimental comparison, cost-benefit analysis and so on. Extensive literature has been published on this approach. In France, a presentation of its ideas can be found in Deleau et al (1986) and in the annual publications of the *Conseil Scientifique de l'Évaluation*. It is also evident in the manuals for the evaluation of socio-economic programmes recently published by the European Union with the aim of facilitating the evaluation of programmes associated with European structural funds.
- The second focuses on the *process of evaluation* and its implementation in terms of improving public management and influencing decision making. A significant number of North American and, more recently, European authors have investigated this question, including Rossi and Freeman (1993) for the US,

Monnier (1992) for France and the collective work of Bussmann et al (1998) for Switzerland.

In Switzerland, policy evaluation has become almost a profession: it is practised by academics at the universities, in private consultancies and can also be found within the administrative authorities themselves due to the creation of a parliamentary and governmental evaluation service (*Organe Parlementaire de Contrôle de l'Administration, Service d'Evaluation du Conseil Fédéral*). A professional association (*Société Suisse d'Évaluation*, SEVAL) monitors the quality of evaluations carried out (meta-evaluations that monitor the adherence to quality, use and ethical standards etc).

This trend is equally evident in France. It is associated with the organisation of evaluation mechanisms at national and regional level and with the development of European policies that require the organisation of evaluation exercises during the implementation of European structural funds, for example. A *Société Française de l'Évaluation* was recently created with the aim of rendering this activity more visible and improving its organisation. However, this movement is finding it difficult to become institutionalised as a standard practice in public administration. The disappearance of the interministerial mechanism that was introduced in 1990 is an indication of this, similarly the absence of transparency in the work of the *Office Parlementaire des Choix Scientifiques et Techniques*. However, it is increasingly the subject of analysis by political scientists (Duran and Monnier, 1992; Lascoumes and Setbon, 1996; Kessler et al, 1998). Thus, the French model for the evaluation of public policy appears to be characterised by the weak involvement of the policy actor and a very much reduced use of the results of evaluation in the modification or conception of public policies, despite the interest of actors in policy implementation.

In the UK the work of the Audit Commission and the increasing use of quantitative performance indicators in education, the health service and local government has had a similar impact (Pollitt, 2003; Audit Commission, 2006).

This evaluative approach is generally accompanied by an explanatory approach, even if it may be conceptually dissociated from it. It is an inspiration for our own model in the sense that it is concerned with the effects of public action – effects that are measured on the basis of the collective problem that a policy tries to resolve.

1.2 Policy analysis as a 'science of action'

Rather than fitting perfectly within the framework of one of the above-described schools, our analysis borrows from all three. It is our ambition to establish a diagnostic approach that demonstrates the factors that explain the 'good' and 'bad' functioning of public policies in terms of public administration production and with respect to the efficacy of its policies and their products. This type of analysis ultimately leads to *describing*, *understanding* and *explaining* the workings of the political-administrative system as a whole and its interactions with private actors. Thus, our approach is mainly based on the explanation of the products or services provided by public administration that are traditionally referred to as 'outputs', and on the explanation of the effects produced by these services on social groups ('impacts and outcomes') that cause and/or are affected by a particular collective problem.

To the extent that it aims to understand the 'logic' of public actions by reconstructing the hypotheses on which public authorities (sometimes implicitly) base their thinking for the resolution of public problems, our intellectual reasoning belongs within the framework of the action sciences.

More precisely, the majority of the concepts presented here are derived from the publications of the *Centre de Sociologie des Organisations* (Crozier, 1963, 1991; Crozier and Friedberg, 1977; Friedberg, 1993) as well as the work of the German social and political scientists of the 1970s (that is, the Frankfurt School), who, in turn, were strongly influenced by neo-Marxism (Offe, 1972; Habermas, 1973; Grottian, 1974). However, this influence is limited to the individual heuristic contributions that are particularly well developed by these authors. This enables us to identify the actors, their networks and their modes of interaction. As opposed to the 'systemic forces' often favoured by these authors, in our approach, the retraceable strategies, ideas, interests and actor behaviour essentially depend on factors connected to their resources and their 'institutional framework' and must all be observed empirically. In this sense, our reasoning strongly resembles actor–centred institutionalism as presented by Scharpf (1997).

The concept of public policy adopted here (as well as most of the definitions and terms used in this book) originate in part from the work carried out in Germany by the *Forschungsverbund: Implementation politischer Programme* at the *Deutsche Forschungsgemeinschaft* between 1976 and 1981 under the direction of Mayntz, Scharpf, Kaufmann and Wollmann[14]; one of the authors of this book was associated with this work. It is also based on texts on the implementation of public policy[15].

The approach presented has been particularly strongly influenced by the international comparison of public policies, in particular because the comparative approach leads to the definition of a common analytical frame that is applicable to different countries and institutional regimes and that constitutes the essential aim of our approach.

As discussed in detail in the following chapters, our approach is mainly characterised by the fact that it:

- tackles a policy from the angle of its 'action logic', thus its starting point constitutes the arena of the political-administrative action and social *actors* who interact in a defined sector;
- integrates the influence of *institutions* on the behaviour of these actors and on the substantive results of the public action (while the first generation of policy analysis tended to neglect the institutional variables);
- pays particular attention to the *resources* mobilised by these actors in order to assert their interests (which facilitates the combination of policy analysis and public management).

Finally, our approach, which is essentially based on a retraceable interpretation of empirical data, differs from other contemporary research currents, in particular:

- neo-Weberianism that supposes that bureaucratic actors benefit from the rigidity or at least inertia of certain structures and administrative rules and try above all to obtain secure incomes at the cost of the content of the policies for which they are responsible;
- neo-Marxism which, despite claiming with justification that in addition to its primary democratic legitimacy the state must ensure a secondary legitimacy through the approbation of the 'quality' of its public policies by actors powerful in resources, interprets the latter as acts of domination of one social class or group over the other. The state and its policies are reduced to an instrument of power and repression controlled by the minority of these powerful actors. We, on the other hand, believe that the public actors have a certain margin for manoeuvre in their choices;
- the theories of rational choice ('public choice', 'game theory') that assume that for political parties and bureaucrats the only value that policies have is as currency during electoral calculations and/or in the appropriation of personal advantages (material and

immaterial). Much empirical data shows that this theory is strongly reductionist;
- neo-corporatism and network theory that suggests that the political-administrative apparatus is in the thrall of organised sectoral groups and that, as a result, the state remains unable to develop and implement redistributive interventions for the benefit of non-organised social groups;
- classical pluralism that defends a vision of the 'the state as service hatch' that is attentive to all social claims and demands and whose public policies reflect the priorities for action emerging from all of the members of civil society. However, as experience shows, numerous social problems are never politically acknowledged as being worthy of a public policy;
- simple systematisation that does not grant policy actors the appropriate autonomy and intentionality. The latter's behaviour is simply seen as a function of the role assigned to them by their direct organisational environment. However, social reality is full of examples that demonstrate the importance of actors even when the scope for manoeuvre is theoretically very limited;
- the comparative approach in terms of political systems ('comparative politics'), which is based on the comparison of statistics and structural data about political systems and different public authorities without really analysing the process and more qualitative aspects of the actual content of public policies (Hofferbert, 1974). We believe these dimensions are too unrefined to analyse the substantive policies that interest us;
- the critical approach that refuses to consider any positive or rationalistic approach to policy analysis and concentrates on underlining the power and domination dimensions implicitly associated with concrete public actions (Fischer and Forester, 1993; Fox and Miller, 1995; Fischer, 2003).

In actively refraining from subscribing to one or other of these theoretical concepts of the state, 'society' or any other 'system' (merely touched on here), our approach remains completely open to all of the hypotheses originating from these theories. The analysis model presented in this book aims to remain as neutral as possible with respect to specific theories so as to be able to accommodate – in terms of working hypotheses to be empirically verified – the broadest possible range of theories developed in trends as divergent as neo-Marxism, neo-liberalism and neo-corporatism, on condition that the researchers take the trouble to use the concepts in accordance with the basic dimensions proposed with respect to their empirical field testing.

Notes

[1] This analysis is adopted in part from that presented in the work *Analyser les politiques publiques d'environnement* (Larrue, 2000).

[2] The 'public choice' school is based on the work of Buchanan and Tullock (1962). A critical review of the main principles of this school can be found in Self (1993).

[3] See Simon (1957); Lindblom (1959).

[4] The neo-Marxist approach was mainly developed in the 1970s by urban sociologists like Castells and Godard (1974) and German sociologists, such as Offe (1972) and Habermas (1973).

[5] The neo-managerial approach is based, for example, on the sociology of administrative elites or, more broadly, the sociology of organisations (Crozier and Friedberg, 1977).

[6] For France, see, in particular, the work of Jobert and Muller (1987) and, for Germany, that of Lehmbruch and Schmitter (1982).

[7] See, in particular, the work of March and Olsen (1984) and our own approach (Chapter Five, this volume).

[8] See Jordan and Richardson (1987); Marsh and Rhodes (1992); Smith (1993).

[9] See, in particular, the review of this phenomenon by Emery (1995), Hood (1995), Pollitt and Bouckaert (2000) and Pollitt (2003).

[10] Quermonne defines institutional policies as policies whose main object is "the production, transformation or decline of public or private institutions" (Quermonne, 1985, p 62); see also Germann (1996, pp 5-6).

[11] See Chevallier's reflections (1981).

[12] Since 1983, policy evaluation has developed significantly in France, from both an institutional and scientific perspective, for example, the article by Duran (1993) and more recently Kessler et al (1998). For Switzerland, refer to the

work of Bussmann et al (1998), which summarises the main message of Swiss National Research Programme no 27 on 'the effects of state measures'.

[13] See Davies et al (2000) and the emergence in 2005 of the journal *Evidence & Policy* (see https://www.policypress.org.uk/journals/evidence_policy/).

[14] See Mayntz (1980, 1983).

[15] Lester et al (1987) present a good synthesis of the implementation analysis models developed in the 1970s and 1980s in the US and in Europe. See also Bohnert and Klitzsch (1980); Parsons (1995); Hill and Hupe (2002).

Part II
Keys to the analysis

In this second section, we present the prerequisites of our policy analysis model. We also define the concepts necessary to our analysis.

More precisely, our approach focuses on the individual and collective behaviour of the actors involved in the different stages of a policy. Thus, we assume that the content and institutional characteristics of a public action (the variable to be explained) are the product of the interaction between the political-administrative authorities, on the one hand, and the social groups that cause and/or support the negative effects of the collective problem that the public action seeks to resolve (explanatory variables), on the other. Apart from respective values and interests, the 'games' these actors play are dependent on the resources they succeed in mobilising so as to defend their positions with respect to the objectives, instruments and development process involved in a public intervention measure. These games can affect equally the substantive content of the public policy and the procedural and organisational modes of its formulation and implementation. In all of these cases, however, the actors must take into account the constraints and opportunities constituted by the institutional rules in force. The (meta) rules established at constitutional level and hence theoretically applicable to all policies, predetermine the more specific rules associated with a specific policy. The latter directly influence an actor's access to both this policy arena and the action resources that can be mobilised. If these specific institutional rules pre-structure the actors' game, it should be kept in mind that they too are (partly) negotiated, mainly during policy formulation, by the actors who are (potentially) affected by the substantive targeted results.

Figure 1 summarises the key elements of the public policy analysis model adopted in this manual.

Before we explore all of the possible relationships between actors, resources and the institutions involved in a given policy, we must define exactly what we mean by these concepts.

Chapters Two to Five provide responses to four fundamental questions: what are the constituent elements of a public policy (Chapter Two)? How can the different categories of public policy actors be identified and characterised (Chapter Three)? What are the different types of resources that the actors can mobilise to influence the content

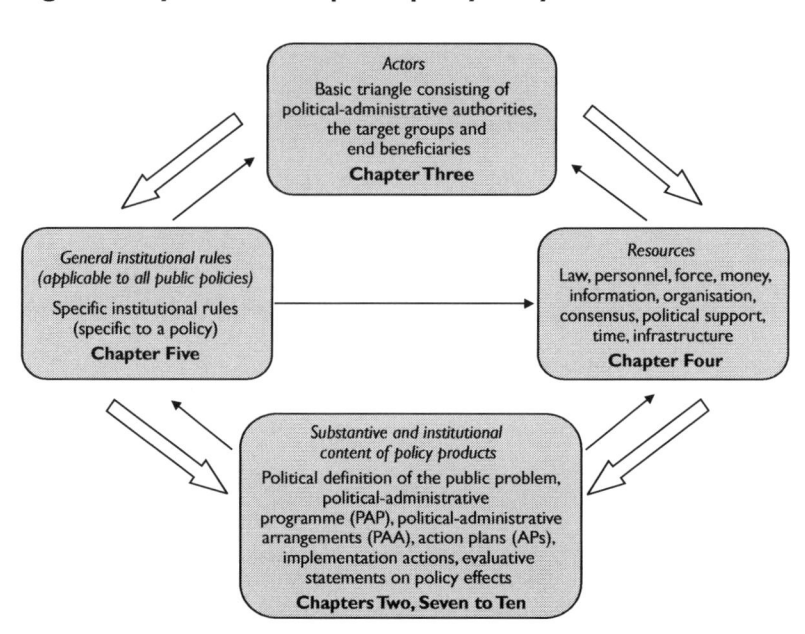

Figure 1: Key elements of public policy analysis

Actors
Basic triangle consisting of political-administrative authorities, the target groups and end beneficiaries
Chapter Three

General institutional rules (applicable to all public policies)
Specific institutional rules (specific to a policy)
Chapter Five

Resources
Law, personnel, force, money, information, organisation, consensus, political support, time, infrastructure
Chapter Four

Substantive and institutional content of policy products
Political definition of the public problem, political-administrative programme (PAP), political-administrative arrangements (PAA), action plans (APs), implementation actions, evaluative statements on policy effects
Chapters Two, Seven to Ten

and development of a policy (Chapter Four)? Which general or specific institutional rules influence the actors' games during the definition of the public problem to be resolved and the policy programming, implementation and evaluation (Chapter Five)?

This sequence of chapters corresponds to a certain degree to the different stages in the evolution of our discipline.

In the early 1970s, policy analysts tried to go beyond the legal analyses of the political-administrative system that focused exclusively on the study of the conformity of administrative measures with respect to the law. These analyses were mainly designed with the aim of providing legal protection for citizens vis-à-vis the state. It was during this period that the use of the term *public policies* enabled the linking of a single group of laws, decrees and directives, on the one hand, and the thousands of activities associated with their concrete implementation, on the other. Thus, during this initial period, policy analysis tried to explain what are known as 'implementation deficits': why a particular law is enforced to the letter in one place and not enforced at all in another. The discovery of implementation deficits led lawyers (concerned about the unequal way in which legislation was applied) and politicians to query the utility of the legislation that had been enacted.

The analysts then tried to explain these deficits. In their quest for explanatory factors, they focused primarily on the role of the public and private *actors* who are involved in the legislation and its implementation. In effect, these actors are human beings with their own values, interests, means of defence and capacities for innovation and adaptation; in short, capable of using policies for their own ends. Thus, the analysts studied the social reality of the actors involved in the policy area whose behaviour was supposed to be predictably and enduringly loyal to the established legal order.

The research carried out on policies and their actors showed that the latter, their umbrella organisations and their representatives enjoyed extensive autonomy. In effect, they appeared to benefit from a very extensive margin for manoeuvre that enabled them to influence policies to suit their own interests. However, the research also quickly revealed that the scope of this autonomy varied considerably from one actor to the next. Thus, the old question of *power* raised its head, hitherto seen as the preserve of the political scientists who study politics, on the far side of the artificially erected barrier between political analysis and policy analysis, a barrier that was very probably the outcome of the legal fiction of the equality of all citizens before the law.

In their quest for an explanation of this phenomenon, researchers more or less simultaneously identified the availability of and accessibility to *policy resources* for the different types of actors and the key roles played by the *institutions* (parliamentary, governmental, administrative and judicial).

Nowadays, while the analysis of resources benefits from the wide range of academic disciplines applied to the public sector that are united under the concept of public management, institutional analysis is supported by neo-institutionalism (Hall and Taylor, 1996), an approach that is strongly rooted in the economic and political sciences and in sociology.

TWO

Public policy

2.1 Policy as a response to social problems

All policies aim to resolve a public problem that is identified as such on the governmental agenda. Thus, they represent the response of the political-administrative system to a social reality that is deemed politically unacceptable.

It should be noted here that it is the symptoms of a social problem that constitute the starting point for the realisation of its existence and of a debate on the need for a policy (for example, decline in the state of forests, drug-associated delinquency, high unemployment). At the initial stage of all public intervention, the actual causes of the collective problem have not yet been defined with certainty or defined consensually by public and private actors. The increase in unemployment levels in industrialised countries and the material precariousness of unemployed people prompt the state to create or revise its unemployment benefit system and to take measures to revitalise the labour market. Air pollution arising from industrial production and the consumption of fossil fuels prompts the state to develop an environmental protection policy. Urban criminality and the deterioration of the physical state of drug addicts are the triggers for new policies on the distribution of heroin under medical supervision. Although this interpretation of policies as institutional responses to (changing) social states that are deemed problematic is dominant within policy analysis, this assumption must be relativised.

Firstly, some instances of social change do not give rise to policies, mainly because they are not visible or expressed (for example, non-visibility of consequences, long-term consequences only, lack of political representation of the disadvantaged groups), or because no mode of state intervention proves feasible and consensual (for example, negative electoral impacts, absence of political-administrative implementation bodies, the inability to influence the behaviour of certain private actors in reality). Thus, the pluralist vision whereby the 'service hatch' state responds in an egalitarian and automatic fashion to all 'social demands' must be rejected.

This point raises questions about the ways in which social problems are defined (Dery, 1984; Weiss, 1989), their thematicisation on the governmental agenda (Kingdon, 1984, 1995; Rochefort and Cobb, 1993), the definition of target groups and the eventual decision not to get involved or apply a collective solution (Bachrach and Baratz, 1963). Numerous filtering processes exist at all of these levels and they represent opportunities for organised actors who oppose the political recognition of an instance of social change to keep the latter outside the political-administrative arena.

Secondly, certain policies may be interpreted, not as collective actions aimed at resolving a social problem (adaptation to or anticipation of a social change), but as simple instruments for the exercising of power and domination by one social group over another. As explained in Chapter One, the neo-Marxist authors believe that state policies aim solely to reproduce or emphasise the divides between the social classes. The neo-Weberian school supposes that state intervention can only enable the satisfaction of the internal interests of bureaucratic actors (administrative inertia). The theory of rational choice defines policy as the (re)distribution of the costs and benefits between the electoral groups in exchange for votes and/or partisan support. Seen from this perspective, substantive policies would be merely currency exchanged in electoral competitions. Finally, the neo-corporatist approach believes that policies protect the interests of organised groups who are able to 'capture' the political-administrative institutions and establish clientelist relationships with them.

As stated in the first section of this book, our position lies somewhere between these two extreme visions of a neutral 'service hatch' state that is attentive to all social demands, on the one hand, and a 'captive' state manipulated by an organised group, on the other. Viewed from this perspective, public policies emerge as a response to a public problem that reflects a social state (in transformation), which has been articulated by mediators (for example, the media, new social movements, political parties and/or interest groups) and then debated within the democratic decision-making process (Muller, 1990). This does not take away from the fact that the problem to be resolved is a social and political construct, even in the case of shock events – for example, the nuclear disaster at Chernobyl (Czada, 1991) or the effects of mad-cow disease (BSE) on humans (Greer, 1999) – because it always depends on the perceptions, representations, interests and resources of different public and private actors (Vlassopoulou, 1999).

There is no linear and mechanical institutional response that would be a function of the objective pressure of a collective problem; this is always a redistributive exercise, a 'mobilisation of bias' (Schattschneider, 1960). Examples of this, which are already well substantiated by empirical studies, include the insufficient police presence in Swiss suburbs with high immigrant populations, which are one of the locations of urban violence, and the priority implementation of traffic-calming measures in residential areas as opposed to working-class areas directly affected by noise and the hazards of road traffic (see in particular Terribilini, 1995, 1999).

2.2 An analytical definition

We have seen that the essential object of policy analysis is not political power in itself, but its use for the purpose of resolving collective problems. Thus, the notion of public policy refers to the power games in a specific institutional context played out between various public actors who make a concerted effort to resolve a collective problem in collaboration with or in opposition to para-state and private actors. Given that these problems are connected with specific areas or sectors, the term 'policy', which has been established in common parlance since the growth of state intervention in the 1930s, is often qualified with the name of the sector or area in question (for example, 'energy policy', 'agricultural policy', 'economic policy', 'social policy').

There are numerous definitions of the concept of public policy. Thoenig lists at least 40 in the introduction to his 1980 analysis of public policies (Thoenig, 1985, p 3). Without replicating this list in its entirety, we note some of these definitions below, ranging from vagueness at one extreme to efforts to be very precise at the other:

- "Public policy is whatever governments choose to do or not to do" (Dye, 1972, p 18).
- "A public policy is the product of the activity of an authority invested with public power and governmental legitimacy" (Mény and Thoenig, 1989, p 129).
- "A public policy is a programme of action specific to one or more public or governmental authorities within a sector of society or a given area" (Thoenig, 1985, p 6; Mény and Thoenig, 1989, p 130).
- "A public policy is the product of activities aimed at the resolution of public problems in the environment by political actors whose relationships are structured. The entire process evolves over time" (Lemieux, 1995, p 7).

Despite being very different, these definitions tend to emphasise the idea of actors invested with public power (see in particular Dye, Mény and Thoenig cited above; also Sharkansky, 1970, p 1; Heclo, 1972, p 85; Simeon, 1976, p 548), collective problems requiring resolution (see Anderson, 1984, p 3; Pal, 1992, p 2) and on the state solutions provided (see Laswell and Kaplan, 1950, p 71; Jenkins, 1978, p 15).

Ultimately, policy experts agree that an 'operational' definition is necessary to qualify the object and field of study in this area (see Muller, 1990, p 24). The definition proposed below, which encompasses the main elements on which consensus exists in the literature (see specifically Thoenig, 1985, p 7; Mény and Thoenig, 1989, pp 131-2; Lagroye, 1997, p 454), is rooted in this perspective.

Thus, within the framework of the approach proposed here, a public policy is defined as *a series of intentionally coherent decisions or activities taken or carried out by different public – and sometimes – private actors, whose resources, institutional links and interests vary, with a view to resolving in a targeted manner a problem that is politically defined as collective in nature. This group of decisions and activities gives rise to formalised actions of a more or less restrictive nature that are often aimed at modifying the behaviour of social groups presumed to be at the root of, or able to solve, the collective problem to be resolved (target groups) in the interest of the social groups who suffer the negative effects of the problem in question (final beneficiaries).*

Thus, when we use the term 'public policy', we are implicitly referring to a large number of legislative and administrative activities aimed at the resolution of real problems. Most modern legislation is only effective when the political, administrative and social actors involved in the different institutional arrangements are involved in the decision making. The desired effects are only attained, however, in the aftermath of a group of complex decisions that form a sequence between the centre and the periphery. It is this set of decisions and activities that we define here as a 'public policy' – decisions taken by public (and sometimes private) actors that are aimed at channelling the behaviour of a target population so that a collective problem that society is not in a position to manage on its own can be resolved by public effort. This set of decisions includes the decisions taken at all stages of public action, and also includes general and abstract rules (laws, decrees, ordinances and so on) and the individual acts and concrete products that arise during policy implementation (administrative decisions, authorisations, subsidies etc).

With a few exceptions, the legislation of the original liberal state was primarily limited to the definition of the frame conditions likely to facilitate the resolution of problems by the agents of the private sector. Thus, public activities were limited to the production of legislation and its occasional enforcement by the courts in the case of litigation. It was only from the 1930s, and in close association with the development of the state, that there were efforts on the part of the public service to design interventions directly targeted at concrete problems. This state interventionism is at the root of the conception of real public policies in the sense of the above definition. It was on the basis of these policies that politicians, public managers and researchers started asking questions about the effectiveness and efficiency of different regulatory, incentive, economic and, more recently, persuasive and informational instruments (Knoepfel and Horber-Papazian, 1990; Morand, 1991).

Our definition of public policy claims to be primarily analytical. However, public administrations themselves consider and increasingly manage their daily activities with explicit reference to this kind of analytical frame[1]. This analytical frame gives the observer a view of all of the different activities that prompt the concretisation and implementation of political and administrative decisions, activities that are considered too often in isolation by the public agents concerned. This frame of reference makes it possible to clarify the distribution of the political and administrative functions and responsibilities of each of the instances at different state levels. Finally, it enables the distinction of those public activities associated with the resolution of a concrete problem through the creation of a particular policy from other state activities that are associated with the management of the entire political-administrative system. Thus, our definition applies to policies referred to as 'substantive' (Bussmann et al, 1998) as opposed to 'institutional' or 'constituent' policies (Lowi, 1972; Quermonne, 1985). In effect, the main object of the latter is the promotion, transformation or disintegration of state or social institutions (Quermonne, 1985, p 62) and not – at least not directly – the resolution of a social problem. We also classify budgetary policies as institutional policies even if budgetary tools are part of the panoply of the instruments of substantive public policies. These exclusions may be problematical in some situations in which institutional or budgetary changes have either explicit problem-solving goals or indirectly have this effect. However, situations of this kind will be complex, and not easily subjected to systematic analysis.

2.3 Constituent elements of a public policy

Several of the constituent elements of a public policy can be noted in the following definition.

The constituent elements of a public policy comprise:

- *A solution to a public problem:* a policy aims to resolve a social problem that is politically acknowledged as public and necessitates the re-establishment of the communication between several social actors that has broken down or is under threat. Thus, the proposed definition presupposes the recognition of a problem, that is, a socially unsatisfactory situation whose resolution is subject to action by the public sector. Nonetheless, problems that have been the object of public policies can return to the private or social sphere and disappear from the political agenda: for example, behaviours that were formerly subject to moral condemnation such as cohabitation were an element of family policy that is no longer relevant today. Furthermore, the situation can arise whereby public bodies created to resolve a given problem are on the lookout for new public problems: hence, the maintenance of a federal Swiss stud farm within the Federal Office for Agriculture's main 'research and popularisation' division which, having initially represented a means of action in the context of military policy, now focuses on a (new) problem: agricultural research.
- *The existence of target groups at the root of a public problem:* all public policy aims to channel the behaviour of target groups, either directly or by affecting these actors' environment. The 'causality model' (see Sections 3.3 and 3.4 in Chapter Three) that underpins the coherence of public policy leads to the identification of the target groups of the policy, that is, the social groups who should be able to resolve the problem by changing their behaviour. A political declaration to the effect that air should be clean, public order restored, unemployment reduced that is not accompanied by the identification of the social groups to be called on to change their behaviour with a view to fulfilling these objectives cannot, therefore, be considered a policy. It should be noted, however, that the target groups of a policy can evolve over time: thus water protection policies started out by defining devils, witches and pagans, households, industrial enterprises and, more recently, farmers, as the target groups at whom public intervention is aimed.

- *Intentional coherence, at the very least:* a public policy is created with a given direction. It presupposes "a theory of social change" (Muller, 1985, 1995; Mény and Thoenig, 1989, p 140) or 'a causality model' (Knoepfel et al, 1998, p 74), which the policy will attempt to apply in its attempt to resolve the public problem in question. It also assumes that the decisions or actions taken are connected. Thus, a lack of coherence will manifest itself in the purely occasional coincidence of measures that are aimed at the same target groups but are not connected to each other in accordance with the legislator's intention. This is the case, for example, when measures to save energy are introduced as part of an energy policy, while at the same time the VAT or sales tax on energy products is increased for exclusively fiscal reasons. In this case, it is not advisable to include the fiscal measure in the energy policy. If the energy policy does not contain any economic measures, due to the lack of intentional coherence, the fiscal measures may not be considered as energy policy means. However, there will be areas of ambiguity, particularly where there are alternative interpretations of policy goals or actors do not make their policy goals explicit. For example, the congestion charge introduced by the Mayor of London was presented, as its name suggests, as a measure to reduce traffic congestion. That did not stop commentators suggesting that the Mayor's primary motive had been to increase the revenue available for his use. Interestingly this policy has been resisted by the various foreign embassies in London, particularly the United States one, who argue that the charge is a tax and they should not pay it as they are immune from UK taxes. The policy analyst is hardly in a position to judge what the 'real' intention was in a situation like this. The solution to this problem, however, must either involve, as in this proposition, the acceptance of stated intentions or the imposition in the analysis of the presumed intention (with the analyst acknowledging that this is their imposed assumption). Hence this example may be quite appropriately explored in terms of the policy's impact on traffic congestions (as it is in practice) but could alternatively be explored as revenue-raising policy. See Section 7.2.1 for further discussion of issues about alternative problem definitions.
- *The existence of several decisions and activities:* public policies are characterised by a group of actions that go beyond the level of the single or specific decision while remaining short of a "general social movement" (Heclo, 1972, p 84). A basic declaration of

government policy stating that AIDS is a public problem that does not also define the social groups affected by the existence of this problem cannot in itself be considered as a public policy. This kind of declaration may (but does not have to) contribute to the emergence of a new policy if it is followed by legislation and its application.

- *Intervention programme:* this group of decisions and actions should – moreover – contain decisions that are to a greater or lesser extent concrete and specific (decisions relating to the programme and its application). Unlike other authors, we are of the opinion that an intervention programme that is specific to one or more authorities (Thoenig, 1985) cannot be considered in itself as a public policy. Thus, Switzerland's proposed measurement plan for the prevention of atmospheric pollution[2] or France's plan for the protection of the atmosphere within the framework of the Law on Air (1996) can only be considered as an element of a policy in themselves if individual measures that are the object of explicit decisions are (at least partially) implemented. A programme of interventions that has no outcome is not a policy; it is merely a – possibly indispensable – product among the other constituent elements of a public policy (see Section 9.3 in Chapter Nine).

- *The key role of public actors:* this group of decisions and actions can only be considered as a public policy to the extent that those who take the decisions act in the capacity of public actors: in other words, the involvement of actors belonging to the political-administrative system or private actors with the legitimation to decide or act on the basis of a delegation based on a legal rule is essential. If this condition is not fulfilled, a group of decisions of this kind (which can, in fact, also impose restrictions on third parties) will be considered as a 'corporative (associative)' or even 'private' policy. Thus, many of the 'policies' adopted by multinational companies (salary scales, environment strategy, environmental management systems) are based on strictly internal decisions and responsibilities.

- *Existence of formalised measures:* a public policy assumes the production of acts or *outputs* intended to channel the behaviour of groups or individuals. In this sense, our definition of a public policy presupposes the existence of a concrete implementation phase for the measures decided on. However, in certain cases, the policy analysis reveals the failure of political-administrative actors to intervene or a lack of recourse to certain intervention instruments.

In this respect, we differ in part from approaches that also consider groups of non-decisions (Dye, 1972) or non-actions (Smith, 1976, p 13; Mény and Thoenig, 1989, p 152) as public policies. According to our definition, these non-decisions can only constitute a policy if they are simultaneously accompanied by formal decisions, with which they will be associated. This is the case, for example, if a service voluntarily refrains from implementing the procedure for serving notice on a polluting company so as to prompt the company itself to self-regulate.

- *Decisions and activities that impose constraints:* traditionally, the majority of actors assume that the decisions made by political-administrative actors are often coercive in nature (Mény and Thoenig, 1989, p 132). If, as Gibert (1985) suggests, the public action is deemed necessary by virtue of the legitimate authority assumed by public power, today, the diversification of the means of action and intervention at the disposal of the political-administrative system is such that this coercive aspect is increasingly less prevalent. Whether they concern the development of conventional public activities (Lascoumes and Valuy, 1996) or contractual activities (Gaudin, 1996; Godard, 1997), the forms of public action adopted today are as likely to be incentive-based as coercive. This has prompted us to modify this aspect of the definition. Thus, many public interventions are currently implemented by means of contractualisation procedures between the state and public authorities (waste management, road maintenance, regional development), between, for example, the state and private or public companies, foundations or cooperatives (service contract for establishments that fulfil public functions such as hospitals, public transport franchise companies, educational establishments etc) (see Chevallier et al, 1981; Finger, 1997).

Figure 2.1 demonstrates the links between the different constituent elements of a public policy. In doing this, it also indicates those elements that will not be considered here as constituent elements of a policy. It is recognised that this seems to eliminate from consideration some actions that are widely seen as public policy decisions. That is not our intention; rather it is to suggest that in these cases systematic policy analysis is probably not feasible. This is an important consideration that highlights elements in the policy process that tend to undermine rational analysis, offering warnings to analysts against getting trapped into pointless evaluative activities or into the legitimation of symbolic or contradictory policies.

Figure 2.1: The different constituent elements of a public policy

Constituent elements of a public policy	Elements that may not be considered
Group of decisions and activities ...	A single decision or activity for example, declaration of political intention without concrete follow-up
... coherent, at least in intention ...	Incoherent decisions or activities (for example, granting planning permission for a construction project on the basis of another policy; increase of tax on petrol imposed for fiscal reasons rather than as part of energy policy)
... taken by public actors ...	Decisions and activities taken by private actors (for example, labelling promoted by a group of companies)
... at different levels of concretisation ...	Decisions that are still purely legislative (for example, intervention principles that are defined without being implemented)
... which translate into individual formalised actions ...	Decisions or activities divorced from concrete policy changes
... which try to shape the behaviour of targeted groups in order to solve a problem	Decisions or activities that are not targeted (for example, general tax increases involving no attention to redistributive effects)

2.4 Policy cycle

Numerous writers (see the review in Parsons, 1995, pp 78-9) have tried to create a diagram conveying the unfolding of the decision and implementation processes involved in the creation of a policy. The overall impression that emerges from the literature is one of a policy 'cycle' starting with the emergence of problems and progressing to the evaluation of the results obtained, as shown in Figure 2.2. The questions posed by the analyst can be differentiated for each of the stages in the policy cycle (see Table 2.1).

This approach based on the policy cycle model should be understood as a framework and not a rigid grid. This is what Muller has in mind when he notes that "the sequential representation of policies should not be used in a mechanical fashion. Instead, policies should be represented as a continuous flow of decisions and procedures, for which it is necessary to find the meaning" (Muller, 1990, p 33). The proposed grid should be understood as an aid in the quest to understand the decisions taken in the context of a policy.

Table 2.1: The different sequences of a public policy

Sequence	1st phase	2nd phase	3rd phase	4th phase	5th phase
Terminology	Emergence of problems	Agenda setting	Formulation and adoption of the policy programme	Policy implementation	Policy evaluation
Content	Emergence of a problem	Selection (filtering) of emerging problems	Definition of the 'causality model'	Application of selected solutions	Determination of eventual policy effects
	Problem perception	Outline and formulation of causality model	Definition of suitable and acceptable solution(s) to the defined problem	Action of administrative implementation agents	Evaluation of extent of impacts, effectiveness, efficiency, relevance, with respect to the original problem
	Definition of the problem and identification of possible causes				
	Representation of the problem	Responses of public powers to problems recognised as being the necessary object of a policy	Filtering between ideal solutions and available resources		
	Request for public action		Selection of instruments		
Analyst's main questions	How is an awareness of the problem reached?	What are the factors that will make the government act in response to the problem?	What are the solutions proposed and accepted by the government and parliament? On the basis of which processes are these solutions formulated?	Have the decisions of legislature and the government been implemented?	What are the direct and indirect effects of the policy?

Public policy analysis

Figure 2.2: The policy cycle

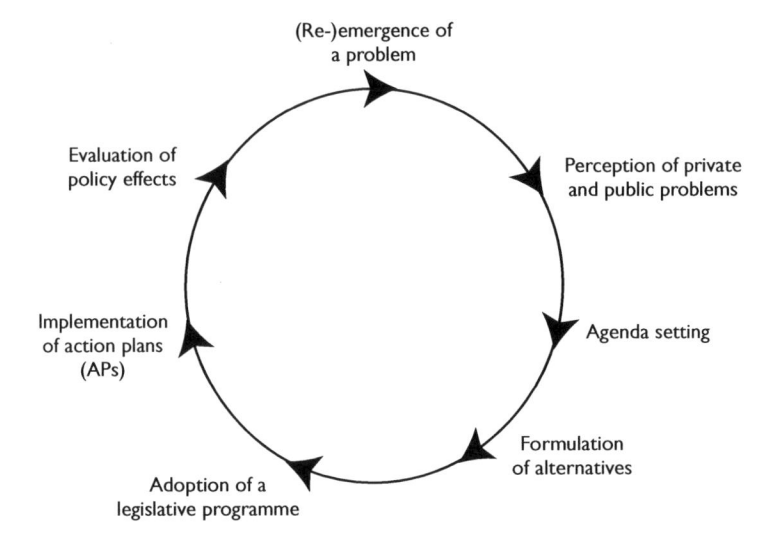

Cycle diagram with the following stages (clockwise from top):
- (Re-)emergence of a problem
- Perception of private and public problems
- Agenda setting
- Formulation of alternatives
- Adoption of a legislative programme
- Implementation of action plans (APs)
- Evaluation of policy effects

We adopt this approach again in a slightly modified form when we present our own theoretical model (Part III, Chapter Six).

Therefore, and more precisely:

- The phase involving the *emergence and perception of problems* is defined as a situation triggering a collective need, an absence or dissatisfaction, which is identifiable directly or via external manifestations and for which a solution is sought (Jones, 1970, p 53). More generally, a problem exists when there is a difference between the current and desired status of a situation. Nevertheless, a significant number of social problems exist that are not the subject of a public policy. The passage from the existence of a problem to its political processing results from a 'social [re]construction' of this problem that itself is related to the extent of the coverage it receives in the media (through scientific knowledge, the dissemination of information, lobbying etc).
- The *agenda-setting* phase corresponds to the consideration by the key actors of the political–administrative system of the numerous requests for action made by social groups or even the public services themselves. This agenda setting could be considered as a mechanism for the filtering of problems by public actors.
- The *policy formulation* phase presupposes, firstly, the definition of the causality model by the public actors (a definition that is

influenced to a greater or lesser extent by the social actors) and the formulation of the political-administrative programme (PAP), that is, the selection of objectives, instruments and procedures to be implemented in order to resolve the problem under consideration. Here again, the existence of a filtering and adjustment mechanism may be considered.
- The *implementation* phase consists of the adaptation of the policy programme to the concrete situations encountered (production of outputs). This phase is generally a lot more complex than it seems. Here again, several filtering mechanisms will come into play (for example, non-execution, selective application).
- Finally, the *evaluation* phase, which we consider as a constituent element of a policy, aims to determine the results and effects of a policy in terms of the changes in behaviour of target groups (impacts) and problem resolution (outcomes).

The interpretation of public interventions as processes (a dynamic vision rather than the static one that is typical of the traditional legal approach) makes it possible to highlight 'filtering' phenomena, such as, for example, the failure to take the initially identified beneficiary groups into account during a development process (for example, a motorway construction project that crosses areas populated by immigrants or other disadvantaged groups, or the construction of high-tension lines at the cost of nature conservation) (see Knoepfel, 1997a). Figure 2.3 identifies the position of the different filtering mechanisms throughout the policy cycle: filtering during the perception of problems placed on the political-administrative agenda, adjustment filtering during the policy formulation phase, implementation filtering and finally, evaluation filtering.

While analysis based on the policy cycle offers certain advantages, it also involves a number of restrictions. The advantages include the following elements:

- The policy cycle approach enables consideration of the existence of retroactive loops throughout the process, for example, the questioning of a PAP as a result of opposition arising during its implementation phase (the case of strong opposition to the setting up of a nuclear power station that results in the redefinition of energy policy; opposition to the extension of a civil airport that affects the basic conception of air transport policy).
- The identification of the stakes and actors involved in each stage of the policy cycle makes it possible to reduce the complexity of

Public policy analysis

Figure 2.3: The public policy process and filtering mechanisms

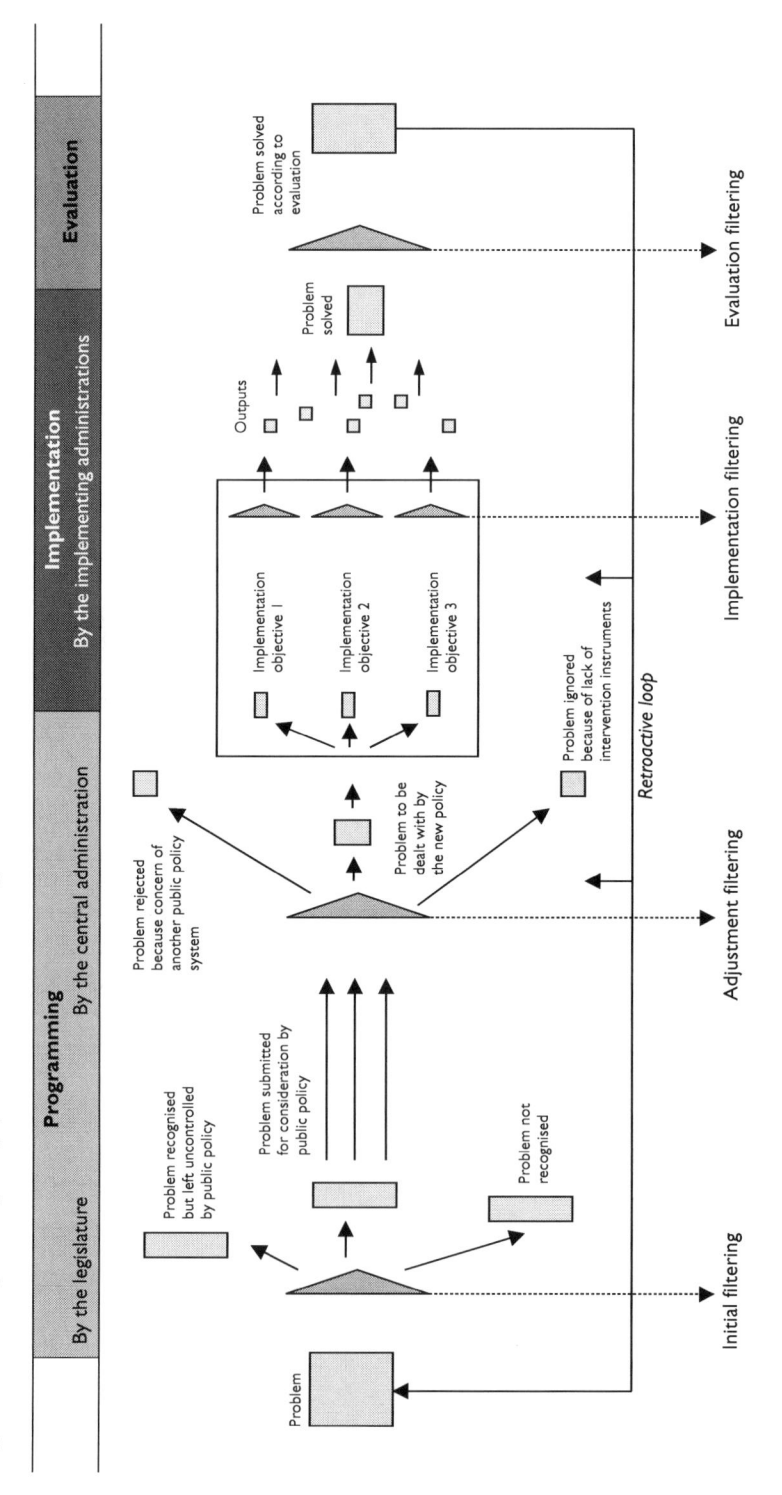

the subjects being analysed. Thus, it is possible to analyse the actor constellation (public/private, central/local) and its variation throughout the policy cycle (appearance and disappearance of actors during each sequence).
- The formulation of analytical questions, hypotheses and partial theories for each stage of the policy cycle makes it possible, in particular, to single out the factors analysed on the basis of different disciplinary fields – sociology, law, political science, economics – and to create sub-disciplines: formulation of public action ('policy design'), policy implementation research ('policy implementation'), and policy programme evaluation ('policy evaluation').
- The possibility of combining policy analysis with a rationalising vision of public action (for example, the linear link between the objectives, means and results that is implicit in management strategies such as the Planning, Programming and Budgeting System [PPBS]). This makes it possible, for example, to detect errors in the identification of the problem or to identify gaps in policy implementation.

This heuristic model may be compared to the stages in the resolution of a (private) problem. This similarity prompts several authors to consider public action as a rational enterprise of problem resolution without necessarily taking the distinctive features of the public sector into account (Table 2.2).

However, the 'policy cycle' model does have certain limits from an analytical perspective (see for example, Jenkins-Smith and Sabatier, 1993, pp 3-4; Hill and Hupe, 2006; Hupe and Hill, 2006).

Table 2.2: Similarities between the policy cycle and the stages of problem solving

Stage	Problem solving	Public policy
1	Problem recognition	Agenda setting
2	Proposal of solution	Policy formulation
3	Choice of solution	Decision making
4	Putting solution into effect	Policy implementation
5	Monitoring results	Policy evaluation

Source: Howlett and Ramesh (2003, p 13)

In effect:

- This is a descriptive approach that can be deceptive as the chronological course of the policy process does not necessarily coincide with the order of the different stages in the model. Thus, a programme may be implemented prior to its precise formulation during the emergence of new problems (for example, in the case of efforts to overcome pollution caused by agriculture in France; see Larrue, 2000). Breaks may also occur in the process with the reformulation of the public problem and the solutions before the measures initially planned are implemented and/or evaluated (for example, in the case of political asylum policy in Switzerland; see Frossard and Hagmann, 2000; there are similarities to this in the UK in the case of the rapid succession of political responses to fears about terrorism, with new initiatives occurring before exiting policies have been properly established).
- This heuristic approach does not enable the development of a true model of the causality of public policies and the identification of logical links between the different stages. It runs the risk of giving an artificial coherence to the policy by prompting the analyst to construct links between elements that do not exist in reality.
- The policy cycle model is in line with a legalistic interpretation of public action ('top-down' approach) and centred on state action, and it fails to take account of an approach that originates with social actors and their context ('bottom-up' approach). Thus, one could be led to incorrectly attribute the reduction in electricity consumption to energy-saving measures when it actually results from an increase in prices or downturn in the economy. Similarly, a number of solutions exist that are looking for a problem: a state service that is due to be closed down (for example, the federal Swiss stud farm) will create a new problem in order to survive (the risk of disappearance of traditional horse races that are part of the national heritage).
- This approach does not make it possible to go beyond a sequential analysis and consider, in particular, several cycles unfolding at the same time or the possibility of incomplete cycles. For example, in order to understand drug policy it is important to dissociate the cycles and identify the different pillars of the policy: crackdown, prevention, survival aid (related to AIDS), medicalisation (with methadone) and medical control.

Nonetheless, in the context of our policy analysis model, we believe it is worth staying with this sequential approach while taking its advantages and limits into account. We see it as constituting a reference framework that can be considered as a tool of a pedagogical or heuristic nature, but which also should be complemented by a more cross-sectional analysis of the stages of a policy. This cross-sectional analysis rests on the detailed study of the main keys for reading policies, that is, the actors, their resources and the institutional framework within which they interact (Chapter Three, Four and Five).

Notes

[1] The terms 'public policy' and 'policy' (or 'government policy') are used synonymously here. It should be noted, however, that certain authors make explicit distinctions here: "For government actors, policy refers to specific actions of an official nature. For teachers and researchers, public policy refers to groups of actions, the majority of which are not considered as policies by government actors" (Lemieux, 1995, pp 1-2).

[2] Federal Ordinance on the Protection of Air (1985).

THREE

Policy actors

We take policy to mean a series of decisions or activities resulting from structured and recurrent interactions between different actors, both public and private, who are involved in various different ways in the emergence, identification and resolution of a problem defined politically as a public one.

In this chapter, we focus on the types of actors concerned by policy, while following chapters will deal with the resources to which these actors have access in order to represent their interests (Chapter Four), on the one hand, and with the institutional context that influences their individual and collective behaviour (Chapter Five), on the other. These three concepts (actors, resources and institutions) constitute the principal focus of our analysis and are the key factors on which we will base our policy analysis model (Part III).

3.1 'Empirical actors'

Given that policies embody the results of the interactions between different public and private actors, we must start by defining the actual concept of an actor. For the purposes of this study, the term 'actor' can be taken to designate either an individual (a minister, member of parliament, specialist journalist etc), several individuals (constituting for example an office or a section of an administration), a legal entity (a private company, an association, a trade union and so on) or a social group (farmers, drug users, the homeless etc)[1].

Note, however, that a group of several individuals constitutes a single actor insofar as, with respect to the policy under consideration, they are in broad agreement and share a common approach as far as the values and interests that they represent and the concrete aims that they pursue are concerned. This consensus can be arrived at, for example, through the hierarchical structure or through the democratic process.

Talcott Parsons (1951) inspired our approach to the concept of actor. In his view, in order to analyse a social action, we must focus essentially on the simplest unit that retains the significance of what Parsons terms a 'unit-act'. This elementary act is undertaken by at least one actor who has an objective (bringing about a future state of affairs with a view to which the actions of the actor in question are directed), and who uses certain means to achieve that objective (Bourricaud, 1977, p 31). Thus, depending on the individual case, the actor concept can apply to an individual, a group or groups of individuals or to an organisation, the latter being defined in terms of the shared ideas or common interests that link its members. As Olson remarks in his book on the logic of collective action: "Without a common point of interest, there is no group" (Olson, 1965).

Every individual, legal entity or social group is considered as an actor once, by virtue of their very existence, they belong to the social field regarded as being relevant to the analysis:

> An individual in a given field does not qualify as an actor by virtue of his understanding of, or control over, events, nor on the basis of his awareness of his interests and scope for action, nor, a fortiori, because he is aware of his place in history or in the process of social change, or because he participates in 'the production of society. (Segrestin, 1985, p 59)[2]

In so far as their behaviour can be shown to contribute to the structuring of this field, they have this status simply by belonging to the field being studied. It is not, therefore, a problem of awareness, lucidity or identification: it is simply a de facto situation, which means that this becomes a question of research (Friedberg, 1993, p 199).

In this way, every individual or social group concerned by the collective problem addressed by a policy can be considered as a potential actor capable of being part of the 'arena' (see Section 3.3.1) of this policy. In fact, the actor's – more or less active – behaviour influences the way in which the public intervention in question is devised and implemented.

This broad definition of the actor concept means that the analyst must consider all individuals and social groups concerned by a specific collective problem. Such a viewpoint has the advantage of taking account of the fact that public and private actors do not all intervene actively and visibly at all stages of a policy: their behaviour is sometimes directly tangible, but equally it is sometimes hard to identify directly. This depends on, among other factors, the process by which they become aware of their own interests, their capacity to mobilise resources and form a coalition to defend their rights and interests and, finally, their strategic decision either to take action or to remain voluntarily outside the decision-making arena. By adopting the concept of 'empirical actors' proposed by Friedberg, we go along with him in rejecting the distinction made by several authors between an *agent*, who is rather passive and whose behaviour is determined by the system in which action occurs, and a *true actor*, who has become active and autonomous in relation to the institutional and social context.

In the same way, our perspective leads to a rejection of a formal opposition between *actor* and *non-actor*. In this regard, we do not contest the fact that, in the context of a policy, different individuals or social groups display different degrees of internal organisation, control different action resources and have different capacities for the mobilisation of external interests. However, we maintain that any individual or social group concerned by the collective problem addressed by the policy under consideration is an actor (at least potentially), even if (momentarily) unable to undertake concrete action in one or more phases of a public intervention. In fact, an actor's passivity, whether deliberate or the result of a lack of resources or of a failure to realise the importance of certain issues, is a factor that explains why one policy is ultimately developed and implemented rather than another[3].

There are also opponents of a policy who only come to the fore in the last stages of its implementation: whether during negotiations with those responsible for the policy implementation (for example, the foresters in the case of the implementation of the legislation on forest clearing analysed by Padioleau, 1982) or through legal opposition (cases involving environmental protection organisations that oppose infrastructure policies).

If analysts only focus on the behaviour of the most dynamic and enterprising actors, stipulating that passive groups are 'non-actors', they run the risk of overlooking certain factors that are central to an understanding of how a given policy is developed. Analysts sometimes adopt too elitist an approach to the actors' game, not taking into account sufficiently the effects induced by the passivity of certain social groups or political-administrative actors who are concerned by the collective problem under consideration. Note, however, that for obvious reasons connected to empirical observation, analysts tend naturally to focus on the behaviour of the most active actors within the context of a policy. It is certainly easier to identify individuals, informal groups and formal organisations who, having access to the necessary resources, participate on an ongoing basis in the conception, adoption and implementation of a policy.

3.2 'Intentional' actors

Adopting a scheme of intelligibility known as *actantial* (Berthelot, 1990, p 76), we acknowledge the *intentionality* of individual action. This takes place in a social context that can be perceived alternatively as a system of interdependence (Crozier and Friedberg, 1977; Boudon, 1979), a historical stage in a process (Touraine, 1984) or a situation pertaining to the here and now. In each case, an actor's behaviour is never reduced to a position, role or other type of fixed category. In other words, in our opinion, an actor always disposes of a greater or lesser margin of discretion and of manoeuvre, depending on the situation in question. Our thesis here is that no social or political field is perfectly structured, controlled or regulated. For this reason, individual and collective actors deliberately exploit 'areas of uncertainty' (to use the expression coined by Crozier, 1963) that are an inherent part of political-administrative organisations, formal regulations and social norms in order to promote their own values, ideas and interests. They possess, therefore, a certain degree of freedom but also resources (see Chapter Four), which enables them to develop strategies and tactics, or even to adopt "goal-oriented behaviour" (Berthelot, 1990, p 80).

Thus, we do not seek to deny the influence – that is sometimes quite considerable – that the actors' *institutional* and *social context* has on their decisions and actions. On the other hand, we believe that these institutional factors do not determine the assessments, choices and behaviour of public and private actors in an absolute and linear manner (see Chapter Five). We reject, therefore, the holistic theses that assume that social phenomena, policies for example, have their own intrinsic nature and their own laws that inevitably lead individuals to act in one way rather than another. On the contrary, we propose that policies should be interpreted as the result of the behaviour of actors who are (partially) autonomous. Thus, we adopt the principles of methodological individualism as developed by the sociologists Boudon and Bourricaud (1990, pp 301-9).

The area of uncertainty is particularly significant in the context of unforeseen crises (for example, the accident at the Chernobyl nuclear power station, natural disasters). The actors who have to intervene in such circumstances are unprepared and have to cope as best they can with no system to fall back on. When this happens, the different public authorities concerned can be observed to react in different ways (Czada, 1991; Keller-Lengen et al, 1998; Schöneich and Busset-Henchoz, 1998), and indeed such disparities can be observed even within one and the same organisation (Müller et al, 1997).

This in no way implies that we interpret actors as totally rational beings, motivated only by the maximisation of their personal utility (both material and non-material) and omniscient, as suggested by the homo economicus model beloved of neoclassical economics. For example, for cognitive, emotional and cultural reasons, the *rationality* of individuals and social groups remains necessarily *limited* (Simon, 1957). An actor's behaviour can never be reduced to its purely instrumental dimension, that is to say to the accomplishment of a predefined objective based on a considered choice and perfect realisation of the best possible course of action. Actors are in part calculating and are motivated by the satisfaction of their personal needs (means-end rationality or *Zweckrationalität*, according to Max Weber) and partly drawn towards the defence and promotion of collective values (value rationality or *Wertrationalität*). It is important to bear this dual motivation in mind when interpreting the behaviour of actors in the field of policy.

Thus, for example, while battling on behalf of unemployed people, civil servants can work to further the interests of their own departments so as to ensure their survival (which might be endangered, for example, by the privatisation of job-finding schemes for unemployed people). In the same way, the social services of a church become involved, for altruistic reasons, in the state system of providing home care for older people, while at the same time pursuing their own agenda of consolidating the role of the church and its message at the local community level (see Gentile, 1995).

We take the view that actors are rational in the sense that they care about the consequences of their own decisions and actions, even if they are unable to anticipate and control all of the effects that stem from these, and especially the adverse or undesirable effects that derive from the cumulative actions and behaviour of individuals (Boudon, 1979). At the same time, we propose a very broad interpretation of the intentions and interests that underlie all human activity: an actor's motivations are manifold, especially because they depend on the experiences and past history of the individual or social group concerned and also on the situation that pertains at a given moment in time and which entails certain constraints as well as opportunities for action. This being the case, we can speak of a *situated rationality*: the analyst being faced with interpreting individual and collective activities in terms of the logic and expectations on which strategic calculations are based and, at the same time, in terms of the actors' ignorance or intuition, their emotions or feelings and even in terms of the weight and impact of historical factors (Friedberg, 1993, p 211).

Briefly, policy actors can be described in the following terms (Crozier and Friedberg, 1977, pp 55-6):

- Actors rarely define clear, explicit or coherent objectives. They change them as they go along, if only because the unanticipated consequences of their own actions and those of other actors in the domain of policy compel them to readjust their objectives or re-evaluate their positions. What was a means to an end at one moment becomes an end in itself at another, and vice versa.
- Although it may sometimes appear erratic, actors' behaviour always has a meaning and a logic of its own that the analyst tries to decipher. Instead of being necessarily rational in relation to predetermined objectives, it is sometimes quite reasonable given the constraints and opportunities afforded by a given situation. According to a subjective appraisal of the institutional context and of the other actors' strategies, the actor adapts behaviour so as to be able to participate in and learn the rules of the 'game' of a policy and be acknowledged socially by the other actors involved. This leads to sometimes strange coalitions or alliances, for example between a company responsible for producing moderate levels of pollution and environmental protection organisations, which join forces in order to protest against a company producing high levels of pollution; or around an issue like wind farms where local residents, nature protection groups and tourist businesses band together (see Carter, 2001, p 281).
- An actor's 'strategic instinct' (to borrow the expression used by Crozier and Friedberg, 1977) is characterised by two complementary aspects. On the one hand, an actor tends to go on the offensive when taking advantage of opportunities to improve a position and further immediate interests (direct intervention on the substantive components of policy). On the other hand, an actor adopts a more defensive approach when seeking to maintain and broaden a margin of freedom, that is, the capacity to act in the way wanted at a later stage (indirect intervention on the institutional components of policy). From this perspective, it can be seen that every actor weighs up the short-term gains and the advantages of a longer-term investment; this encourages participation in one or several phases of a policy. In this way, a right-wing Swiss party which, in spring 1999, aimed to fight against an environmental policy that it deemed to be too strict, did not ask for the prevailing environmental regulations to be relaxed (substantive factor), but instead launched

an attack on the environmental protection organisations' right to monitor and control the way in which the regulations were implemented (institutional factor). The party appears to have been perfectly aware that it had no chance of obtaining a relaxation of the substantive regulations.

3.3 Types of actors

Our concept of policy actors leads us first of all to identify and define the parameters of the arena in which the actors will intervene (see Section 3.3.1). Within this arena, policy actors can be distinguished in terms of their public nature, that is to say, *political-administrative* actors who are vested with public authority (see Section 3.3.2), or in terms of their 'private' nature, that is to say, actors who belong to what are known as *socio-economic* or *socio-cultural* spheres (see Section 3.3.3). But the concepts of public and private need using with some care, as we show below. The second group can be broken down into the *target groups* (the actors whose behaviour is politically defined as the [in]direct cause of a problem or who are able to take action to deal with it), the *end beneficiaries* of a policy (actors who experience the negative effects of a particular problem and whose situation should be improved following the implementation of public intervention) and the *third-party groups*, who are affected indirectly by the policy, either positively (= positively affected third parties) or negatively (= negatively affected third parties). These two latter groups comprise all actors whose personal situation is altered by a policy without having been directly targeted by the policy, either as target groups or end beneficiaries. These three types of actors constitute what we call the triangle of actors (see Section 3.4). It is quite possible for actors to be both targets and beneficiaries (although there may be some problems here about the differences between how they see themselves and how they are seen by *political-administrative* actors).

3.3.1 Policy arena

Our intention here is to deal with policy from the perspective of the solution of a problem considered as pertaining to the public domain. Here we present the different actors found in a policy *context*, a context in which crucial interaction takes place between the different policy actors. The way in which this arena, in which these actors interact, is structured is neither neutral nor without effect on the behaviour of the different actors or the selected modes of public intervention. The policy arena is determined by – among other factors – the logic of the state. Traditionally, and especially since the advent of the welfare state, 'public matters' are managed by the public actors of the political-administrative system. But the principle of the constitutional state and that of democracy equally require the involvement of private actors whose interests and objectives are affected by the collective problem to be resolved in one way or another. Every policy arena inherently constitutes a framework that, to a greater or lesser extent:

- is structured
- is formally defined, and
- contains public actors interacting with private actors,

thus allowing alternative strategies to be developed.

In this way, a policy is designed and managed by public and private actors who together constitute an often highly complex network of interactions, which can experience problems involving horizontal coordination (for example, relationship between actors belonging to the same government level) and vertical coordination (for example, relationship between central, regional and local actors). Although they belong to different organisations and represent interests that are often opposed, if only because of the contentious issues in which they all have a stake, these various actors form *areas of interaction*. The boundaries of these areas in which they interact are often difficult to define, especially if the analyst focuses on peripheral actors. This is especially true of the initial phases of the emergence of new policies. It is these ideas that have been given particular attention in analyses of 'governance' (Pierre, 2000; Richards and Smith, 2002).

On the other hand, in every policy arena it is easier to identify a hard core of actors who, despite potential conflicts, have a (semi-)vital interest in not losing their position and, consequently, in controlling and even limiting new arrivals' access to the area in which they operate. This 'policy community' (Richardson and Jordan, 1979) is often subdivided into different coalitions (the term used by Sabatier and Jenkins-Smith, 1993, is 'advocacy coalitions'). At the same time that they struggle to assert their own interests or ideas, these coalitions together try to differentiate themselves from the individuals and groups outside the policy arena. With this end in view, the actors in a policy arena develop, for example, a language that is specific to 'their' policy, control the way in which information is circulated or try to avoid becoming politicised in case that might overwhelm 'their' ordered world in which a level of cohesion is preserved despite the differences that exist between the different coalitions.

Thus, the agricultural policy arena contains actors that vary from the large international companies that produce animal feed and auxiliary materials (fertilisers, pesticides) to intensive farmers, small farmers and the food-processing industry, including the distribution chains. The public health policy arena not only includes doctors' organisations, hospitals, public health services and health insurance companies, but also manufacturers of pharmaceuticals. The environment policy arena comprises the various polluting sectors of industry, eco-industries (companies producing anti-pollution products), environmental protection organisations and public services.

As a general rule, policy arenas do not change much in their make-up. A coalition that was formerly a minority one can become dominant, or the power relationship between central and local actors can undergo changes, but the configuration of actors and, by extension, the way this is defined in relation to everybody else, is rarely fundamentally called into question.

Examples of changes among the actors in the policy arena may nonetheless be linked to the following:

- *A radical change in the way the problem in question is perceived:* for example, narcotic drug use has gone from being seen merely as an issue requiring a prison sentence to being seen as a health issue, as an aid to survival. This being the case, the policy requires the participation of doctors (as methadone must be prescribed under medical supervision), or even health insurance companies.
- *Strong opposition to a given project on the part of some actors:* for example, the construction of a railway infrastructure that encountered massive opposition from environmentalists and ecologists (for example, Rail 2000 in Switzerland, the Mediterranean TGV in France). The transport authorities have found themselves obliged to systematically include private associations as actors in the arena of rail transport policy.
- *The departure of some actors from the policy arena:* small mountain farmers in Switzerland, who thought that official agricultural policy was too focused on the interests of lowland farmers and who advocated a radical reorientation of this policy, turned their backs on the official policy forum in order to create a new forum where they could express and assert their point of view more effectively. In France, the Confederation of Small Farmers, a very small farmers' union, adopted a similar stance.

3.3.2 Public actors

If there is one common denominator that connects all policies it is the fact that they are constituted by a range of initiatives usually undertaken by *public actors*. Thus, it would seem essential to provide as precise a definition as possible of the characteristics of public actors as opposed to the private actors who are also involved in policies. This is all the more necessary given the fact that the names and titles by which the actors are ordinarily known usually provide little information about what they actually do, whether in a public capacity or not. Furthermore, the definition of public actors must make it possible to differentiate between policies described as 'corporatist' (associative) or 'private'. It should be noted that, in terms of an analytical approach, this distinction will hardly fit in with a prescriptive theory that seeks to define the 'appropriate' role of the state in society. In order for it to work, it is imperative that this definition be inclusive, that is to say, that it should not exclude any of the activities in which political-administrative actors are involved. However this is difficult. Several approaches are possible.

There seems little point in defining public actors exclusively in terms of the legal dimension of their actions. For a long time, the basic element of public activity was considered to be formally constituted by what are known as *administrative measures*. According to the definition of federal Swiss administrative law, for example, the latter are decisions "taken by the authorities in individual cases, founded on federal public law and having the following objectives: (a) to create, modify or annul rights or obligations; (b) to record the existence, non-existence or scope of rights or obligations; (c) to reject or declare inadmissible applications tending to create, modify, annul or record rights or obligations"[4].

The order for civilians to report for military training, tax returns and planning permission are all examples of this. Founded on law, these administrative measures must also comply with it. As such, they may be subject to legal monitoring, usually by an administrative court. However, it can happen that public actors escape, quite legally, from being monitored by the administrative jurisdiction. The state's interest in not being restricted by public law is obvious: by acting in the sphere of *private law*, it escapes the constraints connected with observance of the principles of administrative action (for example, the necessity for a legal basis, equal treatment, proportionality etc) and the principles of public law that govern the administrative domain (Manfrini, 1996). This 'flight' outside the realm of public law prompts the state and the public authorities to acquire shares as a limited company or to create private law foundations or semi-public companies (*Société d'Économie Mixte* [*SEM*]) through partnership with private actors. Today, in both France and in Switzerland, and of course in the UK, more and more organisations based on private law exist that carry out public functions. These are mainly organisations that provide goods and services in the energy sector (*Electricité de France* [*EDF*], *Energie de l'Ouest Suisse SA*), the telecommunications sector (*France Télécom, SWISSCOM*) and the transport sector (*Société Nationale des Chemins de Fer* [*SNCF*], *CFF-SA*) to the general public and companies. At a more local level, such companies provide environmental services (household waste-incineration plants, water distribution services etc) and transport services (local transport companies, contracted companies etc), although it should be noted that they normally do this under contracts to provide services for public authorities.

In the UK these distinctions between 'public' and 'private' are often even harder to make. While in modern times an important range of public or administrative law has developed, the starting point is, as an influential textbook on administrative law puts it, that: "there is no formal distinction between public and private law. The ordinary law of the land, as modified by Acts of Parliament, applies to ministers, local authorities and other agencies of government, and ordinary courts dispense it" (Wade, 1982, p 12). That may partly account for the way in which the implications of developments like those discussed here have received rather less attention in the UK. This topic is further discussed below with reference to Jordan's exploration of this issue (1994).

By having recourse to private law, the state and the different public bodies can successfully avoid being subject to administrative and judicial control. However, this does not prevent them from intervening in their capacity as *public authorities*. In contrast to a restrictive judicial approach, it must be emphasised that 'para-state' policies pursued in this context remain policies and that the administration acts as a public actor.

It should be noted, however, that the flight of the state outside the domain of public law poses a problem in terms of *political control*: the administrative decisions subject to public law can, in theory, be the subject of parliamentary debate, even if they usually come under the jurisdiction of the executive. On the other hand, it is much more difficult for the legislature to monitor all acts of public authority that are not public decisions at the formal level. The degree of effective political control is, therefore, also an inadequate criterion by which to define an actor as public or private, especially in a period of economic liberalisation and deregulation – indeed privatisation – of the different public services (most notably the telecommunications services, railways, postal, gas and electricity services). There are of course many institutional variations around this theme, and in the case of the UK there is an increasing concern about measures that remove quite significant policy decisions from parliamentary scrutiny; these cannot be explored further here but the general point applies across national contexts.

As far as *political actors* caught up in power struggles are concerned, the line of demarcation between public and private actors is an important factor in the development of their strategies. In fact, confronted with a social problem that has not yet been tackled by the state, political actors can either propose the introduction of a new policy (which will be politically costly to a greater or lesser degree), or propose that a 'corporatist' or 'private' policy be established.

There are numerous examples of policies of this latter type. Most notably:

- wage policy (collective agreements)
- the voluntary compliance of companies with manufacturing standards (categorising of companies according to ISO regulations)
- disclosure agreements entered into by bankers who undertake to monitor the origins of certain funds that may be linked with money-laundering operations or tax evasion.

In order to define public actors as a whole, we return once more to the classical term 'political-administrative system' initially proposed by Easton. According to Easton, the political-administrative system comprises all of a country's governmental (parliament/government) administrative and legal institutions, which have the capacity, apparently legitimised by the legal establishment, to structure any sector of society through decisions of an authoritarian nature. These decisions are the result of political-administrative processes that are completed according to precise rules of procedure governing internal and external interactions (Easton, 1965, p 25).

Some aspects of this definition of the political-administrative system and the public actors who constitute its fundamental components, are worth singling out:

- The classical dimension of this definition resides in its affirmation of the *sovereignty of public actors*: the state is supposed to be the only entity entitled to exercise power of restraint over all other sub-systems and over citizens (legitimate monopoly of power – Max Weber).
- The *administrative organisations* of the political-administrative system form an important and relatively independent centre of gravity (for example, in relation to governments and parliaments) in the body of a state's institutions.
- The notion of *interaction* suggests that there are reciprocal relationships between the sub-systems. The political-administrative sub-system *transforms* 'societal' demands (inputs) into restrictive state actions (outputs).

The definition distinguishes between *external* interactions (relationships of reciprocal influence between the political-administrative system and its environment, for example consultation procedures for parliamentary bills, rulings or decrees with regard to people who will be affected by them or the examination of applications for operating licences) and *internal* interactions in the public sector (for example, the consultation procedure for the services linked to 'environmental impact studies' in Switzerland, or the procedures for bringing an issue to the attention of the relevant authorities within the French administration or the planning inquiry system in the UK). Clear procedural rules are generally defined for each type of interaction by the legislation and/or regulations.

It should be noted, however, that several private actors to whom the state delegates some of its privileges belong indirectly to the political-administrative system. In France and Switzerland these actors are generally designated by the term *para-public* (or *para-state*) *administrative bodies*. This phenomenon of interpenetration between the public and private sectors exists in many areas of intervention both in France and in Switzerland (Germann, 1987; Linder, 1987, pp 113-16; Mény and Thoenig, 1989). Many of the examples given below have UK equivalents, even if the legal forms of their designations differ. These para-public administrations can exist in various forms:

- *Autonomous public establishments created by a law and enjoying a certain freedom of enterprise:* in Switzerland they include the cantonal banks, universities, the Swiss Broadcasting Company (SSR); and in France they include public establishments of an administrative nature (such as the water companies and the National Library),

of a scientific, cultural and professional nature (for example, the universities) and of an industrial and commercial nature (establishments that provide all kinds of public services and obtain revenue from these services: airports, the national electricity supplier – *EDF* – and the national railway – *SNCF*).
- *Semi-public and private organisations:* local cooperative style companies for the promotion of the economy, or national organisations like the Swiss cooperative for the study of radioactive waste deposits (*CEDRA*) in Switzerland, and the *Sociétés d'Équipement*, the regional or local development companies, in France.
- *Private organisations:* the central union for milk producers, pension funds, health insurance and social security organisations in France, or any French organisation set up as an association in accordance with the terms of the Law of 1901, as long as it is under the control of political-administrative actors. In the UK professional associations licensed to regulate the behaviour of their members would also come into this category.
- *Social organisations:* Pro Senectute, Helvetas and various mutual aid organisations.

In the UK Jordan has explored this issue in a book in which he writes of "government in the fog". He argues that "the public/private divide is more than a matter of an imprecise boundary and involves a scale of problems that throw the categories into doubt" (1994, p 183).

In order to define public actors, we use the notion of the *political-administrative arrangement* (PAA) (see Section 8.2 in Chapter Eight), an entity that is structured by legal rules governing competencies and administrative procedures and by other relatively informal institutional rules, and which encompasses all *public actors* involved in the development and implementation of a policy. This notion is based on the existence of public responsibility and, consequently, direct government control of these actors, and it does not, therefore, include private actors. For this reason, it is distinct from the notion of 'policy networks' developed most notably in France by Le Galès and Thatcher (1995) following the British analyses dominated by Richardson and Jordan (1979), Rhodes (1981), and Smith (1993). However, it is used here in the context of policy analysis, that is to say that the PAA is analysed from the point of view of its impact on the policies analysed, and not for its own sake (see Chapter Eight).

In order to draw on the defining element of government control, research into public actors also focuses on the *administrative organisations* to which they 'belong' institutionally. The aims and internal workings of these organisations explain, in part at least, actors' behaviour and, more widely, the development and implementation of policies. The structures and procedural regulations of a public administration (for example, the federal offices and cantonal services in Switzerland, the different levels of the administrative hierarchies in France, the law determining the functions of local government in the UK) prevent an individual actor from acting in a wholly autonomous way. The principles of democracy and the constitutional state imply that public actors are subordinate to departments politically responsible for the actors' 'parent' organisations. Therefore, public actors can be 'handicapped' by the administrative context in which they operate when a specific policy is implemented. They will then tend to try to break free of their control and create a political and administrative coalition outside of their formal organisation.

But in order to escape the confines of an institutional framework deemed to be too narrow or restrictive, actors may also create new structures and organisations that will, for example, be able to collaborate more closely with private actors involved in policy. These collaborations can take various institutional forms, which we will discuss in detail later (see 'policy network' and 'public–private partnership' concepts) (see Chapter Eight).

3.3.3 Affected actors

The affected actors consist of target groups, end beneficiaries and negatively or positively affected third parties.

The *target groups* are made up of people (individuals or legal entities) and organisations whose behaviour is required to change. It may be the (in)direct cause of the collective problem that a given policy aims to resolve, or it may be regarded as appropriate that it should adopt the appropriate remedial action. Consequently, the target groups' decisions and activities are – or will be – the subject of concrete state intervention. The policy in question will impose obligations on them or grant them rights. It is presumed that, as a result of such measures, the target groups will alter their behaviour in order that the collective problem can be resolved or at least mitigated. The notion that groups who are the cause of the problem (polluters, providers of unsafe goods, drivers causing accidents) should change is straightforward here; a word of explanation is required, however, on the identification of target groups who are not in this category. For example, schools may not themselves be deemed to blame for illiteracy or doctors to blame for ill health, nevertheless the alteration of behaviour by these actors may reasonably be expected to contribute to the reduction of these problems.

Even formally 'public' actors may need to be seen as the 'targets' of policy inasmuch as the concern is with changing their behaviour. The literature on implementation to be discussed in Chapter Nine has been much concerned with situations in which super-ordinate authorities are seeking behavioural change from public organisations. While in some of this literature the issues involved are about intergovernmental relations, where the political-administrative authority relationship is a matter of dispute (this is particularly true in federal contexts), in other cases it is intra-organisational relationships that are given attention (where professionals claim autonomy or street-level bureaucrats resist instructions). In many of these cases political processes can be involved very like those where private organisations are the targets, with organisations of implementing agencies or their employees participating in the policy process (even in the agenda-setting and policy formulation stages). This phenomenon is increasingly evident as a consequence of administrative reforms that create autonomous entities out of hitherto hierarchically controlled public organisations.

The *end beneficiaries* are the people (individuals or legal entities) and organisations of these people who are directly affected by the collective problem and experience its negative effects. Once the policy has been implemented effectively, these actors can expect a (possible) improvement of their economic, social, professional and ecological circumstances. End beneficiaries are actors who benefit, more or less indirectly and according to the intended objectives of the policy concerned, from the target groups' altered behaviour. In most cases, the individuals who make up this group of actors are far more numerous and more difficult to mobilise and organise than target groups.

Finally, the *third-party groups* comprise all people (individuals or legal entities) and the organisations representing their interests who, without being directly targeted by the policy, see their individual and/or collective situation altered permanently. This change can turn out to be either positive or negative. In the former case, people are defined as *positively affected third parties*, sometimes unintentionally so, of the implementation of the policy, and the corresponding term applied to groups of people who are negatively affected by the implementation of a policy is *negatively affected third parties*. These two sub-groups of actors tend to either support or oppose the policy that is indirectly altering their own situation and circumstances and, as a consequence of this, to form coalitions either with the end beneficiaries (in the case of those who benefit), or with the target groups of the public initiative that has been implemented (in the case of the negatively affected third parties).

This system for the classification of actors is illustrated by the following examples of actors involved in a range of policies:

- The target groups of *environment policy* are polluters (industries, farmers, households and public bodies) whose pollutant emissions need to be reduced; the end beneficiaries are all those whose environment is affected by the different sources of pollution in a given area (human beings, flora and fauna); the positively affected third parties are the industrialists who develop new less polluting technologies (environment-friendly industries), and the negatively affected third parties are those who can no longer market their polluting technologies and the consumers who end up paying more for their products.
- According to the model prevailing in most European countries, the target groups of *agricultural policy* are farmers producing subsidised agricultural products; the end beneficiaries are the consumers who profit from the best market prices. The positively affected third parties are the food-processing industries, while the negatively affected third parties are the environmentalists, who see the environment as being harmed by intensive farming methods, those small farmers whose produce is not subsidised and third countries who import products that compete unequally with their home-grown produce as a result of this agricultural *dumping*.
- The target groups of *policy to combat unemployment* (at least in the micro-economic sense as opposed to broad economy regulation measures) are the companies that need to recruit staff (whose resistance or discriminatory practices are in question); the end beneficiaries are the unemployed people who are likely to obtain employment; the positively affected third parties are the job agencies who act as mediators on the job market; and the negatively affected third parties are those who see their incomes limited by the increase in compulsory deductions designed to fund, partially at least, the measures against unemployment. In this field of policy we may particularly find individuals who may be seen as both targets and beneficiaries: they are required to change their behaviour – undergoing training, participating

in job search activities — but may benefit if they nevertheless acquire desired employment.
- The target groups of *education policy* are schools, colleges and universities (with various statuses in terms of the public/private distinction), parents and employers; the end beneficiaries those who secure more or better education; the positively affected third parties may include some employers and parents; and the negatively affected third parties those who have to pay the costs of these improvements without securing any significant benefits and (perhaps) those whose access to education is diminished as a consequence of efforts to supply more education to others (as in the case of some forms of affirmative action, a topic explored in similar terms to this discussion in an appendix to Stone's *Policy paradox*, 2002, pp 384-414).

Obviously, it is not always easy to define the different categories of actors. In the context of a single policy, disagreements can emerge (between actors) regarding the exact definition of target groups and beneficiaries as they are interpreted from the various actors' standpoints, that is, in terms of the hypothesis of causality that underlies the policy initiative. The boundaries between these and the third-party groups who may, often perhaps without being fully aware of it, pay the real costs or secure the benefits may be obscure. It is worth noting here how public choice theorists have suggested that governments will deliberately try to obscure how costs fall.

While the discussion above suggests that the distinction between public and private actors is often a blurred one, the main issues about targeting and benefits can be seen in terms of the likelihood that the actors in these categories will be private ones. Nevertheless these actors participate equally in the constitution and structuring of the policy arena by virtue of their own responsibility and because they are outside the scope of direct government control.

3.4 'Triangle of actors' of a public policy

These different types of actors constitute what we call the 'basic triangle' of a policy. The *political-administrative authorities*, *target groups* and *end beneficiaries* constitute the three points of the triangle. Actors affected indirectly by policy (third parties constituting either negatively affected third parties or positively affected third parties) are located at the peripheries of two of these three poles (see Figure 3.1).

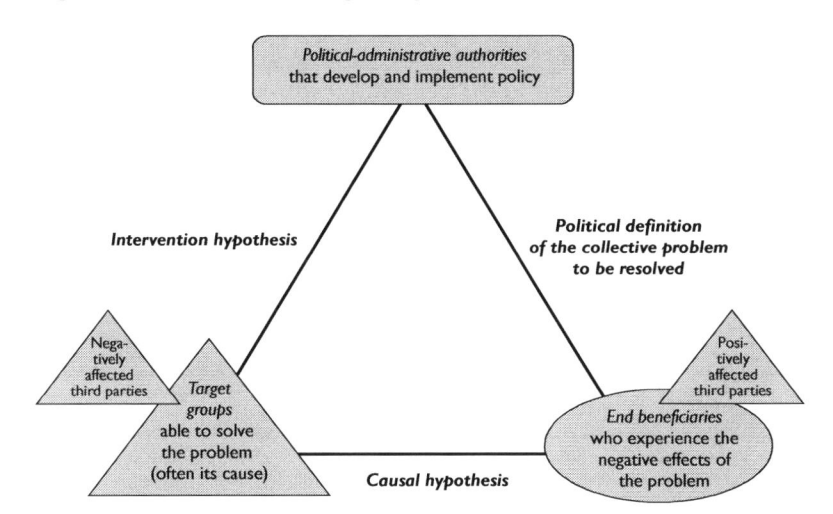

Figure 3.1: The basic triangle of policy actors

Political-administrative authorities that develop and implement policy

Intervention hypothesis

Political definition of the collective problem to be resolved

Negatively affected third parties

Target groups able to solve the problem (often its cause)

Causal hypothesis

Positively affected third parties

End beneficiaries who experience the negative effects of the problem

To add concrete examples to this triangle, the analyst seeks to identify the 'empirical actors' (in)directly concerned by the collective problem to be resolved, as well as the hypotheses (often implicit) on which the public initiative is based. In fact, here we suggest that every policy can be interpreted as a theoretical construction whose consistency and rationality must be questioned analytically, "… in the sense that it implies an a priori representation of the measures implemented, of the actors' behaviour, of the sequence of measures undertaken and of the effects produced on society" (Perret, 1997, p 292). We describe this theoretical construction as a 'model of causality' (Knoepfel et al, 1998, pp 74ff) or as a 'theory of social change' (Mény and Thoenig, 1989, pp 140ff; Muller, 1985, 1995). It comprises a causal hypothesis and an intervention hypothesis, the analysis of which makes it easier to discern the links between the different actors and the ways in which they are altered in the aftermath of public intervention.

The *causal hypothesis* provides a political response to the question as to who or what is 'guilty' or 'objectively responsible' (that is, without subjective guilt) or able to make changes to enable the collective problem to be resolved. Thus, the definition of the causal hypothesis of a policy consists in designating the policy *target groups* and the *end beneficiaries*. This attribution of responsibility is still determined by political value judgements and by the way in which the problem is perceived. Furthermore, uncertainties of a scientific nature with respect to the effective (objective) functioning of the intervention sector greatly limit the possibility of correctly identifying the target groups at the root of the problem.

Thus, for example, within economic theory the individual causes of unemployment remain matters of dispute. The way in which ecosystems function and the development of anthropogenic phenomena within ecosystems (the generation of ozone, the greenhouse effect, global warming) are still subjects of scientific debate. Similarly, the external observer is partially ignorant of the intricacies of heroin trafficking and heroin use, as well as of the profile and behaviour of drug addicts.

It is essential, therefore, for political-administrative authorities to know and understand the factors and effects of social change and the collective problems that stem from these, if they wish to make some impact on them and alter them. In order to do this, the state often depends directly on information that the private actors control and partially produce, especially the target groups at or close to the origin of the social problem to be resolved. This functional dependence of the state on certain target groups sometimes allows the latter to present information from their own perspective and, as a result, to designate the behaviour of other social groups as being the cause of the public problem (that is, to formulate a competing causal hypothesis). For example, for a long time farmers who pollute underground streams by spreading fertiliser were able to evade compliance with government regulations by arguing that the resultant deterioration in the quality of drinking water was due primarily to adverse effects on the environment produced by industry and private households.

The ineffectiveness and adverse effects of certain policies often derive from false or incomplete causal hypotheses. The causality model that was for a long time favoured by agricultural policy was based on the effects of subsidies on farmers' incomes, ignoring both the effects of overproduction of agricultural produce and the impact of intensive farming on the environment. The model used in the area of policy dealing with road congestion assumed that the increase in the provision of facilities for drivers (the building of extra roads and motorways) would make it possible to resolve the problem without taking into account the effects that these new facilities would actually have in real terms (a correlative increase in the number of cars on the roads leading to the same level of congestion). Similarly, the causality model used in public transport policy was initially based on the premise that increased services and lower costs would be enough to persuade drivers to leave their cars at home and start using public transport in large numbers. In the context of Aids prevention policy, the disease was first regarded as exclusively affecting homosexuals and drug addicts before being treated as a general public health problem.

As for the *intervention hypothesis*, it establishes how the collective problem requiring resolution can be mitigated and, indeed, resolved by a policy. It defines the methods of government action that will influence the decisions and activities of the designated target groups so that these will be compatible with the political aims. Thus the state can compel them to change their behaviour (for example, through the imposition of obligations, bans, enforcing compliance with requirements for permission-granting schemes), induce a change of behaviour by positive or negative economic incentives (for example, taxation schemes, tax relief, subsidies), or again suggest it through the manipulation of symbols and information (for example, campaigns to heighten public awareness of an issue, training programmes). The effectiveness of each method of government intervention with regard to the resolution of the collective problem depends, among other factors, on the practical relevance of the behavioural hypothesis that underlies it. This process of pre-emptive evaluation of private actors' capacity to react to government intervention is, however, contingent on the social structure of the target groups (Schneider and Ingram, 1993). In anti-drug addiction policy, the initiatives favoured by private and public actors vary significantly, depending on whether the actors perceive drug addicts as deviants and criminals who should be subjected to police intervention and legal sanctions, or as people who are ill and who should, therefore, be provided with medical help and social rehabilitation. Thus, it is up to the state to anticipate the possible reactions of the relevant target groups if it wishes to modify their behaviour with some degree of predictability.

In order to ensure that such reactions can be forecast with a degree of predictability, the public authorities generally participate in a (pre-parliamentary) consultation and negotiation procedure with the parties concerned and/or adopt a participatory approach to the implementation of the policy. These two strategies, whose aim is to legitimise and to make state intervention acceptable to the target groups, and end beneficiaries and third parties, result in the 'co-production' of certain policies. At implementation level, this then results in the fact that several tasks may be delegated to para-state or private organisations; for example, the management of milk quotas in France and in Switzerland, the monitoring of the origins of bank funds in Switzerland), the provision of psychological and material support for the homeless in France and the supervision of the conduct of doctors in the UK.

The suggestion that a policy is based on a – usually implicit, partial or indefinite – model of causality (that is, hypotheses of causality and intervention) derives from an instrumental and rationalist interpretation of public intervention. This is naturally open to criticism. It must be emphasised, however, that, even in cases where a policy has been adopted and implemented for a reason other than the resolution of a collective problem (for example, in order to affirm the power of the state in a symbolic way, for the purposes of electoral competition, personal, organisational or institutional prestige, selective targeting of a certain social class), the methods applied inevitably generate new framework conditions for public and private actors, and the effects that derive from this can potentially affect the course of social change.

Furthermore, as every policy plays a part in the definition of the relationships between the three defined groups of actors, it is intrinsically redistributive in nature. This being the case, it always brings about a change in the material and symbolic attributes enjoyed by the different actors, by imposing costs (induced by changes in behaviour) on the target groups addressed, and by granting privileges (linked to the improvement of their personal situation) to the end beneficiaries of the public initiative. By objectifying these redistributive effects between individuals and social groups, policy analysis also aims to answer the traditional question put to political scientists: 'Who gets what, when, how' (Lasswell, 1936). At a time when it is no longer simply a question of distributing the fruits of growth, today, it would be necessary to add 'from whom?' to this question.

Up until now, we have argued that policies aim to resolve a collective problem, and, therefore, to have an impact on the process of social change and the way that this evolves. In order to do this, the public actor must designate the target groups whose activities (or passivity) may be one of the (in)direct causes of the situation that is judged to be unacceptable from a political point of view. Having formulated this causal hypothesis, the public actors must then apply – in accordance with the politically conceived intervention hypothesis – certain initiatives and procedures that effectively encourage the target groups to alter their behaviour. Consequently, a policy's causality model always constitutes a normative representation of the way in which society functions and of the behaviour of private actors. Ultimately, its validity can only be tested in the context of policy implementation and the subsequent evaluation of their effects.

This entire discussion presupposes, nevertheless, that a social problem has been defined politically as a public one and that, consequently, a public intervention measure of a redistributive nature is imperative.

This precondition concerning the link between the beneficiaries of public initiatives and political-administrative actors is not necessarily a given in everyday reality (see Chapter Seven on the political definition of a public problem).

Notes

[1] Note here that every group is always a social (and political) construct. With regard to this point, refer to the example of the typology of social groups developed by Schneider and Ingram (1997).

[2] While, in conformity with contemporary practice in English, gendered pronouns have generally been avoided in situations where the actor could be of either gender, there are situations like these where they have been kept because an alternative formulation would substantially change the form of a translated quotation from French.

[3] Just as a 'non-decision' expresses one of the forms of power (according to the thesis of Bachratz and Baratz, 1963, 1970; see also Wollmann, 1980, p 34), a passive attitude ('non-action') is one of the possible modes of behaviour that policy actors may adopt. It should also be noted that some discussions of this topic, such as that by Lukes (1974), go further to try to identify 'interests' that are entirely suppressed (see the discussion in Hill, 2005, pp 33-5).

[4] Article 5 of the Federal Law on Administrative Procedure of 20 December 1968 (LPA, RS 172.02).

FOUR

Policy resources

In this chapter, we present the resources that motivate public and private actors to assert their values and interests in the course of the different stages in the policy life cycle. In the traditional policy analyses, resources are generally considered as specific elements of political-administrative programmes (PAPs), or as means of action specific to actors' efforts to resolve a collective problem.

In reality, a policy is not created or realised in a void. From the outset, the available resources exert a significant influence on the intermediate and final results of a policy. Even before the first intervention plans have been drafted, civil servants, politicians and private actors already see themselves as confronted with the 'conditions of production' for a proposed public action; they find themselves situated on a 'building site' with limited but necessary resources for the structuring and 'construction' of a public policy.

Until recently, the only policy resources considered by analysts were the law (legal and regulative bases), money and personnel. However, research carried out in recent years by representatives of the administrative sciences working in the area of organisational sociology, human resources and information systems shows that information, organisation, public infrastructure, time and consensus can also be considered as resources employed by policy actors. Political scientists also stress the importance of the political support or power that can be mobilised as a resource by different actors.

The availability of different resources to the actors involved in a policy process, their production, management, exploitation, combination, and even their substitution or exchange, can exert a significant influence on the processes, results and effects of a policy. In a number of variants of the New Public Management model the distribution and 'management' of resources at the disposal of policy actors is seen as a matter of choice for the executive. This approach involves treating such important resources as, for example, organisation, consensus, time as the sole responsibility of executive bodies and aims to limit the influence of parliament. Decisions about these have political elements; hence this approach may undermine democracy (Knoepfel, 1996, 1997b). As we shall demonstrate in this chapter, in our opinion,

Public policy analysis

it is an excessively narrow vision of the role of policy resources and their influence on the quality of policy implementation and its effects.

4.1 Different types of resources

The relative weight of the different resources can vary from one policy to the next. The actors will exchange a number of the resources that they have at their disposal or will mobilise them in order to achieve their objectives. This exchange of resources constitutes the essence of the interactions to be analysed (Wälti, 1999). In effect, the status of resources can change appreciably in the course of such exchanges: private information becomes public when it is placed at the disposal of all of the actors involved in a given policy process. The right of appeal, which is granted to certain actors while excluding others, limits the use of the resource of law and so on for those who are excluded from this resource.

Thus, it is necessary to analyse in detail which resources are available for which types of actor, and which modifications with respect to the access to and use of a resource (exclusivity versus non-exclusivity) and the quantity of the resource (rivalry versus non-rivalry of consumption) are established by the institutional rules pertaining to a public policy. In this context, the analyst asks whether a resource constitutes a public or private commodity, and how the public or private nature of a particular resource develops over time.

A copious literature exists on the resources at the disposal of different actors. For political scientists and sociologists of organisations, these resources are mainly constituted by constraint and legitimacy (Bernoux, 1985, p 161); for economists they are represented in terms of work, capital (natural and artificial) and organisations; for lawyers these resources are expressed in terms of, for example, the right of intervention, participation and decision.

Our concept of resources is specific to the analysis of public policies: thus, we propose to define 10 resources that public and private actors will be able (or not) to produce and mobilise in the course of the policy formulation and implementation processes. This typology is based on different sources but particularly the classifications developed by Crozier and Friedberg (1977), as well as those of Klok (1995), Dente (1995) and Padioleau (1982).

While these resources are sometimes accessible to all, they are unequally distributed among the actors participating in the different stages of a policy life cycle. For example, even if the resource 'law' is primarily available to political-administrative actors, the right of appeal

Policy resources

that may be granted to a private actor (by the laws concerning administrative procedure or judicial/legal organisation) will also constitute an action resource of a legal nature for this actor.

Figure 4.1 shows the different resources at the disposal of policy actors, while leaving open the possibility that other types exist that have yet to be discovered or clarified. We are not concerned with providing an exhaustive account of these ten resources and their specific contribution to public policies. Instead, we will underline certain specific aspects of these (generally rare) resources.

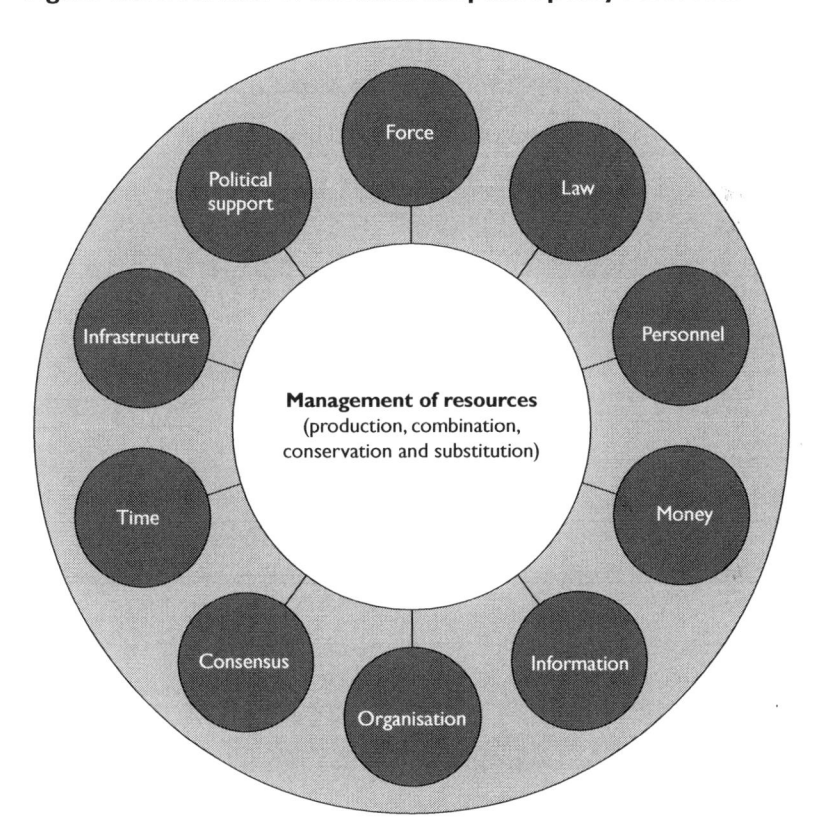

Figure 4.1: Overview of the different public policy resources

Ring of resources: Force, Law, Personnel, Money, Information, Organisation, Consensus, Time, Infrastructure, Political support — surrounding "Management of resources (production, combination, conservation and substitution)".

4.1.1 Law or the 'legal' resource

The law differs from the other resources in that it is mainly (but not exclusively) at the disposal of public actors. The law constitutes the source of legitimisation *par excellence* for all public actions (Bernoux, 1985, p 161). It provides an important resource for public actors in the form of 'legal and regulatory bases' and in the absence of this resource, administrative measures can be contested and even invalidated by decisions of administrative courts.

In the context of policy resources as a whole, the law occupies a prominent place because it constitutes the normative raison d'être of the PAP that organises both the content (definition of objectives and behaviour of target groups) and choice of other resources (organisations, procedure or financial provisions).

The endowment of different actors with legal resources is defined by the combined rules of law adopted by the legislature and the executive. In democratic regimes, the legislature generally finds itself involved in the process of the production of this resource. However, in the majority of cases, parliamentary decisions are limited to its allocation in terms of money and rights. Nevertheless, through the attribution of these two resources, the legislature equally decides – at least in part – on the endowment of other resources (inasmuch as they consider them important).

Despite its relatively high degree of objectivisation, statute law requires reproductive and management activity. Like the other resources, the law can lose its 'value': when it is used in an excessively intensive or abusive manner it is no longer a source of support for public policies. Thus, excessive formalism or extreme normative density may deprive the regulations of sense and, consequently, lead to their questioning by those at whom they are directed, or even by the administration that is supposed to enforce them. Thus, the law loses its legitimacy. This was (or sometimes still is) the case in the former Eastern-bloc countries where over-regulation in the different areas of public intervention led to the absence of respect for law.

More generally in order to retain its normative character and thus avoid becoming completely devalued, the law needs to be 'stated' and 're-stated' (Moor, 1997) through administrative and legal practice.

4.1.2 Personnel or the 'human' resource

This resource, which may be either quantitative or qualitative in nature, is a function of the recruitment services and personnel training services. Crozier and Friedberg (1977) classified it as one of the four resources at the disposal of organisations when establishing their power[1]. For this reason, it is traditionally the object of human resource management (see Emery and Gonin, 1999, p 13).

Policy actors develop a language specific to their activity that is based on the technical terminology used in their specific field of intervention. The people involved in a policy should, therefore, have a flair for communication and (increasingly) expert professional qualifications.

In order to avoid becoming too technocratic, human resource management must also ensure that no actor (public or private) is systematically excluded from the process of the development and application of these new languages. In this regard, it is argued that the organisation of courses to be taken jointly by the representatives of the administration, the economy and professional and scientific bodies is essential, particularly in the case of policies of a highly technical nature (for example, spatial planning, environment, energy, transport, health, drugs).

In many countries, the close links between the qualifications necessary for policy management and personnel training have led to the establishment of specific training programmes by the administration. In France, the relationship between training and administration is particularly well developed because of the existence of the third-level *grandes écoles*. Be they technical (for example, *Ecole polytechnique et ses écoles d'application, Ecole nationale des ponts et chaussées, Ecoles des mines, Ecole du génie rural des eaux et forêts*), administrative or legal (*Ecole nationale d'administration, Ecole de la magistrature*), these colleges provide a breeding ground for civil servants involved in the conception and implementation of public policies. The training programme at these colleges is specific with most of the teaching provided by active members of the administration. Thus, the language and doctrines of existing and practised policies are transmitted directly to the students. Furthermore, further education and training programmes for established civil servants are regularly organised either by these colleges or by bodies attached to ministries (for example, the *Centre Interrégional de formation professionnelle du Ministère de l'équipement*).

In the case of the Swiss Confederation, several courses of this nature have been created at the universities and other institutions: for example, the diploma courses provided by the *Écoles polytechniques fédérales* that reflect the need for the professionalisation of national policies (for example, graduate diplomas in food chemistry, engineering, environmental sciences, forestry, agronomy etc) and the courses and qualifications recognised by the Federal Office for Professional Education and Technology (for example, the qualification of 'specialist in nature conservation', which is awarded by the Swiss Centre for Nature Conservation and Environmental Protection that was founded by the Swiss Academy of the Natural Sciences, and other certificates of proficiency in the areas of health, telecommunications and social policy).

While in the UK public authorities have had similar concerns about staff training, course development has been less systematic. This seems to be partly a consequence of the influence of the view that 'management' is a generic skill, applicable to both public and private organisations, with the latter having a great deal to teach the public sector. Officials from local government and the health service have been encouraged to take MBA (Master of Business Administration) courses, only some of which have had a specific public sector orientation. Within central government, at the same time, training for civil servants has been largely kept 'in house', within a National School of Government (formerly known the Centre for Management and Policy Studies and before that the Civil Service College), which does not offer specific qualifications, or within individual departments.

In France several sociological studies (Padioleau, 1982; Thoenig, 1985; Vlassopoulou, 1999) have stressed the negative effects arising from the presence of a socio-professional 'corps' in the public policy arena. These negative effects include isolation, a lack of transparency and democratic control due to a defensive technicisation and the risk of cronyism and *pantouflage* (rotation of senior civil servants between the public and private sector). In Switzerland the relative absence of rotation between sectors means that there is a risk of professional 'blinkering'. In the UK these arguments about isolation are also found, but efforts have been made to encourage open recruitment to senior posts within the public sector.

The definition of qualifications required to manage a given policy is generally considered as the concern of the administration and the task usually falls to the human resources services of the bodies concerned with the policy in question. These services generally wish to define these qualifications alone rather than having them approved by centralised personnel services whose task is to implement a coherent institutional policy for the entire administration. This occurs in France when organisations (state services such as local authorities) have the (increasingly rare) possibility of recruiting 'contractors', whose professional profiles are more specific to the policies for which the organisations in question are responsible, instead of using permanent employees whose job descriptions are less flexible.

In certain cases, criteria are specifically defined in the PAP for a policy: this occurs, for example, in policy matters concerning the health sector, where medical graduates are required for certain posts. There has been a long tradition of this kind in the UK – particularly in

Policy resources

relation to education and health, and in regulatory activities where scientific expertise is relevant. Interestingly in this case the modern concern for greater flexibility in career patterns in government has encouraged movement from specialist posts to generic ones.

It should be noted that an increasingly important role for private actors is arising, where such people are called on to comment within very short periods on, for example, proposed regulations, plans and evaluation reports. Thus, even the secretaries of medium-sized organisations of regional scope maintain specialised management staff whose tasks consist in the ongoing follow-up of the public policies that concern them. These experts and quasi-policy practitioners are often recruited from the public service.

In terms of the exchange of resources, the lack of personnel with appropriate qualifications within the public sector can be counteracted through the purchase of these specific competencies from outside the administration: this is the case when an administration acquires expertise from private or public consultancies and is generally referred to as 'outsourcing'. This practice appears to becoming more common, in particular as a result of decisions to reduce personnel numbers in administrations (for example, *Personalstopp* or moratorium on recruitment by the Swiss Parliament), a measure that affects the personnel resources available to a greater or lesser extent and hence also the services at the disposal of an entire group of public policies. In the UK the development of agencies (initially stimulated by the 'Next Steps' initiative in the 1980s) has a similar impact. In practice agencies vary in the extent to which they are required to maintain civil service practices in relation to the recruitment and promotion of staff. Actually classifying UK governmental organisations, in relation to debates about the actual size of the civil service or – more seriously – concerns about public accountability has become a difficult and obscure activity (Jordan, 1994; Drewry, 2002).

4.1.3 Money or the 'financial' resource

This resource is clearly one of the most obvious for all concerned. It is raised and allocated not only in the case of distributive policies, but also in the case of regulatory or constitutive policies. Without the finance to pay for salaries, accommodation, office and IT equipment and the necessary analysis tools the effective implementation of a public policy is impossible. Numerous central, regional and local authorities engage in the practice of 'outsourcing', that is, the purchase of work, advice, expertise and other services from external private consultancies and laboratories. Several policies use different types of financial incentives to prompt private individuals or public bodies to adopt the behaviour desired by the policy. This practice is particularly common in decentralised federal states: thus almost 60% of the Swiss Confederation's budget consists of subsidies granted (in the form of financial payments or compensation) in return for the implementation of federal policies. This practice is also becoming more common in France, a more centralised country, and being implemented through contractualisation processes being established between public bodies (that is, contracts between the state and the region, for example, *contrat de plan Etat Région, Contrat de Ville*) (Gaudin, 1996). In the UK central control over the resources available to local government (where over three quarters of local income is either directly allocated from central taxation or from local taxation controlled by central government) is important alongside legal controls for an explanation of central dominance over policy. Similarly the limited character of devolution to Scotland flows particularly from the minimal granting of additional tax-raising powers.

Therefore, the provision of public (and sometimes even private) policy actors with financial resources is considered as an important political measure, in which the legislator engages on a regular and very concrete basis.

According to our approach, this provision of finance for public actors should feature in the PAP defined for a policy by a parliament. However, in general, the link between policies and budgetary decisions remains very indirect, although perhaps less so in the UK than in France and Switzerland. Budgetary categories only partly reflect policies and their specific services because they are conceived on the basis of types of spending (classification by nature of spending) and often not with an eye to the creation of specific policies (a more functional classification). In addition, in many cases, these categories apply to all of the administrations within the authorities in question (that is, those dealing with salaries, equipment, expertise and subsidies). Thus, the traditional budgetary process does not facilitate the precise control of the funding of different policies implemented by administrations. The annual nature of the budgetary process (despite increasingly frequent attempts to develop financial planning that runs over several years) and difficulties in changing the financial accounting categories hinder any major change (despite the trial introduction of analytical accounting) and only rarely facilitate the combination of resources from different budgetary categories. This accounting system has been criticised for its rigidity in the past by public finance experts and, today, by the supporters of New Public Management, who propose its replacement with service mandates or contracts and budgets extending over several years to be defined in an ad hoc manner for each public policy on the basis of proposed services. The shift to a cost accounting system (developed on the basis of the estimation of the cost of administrative products) gives rise to profound changes at the level of how the organisation of the public administration works (structuring according to administrative product categories), and at the level of state financial policy. In effect, cost accounting tends to prevent MPs from monitoring the different types of accrued expenses that represent important factors for the management of economic, fiscal or budgetary policies, which – in periods of economic recession and financial crisis – are the focus of the attention of parliamentarians. Furthermore, it may be noted that in many instances, parliament is more interested in the way in which state resources (in particular, money) are used than in the purpose of the spending in question (policy objective). For example, the Swiss programme for the construction of water treatment plants prescribed by the legislation of 1972 on the protection of waters against pollution and the programme for the construction of national and cantonal roads (from 1961) subsidised by the Swiss Confederation were passed almost unanimously on the basis of their positive effects on the regional economy, as opposed to concerns about water quality or the extension of the road network. In France, the failure of recent attempts to introduce parliamentary control of public spending from the point of view of its appropriateness bears witness to the difficulties facing reform in this area (Migaud, 2000).

In general, monetary resources are the most easily quantified and exchanged with or substituted for other types of resources. However, money is probably also the resource that is most unequally distributed among private actors, and one of the most essential in terms of the real political power of a policy actor.

4.1.4 Information or the 'cognitive' resource

Knowledge is one of the foundations of public and private actors' intervention capacity. Scarce and unequally distributed among public policy actors, this 'cognitive' resource consists of information acquired in relation to technical, social, economic and political data concerning the collective problem to be resolved (Padioleau, 1982). This 'raw material' comprises factors that are indispensable to the good management of a policy at all levels (political definition of the public problem, PAP, implementation and evaluation of effects).

Knowledge provides an essential basis for decision making. However, it is often expensive to produce and maintain and should, therefore, be considered as a scarce commodity in the majority of decision-making situations. In relation to a number of policies today, a kind of 'monitoring' is implemented to enable the ongoing observation of the evolution of the targeted problem. This is particularly true of environment policies, health policies and social and economic policies. Certain policies have their own services equipped with high-quality technical instruments for the production of the information necessary to their implementation (for example, agricultural research bodies, ministerial forecasting services).

The production, reproduction and dissemination of this resource require the provision and management of increasingly sophisticated information systems, which in turn require specific qualifications on the part their users. This state of affairs is at odds with the notion (partly rooted in the right of users to information) that all public and private actors must have equal access to the information. As research on implementation processes show, equal levels of information among all actors is a sine qua non condition for the effective functioning of policies (Kissling-Näf, 1997; Kissling-Näf and Knoepfel, 1998).

In the context of public policies, the distribution of this knowledge, which is financed by a state service, among private or public users on the basis of the laws of the market (for example, payable services) would be inappropriate. However, 'markets' or 'quasi-markets' are emerging today for all kinds of public data (for example, inventories, statistics, campaign results, results of publicly financed research). Moreover, it is possible to observe practices involving the withholding of information between services (national, regional and/or local) that are not solely motivated by strategic intentions (obtaining an advantage based on a file), but also by financial ones ('our service paid for the production of the data'). This tendency could be reinforced in the case of the application of the principles of cost accounting and the distribution of budgetary funding to different policies.

Traditionally, the production and – above all – the processing and distribution of statistical data on policies is the responsibility of special services (for example, the Federal Statistics Office and the cantonal and local authority statistics services in Switzerland; the National Institute of Statistics and Economic Studies in France; National Statistics [a body that has had regular changes of name in recent years] in the UK). This situation is justified by the need for scientific quality and (hopefully) independence on the part of these bodies and their services. Given the increasing importance of the information as a resource in the context of the daily conduct of various policies (for example, health, employment, spatial planning, energy, transport, environment), the public actors responsible for a particular policy have also been driven to managing their own data. This development has necessitated the adaptation of the relationships between the official statistics services and those of specialised public policies and has resulted in either the creation of a specific service (in the case of France, the creation of the French Institute of the Environment [*IFEN*], a statistics service specialising in the area of the environment, and the French Ministry for Agriculture's Central Service for Enquiries and Statistical Studies, a statistical service specialising in the area of agriculture) or in the establishment of specific agreements between different public services to share data.

The question of the level of cognitive resources available to policies goes back to the role of expertise in public decision making (see in particular, Callon and Rip, 1991; Latour, 1991; Theys, 1991; Barker and Peters, 1993). In situations characterised by growing uncertainty, the control of information is set to play an increasingly important but also controversial role. This is particularly true of the surveillance of radioactive fallout in France that is the subject of controversy and has prompted environmental protection organisations to set up their own monitoring body working in parallel to the state services. Similarly, the question of the carcinogenicity of certain food products necessitates very expensive research and does not always provide unambiguous results (the case of nitrates in drinking water and plants: Knoepfel and Zimmermann, 1987, p 81). A similar situation exists in the area of the environment with respect to climate change where significant uncertainty continues to exist despite considerable research efforts.

There are also a number of worldwide bodies involved in the collection of statistics (particularly the Organisation for Economic Co-operation and Development, the World Bank and various organisations linked to the United Nations) and within Europe the data relating to the countries of the European Union is collated by Eurostat. In the context of global efforts to influence national politics on matters like market regulation and environmental pollution, and of EU concerns with the coordination of economic (and to some extent social) policies, these activities – although inevitably influenced by state data collection – may provide important policy resources.

4.1.5 Organisation or the 'interactive' resource

This resource is more difficult to identify. It corresponds in part to the resource 'use of organisational rules' proposed by Crozier and Friedberg (1977).

Organisation is a resource constructed on the basis of the individual actors present, the quality of the organisation of the administrative or societal structures to which they belong and the existence of networks of relationships between the different policy actors. From the perspective of policy actors, this resource is also based on the internal structures of the political–administrative arrangement (PAA), that is, the actors' capacity to organise the interaction processes between them, and on the presence of collective values that are usually shared and constantly updated in the course of action ('learning organisation': see Levitt and March, 1988).

In the policy analysis context, we consider actors (possibly a group comprising several individuals) who fulfil the specific functions associated with the conduct of a public policy as fundamental elements of public organisation (in the broad sense). These actors are located within one or several administrative organisations (for example, public corporations, departments, devolved services, central ministries), and even outside administrations. This resource varies on the basis of the characteristics of each individual actor and the quality of the network that links the various actors to each other. Each type of organisation can contribute in a different way to the success of the policy in question. Suitable organisations may improve the quality of services or spare other resources (for example, personnel or time), or increase their availability (for example, consensus or information). For this reason, we consider organisation as a resource that is different to a 'human resource'; the latter can be of a very high quality but nonetheless so badly organised that the services it provides are ultimately mediocre and expensive. Thus, this interactive resource requires creation, follow-up and adaptation strategies that differ to those required by 'human resources'.

Every policy is likely to have to own distinctive organisational form. The 'interactive resource' at the disposal of policy actors is of major importance in terms of the quality of services. Despite this, large-scale changes in the public sector (for example, the creation of new departments and ministries, amalgamations, elimination and reassignment of policies to other structures) are generally carried out without the involvement of parliament. Thus the new Swiss law on the organisation of the federal administration delegates a very large part of the organisational competencies – creation, modification of federal departments and their responsibilities – to the Federal Council (Swiss government). In the UK departmental arrangements are often changed more or less on the whim of the Prime Minister when Cabinet reshuffles occur.

The main organisational units that accommodate the public actors generally have several hierarchical levels (in Switzerland: the federal 'office', directorate, main division and division or sector; in France: ministry, central administrative body, department, service and authority; in the UK arrangements are more varied, complicated by the importance of agencies). Empirical research has shown that the existence of a strong hierarchy tends to hinder the development of a sense of responsibility among officials working at the bottom of the agency in direct contact with the partners of the administration ('clients'). Furthermore, it tends to divide and fragment the processing of files, thus giving rise to administrative services with a low degree of coherency. More generally, such rigid hierarchical structures do not accommodate the introduction of transverse functions whose task is to systematically monitor the coherency of policy programming and implementation.

As a result, organisations based on a strong hierarchy and a sedimentation logic associated with legislative history are increasingly replaced by structures with two or a maximum of three hierarchical levels that give greater responsibility to the people who actually deal with the files. Moreover, the organisational structure takes into account the types of services and different target groups of the policy in question so as to avoid the multiple passing of files from one service to another. Thus, the basic units unite teams capable of integrating all of the aspects to be dealt with into a coherent end product. Experience shows that because it involves 'generalists' who also need to have relatively advanced specialised knowledge at their disposal, this transformation of the resource organisation requires significant effort in terms of education and training (Baitsch et al, 1996).

A key concern for modern British government has been a search for organisational forms that will facilitate collaborative arrangements in the implementation of closely related policies. But there are doubts as to whether there are readily recognisable optimal solutions. The consequence has been repeated organisational change that may detract from the value of organisation as a resource (in the National Health Service, for example, coping with frequent organisational change has been seen as a source of inefficiency in policy delivery; for discussions of these issues see Newman, 2001; Pollitt, 2003).

4.1.6 Consensus or the 'confidence' resource

Consensus is a resource that every actor may or may not have at their disposal. Conflicts and obstacles arise in the absence of consensus. This confidence-based resource adds a degree of secondary legitimation that is not provided by majority democratic suffrage (see the resource 'political support'). It may even counterbalance or reinforce this democratic legitimacy of the state during concrete public intervention processes (Knoepfel, 1977, p 222). This resource is generally widely exchanged between actors during policy implementation. Consensus represents an increasingly important issue in the development and execution of infrastructure and environment policies (for example, national roads, high-voltage power lines, nuclear waste) with spatial implications (see Terribilini, 1999; Wälti, 1999; Knoepfel et al, 2001).

(Relative) consensus between the political-administrative actors, the end beneficiaries and target groups with respect to the production modalities and contents of implementation measures (outputs) has become a basic resource for all policies. Given the strength of policy target groups and – increasingly – end beneficiaries, administrations find themselves increasingly less capable of conducting a policy in the face of open and firm opposition from one of these social groups, even if the associated law enjoys significant political support. A minimum level of consensus is required for an administration to be able to implement its policies reasonably and efficiently.

As mentioned above, for public actors, consensus as a resource differs from the legitimacy constituted by political support from the legislature or the democratic majority that can be described as primary (see Section 4.1.9). In effect, democratic legitimacy, conveyed through voting processes, solely defines the objectives and rules of play for actors participating in the policy implementation process and does not determine (in detail) the specific modes of production of formal measures and their concrete content.

Traditional administrative procedures did not include provisions for specific rights of participation for all concerned parties; the general principles governing administrative procedures merely guaranteed a right of hearing to the subjects of administration whose legal rights were violated. In most cases, this exclusively concerns target groups to whom administrative practice granted a minimum right of inspection of the public action. These rights of participation[2] were extended to end beneficiaries in the course of the 1980s (in particular in areas such as spatial planning, planning of major infrastructure, environmental protection, social policy, consumer protection; see Knoepfel et al, 1999 for examples involving military structures and installations). The raison d'être of this movement was the recognition of the necessity for a double legitimation of public action by the sovereign power (primary legitimacy) *and* its direct (target groups) *and* indirect (end beneficiaries) (secondary legitimacy) addressees. This minimum level of consensus was considered necessary to avoid actual physical impediments (for example, occupations of sites, open battles in the streets, disregard of administrative orders) and avalanches of appeals at the administrative courts.

Consensus is an important resource that makes it possible to make savings with respect to other resources (in particular law, money and time), and as such deserves particular attention. Current administrative practice and the social sciences now offer numerous strategies in this area under the headings of information, consultation, participation, negotiation and mediation (Hoffmann-Riem, 1989; Hoffmann-Riem and Schmidt-Assmann, 1990; Weidner, 1993, 1997). All of these socio-technical 'public marketing' procedures hinge on the creation and conservation of consensus.

Thus, it would appear that this resource is not merely precious; it is also very fragile. Research from the 1970s on participatory approaches demonstrates that a 'culture of consensus' requires a certain level of temporal continuity, equal access for all actors, organised conflict-regulation approaches, the concern of a tolerant political-administrative practice – enabling the management of variable majority ratios – and, finally, a guarantee of adequate exchange between the participating bodies so as to avoid structures becoming too closely associated with individual cases (Weidner, 1993).

Recent examples of specific measures aimed at strengthening this resource include 'conciliation groups' in Switzerland that were established in the area of energy policy (nuclear waste, hydro-electric power and high-voltage power lines; see Knoepfel et al, 1997). Special structures have also been created in France, such as the National Commission of Public Debate, introduced by the law of 1995, which makes provision for the prior discussion of potentially controversial planning projects, and the so-called 'Bianco' commissions that were set up as part of the application of the law on interior transport (1982) in the case of major road and rail infrastructure projects. Consultative practices are widespread in the UK, given specific forms in bodies seeking consumer opinions about the privatised utilities and about the NHS, and in central government requirements that local authorities consult widely. There have also been long-standing arrangements for statutory public enquiries on potentially controversial planning matters – for example, new roads or airports, nuclear power installations.

4.1.7 Time or the 'temporal' resource

Some authors do not consider time as a resource in itself. However, having been made aware of its 'volatility' in the course of a policy life cycle by our empirical analyses, in particular in the area of planning policy and environmental protection, we decided to include it in our typology of resources.

It is not uncommon to hear statements to the effect that the construction of a policy 'takes time'. It is certainly true that teaching and learning about the myriad communication processes involved in public policies take more and more time. It should also be noted that this temporal resource is generally referred to with negative connotations in political-administrative language ('lack of time'). The need for this resource for all public policies is incontestable. In effect, policy participants find themselves drawing up a clearly defined 'time budget'. Thus, deadlines are generally defined for the compliance of installations in the context of environmental protection policy and in the enforcement of wage policy (the case of the French law on the 35-hour week, for example, whereby different application deadlines were defined according to the category of company). Indeed the controversial element in cases of compliance centres less and less on the requirements themselves and increasingly on time allocated to proceed with the necessary reorganisation measures. It is surprising to see how seldom this question has been addressed, be it at political or academic level, although 'lack of time' warrants a mention in almost all government and parliamentary reports. In addition, time is the essential object of conflicts surrounding the implementation of new policies (for example, transitory and agreed deadlines, crisis situations, coordination constraints affected by time).

The distribution of this 'temporal resource' among policy actors is generally unequal. Public actors who, due to their function, have more time at their disposal than representatives of social groups working on a voluntary basis, frequently tend to underestimate this resource in their calculations and in doing this to outperform those who suffer from a lack of time. Such dysfunction may be avoided through a more equitable distribution of this resource among the actors, that is, by allocating more generous deadlines to the private actors.

Finally, time is also relevant in terms of the stakes and synchronisation problems involved in the policy process. Thus, public and private actors can capitalise on time by indicating that they will only act if the other actors act first, simultaneously or subsequently.

4.1.8 Infrastructure or the 'property' resource

The resource infrastructure includes all of the tangible goods or property at the disposal of the different actors, including public actors, whether the actors are the owners of these goods or have acquired a right of use to them (by means of a rental contract, for example). The goods relevant to the public domain are, therefore, very diverse: they vary from a road to a river or state forest and various old (historical heritage) or new (administrative, cultural centres etc) buildings. All policies benefit from an allocation of public goods to a greater or lesser extent: the least well-endowed benefit only from the buildings that house the services responsible for their development or implementation and the better-endowed benefit from vast expanses (state forests, for example). Certain policies explicitly aim to increase this allocation of goods. This is the case with town planning policy that deals traditionally with property reserves, for example, or housing policy that is concerned, in part, with the construction of social housing.

Two main 'benefits' may be associated with this resource. The first concerns the capacity of public actors to directly mange a service or, more directly, to impose restrictions in cases in which the state or public body is the owner or manager of the goods in question. Thus, it may be easier to close an environmentally sensitive area to the public if it is owned by the state than if it is 'private' property. In France and in the UK, the policy of nationalising large companies in the postwar period and in the early 1980s corresponded to this desire to base the state's policies on companies directly controlled by it (for example, the railways and the gas and electricity supply companies). The waves of liberalisation and privatisation that unfolded in the late 1980s have resulted in the re-examination of this strategic option.

This logic, which was pushed to extremes in Communist countries over the past 30 or 40 years, still exists in part in certain countries; for example, environmental protection policy in the Ukraine is based on the imposition of restrictions on the users of land and facilitated by the fact that for the most part land is still in collective or state ownership.

The second 'benefit' concerns the communication capacity that these infrastructures provide for the actors of the political-administrative system.

Administrative property includes a vast range of physical equipment necessary for government, and, in the language of policy analysis, necessary to produce implementation measures on the interface between the state and civil society. It is true that the characteristics of this equipment depend largely on the use made of it by actors who manage the organisational and cognitive resources. Thus, administrative buildings represent a production space that facilitates the myriad communications between the individual members of the administrative organisation in question and the target groups and end beneficiaries of policies. And a wide range of administrative equipment is used to facilitate communication in modern administrations including paper, forms, computer software and hardware, works of art, plants and even equipment used for catering and security services, fire services and care-taking services. According to their official purpose, at least, all of these facilities make it possible to facilitate communication between public actors and society.

However, infrastructure or the 'property resource' is not limited to material equipment. The administrative building is also the physical incarnation of the interface between policy and the real world. The building is in fact the site where communication takes place between the state and its citizens. Thus, all of the external communication aids, both individual (post and telecommunications system, that is, telephone, post, email, fax) and collective (meeting rooms, conference rooms, press conference rooms, television distribution network) belong to the resource infrastructure. The apparatus associated with administrative buildings is becoming increasingly complex and its management an increasingly important resource at the disposal of policy actors. This is due, among other things, to the fact that a growing number of policies work on the basis of persuasive instruments and, furthermore, that numerous formal administrative measures must now be accompanied by an explanatory communication.

The availability of infrastructure and the communication it facilitates varies in time and space. In times of crisis or disaster, its absence may prompt the questioning of an entire policy (for example, incapacity of emergency services to disseminate an evacuation order in a disaster area due to a lack of telecommunications resources), despite the availability of the resource information (for example, knowledge of the imminent arrival of a hurricane on the part of meteorological forecasting services). Similarly, the non-availability of a room or software programme necessary for holding negotiations with opposition actors at a given time or in a specific place may strongly undermine the success of a controversial infrastructure policy (for example, lack of an appropriate room for receiving several hundred opponents of a road construction project and lack of a software programme capable of quickly mapping possible variations for a contested stretch of road in the context of such a mediation meeting). The lack of representation of the central administration in districts/provinces/neighbourhoods or an inappropriate territorial network may distance citizens from their administration and thus create a physical barrier between public policy and the real world that is detrimental to the success of negotiations.

All of these examples demonstrate the crucial role played by the infrastructure at the disposal of public policy actors. This has largely been acknowledged in the reality of modern administrations. For some time now, certain public administrations have been establishing specific functions, such as (centralised or decentralised) IT services, press services, government publishing offices, office equipment services, services for the construction of administrative buildings and special state telecommunications services for the purpose of creating, managing and using this resource.

Today, the management of the resource infrastructure is a cause of controversy between trades unions and public service management and between central ministries and their devolved services. In effect, the trades unions are opposed to proposals for the privatisation of individual components of this resource (for example, cleaning services, canteens, office equipment, IT services) while the management bodies oppose the centralisation of this resource at the level of the general ministerial secretariat (IT service responsible for all IT functions in the public administration; centralised press service). Finally, it should be noted that unlike the majority of other public resources, like time, infrastructure is seldom the object of research or teaching. The 'communications/public marketing' sector appears to remain underdeveloped, which is all the more regrettable as this resource has made an important contribution to the conception and support of other resources (for example, consensus, time, organisation and information), and is now subject to restructuring as a part of privatisation measures, whose consequences have not been clearly established.

4.1.9 Political support or the 'majority' resource

According to the rules of the democratic state, during its creation or any major change in its content, every policy needs legal bases that are approved by a majority of parliamentarians (or citizens and, possibly also, the cantons in the case of Switzerland). This approval lends it a primary legitimacy (as distinct from the secondary legitimacy associated with the appreciation of its services by social groups; see Section 4.1.6). This production of legal bases indicates at a given time the majority political support enjoyed by all of the actors involved in a policy. Furthermore, it is with the help of such legal bases that public actors associated with a given policy may assert themselves if necessary over minority social groups. However, any observer or public policy actor will confirm that despite the existence of a legal basis comfortably approved by parliament, a policy may be subject to periods of crisis, during which it risks losing this majority support if it is subject to another vote in parliament. A time-lag can sometimes be observed between the legitimation of the law and its real legitimation.

The resource 'political support' concerns this second aspect of primary legitimation and consists at any moment in its existence in the potential acceptability of the policy in question by a parliamentary or popular majority. This predominantly involves strongly contested phases that generally manifest themselves in terms of the loss of the resource consensus at implementation level. The reasons behind the loss of this resource are often foreseeable.

Thus, a policy may lose its acceptance by a majority if its services and projects are re-examined. This may be due to:

- negative effects (for example, the very different way different Swiss cantons apply the Federal Swiss Law on the Acquisition of Property by Foreigners; see Delley et al, 1982);
- effects contrary to the policy objectives (loss of policy coherence, for example agricultural overproduction);
- implementation deficits that are evident or arise as a result of a change in the values or customs in the area of intervention of the policy in question (for example, penalisation of so-called 'soft' drug consumption, abortion, cohabitation or passive euthanasia).

The effective loss of the resource 'political support' may arise as a result of the subjection of individual cases to public debate (particularly in the media), or by means of parliamentary intervention in the form of questions or motions demanding changes in policies that have become highly politicised. Thus, the question of 'how to produce or reproduce the resource political support' arises among the actors concerned. Numerous resources have already been developed to try to overcome such a loss: for example, the establishment of an evaluation process (to 're-establish' coherency), efforts to provide public explanations, the mobilisation or modification of symbolic values that could muster a new majority, the disparagement of opponents thus placed in a minority position.

Recourse to symbolic values shared by the majority appears to be a common means of producing and reproducing this resource: for example, political support for agricultural policy may be re-established by referring to the role of agriculture in 'supplying food for the country in periods of crisis' and, hence, the defence of the nation, in contributing to the export market and hence the balance of payments (in France) and in the management of the countryside (a salient argument in the UK where the decline of agriculture has weakened the use of the other arguments).

The repetition of these symbolic values contributes to the stabilisation of the relationships between a political majority and political support for a particular public policy. It should be noted that it is possible to substitute new symbolic values for defunct values without modifying the policy in question one iota. Thus, the symbolic communication of a policy would appear an almost indispensable means for the reproduction of its resource 'political support'.

The availability of the resource 'political support' makes it possible to save on other resources, while in the case of its absence, it may lead to the increased use or abuse of other resources. Policy actors who enjoy broad political support may (temporarily) manage without consensus as a resource (nuclear power policy in France in the 1970s), or law as a resource (security policy, particularly in the UK since 9/11 and the 2005 London bombings), time as a resource (rapid interventions short-circuiting procedures deemed too time consuming) or information as a resource (if the conviction of the majority replaces the serious quest for the causes of the existence of a collective problem).

All of these substitutions show the primordial importance of the resource 'political support'. This is particularly applicable during the first phase of a public policy that consists in the (re-)definition of the public problem to be resolved and the identification of its causes. In fact, in many cases the symbols used convey implicit causal hypotheses largely shared by the political majority without necessitating specific reasoning. Thus, it is not necessary to prove that everything that is ecological is good and that all those who contribute to national defence contribute to the wellbeing of the country because ecology and national defence are part of values shared and accepted by the majority of citizens.

4.1.10 Force or the 'violent' resource

Just like money as a resource, legitimate constraint by physical force is easy to understand. It is even a primordial element of the policies adopted by dictatorial regimes.

Many public policies do not avail of this resource, which is often considered as an extreme. Nonetheless, some of them are specifically based on physical force, in particular security or defence policies. The capacity of public actors to physically restrain an individual or a policy target group to change behaviour should not be underestimated: the closure by the authorities of installations considered as operating outside of the law, the physical control or legitimate violence of the forces of order in response to opposition from target groups or end beneficiaries, even if they constitute a legitimate constraint by the law and are generally dependent on personnel, may be conceptually dissociated from other resources.

Nevertheless, physical force is a resource rarely used in its own right. It is generally exchanged for consensus. However, the threat of recourse to force may be a determining factor during the implementation of certain policies, in particular those based on legal obligations. For both target groups and end beneficiaries, force may represent a resource that allows the expression of profound disagreement (violent street demonstrations, for example) or the blocking of a property resource at the disposal of another actor (a strike picket in front of a company premises, for example).

The management of the resource 'constraint by force' is a highly sensitive matter. Its use generally requires an association with majority political support; in the absence of the latter it risks being the source of the loss of the resource consensus for a considerable period of time. Furthermore, in certain situations, the recourse to violence must receive extensive media coverage to be effective: in the case of road security, for example, it would appear to be impossible to physically control all those who break the rules of the road in all places at all times. On the other hand, however, the deployment of the police to reinforce controls during holiday weekends in France when road deaths are a frequent occurrence has a real impact if it is accompanied by extensive media coverage targeted at the motorists concerned.

4.2 Management of resources

4.2.1 Principle of the sustainable management of resources

The link between the analysis and management of public policies and the public management sector consists in the processing and management of the above-listed resources. Each resource has its own 'laws' that govern its production, reproduction and utilisation. Today, relatively well-developed disciplinary knowledge exists in the areas of personnel management ('human resources management'), money ('public finance'), organisations ('sociology of organisations', 'organisational learning') and information ('information systems management').

The same more or less applies with regard to the management of the law as a resource law ('jurisprudence' – legislative techniques), although to our knowledge a real 'law management' sector does not yet exist. The management of consensus or 'social engineering', which is necessary for the reasonable management of conflicts, would appear to be still at an early stage in its gestation at present. In effect, although almost endless improvements have been made to legal procedure, this discipline is still relatively underdeveloped in the area of political and administrative procedure (for example, the case of 'mediation' and 'participative evaluation'). With regard to the management of time as a resource (logistics) highly sporadic achievements have been realised without, however, leading to the creation of an actual 'discipline'. In our opinion, all researchers and practitioners working in the area of policy analysis must be familiar with the specific features of the sustainable production and management of all of the state's action resources.

According to the theory of sustainable development, which originated in the field of environmental policy and subsequently became more generalised, all scarce resources, be they public or private, natural or artificial, must be utilised in a moderate manner with an awareness of the long-term perspectives. The adoption and implementation of this perspective will have important consequences for the public sector as a whole because it would appear that our public resources are currently managed in an abusive and non-sustainable manner.

Can it not be said that we are abusing time as a resource in our companies and administrations that tend to accelerate the rhythms of production with the result that nobody can allow themselves time for reflection? Are we really managing law as a resource in a sustainable manner when we increasingly have people believe that information deemed true or admissible today will be false or prohibited tomorrow? Does the increasingly abundant and decreasingly targeted production of information correspond to the ideal of the sustainable management of this resource? Do we not abuse human resources when we demand more public sector personnel without offering adequate possibilities for training? And what does it say about our use of consensus as a resource when it is accelerated and used almost without reflection and leads to results devoid of either sense or legitimacy in the eyes of citizens?

4.2.2 From resource management to policy management

The management of public resources must first and foremost be carried out on the basis of knowledge, techniques and rules that are specific to each individual resource. In order to manage public finances, it is necessary to master and practice the techniques of cost accounting and budgetary processes; human resources cannot be managed without knowledge of the psychological motivation of personnel, for example.

However, this vision is merely partial and it involves two risks:

- The first concerns the extraction of each of the resources concerned from its context, with the result that it is distanced from its ultimate aim, that is, to contribute to the process of policy realisation. An approach leading to the isolation of the different resources risks dissociating them excessively from the policy products and, hence, giving them the status of a private type of management without taking account of the public nature (and thus their specific characteristics) of the policies to which they contribute. This leads to aberrations because if the production, reproduction and utilisation of public resources are to be subjected to the demands associated with the quality of the end product, they must also respect the democratic and social constraints of the democratic state (for example, transparency, political responsibility, equality of treatment, equity), which are not comparable to those that rule the resources of private or corporative (associative) policies.
- Furthermore, an isolated 'approach by approach' management of resources carries within it the seed for internal abuse of policies. In effect, this approach may lead to the utilisation of these resources for aims other than those of the policy in question: in this case, the actors will concentrate their efforts on the

distribution of a category of resource that is favourable to their clientele and not on the utilisation of all the resources available as a function of the objectives of the policy in question. The known consequences of this can be seen, for example, in the way in which motorways are built with the sole aim of promoting the regional construction industry, impact studies are commissioned to support eco-business, or arms are produced to pursue economic policy aims without giving any real thought to national defence policy. The aims of substantive policies in themselves, which with the exception of financial and economic policies will never consist of the simple allocation of a resource (in particular finance), become secondary with respect to the primary aim of the allocation of resources to certain types of actors.

As the research on policy implementation has shown, policy resources are in part substitutable. Situations are often encountered whereby actors reach an agreement on a solution without having a clear legal basis; thus law as a resource is – partly – replaced by the consensus. In other cases, opponents voluntarily renounce their right of appeal (law as a resource), which is likely to slow down the decision-making process considerably, in exchange for the modification of a project (time as a resource), financial compensation (money as a resource) or benefit in kind (property/infrastructure as a resource).

This observation offers another reason for the adoption of a global approach that consists in the real management of public policies. This latter consists in the strategic, intelligent and economical combination of the different public resources so as to obtain a product that is likely to resolve the collective problem being targeted. In doing this, public actors should take account of the imperatives of sustainable management individually applicable to each of the categories of resources described above. It is true that this concern, that may be described as the 'policy management', should take account of the limited availability of resources inasmuch as this is decided (at least in part) by the legislature. Thus, there will be no miracles: these resources cannot be multiplied at will, even if they are in the hands of the best possible managers. However, experience shows that even with an equal initial allocation of resources, some actors manage to meet the defined objectives in full while others fail in the implementation of their policies. And the difference often resides in the more or less astute combination of habitual resources with 'sensitive' resources, which, in most cases, appear to be the resources of time, consensus and organisation, all of which remain largely acknowledged and understood. This kind of management presupposes the monitoring and detailed analysis of the development of the collective problem to be resolved, an evaluation of the results and effects of political-administrative activities, a strategic capacity to combine and exploit the available resources and to sustainably manage each of the resources used.

At this stage, we would like to stress that the resource concept presented here allows us to distinguish clearly between actors' resources, the means of action (or instruments, that is, 'policy tools')[3] availed of in the policy process and the measures (or outputs) it produces:

- *Resources* represent a store of raw materials on which public and private actors draw to fashion their actions.
- *The means of action* themselves represent the concrete result of the combined use of these resources based on the selected mode of intervention (for example, regulatory, incentive, persuasive, contractual or reflexive). The intervention instruments are based, among other things, on the strategic objective of the policy in question and the priorities in time and space. The choice of means of intervention (generally specified in the PAP) will result in the prioritising of the use of one or other of the available resources. Thus, the regulatory mode will make more use of the law as a resource, the incentive mode will tend to use money and the persuasive mode will favour the cognitive and communicative resources. However, the mode of public intervention does not fully dictate the dosage and combination of resources adopted for the action in question. Thus, the regulatory mode may be applied with the more or less extensive utilisation of the property resource. The same applies to the other intervention modes that may be more or less effective according to the combination of resources used.
- *The implementation measure (output) produced by the public policy* represents the material and immaterial result of the use of resources on the interface between the administration and civil society. Applied to an individual case, the administrative end product may contain a clearly identifiable resource (for example, the money paid to farmers in the form of direct payments, the law 'applied' and thus 'repeated' in the context of planning permission or the information circulated in a public health warning issued by the state). Similarly, the product of administrative activity always 'contains' a mixture of fairly recognisable resources and other resources used in its production

process that include, at least, for example, its acceptability (for example, resource consensus) and legitimacy (for example, resource political support).

Notes

[1] According to these authors, the other three resources at the disposal of organisations are: control of relationships with the environment, communication and the use of organisational rules. We have adopted these resources in our typology; however, the forms we use sometimes differ.

[2] Pierre Moor does not share this point of view. According to him, it is not the constitutional state that demands participation, but the deficit of the constitutional state, which was prompted to create a kind of 'compensation' through procedure thanks to the influence of democratic movements (see Moor, 1994, pp 300ff).

[3] It should be noted that there is a literature that addresses some of the concerns of this chapter using the more limited notions of 'tools of government' (Hood, 1986) or policy instruments (Howlett, 1991; Howlett and Ramesh, 2003, chapter 4). This usage corresponds rather to the explicit topic of the selection of instruments explored in the discussion of 'operational elements' in Section 8.1.1.

FIVE

Institutional rules

In Chapter Two we outlined the reasons why we believe it necessary to analyse the institutional rules that frame the interaction of policy actors. In this chapter we discuss how analysts working in the social sciences have explored the influence of institutional rules on individual behaviour and on public policies. We then present the definitions of institutions proposed by the different neo-institutionalist schools, as well as the various hypotheses that have been formulated to explain these institutional changes. Having completed this review of the literature, we then operationalise the concept of institutions so that it is directly applicable to the analysis of specific public policies.

5.1 Institutional analysis

5.1.1 From institutionalism to neo-institutionalism

Contemporary political science has been dominated by three successive paradigms dealing with the role of institutions. These paradigms are important for understanding the influence of institutional rules on the behaviour of actors and, consequently, on public policies. The traditional institutionalist paradigm assumes that democratic institutional rules determine individual and collective decisions. *Homo politicus* 'makes policy', but always in the context of constitutional institutions and in accordance with formal rules. The political scientist describes – mostly in legal language – the structures and procedures of the organs of parliament, government and the administration as well as the functioning of political parties and interest groups. However, traditional institutionalism gradually devoted itself to the identification of the legal aspects and organisational structures of (informal) rules that relate to collective decision making (Duverger, 1968, pp 7-8; Chevallier, 1981, pp 3-61).

Making a fundamental change from that paradigm with respect to the selected unit of analysis, the behaviourist paradigm assumes that the social roles, informal norms and personal values of individuals determine their political behaviour. In its more radical version, institutions are defined as 'empty shells' (Shepsle, 1989, p 133). The

Public policy analysis

paradigm of rational choice (for example, public choice and game theory) interprets political actions by applying the theories and methods of neo-classical economics. According to this approach, the field of politics corresponds to a market; collective decisions represent the equilibrium resulting from the aggregation of individual behaviour. *Homo oeconomicus* makes strategic political choices that aim to maximise personal utility (material and immaterial). The institutional arrangements do not influence the formation of individual preferences but may channel them and constitute a means of resolving collective action dilemmas (for example, 'free-riding', 'the prisoner's dilemma' and 'the tragedy of the commons'). Empirical applications of these theories deal with the electoral strategies of political parties (Downs, 1957), the maximisation of bureaucratic budgets and prestige (Niskanen, 1971), the creation of interest groups (Olson, 1965) and political decision making (Buchanan and Tullock, 1962).

Since the 1980s, it has been possible to observe the emergence of a new research trend that aims to integrate the ideas of the public or rational choice school with those obtained from the analysis of public institutions. This reorientation envisages a cumulative development of knowledge in the political sciences. While the supporters of the paradigm of rational choice emphasise the stabilising role of institutional rules, for example in parliamentary decisions (Shepsle, 1979; Riker, 1980)[1], the proponents of the traditional institutional paradigm look at the strategic interactions between individuals within institutions, for example in interest groups (Moe, 1980; Walker, 1983)[2].

Neo-institutionalism suggests, therefore, that actors and institutions influence each other. 'Embedded' or 'trapped' in formal and informal institutional rules, *homo institutionalus* adopts political behaviours that are appropriate to the values and expectations conveyed by these rules, at the same time, modifying them gradually on the basis of his or her own decisions and actions. In order to account for this multi-causality, the political scientist simultaneously analyses the individual behaviour and the institutional structures or rules.

5.1.2 Definitions of institutional rules (that is, institutions)[3]

It is then appropriate to differentiate between the three neo-institutionalist schools – referred to as sociological, economic and historical – rather than speak of a theoretical approach that has already been consolidated (Koelble, 1995; Goodin, 1996; Hall and Taylor, 1996; Lowndes, 1996; Norgaard, 1996) (see Table 5.1). Each of these movements defines the concept of institutions or institutional rules in a specific

Institutional rules

Table 5.1: Synopsis of neo-institutionalist schools

Schools	Sociological (cultural approach)	Historical (structuralist approach)	Economic (calculating approach)
Major authors	March and Olsen (1989); Powell and Di Maggio (1991); Scott and Meyer (1994)	Evans et al (1985); Hall (1986); Steinmo et al (1992); Weaver and Rockman (1993)	Williamson (1985); Ostrom (1990); North (1990)
Analytical definition of institutional rules	Cultural values, social norms, symbols, rites, habits and so on that limit the cognitive capacities of actors who define the roles of the members of an organisation and provide the social legitimacy of institutions	Formal and informal procedures, routines, legal norms embedded in the structures of the political system that reflect the power relationships between actors and that pre-define access to the decision-making arena	Voluntary contracts or arrangements that are the result of repeated interaction between the actors that stabilise individual attempts ensuring a certain degree of predictability to the results of collective actions
Epistemological status of institutional rules	Independent variable (macro level): Institutions → individuals	Independent and dependent variable (meso level): Individuals ↔ institutions	Dependent variable (micro level): Individuals → institutions
Creation of institutional rules	Immanent: institutional rules (re)produced by individuals, groups and organisations	Contingent: rules develop among the existing institutional rules	Functional: institutional rules created to serve the interests of its members
Institutional change	Institutional rules influence the world vision of actors who, during institutional change, adopt a new reference framework among several options available	The institutional rules have, above all, a stabilising effect while certain institutional constellations offer opportunities for change at any given moment	Institutional change aimed at re-establishing the balance if actors' preferences change and in reducing the negative effects caused by former institutional rules
Strengths of the approach	Focus on organisational sociology and on social attitudes and roles	Combination of several decision-making logics, taking into account structures	Conceptual clarity and coherency, formal and deductive theory
Weaknesses of the approach	Ambiguity with respect to the true nature of relationships between social norms and (formal) political institutions	Inductive approach not yet theoretically consolidated, risk of structural determinism	Limited capacity for explaining institutional (non)-change, limits inherent in 'public choice' models, functionalism

Public policy analysis

way and hence proposes different hypotheses with respect to their influence on individual actors and the conduct of public policies.

- *Institutional rules as social norms:* adopting a *cultural* approach, sociologists define institutions not only as the internal formal rules and procedures within an organisation, but also, and above all, as the latter's value system, symbols, cognitive patterns and behavioural norms. Institutions are essentially cultural and they provide the members of an organisation with a frame of meaning that guides individual actions. Thus, social conventions predefine the role of actors at the same time as updating the legitimacy of organisations.
- *Institutional rules as voluntary contract norms:* in contrast, economists adopt a *calculating* perspective. Institutional rules are defined as voluntary arrangements between individuals. These (incomplete) contracts make it possible to reduce the uncertainty that is inherent in all collective decisions and stems from inaccurate information and the limited cognitive capacities of actors. In the absence of an institutional frame, the desire to resolve this uncertainty would involve excessive transaction costs. Therefore, individuals freely negotiate formal rules and/or accept informal codes of behaviour. The aim of these institutional rules is to provide a certain degree of predictability with respect to the behaviour of other actors and the outcome of collective action.
- *Institutional rules as state structures:* historians turn to *structuralist* theories in their approach to institutions. They apply them to the constitutional and legal norms, to the formal political-administrative procedures and to the informal conventions that define the rules governing the interaction between actors. The institutional rules of a democratic regime reflect the power relationships between the social groups and provide some of them with privileged access to the arenas of policy decision making and implementation. If they do not in themselves determine actor participation and the substantive results of state actions, they nevertheless offer opportunities for selective and distorted action. In reality, historical neo-institutionalism represents a happy medium between the cultural approach of the sociologists ('logic of appropriateness') and the calculating approach of the economists ('logic of consequentiality'). The institutional rules affect the preferences and identity of individuals while, at the same time, the latter exploit them from a strategic point of view to assert their interests.

In addition to highlighting the differences between these three neo-institutionalist schools – deliberately presented here as ideal types – we note that the major authors agree on at least three points.

Firstly, all of these research movements define institutional rules as both structures and rules that are formal, explicit and generally legally formalised *and* as informal norms that are implicit but shared by the members of an organisation or community. Consideration of both of these types of rules is necessary as the informal norms may replace the influence of formal rules or even prove to be more stable (more 'mythical') than the latter (see Knight, 1992, p 17; and also North, 1990, p 4). An MP may vote against the party line for personal and ethical reasons (for example, on abortion). Administrations sometimes also tolerate the breaching of their regulations for cultural reasons (for example, lax application of state regulations in certain French-speaking Swiss cantons, or certain French regulations in regions like Corsica). Policy analysis must, therefore, accommodate this dual dimension and question the relative influence of formal and informal institutional rules on political behaviour, their respective stability and the conflicts that may arise between these two categories of rules.

Secondly, and as demonstrated by the empirical work carried out by the historical school of neo-institutionalism, institutional rules establish structures and procedures that facilitate or limit the political participation of individuals and groups (for example, the right to launch a popular initiative or facultative referendum in Switzerland, the right to a hearing in an administrative procedure, the right of a linguistic minority to be represented in the Swiss government) and the efficacy of policies (for example, inequalities in implementation associated with federalism of execution, compromise solutions negotiated to avoid appeals). Furthermore, they substantiate and define in temporal terms the power relationships between the social groups (for example, under-representation of women in executive and legislative bodies, clientelistic relationships between an administration and an interest group, consultation of employees in the context of collective agreements). Even if they appear to display a very high level of stability, institutions are not, however, completely frozen and immovable. Developments may prompt changes in social reality (for example, recognition of the right of appeal of environmental protection organisations, granting of the right to vote to women and foreigners) or repeated statements on the inefficacy of the institutional rules in place (for example, reform of consultation procedures, revision of the Constitution and democratic rights, attempts at reform by the government and parliament). Without going into the reasons for the stability and transformation of institutional rules in detail here, it should be noted that with regard to policy analysis this involves understanding both of these stages in the life cycle of an institution as well as the reasons for the selection of one institution over another ('institutional design' according to Brandl, 1987; Weimer, 1995; Goodin, 1996).

Finally, a consensus emerges with respect to the necessity to interpret political behaviour as actions that are strategic *and* guided by social norms. Understood in its broadest sense, the rationality of actors is, therefore, limited in cognitive terms ('bounded rationality') and in institutional terms ('bound rationality'). In other words, individuals are rational to the extent that they have concrete and rational aims and try through their behaviour to forge a social identity for themselves and to win the recognition of a group or an organisation. As Norgaard (1996) suggests with his concept of 'reasonable rationality', political actors act in an intentional and reflexive manner. They also formulate their strategies on the basis of the opportunities provided by institutional rules. Thus, what we need to establish is how the institutional rules influence this double motivation. For each concrete case, it is a question of determining whether an institution influences a specific individual behaviour by increasing the information and knowledge available to actors, from a perspective of institutional transformation (strategic behaviour), and/or in suggesting a behaviour that is compatible with the conveyed social norms, from a perspective of cohesion and socialisation. The relative weight of these two mechanisms appears of equal importance in explaining not only the individual decisions and actions, but also the institutional transformations. In this respect, Lowndes (1996, p 195) for example, suggests that strategic actions are decisive for initiating an institutional change while the behaviours guided by social norms tend to strengthen the institutional rules in force.

Three elements (at least) of institutional rules must be kept in mind when analysing a given policy: it is necessary to differentiate between formal and informal rules, between stable and dynamic institutions and between strategic behaviour and behaviour that is guided by social norms. The intersection of these three analytical elements enables the formulation of several concrete hypotheses. One could, for example, suppose that the institutional changes are prompted by the existence of an excessive gap at a given time between the formal and informal institutional rules, or that different formal rules offer more or less scope for manoeuvre to individuals to adopt strategic behaviour that social conventions do not do (for example, the impact of whether ballots are secret or open on adherence to official lines taken by political parties).

5.1.3 Institutional changes

How do institutional rules originate and evolve over time? Several alternative theoretical propositions have been formulated to explain the emergence, stability and transformation of institutions. We will refer to four main arguments influenced by the neo-institutionalist schools described above (see Table 5.1).

1. *Opportunistic calculations and institutional heritage.* Firstly, the authors inspired by the public choice rationale explain the emergence of an institution as the intentional choice of individuals to maximise the predictability of their interactions. Thus, by means of a voluntary act, the actors create an institution representing "an ex ante bargain, the objective of which is to enhance various forms of co-operation and to facilitate the enforcement of agreements. [...] The ex ante rational institutional choice is the one which the collective believes, on average, will generate the least ex post regret" (Shepsle, 1989, p 139). Created for a functional end, an institution will survive for as long as it produces more benefits for the interested individuals and groups than the competing institutional forms; if this is no longer the case, the existing institution is abandoned in favour of a more efficient institution (for example, reform of ad hoc parliamentary committees in Switzerland in favour of permanent commissions that offer greater weight in the legislative process and better information for their members; see Lüthi, 1997). Thus, in the final analysis, institutional changes can be explained by the fact that an institution gives rise to negative effects in the long term that were not predicted in the short term. Out of concern for efficacy and the correction of these negative effects, the actors engage in processes of institutional change. The success of these reforms in itself depends on the resources of the coalitions that have a specific interest in operating them.

    This voluntarist interpretation of institutional changes is in line with an institutional Darwinism. It was partly challenged by North's theory (1990) on changes dependent on the path taken ('path dependence'). If there were no transaction costs (or a perfect situation with respect to information) the interactions between the actors would be direct and there would be no need for institutions. Similarly, if the transformation of institutions does not give rise to any costs, the institutional changes would be immediate. Despite obvious dysfunctionality, both the existence of institutional rules and their great stability must be confirmed. The stability of institutions and their incremental reforms can hence be explained in terms of the costs accepted by the initiators of the proposed change. The innovators should be prepared to pay dearly for breaking with a social norm (for example, reform of popular 'sacrosanct' rights) or for the losses associated with the possible negative long-term effects of a new institution (for example, instrumentation of the optional referendum by all-powerful sectoral interest groups). According to North, institutional progress only clears a way for itself very slowly. This stems either from the migration of certain actors, who in a quest for efficiency, move towards more effective institutional systems, or from imitation, through a process of emulation of the most efficient systems. The most effective institutions do not automatically undermine the less efficient ones; the development tends instead to unfold as a 'shaky-handed evolutionism' (Dockès, 1997).

For these two economic approaches to the evolution of institutions, institutional creation and reform are ultimately explained by the motivations and actions of individuals and groups. The authors of this school of thought confirm, nonetheless, the existence of a significant hiatus between the initial intentions of actors during the creation of institutional rules and their long-term and undesired consequences. Starting similarly with this fact, other theorists suggest structural – rather than individual – dynamics to explain institutional changes.

2. *Social demands and structural barriers.* In this second theoretical trend, institutional innovations are explained by inconsistencies, at a given moment in history, between different institutional rules (for example, collisions between federalist and democratic principles according to Germann, 1991) and/or between one given institution and others in social reality (for example, political non-representation of certain social groups). This time-lag is due to the fact that political and social structures do not necessarily evolve at the same speed. Thus, the stabilising, or conservative, effects of an institution can no longer respond to the social demands expressed. This inadequacy may also concern both the efficacy of the results of the collective action and its legitimacy and that of its members. A critical situation of this nature necessitates institutional reform that translates as a bifurcation in the historical development. The creation, stability and institutional changes are thus interpreted as alternation between long phases

of equilibrium and shorter phases of imbalance and institutional crises (Krasner, 1984).

This approach explains institutional change mainly in terms of the non-satisfaction of (new) demands made by certain social groups. However, it stresses two reasons why institutions tend to resist change. First, they often structure how decisions about their eventual reform may be taken (for example, a popular vote as obligatory for the reform of the instruments of direct democracy). Second, the power relationships that are contained in the institutional rules limit the opportunities for certain social groups that are excluded from the decision-making arena from participating in institutional transformation. This argument tends, therefore, to explain why inadequacies between the social demands and institutional responses may certainly emerge but may not be resolved quickly.

March and Olsen (1989, p 168) stress that institutional changes translate primarily into processes of adaptation and learning. Given the structuring effects of the institutional rules in place, it is above all necessary to expect incremental changes. The proactive exploration of alternative institutions proves less common than changes on the periphery. This hypothesis is strengthened further by the fact that a specific institution often finds itself in a position of interdependency with other institutional rules. Hence, it is not just a question of improving the efficacy of an institution, but also of ensuring that the institution in question is compatible with the principles rooted in other institutions (for example, the trade-off that exists between the rights of direct democracy and electoral rules in parliamentary systems; see Linder, 1994, p 133).

3. *External pressures and internal mediation*. A third hypothesis assumes that institutional change is prompted by *external shocks* to a political system (for example, the impact of the evolution of the EU on Switzerland) and/or by the evolution of its physical, environment (for example, globalisation of the economy). This approach often remains vague in that the analytical definition of external or environmental shocks depends on the level of the analysis applied. In effect, the explanations would not be the same if a single institution and the global institutional system were considered. It is still necessary to take the context – in the broadest sense – into account as this redefines the collective problems with which a country is confronted. However, these contextual variables are always mediated by the institutions already in place that politically redefine the problems to be resolved.

Furthermore, they do not indicate the type of institutional reform required in a linear way. To analyse these elements, it is hence necessary to apply the two types of argument mentioned above.

The question of institutional change is crucial to ensuring a certain coherency in neo-institutionalist approaches and, in particular, to avoid interpreting institutions as exogenous variables (note the neo-institutionalists' criticism of the public choice proponents that they define the preferences of individual actors as given). As a result, an empirical-analytical theory of institutional design should formulate and test hypotheses on the factors of change, for example, as a function of the frequency, scope and level of observable reforms (for example, the distinction between the constitutional institutions concerning collective choices and related to the operational decisions of public policies, according to Kiser and Ostrom, 1982). Rather than aiming to develop a universal explanation of historical change, it would appear to make sense to distinguish analytically different types of institutional transformation and then explain the extent to which such institutional rules in themselves constitute barriers to their own reform or that of other institutions, in other words, which external shock influences which institutional reform.

4. *Ideological paradigm shifts*. The sociological approach, with its emphasis on culture, has contributed to a view of institutional influences as ideological. This has led on to suggestions that crucial ideological paradigm shifts occur from time to time. Thus Hall, who argues that "politicians, officials, the spokesmen for social interests, and policy experts all operate within the terms of political discourse that are current in the nation at a given time …" (Hall, 1993, p 289), goes on to see policy change as stemming from these shifts. He presents Keynesian economic theory and then monetarist theory as successive dominant paradigms (see also Hall, 1986). Taylor-Gooby and his colleagues (2004) have given similar attention to the emergence of privatisation in social policy. But in using notions of dominant ideas or paradigms, these theorists face questions about the extent to which these shifts can be explained independently of other events. Surel argues that there is a need to see exogenous influences as important for this. For him, "transformations of economic conditions, and/or a serious crisis are important" (Surel, 2000, p 503). If this is the case then ideological paradigm shifts involve simply the internal mediation consequent on external shocks (as suggested by the third argument above). Yet were Keynesian ideas and notions of

public provision so universally discredited by economic changes and related crises, or was there not perhaps a form of contagious ideological change to which we need to turn to explain what happened? It is hard to test such arguments; institutional change theories face the problem that they function best as explanations benefiting from hindsight.

We consider institutional rules as a factor that influences the behaviour of actors and, hence, the actual substance of policies. At the same time, while not being easily able to explain that fact, we also consider the institutional frame as something that is not fixed but evolving. Also it would appear to be of interest to take into account the weight of the substantive results of public action that are sometimes at the root of a serious attack on general institutions ('institution-killing policies'; see Knoepfel, 2000). The links between substantive and institutional policies are complex and always mediated by actor behaviour.

5.2 Operationalisation of the concept of institutional rules

What is involved here is the operationalisation of the concept of institutional rules in order to facilitate empirical research. To do this, we propose to combine two approaches: the first, inspired by the legal and administrative sciences, is mainly based on the idea of a hierarchy of norms and institutions; the second, inspired by new institutional economics, aims to inventory the different types of rules that actors negotiate – sometimes on a purely voluntary basis – among themselves for the purpose of managing their interactions. In combining these two approaches, we suggest that the institutional rules sometimes represent constraints and sometimes opportunities for policy actors. If certain institutional rules directly limit their scope for manoeuvre, others offer new possibilities for participating in and influencing the development and/or implementation of a given policy.

5.2.1 Hierarchy of institutions: some constituent principles of concrete action

Adopting the slogan 'Bringing the state back in' (Evans et al, 1985), the so-called 'state-centred' theories define legislative, judicial and executive organisations as *autonomous actors* who pursue their own objectives and as structures *inherited* from the past that define in a stable way the rules governing the mediation between social interests

(Skocpol, 1985, p 28; Weir and Skocpol, 1985, pp 117-19). The empirical work produced on the basis of this approach aims, among other things, to evaluate the extent to which formal institutional rules (for example, parliamentary or presidential rule, electoral system, form of government) limit or extend the state's capacities for the conception and application of its policies (note the work of Weaver and Rockman, 1993)[4].

Considering the state as an actor in its own right and its institutions as a lever for action amounts to the refutation of both the pluralist theories of a 'service-hatch state', which is attentive to all social demands, and the neo-Marxist theories of an 'arbitrary captive state', which, through its public policies, merely seeks to reproduce the divisions between the social classes or to favour the interests of an organised group (see Chapter One). On the contrary it recognises the political-administrative system's proactive role in the definition and resolution of social problems.

Decisions and collective actions are not solely determined by autonomous individuals and/or the evolution of the context (for example, the physical environment, or economic situation). The state is not just a passive agent that reacts to external shocks, responds to social demands and arbitrates in a neutral manner the conflicts of interest expressed by well-organised groups. It is our belief here that public actors relish their capacity to structure the redistributive stakes between private actors and influence societal development by means of their policies. When it comes to understanding public policies, it is not sufficient to identify the private actors concerned by a collective problem, their degree of organisation and the interests at stake; it is also necessary to analyse in detail the determining weight of public actors and the institutions that lend them this weight (Majone, 1996).

By adopting a 'top-down' perspective, the policy analyst can identify the following three levels of institutional rules in all political systems (see Figure 5.1).

1. *The institutional frame* comprises the constitutive rules of a public policy. In concrete terms, it involves principles defined by the constitution with respect to general functions (for example, direct democracy, federalism, constitutional state), individual liberties and legislative, executive and judicial authorities (for example, composition of parliament, responsibilities of the executive, powers of respective tiers of government, competencies of the courts). The institutional rules defined at constitutional level aim to define the frame conditions for the democratic arbitration of

Institutional rules

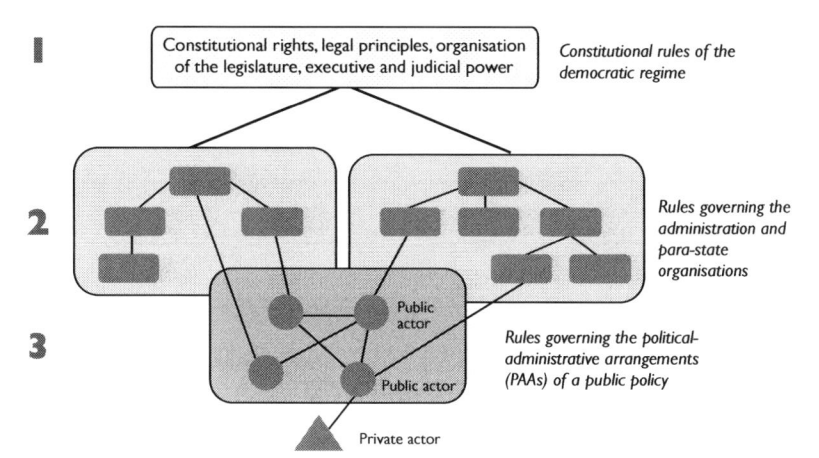

Figure 5.1: The hierarchy of institutional rules

1 — Constitutional rights, legal principles, organisation of the legislature, executive and judicial power — *Constitutional rules of the democratic regime*

2 — *Rules governing the administration and para-state organisations*

3 — Public actor / Public actor / Private actor — *Rules governing the political-administrative arrangements (PAAs) of a public policy*

conflicts of interests on specific subjects. They apply to all public policies.

2. At a lower level, *institutional rules govern the administrative organisations* that embody the 'apparatus of state' (Germann, 1996), that is, the tools and resources at the government's disposal for carrying out its actions 'in the social terrain'. What is involved here is the consideration of the rules that govern all public actors (administrations, agencies) who, based on the legislation or practice, have administrative resources at their disposal that enable them to make an indispensable and autonomous contribution to policy formation and/or implementation. The hierarchical organisation of ministers and ministries and the legal status of public establishments are examples of this. Thus, policy analysts must examine para-public organisations (which are invested with public power) as well as the main public institutions, for example during policy implementation (Germann, 1987). These formal institutional rules are governed by rules developed in accordance with an *organisational and procedural logic*. The members of administrative organisations and para-public establishments carry out their tasks in accordance with the hierarchical delegation of competencies and major principles of administrative law that ensure a certain regularity and predictability of public intervention.

3. The *political-administrative arrangements* (PAAs) specific to a public policy constitute the structured group of public actors charged with the development and/or implementation of a particular

policy. These arrangements are governed by specific institutional rules based on an *action logic* that prompts the public actors to coordinate their decisions and actions with the aim of resolving a substantive problem. Thus, one can consider administrative organisations as places with a high concentration of institutional rules (from the second and of this third level) necessary to orient the public actors brought together to manage the policies in question.

This operationalisation of institutional rules, which are organised on a hierarchical basis, suggests the following logic: the institutional rules involve decisions taken by actors at a higher level representing (positive or negative) constraints for the lower levels. Thus, a PAA cannot be constituted independently of the functional organisation of the state; this may give rise to problems of coherency or intraorganisational coordination as well as a liberation of certain actors of the PAA vis-à-vis the administrative organisations to which they belong. The tensions between constitutional rules and the rules governing the arrangements of specific policies may be associated with a greater or lesser degree of centralisation of the specific PAA, which is itself defined by general rules defining the relationship between the central state and its regions (in accordance with the principle of 'federalism of execution' in Switzerland, the principles of decentralisation of 1982-87 in France and the laws governing devolution in the UK). These tensions may also be associated with a more or less extensive application of the principle of formal legal requirements for specific policies and specific administrative procedures (for example, planning permission).

Furthermore, this interpretation of institutional rules rests implicitly on the argument that the higher the decision-making level, the wider the field of application, and the more indirect the link with the substantive content of the policy, the less frequent the changes. In view of this stability or inertia, institutional rules constitute above all constraints for public policy actors. In fact, they translate the historical process of accumulation and sedimentation of the rules of functioning of the state. Finally, they may be operationalised in terms of pre-existing structures within which all policies must find (or create) their place.

5.2.2 Tensions between the institutional policies and institutional rules specific to public policies

While the institutional rules governing the PAA are generally a part of substantive public policies, the development and transformation of general institutional rules (constitutional rules and institutional rules governing administrative organisations; see Figure 5.1) constitute the object of policies known as institutional. In effect, *institutional policies* may be defined as all of the decisions and public activities whose objectives are to guarantee and improve the functioning of the state apparatus. These policies not only concern the government and the administration; they also concern the parliament and the law. To these are added the decisions connected with constitutional principles such as legislative and executive federalism, the constitutional state and democracy (Salisbury, 1968, p 120; Quermonne, 1985; Mény and Thoenig, 1989, p 363; Germann, 1996). The aim of institutional policies is the provision of frame conditions for the accomplishment of state functions. The conduct of substantive public policies is one of the most important of these functions.

These institutional policies are hence applicable to the definition and management of all concrete substantive policies. No policy can disregard the relatively restrictive requirements of the state with respect to regulatory policies, in particular (for example, clear legal bases, right to be heard for target groups). Thus, for example, in Switzerland, a federal policy that would substitute for the formal application of a law in the cantons would obviously violate the principle of federalism of execution and the executive sovereignty of the cantons. Similarly, in France, local public bodies are subordinated in terms of rules of attribution of competency between bodies, to subsequent monitoring on the part of the state services, for example. In the UK, local governments operate specific policy responsibilities within a framework of law governing their activities as a whole.

Even if these general institutional rules go against the functional needs of a given public policy, in the case of contestation, legislation would be required to correct these violations of general institutional rules enshrined in constitutional law.

A look at relatively recent policies, such as policy to control illegal drugs, spatial policies or policies that have international repercussions, shows that the majority of actors involved in these policies are convinced that they need specific institutional rules that can, if necessary, contradict the general rules for the good functioning of their policy. This is how the need for new administrative instruments, new resources and (public and private) actors that are not exactly compatible, for example, with the principle of impartiality of the public function or that of state action prescribed by administrative law is put forward. These observations bear witness to the birth of particular new formal or informal rules in a growing number of substantive public policies.

Thus, for example, in Swiss anti-drugs policy, major cities have been observed to adopt a position never before seen in the history of Swiss policy, whereby a powerful axis is created between the local and federal levels and a strong public–private partnership is established for which there is no precedence in the rules concerning federal collaboration. Such new practices can also be found in the case of social policy in France and have given rise to the establishment of new partnership relationships between the state, the local public bodies and the administrative departments (in the context of the *contrats de ville* or state–city/town contracts in particular); however, these new partnership-style relationships are not in receipt of suitable budgetary support. Likewise, when confronted with the uncertainties with respect to the risks posed by advanced technologies, policies concerning the regulation of these technologies (for example, genetic engineering, hazardous waste) are not in a position to respect the requirements of the principle of the constitutional state in terms of precise legal bases, (creation of ad hoc ethical committees, for example). In the UK the ease with which central government can alter formal arrangements (making it what Dunleavy, 1995, has called 'the fastest government in the West') makes such explicit contradictions less likely but has aroused a concern among lawyers that the protection of citizens' rights may be violated by uncheckable administrative flexibility (see Jowell and Oliver, 2002). This is thus an argument for more institutional constraints.

It would be possible to go on adding to this almost ad infinitum. In practice, this friction between general institutional rules and the rules specific to the substantive policies arising from them does not go unnoticed. It is manifest in the form of tension between the administrative services responsible for institutional policies, such as legal, financial or personnel services, and the public actors within the substantive policies' PAA. Thus, situations akin to the following are not uncommon: the substantive policy emerges victorious and hence becomes an 'institution-killing policy'. In this case, the internal dynamics of the substantive policy resist the application of the institutional rule or a modification of this rule by a new – budgetary, organisational or legal – institutional policy, thus the new policy's institutional arrangement forms an erratic block in a country's institutional landscape: for example, the rules specific to the operation of water basin agencies in France (instituted by the Law of 1964 on Water Pollution) contravene the constitutional rules for the definition of taxes by the parliament; in effect, it is the Water Basin Committees and not the national parliament that define the base and rate of the taxes levied on pollution discharged and on the consumption of water. This constitutional irregularity has existed for a long while.

It is also possible, however, to imagine the opposite scenario whereby the community of dominant actors associated with a substantive policy fails to impose its will. It is then ultimately obliged to fall into line with the general rules while having to accept a loss in efficacy or even the outright disappearance of the policy. Thus, to adopt the metaphor used above, in this case, the institutional rule becomes a 'policy-killing institution'.

It is possible to confirm that over a period of years, a substantive policy will accumulate 'capital' in the form of actors and institutional rules that are increasingly resistant to change as they progress from the development phase to implementation and evaluation. Embryonic, malleable and easy to handle in the initial phases, in parallel to the organisation of the public and private actors, these specific institutional rules solidify and become increasingly dense, more structured and more resistant to external attempts at modification. It is likely as a result of the increasing predominance of such specific institutional policy capital in the implementation phase that the general institutions, which in the past constituted constraints and opportunities for the actors involved, will themselves become the object of negotiations.

It is true to say that in the past this process of renegotiation of the general rules of play was, essentially, the object of institutional policies guided by objectives such as, for example, the good governance of the country, the improvement of semi-direct or representative democracy, the good functioning of the governmental system of concordance or competition, the improvement of the efficacy of representation arrangements or efficiency of the administration. Today, in contrast, the situation appears to have taken an about-turn. In reality, at least, reforms are increasingly set in motion at the interfaces between the public and private actors of substantive policies, at the level of administrative implementation activities, that is, at the level of the services provided for citizens, administrative decisions or other contacts with target groups or beneficiaries.

These changes have multiple origins. Depending on the circumstances, they may originate in participatory movements, public–private partnerships, other modes involving the integration of civil society, the respecting of minority interests and the appropriation of public power by peripheral interests. All of these movements appear to us to express a growing need for the secondary legitimation (see Section 4.1.6) of policy implementation acts. In effect, however strong their legitimation in terms of their legal basis, the implementation of substantive policies would appear increasingly impossible to achieve in the absence of this secondary legitimation.

For these reasons, it is probably impossible to avoid friction or breakdowns between the institutional capital of substantive policies and that of the state as a whole, even if the latter is acknowledged as being subject to incremental changes.

However, the question remains as to the extent to which each substantive policy can be allowed the right to forge its own institutional capital according to its specific needs for secondary legitimation.

5.2.3 Typology of institutional rules: from the actor to the institutional arrangement

The other approach adopted here for the identification and operationalisation of the institutional rules that influence public policies is based on a 'bottom-up' type process. The analyst adopts the point of view of the actors affected by the collective problem dealt with by the policy under scrutiny. He or she then poses the question as to which institutional rules are necessary to solve the problem in question in a concerted and targeted fashion. These rules are often implicit and follow decisions taken during earlier phases of the policy life cycle. For example, if the causal hypothesis is adopted that unemployment is primarily due to a low level of educational qualifications among unemployed people, it will be necessary to include professional training establishments in the policy's PAA by means of the relevant institutional rule.

Thus, it is not a question of considering all the existing institutional rules and their hierarchical links. Instead it is necessary to identify the formal and informal rules to which private and public actors have concrete access so as to assert their interests, manage the modes of their interaction and, ultimately, ensure the efficacy of the public policy in question. These rules in their entirety are generally described in the literature as the 'institutional arrangements':

> In analyzing the structure of an institutional arrangement, the analyst investigates what participants are involved, what their stakes and resources are, and how they are linked to one another and to outcomes in the world. Specifically, the analyst identifies the types of actions the actors can take, the type of information available to them, how actions lead to outcomes, and how rewards and punishments are allocated in light of the outcomes achieved and the actions

taken. Then the analyst predicts the actions and aggregated outcomes that are most likely, given the structures of the incentives. (Ostrom et al, 1993, p 127)

Thus, the institutional rules are defined operationally as rules developed and applied by a group of actors so as to structure repetitive activities that produce (if possible predictable) results involving these actors and potentially other actors (Ostrom, 1990, pp 53ff). The establishment or negotiation of these 'rules in use' proves a dynamic process whose evolution is highly dependent on the present or past situation. Taking the specific case of the management of natural resources (for example, water, forest, pasture land), Ostrom identifies several rules that actors negotiate voluntarily or respect consciously in order to sustainably exploit a common good[5].

We feel it would make sense to simplify the categories of institutional rules initially proposed by Ostrom (set out in note 5) for the self-organised management of certain natural resources so that they can be applied to all public policies. We propose, therefore, to classify the institutional rules applicable to public policies in terms of the following three categories:

1. The rules defining access to policy resources (see, in particular, Chapter Four on the resources of law, money, time and information and Chapter Eight on the political-administrative programme [PAP]).
2. The rules defining the competencies and nature of interaction between public and private actors (see, in particular, Section 8.2 in Chapter Eight on PAA).
3. The rules defining individual behaviour (see, in particular, Section 9.5 in Chapter Nine on the implementation of public policies)[6].

Notes

[1] The 'public choice' authors face the following paradox: the decisions of the North American Congress display a certain stability while, according to the theories of rational choice, it should be difficult, if not impossible, to obtain stable majorities for the voting on laws in Congress. This paradox can be resolved by taking the procedural rules and commissions of Congress into account as institutions.

[2] Traditional institutionalists come up against the empirical fact that formal norms and informal rules cannot in themselves explain a phenomenon such as

'free-riding', but that it is also necessary to turn to the actual nature of goods (private versus public, material versus axiological) that they produce, as well as the opportunistic calculations of certain individuals, as an explanatory variable for the existence of institutions and the activities of their members.

[3] To avoid confusion between the terms 'institution' and 'organisation', we prefer to use the term 'institutional rules'. When used in this text, the term 'institution' is considered as a synonym for institutional rules.

[4] There is also a substantial comparative literature that explored the impact of institutional systems on political participation, highlighting the impact of both federalism and the rules used to aggregate voting choices (majoritarian or consensus) (see Lijphart, 1999; Lane and Ersson, 2000).

[5]
1. The rules of scope define the boundaries of the domain concerned, that is, the perimeter of the collective problem that the public policy seeks to resolve.
2. The rules of boundary define the actors and the conditions, under which they have the right to participate in the collective resolution of the collective problem.
3. The rules of position assign a particular role or position to a specific actor.
4. The rules of enforcement prescribe the connection between the permitted position and decisions or actions, that is, the hierarchy of positions and activities.
5. The rules of information define the information channels and language used by the actors.
6. The rules of decision establish the modality for the weighting of individual voices during collective decision-making processes.
7. The rules of appropriation stipulate how the benefits and costs that result from the resolution of the collective problem are redistributed among the actors on the basis of their positions and activities.

[6] Hill and Hupe have developed a similar approach based on Ostrom's work in which they write of 'constitutive governance', 'institutional governance' and 'operational governance' (Hill and Hupe, 2006; Hupe and Hill, 2006).

Part III
Analysis model

Part III presents in detail the logic behind our analysis model and the variables and hypothesis that constitute it. Our approach is designed to take into account both substantive ('how can the public problem be resolved') and institutional ('which actors will get involved, which resources are required and which institutional rules apply?') dimensions.

We start this section of the book by presenting the framework that facilitates the empirical analysis as part of a comparative approach (Chapter Six). This is followed by the definition of the dependent variables (or social phenomena to be explained) based on the four main stages of a policy: agenda setting (Chapter Seven), programming (Chapter Eight), implementation (Chapter Nine) and evaluation (Chapter Ten).

In the context of these policy phases, we identify six types of products to be analysed:

1. The political definition of the public problem (PD).
2. The political-administrative programme (PAP).
3. The political-administrative arrangements (PAAs).
4. The action plans (APs).
5. The formal implementation acts (outputs).
6. The evaluative statements on the changes in target group behaviour (impacts) and on the effects achieved in terms of the resolution of the problem (results or observable outcomes among end beneficiaries).

These six products are analysed in each of the above-listed chapters in terms of their substantive and institutional dimensions.

The last chapter of Part III (Chapter Eleven) presents the different working hypotheses on the possible links between these different products, the games played by public and private actors, the resources mobilised and the (general and specific) institutional rules associated with policies. Chapter Twelve provides an overall conclusion to the volume.

SIX

Analysis model

6.1 Policy cycle and its products

Based on the keys to the analysis presented in the previous section, we interpret a public policy as a set of decisions and activities resulting from the interaction between *public* and *private actors*, whose behaviour is influenced by the *resources* at their disposal, the *general institutional rules* (that is, the rules concerning the overall functioning of the political system) and *specific institutional rules* (that is, the rules specific to the area of intervention under scrutiny).

The adoption of such an approach leads us to differentiate our analysis variables as follows:

- the specific scope and content – both substantive and institutional – of the different policy products constitute the dependent variables, that is, the social phenomena to be explained,

while

- the actor constellations and behaviour, which are themselves directly influenced by mobilisable resources and the general institutional context, constitute the independent variables, that is, explanatory social phenomena.

In order to concretise this meta-hypothesis by means of an analytical model that can be applied in the context of practical studies 'in the field', we must first identify the nature of the substantive and institutional results of public actions. In order to operationalise these dependent variables, we adopt the concept of the policy cycle (see Section 2.4 in Chapter Two). Thus, we interpret the unfolding of a policy process in terms of the following four main stages: (1) the placing of the problem to be resolved on the governmental agenda; (2) the legislative and regulatory programming of the public intervention; (3) the implementation of the political-administrative programme (PAP) by

Public policy analysis

means of action plans (APs) and formal acts (outputs); and (4) the evaluation of the resulting effects (impacts and outcomes).

Figure 6.1 presents the six products of a public policy as a function of these different stages.

Thus, the analyst must try to identify these six types of products for all policies in accordance with the following characteristics:

- The political definition of the public problem (PD) not only includes the decision on political intervention, but also, and above all, the delimitation of the perimeter of the public problem to be resolved, the identification of its probable causes by the public actors and the kinds of public intervention envisaged.
- The PAP includes all of the legislative or regulatory decisions taken by both central state and public bodies and necessary to the implementation of the policy in question.
- The political-administrative arrangements (PAAs) define the competencies, responsibilities and main resources at the disposal of public actors for the execution of the PAP.
- The APs establish the priorities for policy implementation in the context of geographical and social space and with respect to time.
- The implementation acts (outputs) cover all activities and administrative decisions involving the application of measures.
- The evaluative statements on the effects of a given policy objective to demonstrate the changes (that may have taken place) in the

Figure 6.1: Policy stages and products (postulate no 1)

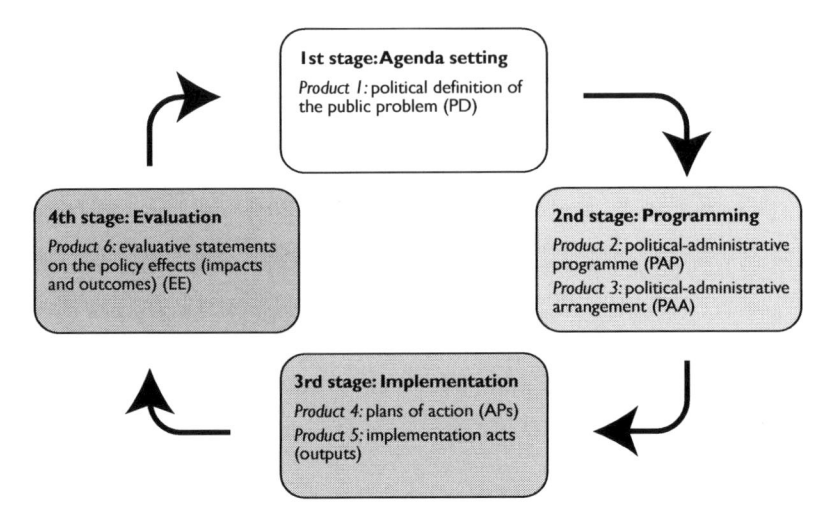

1st stage: Agenda setting
Product 1: political definition of the public problem (PD)

2nd stage: Programming
Product 2: political-administrative programme (PAP)
Product 3: political-administrative arrangement (PAA)

3rd stage: Implementation
Product 4: plans of action (APs)
Product 5: implementation acts (outputs)

4th stage: Evaluation
Product 6: evaluative statements on the policy effects (impacts and outcomes) (EE)

behaviour of target groups (impacts) and the effects triggered among the end beneficiaries (outcomes), and to scientifically and/or politically appreciate the relevance, efficacy and efficiency of the policy that has been implemented (to a greater or lesser degree).

All of these policy products are the results of a specific decision-making process, involving repeated interactions between identifiable actors who mobilise different resources. These decision-making processes are governed by numerous institutional rules that are general or specific to the domain of intervention involved.

During these decision-making processes, the public and private actors establish institutional arrangements (starting during the stages involving the political definition and agenda setting, and being developed in a more sustained manner during the formulation of the PAP, its implementation and, finally, its evaluation). These institutional arrangements prove particularly important during the policy implementation stage which is why we consider the establishment of a PAA as a product in itself that often results in a series of – more or less conscious – ad hoc and pragmatic decisions. This appears all the more significant and justified given that as a general rule implementation arrangements often only emerge in their definitive forms at sub-national levels. Thus, they often differ significantly from one area to the next. Furthermore, the public actors generally consider the constitution of these arrangements as strategic acts leading to the definition of new substantive contents for the policy under consideration.

We insist here on the fact that each of these six products be defined from two perspectives, that is, substantive (how can this problem be resolved?) and institutional (which actors, according to which rules of play and with which resources are going to contribute to the next stage of the resolution of the problem?). Up to now, this duality of the stakes involved in all policies has been more or less recognised at the level of the formulation of the PAP; however, it has been neglected at the level of the other policy products (particularly with respect to agenda setting, APs and ultimate outputs, and even evaluation).

At the same time, it should be stressed that this duality between the substantive and institutional aspects is also found at the level of the a priori purely institutional product, the PAA established for policy implementation. In effect and as already mentioned, the main issue in this decision-making process concerns the designation of the political-administrative authorities as competent to implement the measures associated with a policy. By definition, what is involved at this stage are questions of a more institutional nature. Nonetheless, the substantive dimension of this product should not be neglected because the political decision makers often nominate a particular public authority while – implicitly – expecting that it will adopt a particular direction in the course of policy implementation. For example, in England policies for the protection of children – while enacted in a context in which there are strong efforts to secure policy coordination between departments – are likely to require contributions by ministries whose main concerns are education, or health, or law and order or even income maintenance. Nevertheless designation of the lead department – in the past health but generally now education – will have repercussions for implementation from a substantive point of view.

The causal relationships assumed between the institutional rules (both general ones and those specifically contained in the products of the preceding stages), the actors and their resources (independent variables) and the six products of public action (dependent variables) may be analysed in isolation for each of the four stages of the policy cycle. However, our analysis model aims to describe, understand and explain public policy in its entirety, from the initial perception of a social problem to its eventual resolution through public intervention (see Figure 6.1): thus, we postulate that *the substantive and institutional results of a stage of a public policy (for example, programming) directly influence the content of the subsequent stages (for example, implementation)* (postulate no 1).

This first postulate would seem to be a matter of common sense. In fact, it implies a vision of public action that, if not linear, is at least rationalistic. Thus, insofar as a policy aims to resolve a social problem satisfactorily, it springs from (at least intentionally) concerted and targeted decisions and actions. In order to ensure a certain degree of continuity and predictability in public action, the political-administrative activities of a stage in the policy process will tend to limit the scope of what is possible in later stages. Apart from this, postulate no 1 is also concerned with the explicit recognition of more structural factors associated with, among others, the phenomena of political-administrative inertia (for example, difficulties in revising a law or changing the organisational practices of an administration) and with procedural factors imposed as a result of the application of the rules of the democratic game (for example, the need to apply the major principles of administrative law, such as legality, non-retroactivity).

In other terms, this initial postulate means that the substantive and

Analysis model

institutional results of a stage are directly influenced by the decisions and actions taken during the previous stages of the same policy.

6.2 Effect of the games actors play on the substantive and institutional elements of a policy

However, this interpretation only represents the first constituent element of our theoretical model. Thus, we also suggest that *during each stage in the policy cycle, the actors involved may use the institutional rules in force and the resources not yet used in an attempt to influence the content of that stage* (postulate no 2). As a result, they will try to adjust, modify and even cancel matters that have already been concretely defined, decided or initiated during the preceding stages.

At each stage in the policy process, new actors may appear in the policy arena (or disappear from it) and/or actors who were previously in the minority may – alone or by means of (new) coalitions with others – use (new) institutional rules and exploit (new) combinations of resources to finally assert their interests, ideas and rights. This may then translate into a significant modification of the policy (see Figure 6.2).

It should be noted here that the actors' games also affect the two key stakes identified above, that is, the substantive and institutional aspects. This is particularly true of the agenda-setting and policy programming

Figure 6.2: The direct and indirect influence of the triangle of actors on the first two stages of a public policy (postulate no 2)

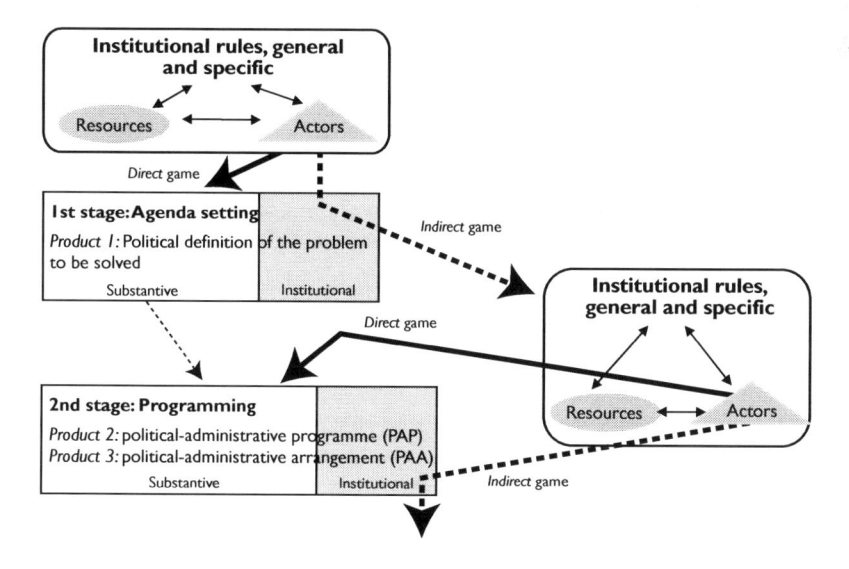

stages, in the course of which actors try to obtain a key position, to establish favourable rules and to obtain abundant resources for the implementation and evaluation stages. Agricultural policy is an example of this type of behaviour: be it during the formulation of the policy or during its implementation, the agricultural lobbies and their representatives within the administration will try at each stage to ensure that they obtain instruments that are favourable to their interests (for example, subsidies and monitoring conditions).

This second postulate suggests, therefore, that public action is never linear nor perfectly determining of individual and collective behaviour. Inaccuracies and areas of uncertainty always exist and, as a result of these, provide scope for assessment and manoeuvre on the part of policy actors. In view of the social complexity associated with the increasing functional differentiation of society and the state and the institutional difficulties involved in reaching a political compromise between all of the actors concerned, the programming of a policy will not succeed in anticipating all of the possible practical details and stakes involved in its implementation. As a result, the conflicts that are unresolved or not predicted during the adoption of a PAP, re-emerge – sometimes in a different form – during the phase of execution. Studies on the implementation of public measures and evaluations of the resulting effects tend to show that the implementation of all policies is essentially a socio-political process whose course and substantive and institutional results are often highly unpredictable.

In other words, this second postulate means that the substantive and institutional results of a policy stage are also influenced by changes in the institutional frame, resources, the constellation and behaviour of actors directly involved in the stage in question, and not only by decisions taken during the preceding stage (postulate no 1).

6.3 Integrated theoretical model

The two postulates on which our model is based are the product of theoretical reflection and have been validated by the results of several empirical studies. They apply to all of the links that exist between all of the stages of the policy cycle.

Thus, the initial definition of the collective problem to be resolved already contains a 'causal history' (Stone, 1989), which identifies those responsible for the collectively perceived problem or able to take action to deal with it, and which, as a result, influences the type of solution adopted during programming. Nonetheless, the social actors identified as the target group of the proposed state intervention (particularly when their behaviour is defined politically as the cause of the collective problem) rarely remain passive during the programming phase: on the contrary, they may actively try to attribute the cause of the problem to another social group, or to at least share the responsibility for the problem with this group (symmetry of sacrifices) so as not to have to modify their own behaviour too dramatically, for example.

Numerous examples of such behaviour can be found, particularly in the area of the environment where polluters, be they industries, farmers, car drivers or even local public bodies, who are identified as a target group never cease to remind us of the existence (and responsibility) of other polluters. Similarly examples may be found when services are deemed to be ineffective, for example an alleged healthcare problem may be attributed to factors outside the health service's control and alternatively portrayed as a social care or income maintenance problem.

This recognition of the duality of the substantive and institutional stages prompts the analyst to question the direct and indirect links between the different products for each stage of the public policy being studied as well as the links between the products and the nature of the interaction between public and private actors. In effect, decisions and activities of a substantive nature may strengthen or weaken decisions of an institutional nature. The coherency between these two dimensions will have a decisive influence on the (institutional and substantive) results obtained during the next phase of the policy process. Thus, the introduction of new actors (for example, environmentalists in the context of agricultural policy) or modification of the rules of the institutional game (for example, the inclusion of the right of appeal to end beneficiaries or third parties) will have repercussions on the application of a piece of legislation.

Figure 6.3 shows an integrated theoretical model that unites the elements presented in Figures 6.1 and 6.2.

The proposed model makes it possible to carry out a diachronic analysis (in time) on the identified stages (agenda setting, programming, implementation, evaluation) based on the following issues:

- *The concretisation of the 'substantive content' of the public policy:* to the extent that a public policy tries to resolve a collective problem, the activities and decisions taken are directed at this final outcome. Thus, the analyst must be able to confirm empirically a concretisation of the actual content of the public action in the course of the different stages. The objectives established during programming, for example, must be defined in terms of the

Figure 6.3: Theoretical model for the analysis of a public policy

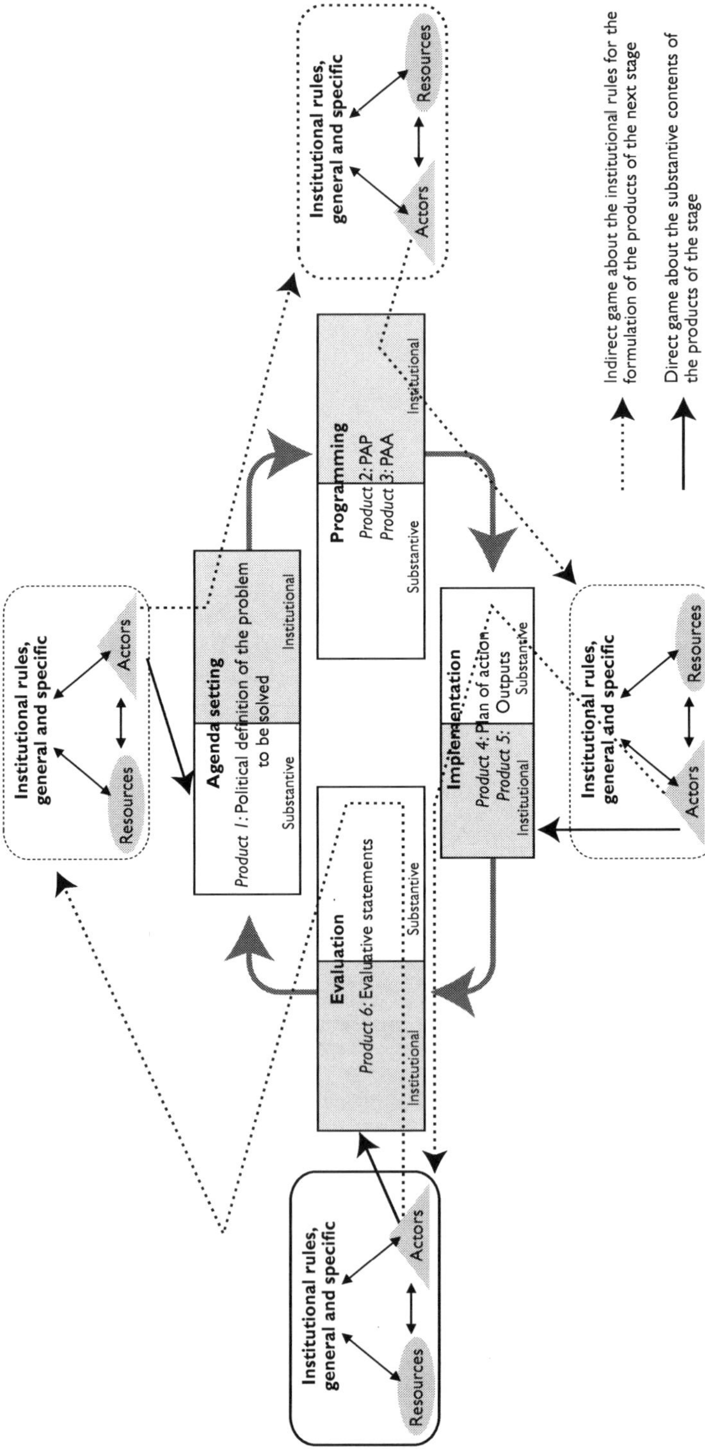

dimensions of the problem to be resolved as perceived politically when it was put on the governmental agenda. Likewise, the evaluation of the effects of implementation measures should be concerned with their contribution to the resolution of the same public problem identified at the outset. This substantive coherency is a sine qua non condition of the efficacy of public policies, if not of their actual existence. In reality, this condition is often far from being fulfilled. There are, for example, shifts in the definition of the problem in the course of the policy process; or the establishment of evaluation criteria other than the objectives defined in the political-administrative programme.

- *The consolidation of 'the policy arena'* (see Section 3.3.1 in Chapter Three): if the boundaries of the arena associated with the actors who are concerned with the emergence of a new collective problem remain generally blurred and very permeable when it is placed on the political agenda, the evolution of the policy over time will give rise to a progressive stabilisation in the number and type of actors involved and also in the frequency and quality of their interactions. In analysing the strictly relational dimension of policies, based on the basic triangle of all state intervention (state, target groups and end beneficiaries), the observer should, therefore, be able to confirm the beginning and then the consolidation (the more or less exclusive delimitation) of the policy arena analysed (Clivaz, 1998, 2001), which also includes third-party groups (positively and negatively affected third parties).
- *The constitution of 'institutional capital'*: the institutional rules influence actors' strategies because they delimit and channel their possibilities for action, just as they stabilise their efforts in relation to the decisions and activities of the other policy partners. In this sense they are stabilising factors with regard to individual behaviour, interaction between the actors and the substantive results arising from them. In focusing on the institutional aspect of the public action, the analyst should, however, be in a position to identify the 'institutional capital', constituted not only by the constitutional rules and those governing the administrative organisations of the political-administrative system concerned, but also and above all by the (in)formal norms that the actors involved in a specific public policy prescribe for themselves (see Section 5.2 in Chapter Five).
- *The exploitation of the entire 'range of resources'*: public and private actors resort to multiple – combinations of – resources so as to assert their interests. A priori, the 10 resources identified earlier

(see Chapter Four) vary in relevance according to the stage of the policy involved (for example, the 'information' resource during the definition of the public problem, 'law' during programming, 'communication' during implementation). They also depend on the nature of actors (for example, the privilege of law for political-administrative authorities, the partial control of the resource 'consensus' by private actors). Nonetheless, it remains impossible to anticipate specifically which actor will mobilise which resource for which strategic reason and with what level of success. Questions about which resources will ultimately be used, combined and substituted can only be answered through empirical analysis. In this framework, the analyst will be able to observe that the range of resources effectively mobilised expands in the course of the unfolding of a policy process, that resources are exchanged between the actors (for example, financial compensation versus consensus) and that the status of certain resources may even change (for example, private information becomes public). Finally, the empirical analyses suggest that the combinations of types of resources are observable in certain specific situations for comparable actors.

To conclude, we emphasise that our analysis model takes advantage of several of the undeniable heuristic advantages of the 'policy cycle' concept (see Section 2.4 in Chapter Two). It specifically facilitates the interpretation of public policy as a dynamic process and enables the identification and analysis of the stakes and a limited number of actors involved for each stage in the policy cycle. Although it simplifies the empirical analysis through the segmentation of research questions, variables and hypotheses on the basis of the four defined stages, our model tends, nevertheless, to avoid the obvious limits of a sequential approach to policy. That approach, based as it is on the chronology of political-administrative activities, or the excessively legalistic or 'top-down' vision of public action, fails to take into account external events or collective learning processes (see the criticisms of Jenkins-Smith and Sabatier, 1993, pp 3-4). The possibility of explaining the substantive and institutional results of a stage in the policy process partially independently of the content of the preceding stage extends the perspective of the analysis.

Thus, for the conduct of empirical studies we recommend that analysts adopt a two-pronged explanatory process. Firstly, it would appear relevant to want to explain the substantive and institutional result of a policy stage as following on from the decisions and actions taken during the previous stage of the same public policy (postulate no 1).

Secondly, and above all, if it is established that a fundamental difference exists between the scope and content of two successive stages, it is necessary to explain this empirically observed absence of continuity: that is, which (new) actors intervened with which (new combinations of) resources, which (new) interactions took place with which other actors and on the basis of which (new) institutional rules (postulate no 2).

To stress that – in spite of their strongly varied content – the six products observable in the four stages of a public policy cycle are characterised by a similar structure linked to the duality of the substantive and institutional aspects, the chapters devoted to each of these are structured in the same way:

1. *The general definition* of the product as the result of a particular stage of a public policy cycle (the variable to be explained).
2. *The operationalisation* of the product according to several analytical dimensions, substantive and institutional, necessary for an empirical study (the dimensions to be observed empirically).
3. Summary description of the *decision-making process* leading to the product (what type of actor, which resources and which institutional rules?).

Finally, it should again be noted that this kind of approach facilitates a truly comparative approach. The analytical dimensions proposed here make it possible to compare the actors, the resources used, the institutions in action and the policy products, both throughout the different phases of one and the same policy (diachronic analysis) and in the context of decision-making processes in different countries or in politically or administratively different parts of the same country (synchronic analysis).

SEVEN

Political agenda setting

If, as defined in Chapter Two, public policies consist of a group of activities and decisions taken by different actors with a view to resolving a problem that is politically defined as public in nature, it is important first and foremost to look into the actual concept of 'public problem'.

In this chapter, we discuss the processes whereby a *social* problem is identified and then 'thematicised' as a *public* problem as well as the different characteristics of *agenda setting*. According to our analytical model, the political definition of the public problem (PD) constitutes, in effect, the first product that the analyst must study when tackling the cycle of public intervention in the context of an empirical study.

In reality, the processes involving the political definition – and redefinition – of public problems have not been the subject of theoretical and empirical analyses that are comparable, in number at least, with those carried out on the (subsequent) stages of policy programming, implementation and evaluation. Obviously, the failure to take the stakes associated with the definition of the problem tackled by a policy into account is a definite drawback when it comes to the analysis of this policy, including studies carried out on its implementation:

> Yet we know that the problem definition stage frames and generates virtually everything that follows in the policy process, so our failures to examine problem definition sentences us to operate through a glass darkly (DeLeon, 1994, p 89).

As Anderson (1978, p 20) and others demonstrate, the development of a policy cannot be interpreted as the simple resolution of given problems defined on the basis of their intrinsic characteristics. It also involves the constitution and definition of public problems. This is a political designation process that influences or determines the actors involved in the policy (that is, the public authorities of the political-administrative arrangement [PAA], the target groups, the end beneficiaries and third-party groups), and the actual nature of the public actions carried out (that is, the modes of intervention selected in the political-administrative programme [PAP]).

From this perspective and by way of introduction, we stress the need for a (re-)constructive analysis of public problems (Section 7.1).

Then, in accordance with the structure proposed in Chapter Six, we will move on to the general definition and operationalisation of the concept of the 'public problem' (Section 7.2). Finally, we identify the agenda-setting processes on the basis of the strategies of the actors involved, their resources and the institutional rules that frame this first stage (Section 7.3).

7.1 Social construction of problems

In order to analyse a problem relevant to the public sphere and on this basis legitimise public intervention, it is necessary to adopt a constructivist approach. In effect, it is reasonable to assume that no objective fact constitutes a problem in itself (Cobb and Elder, 1983, p 172; Dery, 1984, p xi). The (social and then political) definition of a problem always represents a collective construction directly linked to the perceptions, representations, interests and values of the actors concerned on an individual basis and/or as part of organised groups. Thus, all social reality should be understood as a historical construction, situated in time and space. It always depends on the constellation of the people affected by the problem and/or those whose behaviour may need to change to solve it.

It is important that the reader fully understands what we are saying here: it is never a question of denying the objective conditions that constitute a problematic situation (for example, the existence of an elevated level of carbon dioxide emissions that represents a threat to climate stability, the permanent nature of the situation of a growing number of people seeking employment whose material and psychological situation becomes precarious, the high frequency of acts of violence in urban areas, the massive influx of war refugees at borders), but of stressing that these established facts only represent one of the dimensions – even if it proves fundamental in some cases – that constitute a social problem. Thus, the role of the policy analyst consists in identifying the processes, actors and arguments by means of which these objective conditions are perceived and are defined as problematic and requiring state intervention.

The adoption of a constructivist approach to the reality of social problems and policy has at least three implications for the manner of analytical consideration – that is, the reconstruction and interpretation – of public actions (see Vlassopoulou, 1999, pp 13-17) and, even more specifically, the policy products.

1. *The limits of the rationalistic approach:* according to what is known as the 'definitional' approach (Spector and Kitsuse, 1987), it would not be possible to compare *public policies* with *precise action programmes*. Such comparisons are, however, quite common in the North American research tradition. Action programmes presuppose a prior and clear definition of the objectives of the public action in question. If necessary, their objectives are externally defined (for example, on the basis of objective criteria concerning the scope of the problem to be resolved), the political challenge consisting solely in selecting the means that would enable their realisation. This rationalistic vision of public policy, which was pushed to extremes by the Planning, Programming and Budgeting System (PPBS) approach and other attempts to apply scientific planning to policy processes, assumes that the problem to be resolved is defined for once and for all and that the objectives of public actions are never questioned. Without doubt, the action programmes concretise the intentions of the legislator and the executive – possibly in the form that is most tangible for the analyst. However, they may not be interpreted as independent of the policy of which they are a part and, by extension, of a social situation that is collectively acknowledged as problematic. In summary, if the analysis is limited to the examination of legislative programmes (PAP – see Section 8.1 in Chapter Eight), it is impossible to pose or answer satisfactorily the question with regard to which social problem the state is ultimately trying to resolve and why one problem as opposed to another is selected as the basis of a policy.

    Thus, for example, a ban on allowing public lighting to be left on after midnight may constitute either a measure for protection against nocturnal air attacks (in the case of a country at war), a measure to reduce energy spending or to reduce emissions that represent a risk to the climate of our planet.

2. *The limits of the sequential approach:* the analysis of a policy on the basis of a sequential model conceived in a rigid and strictly linear manner (agenda setting → programming → implementation → evaluation) tends to suggest that the definition of a problem constitutes an individual and isolated stage in the policy process. If all public policies are based first and foremost on the collective recognition and thematicisation of a particular problem, it is necessary, nonetheless, to keep in mind that the programming, implementation and evaluation stages are also based on the definition – in the sense of a concretisation – or redefinition –

in the sense of a modification – of the public problem defined at the outset (Plein, 1994). The construction of a problem is, therefore, an ongoing, non-linear and open process.

During a diachronic study of a policy cycle, at each stage in the cycle the analyst must pose the question as to the extent to which the content, actors and institutional context of the policy being studied are associated with the initial definition of the problem to be resolved or, conversely, are associated with its political reformulation by the actors concerned (who, in some cases, were deliberately excluded from the decision-making process at the outset of the public intervention). A sequential approach to public policies – adopted in part here for its heuristic advantages – which does not take this ongoing process of (re-) definition into account risks obscuring not only a fundamental challenge of all public action, but also one of the explanatory factors of the eventual substantial and/or institutional changes to the policy along the way. In effect, a redefinition of the problem to be resolved (for example, due to the revised interpretation of the initial objective data or the knowledge of new facts) should translate into a change of policy and vice versa.

The evolution of air pollution prevention policy is one of the clearest examples of this kind of dynamic (Weale, 1992). In the 1950s, this policy was aimed at the emission of pollutants by households, industrial companies and emissions in urban areas. The discovery of the phenomena of long-distance transportation of acid pollution combined with the mandatory erection of high chimneys (to ensure better dispersion of pollution and hence a low concentration of pollutants in the local air) noticeably changed policy in this area to the extent that all sources of emission were considered irrespective of their location – urban or non-urban. The dilution/diffusion principle was then replaced by that of treatment at source that translated into the obligation to install filters in industrial chimneys. In the 1980s, the same policy underwent a second fundamental change due to the emergence of phenomenon of the greenhouse effect and leading to the inclusion of mobile sources (cars that were formerly exempt from environmental interventions) as target groups.

3. *The limits of the sectoral approach:* finally an approach centred solely on programmes and their political-administrative structures tends to interpret policies in accordance with a sectoral analysis framework. If such a public administration is in charge of the programming and execution of a policy, the public problem at

the basis of this intervention comes under the responsibility of a particular sector, predetermined by habit (for example, the logic of a profession and its individual members) and the traditional area of competency of the administration responsible. By taking the organisational affiliation of the administrative actors responsible for policy programming and implementation as the only point of departure, the analyst neglects the critical interpretation of the process of (re-)definition of a collective problem. In effect, a social problem will generally not only concern a single sector of intervention, but several (for example, atmospheric pollution may constitute a public health problem as well as problems that are the concern of environmental protection, transport, production and the consumption of fossil fuel-based energies). Furthermore, if the definition of a problem is interpreted as an evolutionary process, the responsibility for its management within political-administrative structures may, with time, shift from one sector to another. Not to take these institutional changes into account risks limiting the interpretation of a collective problem to just one of its dimensions and, hence, the failure to recognise the evolution of the public policy as well as the problems of coordination that arise between the different public actors responsible for its resolution (note the internal coordination of a public policy and coordination between several public policies).

7.2 Political definition of the public problem (product no 1)

Having justified the necessity for a (re-)constructive approach, we must now define and operationalise what we understand by the term 'public problem' so as to guide the analytical (re-)construction of this first policy product.

7.2.1 Public problem: defining elements

Gusfield (1981) makes a clear distinction between 'social problems' and 'public problems', noting that all social problems do not necessarily become public problems, i.e. the objects of political controversy. Hence, public problems represent an extension of social problems to the extent that, having emerged within civil society, they are debated within an emerging political-administrative arena. In this sense, the definition of a public problem is essentially political in nature. In other words, a problem is only public if it is already on the political agenda. At this stage of the definitional process, public actors (for example, the administration, government, parliament) recognise the need to consider a possible state solution to the identified problem.

Even more concretely, Garraud (1990, p 20) identifies the three following conditions for referring to a problem as public: (1) the constitution of a demand emanating from particular social groups; (2) the development of a controversy or public debate; and (3) the existence of a conflict between organised social groups and political authorities.

The assumption of the transfer of a problem from the social sphere to the public sphere on the basis of a strict chronological model prompts the definition of public actors as orchestrators of the agenda-setting process. Although this vision makes sense because it attributes a proactive role to the public actors, it must, however, be stressed that the passage of a public problem is neither linear nor inevitable.

On the one hand, as Vassopoulou (1999, pp 19-20) notes, "a public problem may involve the recuperation of a former social preoccupation as well as an original political construction". The specificity of a public problem consists, therefore, in the fact that it is placed under the responsibility of the public authorities and not necessarily in the fact that the latter take up a social problem that has already been clearly articulated.

On the other hand, several problematic social situations are never thematicised as public problems requiring state intervention. Contrary to the pluralistic vision of democracy that assumes that every actor may access the decision-making arena to thematicise a particular problem, Bachrach and Baratz (1970, p 6) assert that a specific form of public power consists precisely in the possibility of keeping certain social problems off the public agenda. Described as 'non-decisions', these institutional blocks force the social actors concerned by a problem either to find other points of access, or to manage the resolution of the problem themselves (using corporative or private policies):

> Non-decision making is a means by which demands for change in the existing allocation of benefits and privileges in the community can be suffocated before they are even voiced; or kept covert; or killed before they gain access to the relevant decision-making arena. (Bachrach and Baratz, 1970, p 44)

Political agenda setting

We propose – for all empirical analyses – to study the extent to which a problematic private situation is perceived and then defined as revealing of the social sphere and then the political arena. This kind of analysis aims, among other things, to identify the possible pitfalls (that is, the different types of non-decisions) in the definition process (see Figure 7.1).

The sociological approaches concentrate primarily on the individual factors, the collective conventions and norms that favour or, conversely, curtail the realisation that a private problematic situation may concern the social sphere and, consequently, be defined as a social rather than private problem (for a discussion of this topic using UK examples see Hulley and Clarke, 1991).

The more political science-based approaches mainly analyse the articulation of a problem referred to as social, the resulting demands for public intervention and the approaches to agenda setting adopted by the different actors concerned, that is, private and public, individual and collective. As Garraud (1990, pp 17ff) notes, any analysis of agenda setting that takes this diversity of actors into account will by necessity find itself at the intersection of the disciplines dealing, in particular, with political participation, (new) social movements, the media and decision-making processes.

Essentially, as suggested by Figure 7.1, we only speak of a 'public problem' if a situation is judged politically as problematic and is the subject of political debate. Beyond this very general definition, we present below some dimensions on the basis of which 'the PD' may be described and analysed.

It should be noted, however, that it will sometimes be possible to observe a development running contrary to that described in Figure 7.1, whereby a problem initially identified as public (for example, the legal prohibition of cohabitation in Swiss family policy) is subsequently considered as solely relevant in the private sphere and cannot, therefore,

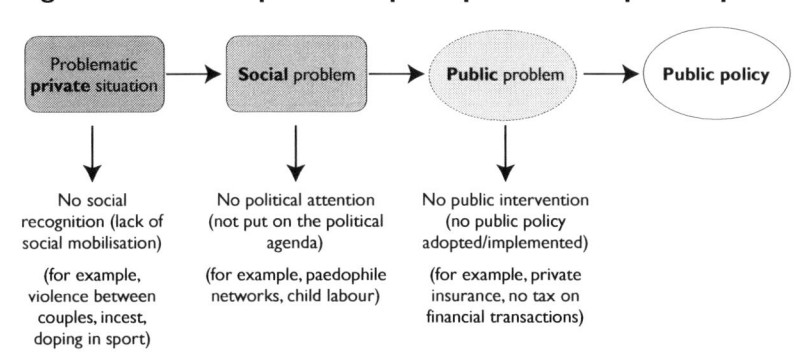

Figure 7.1: Definition process for public problems and possible pitfalls

Problematic **private** situation → **Social** problem → **Public** problem → Public policy

↓ No social recognition (lack of social mobilisation)
(for example, violence between couples, incest, doping in sport)

↓ No political attention (not put on the political agenda)
(for example, paedophile networks, child labour)

↓ No public intervention (no public policy adopted/implemented)
(for example, private insurance, no tax on financial transactions)

be the object of state intervention. Certain sectors historically considered as relevant to the public sphere are being gradually withdrawn from traditional policies and other forms of regulation by the state (for example, competition policy). However, the privatisation of public services may involve the replacement of public provision by extensive public regulatory activities.

7.2.2 Operational analysis dimensions

Policy analysis may identify several constituent elements of a public policy (see Wildavsky, 1979; Gusfield, 1981; Rochefort and Cobb, 1993; Peters, 1998). Let us stress once again that if every problem can be qualified on the basis of the dimensions discussed here, this assessment does not solely depend on the objective conditions of the situation deemed problematic, but also on the evaluation and subjective weighting (that is, of the PD) of the actors concerned. Thus, in evaluating the four constituent elements proposed below, the analysis is trying above all to explain the perceptions of the nature of the problem of those directly concerned by it.

Note also that the agenda-setting stage of a public problem is also something of an 'art' in the sense that for the promoters of a particular policy it involves the combining of substantive aspects (for example, the promotion of out-patient health treatment) with the more institutional dimensions (for example, the reduction of fixed personnel and infrastructure costs in hospitals, altering the roles of various organisations or actors within the healthcare system).

It is also necessary to stress in advance that the operational dimensions discussed above intersect in part; their simultaneous consideration must favour a general interpretation of a public problem rather than partial interpretations.

1. *The intensity of the problem:* the intensity of a problem refers to the way in which the consequences of the problem are estimated at individual and collective level. In this context, the actors involved judge whether it is a serious problem worthy of consideration in view of the negative effects caused (for example, financial costs and psychological distress caused by an increase in unemployment; risk of a nuclear accident; negative effects of tobacco, alcohol and illegal drug consumption on health), or a 'pseudo-problem' that is too insignificant, according to key actors, to galvanise public opinion and/or immediate intervention by the public authorities (previous examples include: difficulty of

access to public places for people with disabilities; disappearance of rare plant species). Note that the degree of intensity acknowledged for a given problem will vary from one actor to the next and at different times.

2. *The perimeter (or audience) of the problem:* the perimeter of a problem consists in the extent (or scope) of its negative effects in relation to the different social groups affected and their geographical location and the development of the problem over time. The identification of this perimeter necessitates knowledge of the circle of people and/or regions that are affected by the negative effects of a particular problem. Obviously, the social and spatial borders of a problem may develop quickly over time.

    This dimension of a problem is closely linked to its public visibility. In effect, if the social groups affected are restricted in number, located in peripheral regions and/or belong to social strata that are not highly politicised, the chance that their situation will be defined as a collective problem is limited. Schneider and Ingram (1997) demonstrate specifically that the manner of definition of a social problem (and the policy intended to remedy it) depends on the (positive or negative) social image and the (strong or weak) public power of the groups that are either touched by its negative effects or responsible for its emergence.

    Thus, it is possible to make a distinction between problems that are perceived as 'clearly defined/concentrated' (for example, water pollution, drug consumption, suburban violence) and problems perceived as being 'without boundaries/diffuse' (for example, the risk of an epidemic in connection with 'bird flu', the human and ecological costs of a nuclear accident, the problems associated with unemployment), and between problems whose perimeter is developing rapidly (for example, the problems associated with AIDS or natural disasters) or slowly (for example, the economic situation of farmers and unemployed people).

3. *The newness of the problem:* while certain problems are new on account of their association with the recent evolution of our post-industrial societies, others are more chronic in nature. The degree of newness of a problem is often considered as a determining factor in its capacity to access the governmental agenda. Downs (1973), for example, suggests that a new public problem will succeed more easily in mobilising public opinion and, hence, in prompting private and public actors to intervene. However, after an initial phase of expansion, the problem in question will gradually relinquish its importance and weight in

terms of the governmental agenda in favour of more recent problems.

The problems perceived as 'new/recent' include, for example, bullying in schools, genetic engineering and environmental problems. Problems perceived as 'old/chronic' include, for example, the problems of illiteracy, public security, price stability and unemployment among people without professional qualifications.

Note that new problems and, hence, completely new public policies are rare. While such situations were still common during the phases of the emergence and affirmation of the welfare state, there is now no choice but to accept that most public intervention is more likely to involve the correction or re-orientation of a previous and (partly) failed policy, or the integration of several previously separate policies.

4. *The urgency of the problem:* a social problem may be perceived as more or less urgent in nature. In extreme cases, often associated with a shock arising outside the political-administrative system (for example, an accidental cause), we speak of crisis management with the state providing an (almost) instantaneous response to the social problem that has quickly become obvious to all. Such contexts should open a 'window of opportunity' (an expression used by Kingdon, 1984) for the 'policy entrepreneurs' who wish to promote policies to address that particular problem.

In the context of problems perceived as urgent, the following are worthy of mention: bird flu, foot and mouth disease, AIDS, the oil crises of 1973 and 1979, the nuclear accidents at Three Mile Island in 1979 and Chernobyl in 1986. The problems that are perceived as non-urgent include, for example, the progressive degradation of the landscape and the ongoing increase in cardiovascular diseases associated with (professional) stress and health issues (nutrition, tobacco, alcohol).

These four dimensions are not claimed to be exhaustive in terms of the operationalisation and comparison of different social and public problems. The analyst may also try to qualify the nature of a problem on the basis of its political complexity (several parties involved/few actors involved), programmatic complexity (several identifiable causes/ a single cause), its capacity to be expressed in monetary form (costs of X million/barely tangible and non-quantifiable effects) or its degree of interdependence with other public problems (isolated problem/ interlinked problems) (see Peters, 1998).

Thus, it is possible to dissociate multi-causal problems, such as air pollution related to motor vehicles, industries and households, from mono-causal problems such as the absence of low water flow in water courses as a result of the production of hydro-electric power (Switzerland) or water shortages as a result of leaks in the water transmission system (UK).

Similarly, it is possible to identify problems that can be expressed in monetary terms, such as the net loss of X billion Euros due to corporate practices with respect to public markets, and problems whose financial costs are not at all tangible such as racist attitudes among certain groups.

Finally, it is possible to identify an isolated problem, such as that of inefficient weather forecasting, from interlinked problems, for example, unemployment that depends on complex links between macro-economic, monetary, fiscal, educational and social security policies.

Without going into these complementary dimensions in more detail here, it should be said that a public problem does not necessarily evolve into a problem of a certain type on the basis of its intrinsic characteristics.

As stated above, the PD results from a symbolic battle taking place between rival groups in an at least partly established institutional context. The dimensions of political agenda setting in respect of a situation judged collectively as problematic are, however, complex and worthy of particular attention.

7.3 Agenda-setting processes

The following paragraphs aim to identify the explanatory factors behind the process of agenda setting. Initially, we suggest that this definitional process may be interpreted as a power struggle whose main challenge is the recognition or imposition of an initial 'hypothesis of causality' which (pre-)structures the development of the future public intervention. We then identify the actor constellations and means of action (resources and institutional rules) associated with different ideal-type processes.

7.3.1 From competing 'causal stories' towards a dominant 'hypothesis of causality'

According to the constructivist approach, all social problems – and to an even greater extent all public problems – are collective constructs. Thus, the definition of the problem that a public policy seeks to resolve emerges in the interaction between the actors concerned by a particular situation. This process of definition most often consists in a power struggle between groups of actors than as a consensual process accepted by all in civil society. The control of the process of definition of public problems and, hence, of the alternative means of their resolution represents a fundamental political challenge (Weiss, 1989), or even the supreme instrument of power (Schattschneider, 1960, p 66). As Stone (1989) states, different social groups are pitted against each other as each tries to impose its own definition of the problem. In other words, the actors concerned clash with each other in their efforts to become the 'owners' or legitimate trustees of the problem (Gusfield, 1981, pp 10-11).

This debate, which is generally conflictual in nature, is expressed in terms of competing 'causal stories' advanced by the different groups of actors:

> Problem definition is a process of image making, where the images have to do fundamentally with attributing cause, blame, and responsibility. Conditions, difficulties or issues thus do not have inherent properties that make them more or less likely to be seen as problems or to be expanded. Rather, political actors deliberately portray them in ways calculated to gain support for their side. And political actors, in turn, do not simply accept causal models that are given from science or popular culture or any other source. They compose stories that describe harms and difficulties, attribute them to actions of other individuals or organizations, and thereby claim the right to invoke government power to stop the harm. (Stone, 1989, p 282)

Thus a 'causal story' is indicated by a social group whose situation is deemed problematic; the group in question also imputes responsibility for this politically unacceptable situation to the behaviour of another social group (Edelman, 1988, p 17). In this context, to define a problem means to identify the groups who suffer its negative effects as well as identifying the origins, that is, which will often involve designating those responsible, whose behaviour gives rise to the problem and who must consequently bear the costs of its resolution. The causal stories create or delineate particular social groups by a process of symbolic designation. In the course of this process, the different actors manipulate images and symbols in order to strengthen their arguments (see, in particular, Edelman, 1964, 1988; Schneider and Ingram, 1997). This is particularly evident in the case of the theories supported by the extreme

Right that deliberately attribute the causes of unemployment, violence and so on to a particular social group, that is, immigrants.

Furthermore, Stone (1989) suggests that public debate generally remains deaf to any excessively complex interpretation or explanation and that (strategic) actors try to put forward simple causal stories. In the majority of cases, the groups affected by a problem try to render credible an 'intentional' cause for their unfavourable situation: the social problem results from a considered human action whose consequences are predictable and desired (for example: "My respiratory problems are due to the fact that industries knowingly produce excessive pollutant emissions and this gives rise to a deterioration in air quality"). If an argument of this type proves indefensible, they aim to identify the causes as arising 'through negligence': the social problem is still the result of a considered human action; however, in this case the consequences are unpredictable (for example: "I contracted the AIDS virus through a blood transfusion because the precautions deemed indispensable by current medical knowledge were not taken"). Conversely, the groups that are publicly defined as responsible for a collective problem advance causes referred to as 'mechanical' or 'accidental' to extricate themselves from all responsibility; in this case, they suggest that the unpredictable and undesired consequences are the product of external events or non-guided human actions (for example, aeroplane accidents were caused by an unknown problem of a technical nature, for which the operating company was not responsible, and it was not caused by pilot error or insufficient security controls; exceptional dry weather caused water shortage not inadequate water conservation and transmission management).

From an analytical point of view, all causal stories have an *empirical-cognitive* dimension (sometimes including a solid scientific basis) and a *moral or normative* dimension. Hisschemöller and Hoppe (1996) combined these two dimensions to develop a typology of public problems classified according to their degree of structuring. Thus, they suggest that, to the extent that the state wishes to effectively resolve it, every type of problem involves a particular type of policy (process) (see Table 7.1).

This typology is useful both to distinguish the processes of definition behind different policies and the formalising of the links between the nature of the problem dealt with and the strategy developed for state action and intervention. Nevertheless, its heuristic range is limited in the sense that, as stated in Stone's theoretical propositions, it focuses almost exclusively on causal histories in its efforts to understand the process of (re-)definition of a social problem.

Public policy analysis

Table 7.1: The relationships between the structuring of a problem and political strategies

At cognitive level \ At normative level	Conflict concerning the norms and values at play in the context of the problem to be resolved	Consensus on the norms and values at play in the context of the problem to be resolved
Ignorance of the actual nature of the problem to be resolved	Non-structured problem (→ strategy based on *collective learning*) Eg effects of genetic engineering or non-ionising waves (mobile telephones)	Partly structured problem: agreement on the objectives (→ pluralist strategy based on *negotiation*) Eg efforts to counteract drug networks, youth unemployment
(Scientific) certainties with respect to the causes and effects of the problem to be resolved	Partly structured problem: agreement on the means (→ strategy of *accommodation*) Eg question of deadlines in the context of abortion	Structured problem (→ interventionist strategy based on *regulation*) Eg efforts to counteract pollution of water by urban, industrial and agricultural pollution

Source: Loose adaptation of Hisschemöller and Hoppe (1996, p 56) with illustrations

In referring us to the basic triangle of a policy (see Section 3.4 in Chapter Three), the concept of the 'causal story' proposed by Stone (1989) displays major similarities with the concept of the 'hypothesis of causality' that we proposed for the identification of the target groups (required to solve the problem and often its cause) and end beneficiaries (that suffer the negative effects of the problem) of a policy. In this sense, what we qualify as a hypothesis of causality (and which is found – at least implicitly – formalised in a PAP) is the causal history that ultimately asserts itself as being the most plausible, based on the knowledge available on the constitutive conditions of the social problem, and/or the most politically desirable one, based on the interests and values of the actors involved in the definitional process. In terms of empirical analysis, the (initial and often temporary) phase of PD may be considered as complete when a causal hypothesis generates political consensus or at least unites the majority of the actors concerned.

In the following paragraphs, we discuss some agenda-setting models for public policy. These propositions identify different actors who mobilise and combine several types of resources, such as the initiators or the 'owners', and engage in the debate on a particular public problem.

7.3.2 Process: actors, resources and institutions mobilised

The study of political agenda setting looks into the factors that influence the fact that one social problem attracts the attention of the actors concerned (and thus becomes a public problem), while another is not subject to public debate or state intervention. In concrete terms, this involves the definition of the actors and processes involved in the agenda setting. Up to now, no general theory has made it possible to explain the constitution and definition of the policy agenda and the ways that the 'initiators' of the debate on a social problem access it. On the contrary, a number of partial models are proposed in the literature, each of which describes a particular process within the overall agenda-setting context. Without making any claim to their exhaustiveness, we present below five ideal types of 'agenda setting'.

Thematicisation through media coverage

The supporters of the 'media coverage' model highlight the decisive role of the media (in particular the press, radio and television and the Internet) and polling institutes (for example, regular polls on problems identified as priorities according to the general public) in the identification of a public problem. The media directly influence public opinion by placing the emphasis on one or other social event, particularly in a crisis situation. This then prompts public actors and the political parties to reappropriate the current topics of debate and to launch a political debate and hence raise their profile among the public (McCombs and Shaw, 1972; Gormley, 1975; Walker, 1977; Lambeth, 1978; Cook et al, 1983; Scheberle, 1994).

Political scandals in France and in the UK that have raised the question of the public financing of political parties and the cases of corruption that led to the regulation of public markets may be quoted in this context. Likewise, a policy can originate from the featuring of a pollution catastrophe on the front page of the newspapers (for example, various shipwrecks leading to severe oil spillages).

Information and communication infrastructure are, without doubt, the main resources mobilised by (private) actors. Furthermore, access to and mobilisation of these two resources express themselves as determining factors behind the actual structures and functioning of the media that are active within a public body. Moreover, 'time' as a resource also appears to play an important role here, because the time chosen to reveal information about a social problem to the public may prove decisive for its inclusion in the political agenda, above all if a problem is presented as new and urgent.

At the same time, it may be assumed that few institutional rules limit or promote the action and the power of definition of the media: the latter can generally take advantage of the freedom of expression guaranteed at constitutional level.

'Mobilisation' or 'exterior initiative'

Assuming that the policy agenda is constituted in response to clearly articulated social demands, a number of authors suggest that the activities of pressure groups and/or (new) social movements are a determining factor. As defenders of often general and long-term social interests (for example, environmental protection, the right to work, anti-racism), these organised actors try to attract public opinion and the attention of political-administrative actors to the social problem to be resolved using both institutional (for example, the popular initiatives and referendums in Switzerland) and extra-institutional (for example, various demonstrations) means. In view of the way that western democracies currently function, this model appears very plausible. It is frequently adopted when the mobilisation of groups is associated with extensive public visibility (Cobb et al, 1976; Cobb and Elder, 1983; Baumgartner and Jones, 1993). For example, the strikes that are organised by public service trades unions and the occupation of nuclear sites by ecologist 'commandos' like Greenpeace correspond to this phenomenon.

According to this model, the (private) actors primarily make use of the resources of 'political support' and 'organisation', with financial and personnel resources naturally acting as indispensable supports to the latter. What is often involved is the setting up of a (new) organisation capable of asserting the interests and values of its members (for example, establishment of a neighbourhood watch group, the creation of a coalition of charity organisations). After this the actors try to thematicise a new problem by opposing an existing policy or a current (infrastructure) project. Unlikely to have access to the resource 'law', that is, not enjoying the right to be heard during the consultation and co-decision procedures, these actors concentrate on the creation, exploitation and combination of other resources such as 'information' and 'time' so as to delay or block a specific project.

From an institutional point of view, (new) social movements frequently avail of legal institutions and/or direct democracy, in particular in the case of the popular initiative in Switzerland, to thematicise (at a national level) a problem that was previously obscured (or perceived at local level only). Although these institutional procedures are on the whole very expensive and uncertain in outcome, they may represent the only means available to individuals and groups to assert themselves as full actors in a defined sector. Finally, it should be noted that several private actors free themselves from all institutional constraints by adopting strategies that although illegal are considered morally justified (for example, a call for civil disobedience motivated by moral values in the case of the non-denunciation of illegal immigrants in France, the occupation of a nuclear site or opposition to NATO military intervention in a foreign conflict). The actors sometimes avail of the resource 'violence' in such situations.

Compared with the 'mobilisation' or 'external initiative' models, let us note finally that the analyst may clearly identify in the case of some policies the existence at local level of 'laboratories of emergence' for a particular problem. The situation is subsequently thematicised at regional and then (inter)national level. In contrast to this 'bottom-up process', 'top-down' processes also exist that introduce collective problems initially discussed at international level to the (infra-)national agenda. This is particularly true of EU directives, one of whose impacts is to introduce public problems that were not hitherto acknowledged to the national or local agenda (for example, the taking into account of air pollution caused by motor vehicles as a result of the enactment of the 'ozone' directive in 1992). Furthermore, the harmonisation of the political agendas at the level of all member states is one of the major impacts of the EU (see, in particular, Mény et al, 1995; Larrue, 2000, pp 49ff; Larrue and Vlassopoulou, 1999).

In the British literature on environmental regulation this external influence is linked with another influence (external to the original policy agenda if not to the country): privatisation. For example, the co-incidence of the establishment of a privatised water industry, requiring specific regulation by government agencies, with European directives on water quality together put water pollution issues on the policy agenda. This provided opportunities for pressure groups concerned with the quality of drinking and sea bathing water (Maloney and Richardson, 1994; Jordan, 1998).

'Policy supply' or 'electoral competition'

Inspired by 'public choice' theory, the policy supply model assumes that political parties do not just respond in a reactive way to social demands that have been articulated already. They may also take the initiative. Hence they may define and formulate public problems with a view to expanding their electoral base through the addition of the beneficiaries of the proposed new policies. Thus, in this context, the policy agenda is constituted on the basis of the topics selected by the main competing parties in their programmes and during campaigns. Various sub-variants of this model are proposed according to which the confrontation between the parties is instead expressed in terms of an ideological dimension (a situation of direct competition according to Downs, 1957 and Odershook, 1986), or in terms of the selective declaration of certain topics, for which one party has greater credibility among the population than another (the situation of indirect competition according to Budge and Farlie, 1983; Klingeman et al, 1994). This is particularly true in the case of the problem of immigration that is thematicised by extreme Right-wing parties in most European countries, the highlighting of the problem of unemployment by the parties of the Left and of environmental problems by the Green parties.

It should be noted that these theories were developed to account for agenda setting in democratic regimes of the Westminster type, in which parties develop clear programmes of legislation that they can realise with the support of a parliamentary majority (Hofferbert and Budge, 1992; Pétry, 1995).

Here, the resources mobilised by political parties generally encompass the resources 'information' (declarations of political programmes), 'organisation' (party apparatuses) and 'political support' (political majorities in power or the achievement of a governing coalition). As the analysis of the financing of political parties and electoral and/or referendum campaigns show, the resource 'money' also plays a decisive role in the capacities of the respective parties to make their presence felt on the political scene and to lead the debate on a given social problem with continuity.

Among the institutional rules that the political parties can use to assert their ideologies and stances, the following should be noted in particular: the constitutional recognition of parties, the instruments of direct democracy (popular initiative and referendums), the electoral rules (majority versus proportional systems) and the informal rules associated, for example, with the Swiss system of concordance (for example, it will be easier for a problem thematicised by a government party to be taken into account than a problem placed on the agenda by a non-government party). Furthermore, it should be noted that the federalist rules or laws governing decentralisation partly influence the internal organisation of political parties (for example, the divergence between the slogans of political parties at national level in Switzerland and those of their cantonal sections).

'Internal anticipation'

The model known as 'internal anticipation' (Garraud, 1990) awards a crucial importance to the administrative actors and public authorities during the constitution of the policy agenda. According to this model, these actors – who are already involved in the implementation of existing policies – would be the best placed to identify the gaps between current state actions and social problems that remain unresolved. Kingdon (1984, 1995) identifies what he calls 'policy entrepreneurs' inside as well as outside the administrative system, perhaps a particular feature of the fragmented system in the US but by no means absent elsewhere. In the UK think-tanks, often with links to the political parties and therefore partly 'inside' and partly 'outside' the system, have played a key role in this process (Denham and Garnett, 2004). Evaluation reports on the effects of a particular policy often constitute essential information support for this kind of anticipation of imminent problems or those that already exist but have not yet been resolved. As a result, the administrative actors propose changes to old policies and/ or new intervention strategies on their own authority. According to the supporters of this model, the internal dynamics of the political-administrative sub-system are strengthened in particular in situations in which a social problem is 'badly' articulated by civil society. In such cases, the public actors replace private actors so as to appropriate and (re-)define the public problem to be resolved. In doing this they also secure for themselves a new legitimacy as a useful organisation as well as support for or extension of their area of competence and their resources (for example, personnel, money, knowledge).

The launch of an awareness-raising campaign targeted at adolescents by the public health authority on the topic of tobacco and alcohol addiction and the ban on advertising of these products is an example of the launch of a new policy (sometimes in the absence of a legislative mandate); similarly the problem of road safety is regularly raised in the media by the public authorities.

In fact, all of the resources theoretically at the disposal of political-administrative actors may be activated and combined in the case of 'internal anticipation'. More specifically, however, it seems that the targeted presentation of information (on a social situation that is deemed problematic) and the privileged position of public actors in initiating a legislative or regulatory process can prove as determining factors in explaining why a given problem ultimately reaches the policy agenda.

Likewise, all of the institutional rules that define decision-making procedures potentially act as procedural supports for the activities of public authorities. Thus, for example, these range from the possibility of establishing a commission of external experts to analyse the data concerning a particular social problem to organising an (informal) consultation (pre-)procedure for certain concerned actors. It should be noted here that the political-administrative actors are perfectly versed in the institutional nuts and bolts of the public sector – particularly the informal ones – a fact that is not necessarily true of certain private actors and more so if they are not organised in a pressure group. Thus, the former potentially enjoy greater room for manoeuvre to assert their own interests (and public policies) or those they represent.

'Silent corporatist action'

While the 'mobilisation' model concentrates on actions involving a high level of public visibility on the part of pressure groups and (new) social movements, the 'silent corporatist action' model analyses the more discreet role of interest groups in the context of the policy agenda. Defending their own (often particular and short-term) interests, these actors, who are very well organised and benefit from networks of influence, seek direct access to the decision-making arena while deliberately avoiding the thematicisation through media coverage and politicisation of the policies they would like to either maintain, introduce or avoid at all costs. This kind of model is based both on the neo-corporatist theories and on empirical studies (Baumgartner and Jones, 1993), which demonstrate that certain administrations and political authorities maintain 'clientelistic' relationships with various private or para-state actors. Cases involving the agricultural sector, the oil industry, the construction sector and public works are the best known in this context.

If the relationships between certain private and public actors are characterised as clientelistic, it may be assumed that the resources 'organisation', 'consensus' and 'political support' are essential to the maintenance of this corporatist equilibrium. In effect, an administrative authority will be interested in negotiating bilaterally with a particular pressure group insofar as the latter offers – in exchange for refraining from thematicising the problem to be resolved – its action network (or an implementing para-state administration) and its support during the adoption of the policy. In fact, the majority of resources mobilised will be mobilised to prevent the information on the problem to be resolved from becoming (too) public or prevent the adoption of (excessively) rigid legal solutions, for example.

At an institutional level, it is the informal rules that will logically influence the nature and content of negotiations between public authorities and private pressure groups. From a more extreme perspective, it may even be assumed that the actors involved will direct all their activities and decisions towards the development of informal conventions or tacit agreements. This is done expressly to prevent the other equally concerned actors from pursuing the option of approaching formal institutions to access the policy in question (see Section 3.3.1 in Chapter Three). This may be observed in relation to issues like sustainable development and food policy, where companies make commitments in efforts to pre-empt government interventions (Cahill, 2002).

7.3.3 Comparison criteria

None of the five models briefly discussed above is sufficiently differentiated and complex to explain on its own the process of political agenda setting associated with a particular social problem. However, by combining these models, the analyst may find it easier to identify the intermediaries to which the social groups (target groups, end beneficiaries and third parties) and public actors may or should appeal to form coalitions at the stage of the PD. To facilitate this kind of comparison, Table 7.2 presents an overview of some of the variables

Table 7.2: Variables for the political agenda setting of public problems

Models / Variables	Thematicisation through media coverage	Mobilisation (exterior initiative)	Policy supply (electoral competition)	Internal anticipation	Silent corporatist action
Actors: 'proprietor' of the problem or initiator of the process?	Various media and opinion polling institutes	Pressure groups and social movements	Political parties and other organisations	Political-administrative authorities	Sectoral interest groups
Clearly articulated social demand?	No	Yes	No	No	Yes
Audience vis-à-vis the problem?	Large	Large	Large	Rather limited	Very limited
Media coverage, appeal to public opinion?	Yes	Yes	Yes	Not necessarily	In no case
Partisan exploitation?	Not necessarily	Not necessarily	Yes	No	No
Main resources mobilised	Information, infrastructure and time	Organisation and political support	Information, organisation and political support	Information and law	Organisation, consensus and political support
Main institutional rules used	Constitutional guarantee: freedom of expression	Direct democracy (and perhaps illegal actions)	Constitutional guarantee, direct democracy and electoral and government rules	Principles of administrative law and traditional decisional rules	Informal rules as a substitute for formal rules

Source: Loose adaptation of Garraud (1990, p 39) with added information regarding resources and mobilised institutions

relevant for empirical studies on agenda setting. It also presents, in the form of hypotheses, the main resources and institutional rules that actors mobilise to promote their causes.

When we consider the different variables presented in Table 7.2, it should appear obvious that a detailed study of the process of the political agenda setting of a public problem must comprise at least three stages:

- An analysis of the actors involved: who is the initiator, the 'owner' and/or legitimate possessor of the problem? What kind of causal history does the latter propose? What are the competing causal histories proposed by the other actors?
- An analysis of the thematicisation processes: which resources and which institutional rules are used by whom and how successfully in order to access the decision-making arena?
- An analysis of the substantive content: what is the influence of the composition of the actors involved and the agenda-setting strategies adopted on the way in which the (social, geographical and temporal perimeter of the) public problem is ultimately defined?

The simultaneous consideration of these substantive and institutional dimensions will facilitate the general comprehension and interpretation of the process of the PD that ensures the passage of a so-called social problem to a so-called public problem.

7.4 Dynamics of the political agenda: competition and change

Up to now, we have discussed the concepts 'social problem', 'public problem' and 'agenda setting' as though every problem would in itself constitute an independent entity. This postulate, which is implicitly found in most of the case studies dealing with a single public problem (for example, on AIDS: Rogers et al, 1991; on global warming: Trumbo, 1995; on economic policy: Kleinnijenhuis and Rietberg, 1995) should not obscure the fact that several social problems are always engaged in (in)direct competition when they aim to access the political agenda.

In effect, in view of the limited resources of the state apparatus and intermediary actors (for example, political parties, social movements, pressure groups), the political agenda cannot process all of the problems articulated by civil society at the same time and with the same intensity. Thus, there is competition between social problems, and some end up being relegated to the queue for inclusion on the list of priorities for public action (for example, environmental questions are often seen as a luxury which should not be dealt with during a period of economic expansion), while others are completely eliminated from the democratic debate (note the concept of 'non-decisions'). In the framework of an analysis of the agenda-setting process for a particular problem, the researcher should bear in mind not only the factors relating to the problem studied, but also the more general conditions relating to the other social problems simultaneously expressed by civil society, in order to explain the access or non-access to the political/policy arena of the problem (Crenson, 1971; Cobb et al, 1976; Hilgartner and Bosk, 1988).

Besides taking into account all of the public problems that constitute the political agenda, it is, finally, also necessary to highlight the importance of a diachronic interpretation of the agenda-setting process. Several different hypotheses have been advanced in this context too. Baumgartner and Jones (1993) suggest that public problems and the policies developed to remedy them do not always evolve in an incremental way. Short periods of radical change alternate with long periods of marginal adaptations or the status quo. This has led to the development of a model described as 'punctuated equilibrium' that is summarised by Vlassopoulou (1999, p 29) as follows:

> Every actor system (policy venue) constituted around a problem and/or challenge represents a particular perception of this problem (policy image). As a result, the diffusion of an alternative vision by a new actor becomes a major element of instability: in asserting itself, it changes, not only the definition of the problem, but also the composition of the actors' system. Thus, each actor configuration reflects a particular definition of the challenge, which suggests that they should not be considered independently: a change of definition is supposed to produce a change of the system of actors and vice versa. In this case, the combination of two elements should be capable of explaining both the stability and rapid change of policy.

According to this approach, by correlating the definition of a public problem and the actors mobilised around it, the analyst should be able to explain a change in the policy agenda. Such an approach has been applied to the process of ecologisation of agricultural policy in France and Europe (see Larrue, 2000).

Rose and Davies (1994) present a rather different hypothesis.

According to them, once in power all governments only have very limited room for manoeuvre when dealing with new public problems. Having inherited programmes initiated by previous governments, a new political majority mainly allocates public funds to the policies that have already been launched. This phenomenon of inertia is even more accentuated by the routines and strategic games of political-administrative actors who try to preserve their prerogatives. Thus, the new programmes primarily constitute an extra layer that is added to the programmes that are already 'sedimented'. As Lascoumes (1994, p 334) also suggests, no public problem is developed on virgin territory. Any change in the definition of a problem and, to a greater extent, of a public policy is undertaken with direct reference to the existing situation that influences the systems of thought, the actor constellations involved and the action strategies. Thus, according to this second approach, political inheritance is a determining factor.

By way of example here, we can quote the sedimentation of agriculture policy that has actually led to an accumulation of subsidies granted to farmers (starting with production subsidies and ranging to hectare subsidies and subsidies for ecological practices).

A third approach, owing much to increasing global influences on policy deriving not only from actual global initiatives but also from the increasing awareness on the part of national government of what others are doing, stresses the role of 'policy transfer'. Policy makers adopt solutions to policy problems from other countries (Dolowitz and Marsh, 2000; Dolowitz et al, 2002). International organisations (for example, OECD, the World Bank) play roles in this process and the literature suggests that wholesale and uncritical policy borrowing will often be problematical. More usually the transfer process involves considerable adaptation under the influence of the other factors examined in this chapter.

In conclusion, all policies are formed 'step by step' and over time, starting with multiple retrospective actions and collective learning processes. During the initial development of a public response to a problem to be resolved, the causal model often proves to be mono-causal and partial. Due to lacunae in these initial causal and intervention hypotheses, the programming of the policy (or the products PAP and PAA) often remains inadequate or at least incomplete. The evaluation of the effects actually arising from its implementation allows the actors involved to learn some lessons and readjust their objectives (that is, to politically redefine the public problem). During this new cycle of the policy, it is thus confirmed that the causal model fills out as also do the institutional elements which flow – in part already – from the sedimentation of successively applied rules in the course of the preceding cycle for the attribution of a given resource and given position to a given actor. Thus, all empirical analyses of the PD should clearly identify the cycle in which the policy being studied is located. The degree of substantive and institutional differentiation of the initial policy product to be explained depends to a decisive degree on this identification.

EIGHT

Policy programming

The first product to be explained as part of the programming stage of a public policy is the *political-administrative programme* (PAP). The PAP defines the legal bases for the objectives, intervention instruments and operational arrangements of the public action. This group of elements also incorporates decisions on the administrative process and organisation of the implementation of the policy, that is, the *political-administrative arrangement* (PAA) that is understood here as the second product to be explained. The PAP then partly (pre)defines the intermediary acts of the policy, that is, the decisions concerning the *action plans* (APs) that define the priorities of the application of the PAP in terms of time and space and between the different social groups. Finally, it provides – more or less precise and restrictive – indications with respect to the administrative production *of more or less formalised final measures* (outputs) creating a direct link, either legal or factual, between the policy's target groups and the competent implementing public bodies. The concepts 'action plan' and 'final formalised measure' will be discussed in the next chapter that deals with the implementation stage and its products (see Chapter Nine).

In effect, we consider that the programming stage of a policy is complete when the two products, the PAP and PAA, are empirically identifiable. Thus, the following paragraphs explore the constituent elements of each of these two pillars of the policy process. As with the product 'political definition of the public problem' (PD), we place particular emphasis on the operationalisation of the dimensions specific to the PAP (see Section 8.1) and the PAA (see Section 8.2) so as to facilitate the application of these concepts in the course of empirical research. Finally, we identify the principal actors, the resources and institutional rules mobilised during the process of formulation and formal adoption of a policy's PAP and PAA (see Section 8.3).

8.1 Political-administrative programme (product no 2)

PAP[1] represents the set of regulatory acts and norms that parliaments, governments and the authorities charged with execution consider necessary for the implementation of a public policy. The PAPs of different policies can vary in terms of their level of detail (variable regulatory density), degree of centrality (national and/or regional/local authority definition of the PAP), and degree of coherence (the internal appropriateness of the constituent elements). In all cases, however, they must respect the principle of legality: all state intervention in civil society and in the private sphere must rest on a legal basis decided on by the competent authority (that is, usually parliament).

A PAP defines in legal terms the political mandate formulated by the legislator by way of a solution to the public problem to be resolved, that is, the objectives to be attained and the rights and obligations imposed on target groups. Thus, these provisions constitute the source of primary legitimation of a public policy (Moor, 1994, pp 31ff, pp 309ff). From a formal point of view, they are composed of several written documents, mainly laws, decrees and orders, implementation orders and administrative directives adopted at different institutional levels. The PAP covers all of these structured legal provisions that usually comprise different layers.

Materially speaking, the provisions of a PAP comprise the normative objectives of the solution envisaged for the resolution of the problem, the definition of target groups and their role during the realisation of the policy (hypothesis of causality), the means made available for this purpose (intervention hypothesis) and the principles of the administrative organisation of the policy implementation. This set of decisions, known as 'legal norms', contains norms that are both general and abstract as well as organisational and procedural provisions. They can also be referred to as the 'normative material' of a policy.

This material is not necessarily constituted in a single stage (this is particularly the case due to the reality of legislative and executive federalism in Switzerland but may be affected by administrative decentralisation in France and the UK). The content of a PAP can comprise several federal and cantonal or central, devolved and decentralised rules associated with different normative hierarchies, and these must be identified at the outset of the analysis. Once inventoried, these different legislative and regulatory acts are interpreted so as to enable the explicit differentiation of the constituent elements of a PAP in accordance with the model proposed below.

It should be noted that this analysis of the decisions concerning the five constituent elements of the PAP presented below can usually only be carried out on the basis of several legal and regulatory documents (for example, formal laws, regulations, orders, memoranda, internal directives). The definition of these varies depending on the country and the policies being considered: decrees, orders,

Policy programming

memorandums, programmes etc for France; orders, federal and cantonal directives etc for Switzerland; Acts of Parliament, Statutory Instruments (regulations), circulars, ministerial letters, codes of practice for the UK.

From a practical point of view, given that policy analysis must be based on the most concrete norms available, there is a need to adopt an approach to this topic from wherever these are set out most clearly. In the Swiss and French cases the most simple approach is to start with directives and ordinances and then 'go up' to the level of formal or even constitutional legislation (principle of the 'consumption' of hierarchically superior rules by lower-level rules; see Knoepfel et al, 2000, p 12; Bättig et al, 2001, 2002). Such a rule may be difficult to apply in the UK context where regulations, while nevertheless vital sources in this respect, need reading in the contexts of the Acts of Parliament to which they relate. Here those Acts are probably the best starting point, although often they are hard to understand without supporting information. The best source of this is usually the White Papers that preceded them, although here there may be a snag that aspects of the policy proposed in the White Paper were eventually excluded from the legislation.

Furthermore, as a policy is frequently based on several legislative acts, it makes sense to take all of the legal basis that may affect the structuring of the PAP equally into account, particularly with respect to the delineation, internal functioning and external relationships of the PAA.

8.1.1 Five constituent elements of the PAP

The analyst who examines the programming of a policy should carry out a detailed study of the relevant PAP as an independent variable. For the conduct of this analysis, we propose a process that has already been tried and tested in the course of empirical research and which, by analogy with the successive layers surrounding a core, identifies the five constituent elements of a PAP (see Figure 8.1). Developed in 1982 by Knoepfel and Weidner (1982, p 93) as an instrument for the comparative analysis of policies to combat air pollution and environmental protection policies in different European countries, this approach was subsequently used in the study of several other policies (see Knoepfel, 1995, p 173)[2]. In the framework of evaluative research, it enables the testing of the exhaustiveness, internal coherence and legality of the PAP.

As indicated by Figure 8.1, as a general rule PAPs comprise five complementary elements that include three substantive elements (the

Figure 8.1: The constituent elements of a political-administrative programme

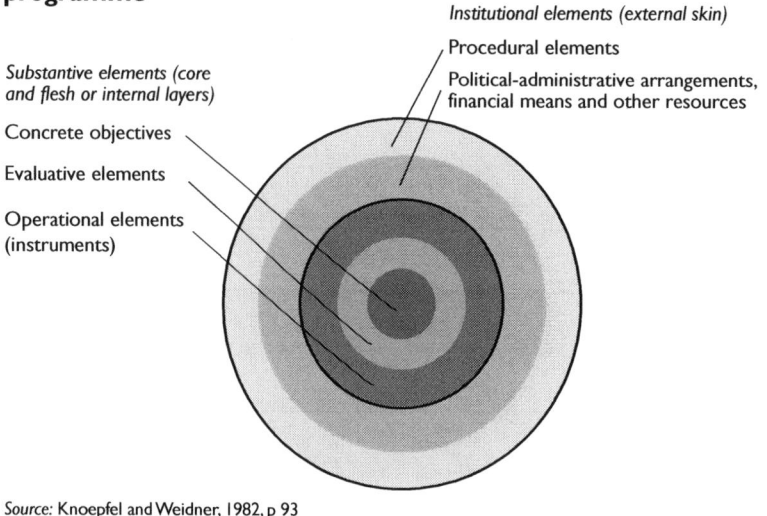

Institutional elements (external skin)
Procedural elements
Political-administrative arrangements, financial means and other resources

Substantive elements (core and flesh or internal layers)
Concrete objectives
Evaluative elements
Operational elements (instruments)

Source: Knoepfel and Weidner, 1982, p 93

objectives, the evaluative elements and the operational elements) and two institutional elements (the PAA and the procedural elements). We shall now discuss each of these elements in succession and then consider them simultaneously as part of a discussion of the different types of PAPs.

Objectives

Each PAP includes a definition of a more or less explicit goal, on the basis of which the public intervention may be conceived as a function of the objectives of the policy in question, which result from the preceding phase, that is, the definition of the problem. The objectives define the status to be attained by the adopted solution that would be considered as satisfactory. They describe the desired social status in a field of action once the public problem is resolved. At the level of the legislation, the objectives are defined in a very abstract way (for example, 'no air pollution that poses a risk to health', 'suitable accommodation'). In contrast, more concrete, quantified and measurable target values (for example 30 μg SO_2/m^3 annual mean for the risk to health posed by atmospheric pollution; $15m^2$ of living space per person considered as the basis for the calculation of suitable accommodation) are found at the level of the regulatory acts (regulations, circulars or administrative directives). An interesting variation on this is applicable in much UK social security policy where the Act specifies the general applicability

Policy programming

of a benefit provision while regulations specify more exactly how entitlement is to be determined. A significant feature of this is the fact that actual benefit rates are likely to be subject to annual revision, taking into account price changes, for example.

The more concretely the values are formulated, the easier it is to establish whether they have been effectively realised (or not). This increases the opportunities open to a policy's end beneficiaries to demand the best solutions to the problems affecting them, through either political or legal means. In effect, legal follow-up is really only possible if the target values are specified in a legally enforceable form. This is why concrete objectives are generally only defined in administrative directives so as to avoid such proceedings. It should be noted that the legal sciences describe programmes for action that have well-defined objectives as 'finalised' (Müller, 1971; Faber, 1974, p 99; Luhmann, 1984, p 201; Morand, 1993; Knoepfel, 1997b).

Concrete objectives imply the definition of units of measure or indicators that refer to the effects of the programmes in social reality (indicators of effectiveness). The latter should not be confused with the indicators that describe administrative measures or activities in themselves. According to this action logic, the aim of a policy is not to produce services/administrative activities in themselves, but to change social reality in accordance with the explicit or implicit provisions of PAPs. It is not the objective of the Federal Swiss Law on Spatial Development to impose an obligation to obtain planning permission for all construction projects, but to achieve "a suitable land-use structure for the country's development"[3]. The objective of legislation on aid to disadvantaged regions does not consist in providing services to these regions, but in improving the conditions for the existence and development of these areas. The same applies to, for example, the guarantee of a stable life, minimum income, or the adequate supply of affordable rented accommodation.

Evaluative elements

The PAPs of policies that work with relatively concrete objectives (and generally display a high level of technicality) often include instructions with respect to the type of data to be collected – so as to facilitate the precise ascertainment of the extent to which the defined objectives have been fulfilled – and with respect to the durations and techniques (natural sciences, social sciences, statistics or economics) for the collection of this data. In some cases, instructions are also given on the way that this data should be interpreted. Examples of this can be found in environment policy (for example, the definition of chemical analysis methods or methods for monitoring minimum flows in water courses), in housing construction policy (for example, the definition of useable living space) and in economic and social policy (for example, the definition of the composition of the 'shopping basket'[4] for the consumer price index).

Despite the fact that the political consequences of such evaluative elements for the substantive management of the public policy may, in certain circumstances, prove considerable, the corresponding political debates often concentrate on the technical suitability and scientific justification of the data on the proposed measures. It is obvious – to all natural and social science researchers – that different results appear to be 'produced' depending on the method applied. The same is true of policy evaluation. A change in the units of measurement sometimes makes it possible to render 'effective' entirely inefficient policies, without any substantial changes being made.

In view of the close interdependence between the methods used to evaluate the extent to which a policy's objectives have been accomplished and the results actually obtained, the choice of the elements for the evaluation of the PAP may strongly influence the normative and political consequences of the objectives to be achieved. The policy discourse tends to neglect this interdependence; thus, this choice, whose political scope is sometimes equivalent to that of the objectives themselves, is often the prerogative of actors who use a technical language to assert their political interests without being obliged to admit this openly. In relatively rare cases, the political consequences of the choice of evaluative elements is commonly acknowledged (for example, the definition of the unemployment rate, a particular matter of controversy in the UK where alternatives used have included numbers registered as benefit claimants, with or without those on training schemes, and numbers actively seeking work, which can be subject to considerable variation according to the actual wording of survey questions on this).

Operational elements (intervention instruments, measures)

The operational elements define the detailed forms of intervention or measures planned to fulfil the objectives of a public policy. Thus, they concretise the intervention hypothesis. Likewise, they clarify the hypothesis of causality in the sense that they define those affected, those to whom the measures will be applied. Without doubt, these are the elements of the PAP that best characterise a policy because they define those affected, its level of interventionism and the type, scope and quality of the proposed public intervention and services.

The choice of instruments is hugely dependent on the mode of intervention selected (for example, police order, direct offer of services, incentives, redistribution, persuasion, creation of social or organisational structures). Due to its more or less extensive effects on the legal situation of those affected, this choice necessitates an explicit legal basis. From both a legal and administrative science perspective, it is important that the operational elements also indicate the conditions under which the measures may or should be applied. In this context, the lawyers refer to conditional clauses. The latter are generally formulated on the basis of an 'if, then' logic: if someone wants to build a house, then such and such a condition must be fulfilled so as to obtain planning permission; if excessive deterioration in air quality is confirmed, then the emissions by the company causing it must be curbed; if someone loses their job due to no fault of their own, then they may benefit from unemployment insurance; if a company creates employment in a particular region, then it can benefit from a tax exemption.

In the frame of the recent debate on New Public Management, the objection is often raised to the effect that policies are excessively controlled by very detailed conditional clauses of this kind while, at the same time, they lack precise definitions of their ultimate purpose (Hablützel, 1995). In fact, the conditional clauses restrict the administration's room for manoeuvre; conversely, they ensure the predictability and legality of policies (Knoepfel, 1996, 1997b).

We use the term 'operational element' here because it defines the means used to motivate those affected (particularly target groups) to comply with the policy provisions. This is the sine qua non condition for rendering a policy operational. Without this indispensable element, even the most legitimate objectives will go unheeded. The precise definition of the contribution of target groups to the change in the situation commonly judged as inadmissible is essential to the operationalisation of a public policy. This 'motivation' can take a number of forms; the following four are the main forms usually identified in this context[5]:

- The *regulatory* mode is based on bans, obligations and the allocation of various rights that may be the object of sanctions in the case of failure to respect them. In this sense, it aims to directly influence the behaviour of target groups. The operational elements cover the general prohibition of an activity (for example, construction), the lifting of a ban by the granting of a permit or

special authorisation (for example, authorisation to use something, authorisation to market something). They also include the general authorisation of an activity (for example, the right to freely express one's opinion in public) possibly accompanied by a ban applicable in particular situations (for example, racist statements, presence of minors). Finally, it may also take the form of a general obligation (to wear a safety belt or safety helmet, for example) with a sanction (for example, fine) imposed in the case of non-compliance.
- The *incentive* mode is more direct than the regulatory mode. It works on the basis of financial payments aimed at influencing the behaviour of target groups by means of the 'price signal'. The incentive may be of a negative (tax, incentive levy) or positive nature (tax relief, subsidy) with the intention of (re)distributive effects.
- The *persuasive* mode uses an information strategy to convince target groups of the proposed objectives. This type of public action often accompanies other forms of intervention. It may, however, become the main mode of action, particularly in areas involving personal liberties that are strongly protected by constitutional rights. This is mainly the case with public health policies (for example, the fight against AIDS, prevention of tobacco use and illegal drug addiction) and efforts to combat racism.
- The last intervention mode involves the *direct supply of goods and services* to the public. This is obvious in the case of many social benefits.

We are aware that these four categories constitute in some ways ideal types that will not necessarily be found in real situations. Furthermore, these categories are not mutually exclusive and in reality they are generally combined in various ways. Thus, for example, a contract represents a combination of a regulatory-type mode (attribution of rights and existence of sanctions in the case of non-respect) and an incentive-type mode (subsidy granted in the event of the fulfilment of objectives). Furthermore, the recent literature contains a multitude of propositions that extend this classical canon of modes of state action through the addition of contractual action (Gaudin, 1995, 1996; Lascoumes and Valuy, 1996), organisational (networked) action (Morand et al, 1991a, 1991b) and so on. Similar approaches are adopted in discussions of the instruments of government by Howlett (1991; see also Howlett and Ramesh, 2003, chapter 4).

The operational elements may be formulated in the PAP in a very concrete way (for example, the listing of industries subject to the intervention and very detailed technical standards), or in more vague terms that leave the task of rendering the policy sufficiently operational to the implementing authorities. The central legislature is, however, responsible for providing clear legal bases at the very least if the public intervention consists in the imposition of obligations or the attribution of significant rights to affected groups. Considerable differences can be observed between countries in terms of the need for the precise definition of these elements (generally more flexible in more centralised countries like the UK and France and more strict in countries with more federalist structures like Germany and Switzerland). There have been some, not altogether successful, attempts to compare national administrative systems in terms of different 'policy styles' (Richardson, 1982; Bovens et al, 2001).

Political-administrative arrangement (PAA) and resources

These provisions of the PAP designate the competent authorities and administrative services (public actors) as well as all of the other institutional rules specific to the implementation of a policy. In addition, they provide some of the (categories of) resources necessary for these new activities. They may also identify the other administrative bodies that will be involved eventually or consulted. In this context, we refer to the distribution of competencies within a policy. This information is found in both the adopted legislation and in the statues and terms and conditions of the administrative services involved. In the case of agricultural, economic and social policies, in particular, these programme elements also define the mandates for associative actors who are invested with public powers of execution (para-state administration).

The implementation competencies (more than the legislative ones) are generally shared between authorities at central, decentralised and devolved levels. This is particularly true in the case of Switzerland where the application of the principle of federalism of execution (Germann et al, 1979) results in a co-management with the cantons (through either 'introductory acts' or 'implementation' adopted at cantonal level). However, it also applies to the more centralised countries.

This is why it is possible to observe the attribution of competencies to a wide range of specialised (professional) services (for example, in the 1980s, the Swiss cantons allocated the implementation of environmental legislation to the public works services, health services, and police) and, as a result of this, the presence of more than one administrative structure for one policy. In the interest of uniformity of implementation, the central legislature may partly overrule this prerogative of regional and local areas and restrictively order them to create specialised administrative services that respond specifically to requirements for similar qualifications (in Switzerland, for example, in spatial development policies, environment policies and, more recently, in the fight against unemployment; in the UK it may be noted how central government has partly overruled local government's prerogatives in respect of departmental organisation in areas like social services and education, sometimes using informal 'advice' rather than legal prescription).

For many policies, this creation of competency structures simply consists in attributing new tasks to existing services; the granting of resources (finance, personnel and others) is then globally decided when the budgets of the services concerned are decided. On the other hand, certain PAPs contain specific finance clauses or establish an entire network of new services that are responsible for the implementation of the (new) public policy.

In Switzerland the subsidies paid to the cantons or local authorities responsible for the implementation of federal spatial planning policy, environment policy or civil protection that result in the creation of ad hoc services (for example, the cantonal economic delegate for regional development policy) are an example of the case in point. The phenomenon can also be observed in France where various taxes on activities giving rise to pollution are used for the benefit of environment protection policy and are managed by bodies specifically created for this purpose (for example, the water agencies, the agency for the environment and energy management [*ADEME*] and the Superior Council for fishing). In the field of social care in the UK there is both funding for new policies through additions to the general grant to local authorities and through specific earmarked funds (Hill, 2000, pp 143-8).

The designation of administrative organisations at the different decision-making levels is not without effect on the conduct of public policies. Unsuitable PAAs can result in considerable deficits in the implementation of objectives defined in the PAP and, as a result, considerably diminish the scope of its substantive elements. Conversely, a particularly well-tailored PAA can trigger an accelerating effect that results in a faster and more advanced resolution of the problem in one region as compared with another (Kissling-Näf, 1997, pp 69, 282). Thus, any decision concerning these institutional elements of the PAP constitutes one of the most sensitive points of a policy. Thus, important political debates on the allocation of tasks and competencies that also concern these substantive aspects of a particular policy, at least in part, are not a rare occurrence.

In Switzerland, if the PAP does not explicitly refer to the provision of resources, the Confederation does not contribute to the financing of policy implementation by the cantons and the latter must finance this from their own budgets. If, on the contrary, legal bases exist to this effect, certain implementation activities carried out by the cantons may be partly financed through the levying of charges on target groups (for example, the financing by users of combustion systems of the expensive monitoring of emissions that is carried out in the context of clean air policy). In France, the allocation of responsibility for the implementation of public policies is generally treated in a more global way in the context of budgetary allocations made by the state to public bodies (in particular, global allocation for operation and equipment). In the UK in policy areas where local authorities are permitted but not required to develop policies they must carry the costs, but in some cases (parking fees, for example) they may recover some or all of this.

The choice of actors for the implementation of the policy defined in the PAA and the allocation of resources, in particular human resources (for example, number of posts, professional qualifications) and financial resources (technical equipment, budget provided to cover ongoing expenses), have considerable repercussions on the extent to which the objectives defined in the PAP will be fulfilled. The selection of a multitude of actors who are difficult to coordinate or of services that are already overburdened due to the lack of adequate allowances can seriously jeopardise the effect of the substantive elements of the PAP, even if they initially seem very 'radical'.

Procedural elements

The administrative services and the authorities that act in the context of public policies have to have regard to specific forms of interaction, both between themselves and with those affected and their representatives. To do this, they are supposed to acknowledge the relevant institutional provisions of the PAP (such as the respect of the principles of the constitutional state and democracy), and to ensure the transparency of the exchange of information, financial resources and services and so on. To this end, PAPs provide policy actors with a limited number of standardised administrative instruments, which they

Public policy analysis

may – or should – avail of in the course of their internal and external communication. These instruments include, for example, the administrative decision, public law contract, various types of plans, environmental impact studies, directives and other special instruments.

This formalisation of administrative activity contributes to the objectivisation, transparency, reconstitution and independence of public bodies and their services. An administrative decision becomes a document with a transferable value (legal title) and represents for its owner a legal resource that can be used against other members of society (for example, planning permission, subsidy agreement). This limited number of possible modes of administrative action ensures the transferability and social recognition of this category of policy products.

With respect to the institutional rules concerning policy instruments and administrative procedures, the PAPs do not necessarily describe administrative realities. On the contrary, they define normative values and standards at which to aim. The actual structure of the PAA may deviate from these normative standards as a result of processes of restriction or expansion adopted in response to the indirect games (see Section 6.2 in Chapter Six). The sudden elimination of posts may cause administrative arrangements to change independently of the PAP. Likewise, considerable discrepancies may emerge between the forms of action planned in the policy programme and those to which the public actors actually resort. For various reasons (for example, savings in terms of administrative costs, withdrawal of procedure from legal monitoring) informal administrative activities may be preferred to formal acts. And the latter may even be sufficient to trigger the desired behaviour among target groups, thus proving more efficient than formal modes of action.

Structure has an influence on procedure. The structure of a PAA does not normally consist in a chaotic mix of different authorities and administrative services that interact with the outside world in continuously changing ways. There will be exceptions to this, some of the sources of which are discussed below. However, it should be noted that contradictory mixes of PAAs has been a focus of some of the classic implementation studies in the US (particularly Pressman and Wildavsky's pioneering work, 1973). There is perhaps here an institutional feature of the US that is less often found in Europe, where in most cases structure determines ordered interactions between the different decision makers. In the interest of creating functional, predictable and stable relationships, the PAPs provide a multitude of institutional rules for managing procedural interaction and access to resources. These rules primarily concern the internal structure of the

PAA and organise, for example, the consultation procedure, the process of administrative arbitration between the different interests of the services.

Furthermore, other procedural elements govern the processes of external exchange between the public authorities and those affected. The provision of public services generally necessitates the observance of minimal procedures, not only for the purpose of creating a consensus with regard to the basic data, but also on account of legal obligations to hear representations from the parties concerned that are generally imposed by administrative law[6]. Thanks to their traditional acceptance, these procedures serve to protect citizens against the arbitrary nature of the administration and attacks on fundamental rights. Furthermore, they should permit the provision to the administration – by the affected groups – of information necessary for policy implementation. Finally, they make it possible to protect the administrative authorities against uncontrollable 'invasion' by the representatives of interest groups.

These procedural elements are not purely technical in nature. Moreover, they are often the subject of controversy, in particular if they concern rights of access to the administrative procedure of the various groups, that is, organisation for the defence of collective interests that do not have the right to express opposition or to appeal to courts or tribunals.

More generally, the procedural elements of policies determine the roles and relative power of policy actors in the context of all implementation processes. In this sense, they should be interpreted as institutional rules, either general or specific to public policy (for example, consumer protection policies, environment policies, labour policies).

Given that we are considering the five constituent elements of a PAP simultaneously, the question of their coherence and legality obviously arises.

8.1.2 PAP: coherence and legality of the constituent elements

The *coherence* between the different elements of a PAP constitutes a central criterion for the analysis and evaluation of public policies. This is imperative in a federalist system like the Swiss one and equally so in a – more or less – centralised system like the French or UK ones, which are also subject to EU directives, because PAPs are generally composed of decisions originating from different public instances (in Switzerland: the Confederation, the cantons and the local authorities; and in the UK: the EU, the UK government, the devolved governments of Scotland, Wales and [hopefully] Northern Ireland and the local authorities). The elements of a PAP may or may not be tailored to each other; in theory, they are supposed to complement and not contradict each other. During the empirical analysis of the programming of a policy, it is necessary to consider the internal logic and reciprocal reinforcement or undermining of the elements of the PAP (level of internal coherence). However, the analyst must also examine its compatibility with other public policies that may eventually contradict it (external coherence). The coherency test may, therefore, focus on the specific policy of which the PAP is part ('intra-policy' coordination) or on the problem as a whole that the PAP is seeking to influence ('interpolicy' coordination) (see Knoepfel, 1995).

The analysis of PAPs on the basis of the five elements described above makes it possible to demonstrate the contradictions that may exist between the constituent elements, for example, between fixed objectives and operational elements, or between fixed objectives and the resources allocated to the public actors of the PAA. These incoherencies may directly influence the quality and quantity of the policy outputs. In such cases, we refer to "(pre-)programmed implementation deficits" (Knoepfel and Weidner, 1982, p 92), for which the bodies responsible for a policy's conception, as opposed to those responsible for its implementation, may be held responsible. Thus, the absence of formal policy implementation measures (outputs) may be explained, for example, by the fact that the PAP defined an 'unsuitable' executive PAA incapable of realising the objectives and services planned for the policy. This occurs, for example, in the context of the implementation of certain EU directives in France that are 'parachuted' onto unsuitable implementing PAAs. Thus, the implementation of the directive on air pollution by ozone (managed by the *Direction régionale de l'industrie de la recherche et de l'environnement*) was initially based on industrial pollution while the ozone directive required action on automobile traffic. The law on air of 1996 then prompted a change in the composition of these PAAs as a result of the introduction of mandatory atmospheric protection plans at agglomeration level and regional air quality plans at regional level.

The 'erroneous' definition of target groups that, in turn, may be based on inadequate analyses and, hence, 'deficient' causal hypotheses provides another possible explanation for (pre-)programmed implementation deficits. This type of programming 'error' results from an inaccurate identification of the behaviour of a social group as the cause of the public problem to be resolved – the behaviour in question being only partly or not at all responsible. This kind of attribution error is demonstrated by policies conducted against automobile traffic associated with commuting patterns in agglomerations: these policies try to reduce public parking places but in situations in which the vast majority of commuters have private parking they are not, therefore, prompted to change their behaviour even if the state reduces the number of public parking spaces available (Schneider et al, 1990, 1992).

There are related issues in respect of the use of forms of taxation to deal with undesired behaviour. Carter analyses the use of petrol taxes in these terms suggesting that "A few countries, including Britain, the Netherlands, Norway and Sweden, have increased fuel taxes for explicitly environmental reasons, but with little impact on consumption" (2001, p 309). He suggests the same may apply to road pricing: "User charges may simply persuade people to visit a different city for shopping and entertainment ..." (Carter, 2001, p 309).

It is generally difficult for policy decision makers to estimate the extent to which the objectives they formulate may be effectively achieved using the proposed operational elements. This is also due to the fact that the debates on the measures planned on the basis of the intervention hypothesis do not for the most part concern their contribution to the realisation of objectives, but instead relate to their 'level of intervention' and, therefore, their ideological connotations, which are more or less compatible with the competing partisan ideologies, or, again, the financial costs of their administrative implementation (Varone, 1998a, pp 325ff).

This kind of disconnection between objectives and instruments may also be observed during highly technical processes of programme formulation. The legal processes of standardisation associated with planning and the environment provide examples of this. In response to the political pressure exerted by sectoral associations, environmental law may define the maximum levels of polluting substances authorised for different types of installations (emission limit values) at a level that is so high that simple physical calculations will be enough to demonstrate that the target value ('imission' limit value) will be exceeded in urban regions with high density individual activity generating emissions (for example, households, private vehicles). Thus, the targeted objective is already doomed to failure at the level of the PAP.

Similar programmatic contradictions may be observed between the resources attributed to the public actors of a PAA and the policy objectives or intervention measures. Given the phenomenon of increasing professionalisation and growing requirements in terms of technical equipment within authorities, the costs of policy implementation are rising. Thus, corresponding priorities must be defined as part of the management of administrative posts and budgetary planning. Decisions that play a decisive role in the efficacy of a policy are often taken in this context, that is, far removed from the central actors of the programmes in question. Parliaments have very little awareness of the real effect of such decisions during the stages of policy implementation and evaluation. It is widely admitted that the provision and use of the resources necessary for policy implementation (for example, civil servants' salaries, infrastructure investments) constitute an important action dimension of the state's general economic policy. The impact of the latter does not follow the same rules as those applied to the substantive public policies involved. This is why it is not always easy for external observers to differentiate between motives that are purely based on economic policy and those of a substantive nature based on budgetary decisions.

Along with the criterion of coherence, the criterion of *legality* also plays an important role in the construction and critical analysis of PAPs. In political systems based on the rule of law, almost all policies are rooted in a legal basis and their formulation, in particular their intervention instruments and administrative procedures, is regulated on a legal basis. The policy analyst must not ignore this normative-legal dimension. In practice, the regulation often constitutes a central element or – at least – an important point of departure. A PAP that is incoherent in legal terms (for example, lack of proportionality between the operational elements and objectives, based on a regulatory decision contrary to the law) may, if necessary, be modified through the intervention of a decision by a court and, hence, considerably reinforced or, conversely, undermined[7]. This is particularly applicable in the case of the EU member states: provisions made at national level must be compatible with European law, otherwise the state in question may be brought before the European Court of Justice. Thus, several decisions by the French government aimed at helping commercial companies were abandoned due to their incompatibility with European competition laws (so as not to interfere with competition between companies operating on the Single European Market).

The examination of the coherence and legality of the normative material of a policy may be carried out both before and after the political decision making. In that way, it can be prospective (and also preventive) or retrospective. The preventive evaluation of the legality of legal provisions may be ensured by internal administrative bodies and procedures. This is the case in France and Switzerland, but not generally in the UK. With regard to the federal level in Switzerland, the legality of all legislative projects is examined by the Federal Office of Justice[8]. In France, this same monitoring function is carried out by the Council of State (compatibility between the decisions of the executive and legislature) and the Constitutional Council (compatibility of legislative and regulative texts with the constitution).

In the case of countries based on federal systems, the controls of legality carried out, for example, by the Swiss Confederation during the process for the approval of cantonal laws should also be mentioned here. As already mentioned, in Switzerland, PAPs very often contain elements anchored at different state levels and the task of administrative execution generally falls to the cantons and local authorities. The term 'cantonal execution' is not restricted to the application of norms – in the sense of 'implementation' otherwise used here – it also involves the passing of substantive, organisational and procedural legislative provisions that form an integral part of the PAP. These provisions are submitted to the Confederation for approval if this is required by the relevant law[9]. Thus, this approval is constitutive in nature – at the same time it may also be a condition of validity so that the verification of conformity with federal law carried out in this context has a preventive function.

In France, the state imposes extensive control on the decisions of local public bodies. Since the enactment of the decentralisation laws, these controls are implemented after such decisions are adopted. The *préfet* (general administrator of a *département* or administrative division) is thus able to submit a municipal or departmental decision to an administrative court. Likewise, he or she may reject a municipal decision taken with respect to an area that is not relevant to the competency of the body in question: for example, the *préfet* may rescind a municipal order for the closure of a company causing pollution within a local authority area because it is based on the legislation governing classified installations and thus comes under the competencies of the *préfet* and not the local authority.

Once again the system of control of this kind in the UK is generally weaker; legal challenges of the kind described here are possible but depend on retrospective actions by those disadvantaged by these decisions (of course in practice possibly aided by an organised group). In general then the aggrieved person needs to prove that the authority has acted *ulta vires*, that is, beyond its statutorily defined powers.

8.1.3 Operational analysis dimensions

The following three main analysis dimensions have been derived from international/regional and intersectoral comparisons of the PAPs of policies aimed at the resolution of similar problems.

(a) Detailed PAP – framework programme

As a set of decisions, PAPs can vary considerably from one country or region to another based on their more or less limited substantive content. If the structure of the public problem to be resolved is similar and the number of individual interventions more or less equivalent, such variations in the PAP reflect a different conception of the implementation activity:

- A PAP with *limited substantive content* reflects either a generally very weak level of concretisation (general clauses) or a limited number of substantive elements regulated at the level of the PAP itself. This leaves considerable room for manoeuvre to the implementing actors who may take specific local circumstances into account during the resolution of individual and particular cases. The competent political-administrative authority then decides, at the moment of the conception of the public intervention, for one or several concrete cases and, at the same time, the general criteria to apply and their individual application. Such regimes enable the development of very different implementation approaches for one and the same (national or even regional) policy.
- A PAP with *extended substantive content* is characterised either by extensive regulation of the majority or all of its constituent elements or by a very high level of concretisation. This philosophy is indicative of the intention on the part of the actors responsible for the policy programming to leave only a weak margin for discretion to the implementing authorities. The aim of such regimes, which can be found in the German federalist system, in particular, and also in the relatively centralised French system, is to limit the variations between the implementation strategies and practices in the regions and hence avoid inequality of treatment among the subjects of administration through selectively homogeneous policy implementation practices. While in the UK a policy style has been identified that is more flexible and adaptive (Jordan and Richardson, 1982), various factors

including the influence of the EU and the strong internal preoccupation with 'territorial justice' has been an important source of contemporary efforts by the national governments in the UK to define the powers of local governments and other decentralised actors more strictly.

The distinction presented here (see Figure 8.2) will often go hand in hand with that between substantive and institutional PAPs described under (c).

In effect, the more restricted the substantive content of a PAP due to legislative traditions or the political-administrative structure of a country, the more likely one is to encounter institutional rules created with the intention of counteracting the risk of (excessively) heterogeneous practices and, hence, the presence of indirect actor games.

Figure 8.2: Detailed and framework political-administrative systems compared

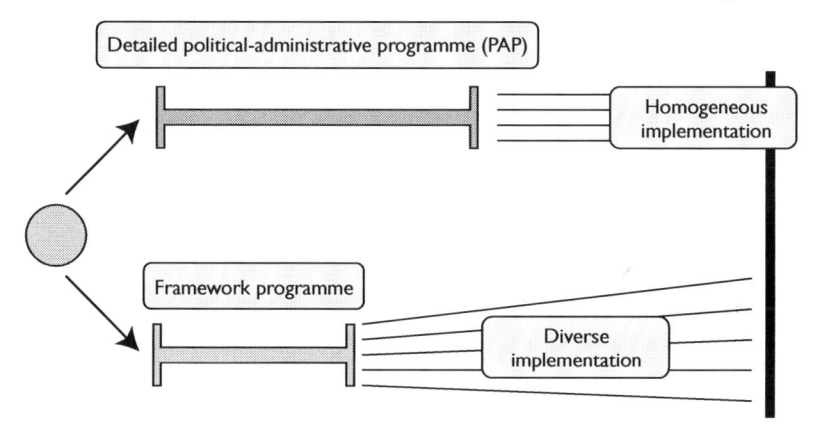

(b) PAP and state levels (centralised/decentralised PAPs)

The distribution of decisions of a legislative and regulatory nature aimed at influencing policy implementation may vary between different levels in different countries: in one country, the essential part of the PAP will be assigned at national level, while in others the legislative part is more important at regional or even local level (for example, legislative federalism in Switzerland). In the UK it is generally the case that this is a national level issue (although in the context of devolution in some areas of policy 'national level' may be taken to mean England, Scotland, Wales or Northern Ireland).

(c) Substantive–institutional PAPs

It is important to note that all PAPs contain not only substantive elements, but also institutional decisions regulating the organisation of their implementation, the provision of different actors with resources and the definition of the administrative and legal procedures to be applied. These rules primarily concern the internal function of PAAs and their interaction with those affected. Empirical observations support the hypothesis that the implementation process may be controlled by different types of PAP.

Thus, the implementation process may be controlled either:

- by a PAP that concentrates on the substantive elements of the problem to be resolved and that expresses itself clearly on the objectives to be attained, the evaluative elements and the operational elements (German tradition);
- by a PAP that places the emphasis on specific institutional rules and that defines as fully as possible the PAAs responsible for the resolution of problems and the procedures to be adopted (English tradition); or
- by a PAP that concentrates on a particular combination of substantive, organisational and procedural elements.

Figure 8.3 provides a schematic representation of how the five constituent elements of a PAP may be counterbalanced by political decision makers.

Thus, the ideal type of the mixed PAP corresponds to the Swiss federal programmes that leave many of the decisions about organisation

Figure 8.3: Political-administrative programme – substantive, institutional or mixed

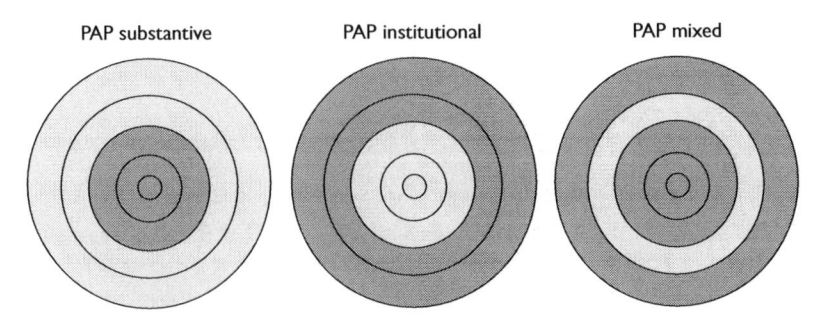

PAP substantive   PAP institutional   PAP mixed

Note: The circles represent the five layers of a PAP as presented in Figure 8.1. The darker colouring indicates detailed provisions, the lighter that they are missing or ill-defined.

to the cantons (although increasingly fewer on procedures). The 'ideal type' of the institutional PAP corresponds to the federal programmes found in the US, which say little on the concrete objectives (their definition is left to the 'rule making' of the federal agencies, which are often independent of the central administration), but provide a concrete definition of the organisation or procedures and so on.

The above observations and suggestions are based on the simple application of a more general rule that specifies an interdependence between the container and the content, on which our entire analytical process rests (institutional rules and substantive rules). However, in the context of everyday legislative discourse, it would appear that the substantive content of the PAP prevails. Decision makers are primarily interested in the objectives to be realised and even more so in specific responsibility for the operational elements. Thus, even if they may ultimately prove the most influential in terms of the quality of the policy implementation and resulting effects, organisational and procedural questions are generally only of secondary interest.

When applied with the aim of comparing the PAPs of different countries and/or regions, the concept proposed here may enable the identification of gaps in certain PAPs as well as facilitating the classification of PAPs so as to enable a better debate on their impact on policy implementation and, more specifically, on the protection of the interests of the policy's end beneficiaries. Thus, the analyst may be guided by two questions: what are the interdependencies between the different elements of the PAP that exercise a particular influence on the impact of its core (strengthening/weakening)? What are the political stakes of the different combinations of specific elements and the strategies of the actors involved with respect to these stakes?

8.2 Political-administrative arrangement (product no 3)

The PAA of a policy represents the structured group of public and para-state actors who are responsible for its implementation. The majority of decisions concerning the designation of the competent authorities and services are already taken at the level of the PAP (see Section 8.1). Nonetheless, it is possible that certain new decisions – arising from the indirect games of certain actors (see Section 6.2 of Chapter Six) – will result in the concretisation or modification of these legal and regulatory provisions. These decisions tend to concern, in particular, the distribution of formal competencies (that is, the attribution of responsibility for the new policy to existing or newly created administrative services), the allocation of various resources, that is, financial, human etc, which are at the disposal of the implementing authorities and also the intraorganisational and interorganisational management of the administrative units involved.

There is in this case an issue that may arise (taking us back to the point made at the end of Section 2.2, Chapter Two) in which changes are made to a PAA of a kind that might be seen as involving 'institutional' or 'constituent' policies rather than substantive policies. These, however, may be directed primarily to the resolution of a concrete policy problem. In the UK, adjustments to the structure of the NHS and to the organisation of state education have been presented as appropriate responses to concerns about specific aspects of health or educational performance, such as inadequate attention to inequalities.

8.2.1 Constituent elements of the PAA

A PAA incorporates not only public actors, but also all of the private actors who may be assimilated into it due to the fact that they are invested with public power, and who, based on this delegation of responsibility, participate on an equal footing in the production of concrete actions (outputs) associated with the policy in question. In fact, the PAA links these actors through formal or informal institutional rules governing the assignment of specific functions with respect to the action to be taken in the relevant social area. These rules facilitate the (positive or negative, proactive or reactive) substantive coordination between the different services that perform the multiple administrative tasks required under the targeted application of a policy. This is reinforced by procedural rules that give rise to a network of horizontal and/or vertical interactions between the actors (procedural coordination). As a result, a PAA may be interpreted as the organisational and procedural basis of a policy. It represents the network of public and private actors responsible for the implementation of a policy without, however, encompassing the entire group of actors in the 'policy arena' (see Section 3.3.1, Chapter Three), who are affected by the problem dealt with by the policy in question (policy network). Thus, despite undoubtedly participating in many aspects of a policy being analysed, all of the private actors involved will not generally form an integral part of the PAA; this rule is applicable almost without exception.

A characteristic of public actors is that they have a very close – often legal – association with the public policy. Their departure from a PAA creates greater difficulties than is the case for private actors, whose involvement is generally less obligatory and/or consistent. Furthermore, the freedom of public actors is limited by the fact that they belong to formal administrative organisations (ministries, departments, services etc). In exchange for this restriction in their room for manoeuvre, these organisations provide them with a level of public legitimacy and resources that the private actors may not necessarily have at their disposal (for example, the law). This observation highlights one of the essential differences between the approach adopted here and the 'policy networks' approach, which deliberately includes private actors (Clivaz, 1998). However, we would also like to stress that our analysis of the exchanges between public and private actors, both within and outside PAAs, adopts several concepts from the policy networks approach.

Public actors are the basic units of PAAs (see Section 3.3.2, Chapter Three). Using an analogy from Newtonian physics, the public actors can be defined as the smallest unit of action in a system and a unit that, due to its internal homogeneity, may not be subdivided into smaller units (see Section 3.1, Chapter Three). This basic unit is defined by an internal hierarchical structure or by the voluntary cohesion of a group of people united in the aim of accomplishing a function that is specific and indispensable to a given policy. Despite their integration to a greater or lesser extent into administrative organisations and despite their hierarchical subordination to political-administrative superiors, all such basic units enjoy a certain autonomy of function. Thus, they have the competency to make statements on all subjects that come within their area of responsibility without always having to obtain the explicit agreement of other possible actors.

Staying with the physics analogy, the PAA may be visualised as a molecule composed of actors (indivisible atoms). While the cohesion of the molecule is provided by basic forces, that of the PAA is based on the obligation and/or will to belong to the network of interaction that emerges around a structure of (formal and informal) competencies and cooperative procedures. As is the case in the physical world, this structure is more or less fragile and may undergo important modifications, in particular as a result of changes in the external framework conditions.

In general, in the case of federal states, PAAs bring together federal, regional/cantonal and even local actors, and, in the case of centralised countries, central and devolved actors, and to a lesser extent, decentralised actors. These actors belong to different administrative organisations (federal offices, regional/cantonal services, ministries and departmental head offices), between whom coordination or actual cooperation must be established so that the PAA is in a position to apply the different substantive elements of the PAP adopted by the political authorities (see Figure 5.1, Chapter Five, on the hierarchy of institutions).

8.2.2 Operational analysis dimensions

To carry out a comparative analysis of PAAs, we identify several *internal* dimensions – enabling the definition of the functioning of the PAA itself – and *external* dimensions – helping to locate the PAA with respect to its environment. It should be emphasised here that, like policy networks, PAAs vary on the basis of numerous dimensions, and the different authors do not agree on the relevance and explanatory capacity of the latter (see the summary of the 'policy networks' debate by Le Galès and Thatcher, 1995; Clivaz, 1998).

To be more exact, we consider that there are five internal dimensions that characterise the structure of a PAA: (a) the number and type of actors; (b) the degree of horizontal coordination; (c) the degree of vertical coordination; (d) the degree of centrality of key actors; and (e) the degree of politicisation. These five dimensions are obviously not mutually exclusive, and instead constitute different facets of a PAA. They may provide a basis for the outline of the typology of PAAs or policy networks. This is not our intention here, however, as we are instead interested in the fact that these dimensions exert an influence on the results of a policy (APs, outputs): as several empirical research projects have shown, they undoubtedly constitute one of the explanatory variables of the intermediary and final products of the policy. We suggest, for example, that the acts produced within a PAA differ according to whether it involves a large or small number of (vested) public and/or private actors, and whether it is integrated or fragmented, mixed up or compartmentalised, centralised or egalitarian, bureaucratic or politicised. The internal dimensions of a PAA are discussed in detail below.

Number and type of actors: single-actor or multi-actor PAA

Analysts may identify both 'multi-actor' PAAs and PAAs composed of a very limited number or even a single actor in the course of their daily work. The greater the number of actors, the greater number of precise mechanisms the PAA must have for the negotiation and definition of competencies and procedures necessary for the coordinated management of multiple activities. The acts produced may be contradictory (for example, in the area of conditions for planning permission) in the absence of such mechanisms. To be considered as such, a multi-actor PAA must display a certain institutional stability and, in particular, the ability to cope with pressure from outside.

Along with the number of actors involved in the implementation of a policy, the analyst must also identify their origins, that is, membership of administrative bodies or private organisations. The greater the number of para-state or private actors included in a PAA, the less the extent to which the rules for the internal functioning of administrative services will apply and be adhered to during the realisation of the policy. However, the outcome of the implementation of a PAP by a mixed PAA composed of public and private actors may be less predictable than in the case where the implementing PAA is constituted entirely of public actors. Alternatively it may be that co-production tying targeted private actors into the decision-making process may increase consistency. Traditional energy policies based on the intervention of a monopolist actor generally supported by a 'single-actor' type PAA are an example of how this first dimension is applied in practice. In contrast, more modern style or multi-sectoral policies such as environment, economic and social policies tend to be based on PAAs with large numbers of actors.

Degree of horizontal coordination: integrated PAA versus fragmented PAA

Among the multi-actor PAAs, a distinction is currently made between integrated PAAs and horizontally fragmented PAAs. The political-administrative fragmentation is not automatically the result of a complex structure including numerous actors. It is far more manifest in the absence of substantive (horizontal) coordination which, in turn, may result in the membership of actors from different administrative organisations or 'regional milieus'[10] or actors who are blatantly opposed on account of their respective primary tasks and the interests they represent and defend. This kind of fragmentation may also be due to a lack of rules of procedure. In many cases it is also the direct consequence of the amalgamation of formerly separate policies (for example, clean air, heavy-goods vehicle traffic regulation and national road construction policy). There is a substantial British literature that has identified different central government departments as having distinct cultures, ways of working and, of course, networks of public and private actors to which they relate (Dorey, 2005, pp 91-7 provides a good discussion of this topic).

PAAs that are not horizontally coordinated tend to be characterised by a lack of will on the part of the key actors to establish the coordination necessary for the application of the PAP, or even an explicit strategy of non-cooperation. Apart from differences in terms of values, functions and objectives, the private clients of these public actors are also often opposed to the coordination and 'integration' of 'their' services into a new PAA. Despite this, the actors belong to the arena of the policy in question (see Section 3.3.1 in Chapter Three) and do not want to leave it without a specific reason for doing so. Such horizontal fragmentation also risks giving rise to contradictions in the content of APs (product no 4) or formal implementation measures (product no 5). This is a topic that has been given considerable attention in the UK. The characteristic response to it from central government has been to seek a variety of ways of securing collaboration and partnerships, sloganising this in terms of a need for 'joined-up' government. Nevertheless there are grounds for suggesting that a widespread problem remains. Actual forms of collaboration vary greatly in strength and effectiveness (Glendinning et al, 2002).

Different quantitative analysis techniques enable the evaluation of the degree of horizontal coordination of a PAA. They actually measure its 'density'; that is generally defined as the closeness of the links (or the existence and frequency of relations) between the different actors belonging to one and the same hierarchical level.

Degree of vertical coordination: entangled/overlapping or compartmentalised PAA

A PAA may also be analysed on the basis of the degree of vertical coordination between the political-administrative levels (for example, the federal, cantonal/regional and local authority levels). Federalism in Switzerland has three main characteristics: (1) the coexistence of three formally different levels, with the lower levels enjoying a degree of autonomy in accordance with the principle of subsidiarity; (2) executive federalism as the dominant mode of implementation of federal policies by the cantons and local authorities; (3) the frequent quest for consensus between the state levels (Knoepfel et al, 2001). In short, the Swiss system may be described as 'cooperative federalism', although considerable differences may be observed between one policy and the next (see Wälti, 1999).

In France, the relationships between the national, devolved and decentralised levels were traditionally founded on a model described as 'hybrid regulation' (Crozier and Theonig, 1975) that is based on a system of exchanges and arrangements between the elected directors of local public bodies and state services. This system was based on a high degree of vertical coordination provided by the state and conducive to the production of a joint doctrine of action throughout a given territory. However, the decentralisation movement that emerged in the early 1980s challenged this mode of functioning (Duran and Thoenig, 1996). While the degree of vertical coordination is still as prevalent within the state services, it is no longer accompanied by the same degree of horizontal coordination and hence leads to a more effective institutionalisation of the negotiation relationships between the central, devolved and decentralised actors.

Issues about horizontal collaboration in the UK have been noted above. The available literature suggests that these are compounded by concerns about vertical collaboration. Efforts to enhance vertical coordination tend to undermine horizontal collaboration. This is particularly evident where there is, on the one hand, a largely nationally coordinated organisation (such as the NHS) that needs to collaborate in respect of policy delivery with relatively autonomous local organisations (local governments) (see Exworthy et al, 2002; Glendinning et al, 2002). In this context Hudson and Henwood (2002, p 164) write of the field of health and social care as one where "Notions of 'levels' and 'tiers' of command and control, of restructuring and 'compulsory partnerships' are all ill-suited to relationships that are more akin to spheres and networks". This last is a topic that will be revisited in the discussion of the 'bottom-up' perspective on implementation in the next chapter.

Thus, when analysing PAAs, it is a question of identifying the degree of effective coordination between the authorities and services on the levels of the state system. A PAA will be qualified as entangled or overlapping if the central state and regional bodies share not only legislative and regulatory, but also implementation competencies. On the contrary, a PAA is defined as compartmentalised if the infra-national public bodies have extensive autonomy during policy programming and/or execution. In this last case, the regional and local actors may adapt the policy to their own needs without having to be concerned about preliminary or concomitant decisions by actors at higher levels. Research carried out on policy implementation in Switzerland and France demonstrates the capacity of certain local actors to appropriate federal policies (Terribilini, 1999), or to use them for ends entirely different to those initially desired by the national legislator (Duran and Thoenig, 1996). More generally, the degree of vertical integration varies between policies.

Degree of centrality of key actors: centralised or egalitarian PAA

The analyst may also identify PAAs in which the actors' influence and power is distributed on the basis of an egalitarian model, and PAAs in which one or more key actors predominate. This central position, which may be held by a national or regional actor, is reflected in the way that its holders are able to intervene against the will of the other actors involved in the PAA and unilaterally impose their point of view. However, in most cases, the dominance of one actor (referred to as central) is not usually met with pure and simple submission on the part of other actors (referred to as peripheral): the threat of unilateral intervention on the part of the central dominant actor is often followed by bilateral or multilateral negotiations with the other public and private actors of the PAA ('mediatory federalism', according to Wälti, 1999). As already mentioned above, most PAAs for the implementation of French policy up to the early 1980s were characterised by a high level of centrality. In many respects now it is the UK (notwithstanding devolution) that stands out as the most centralised in this respect.

Actor centrality, which is an important concept in terms of the explanation of certain policy products, relates to both the vertical and horizontal dimensions of the PAA. An actor may prove dominant at a specific level in the hierarchy, that is, with respect to all of the actors at this level, and/or centrally at all state levels, that is, with respect to all of the actors on the other levels.

It is possible to measure the three types of actor centrality more accurately by adopting the quantitative methods proposed for the analysis of policy networks. 'Degree centrality' indicates the number of actors with whom an actor has direct contact. 'Closeness centrality' indicates the level of closeness between an actor and all other actors in the network. The index measures the minimum number of steps an actor must take to reach another actor (that is, the geodesic distance). Finally, the analyst may try to identify actors referred to as intermediaries through whom everything passes and who cannot, in fact, be ignored in the context of policy implementation. This other measure of the centrality of a key actor ('betweeness centrality') may serve as an indicator of the power of actors in the sense of their capacity to control the behaviour of other actors of the PAA (Scott, 1991; Sciarini, 1994).

While the PAAs of policies with important strategic stakes, such as military or nuclear policies, generally display a high level of vertical centrality, the PAAs of policies with significant spatial stakes, such as infrastructure policies, show a high level of horizontal centrality. In contrast, policies whose stakes are more territorial in nature display a weaker vertical centrality with combined weak horizontal centrality due to their highly sectoral nature.

Degree of politicisation: politicised or bureaucratic PAA

In trying to explain the differences in the generation of the PAAs of policies with similar or identical goals, analysts will often find themselves confronted with the fact that PAAs also differ from the point of view of the role played by so-called 'political' actors (for example, individual members of parliament, government, organisations and expert commissions), whose behaviour differs – in appearance at least – from the more 'technical' behaviour of bureaucratic actors. In the case of the politicisation of a PAA, the products tend to be less predictable and more likely to contradict each other than the products of a PAA that is purely bureaucratic in nature.

The analysis of the degree of politicisation of a PAA should be approached with caution because, more than the four previously discussed dimensions, this dimension is one rooted in fact rather than law. Furthermore, it is sometimes subject to extremely rapid and unpredictable diachronic variations. This unpredictability is due to the simple fact that legally competent actors may be made aware of their political responsibilities at almost any moment in a policy life cycle (for example, the impact of natural disasters). The implementation PAAs for large infrastructure projects quickly become politicised when they are contested.

In addition to the five internal dimensions already discussed, it is also necessary to identify the two major external dimensions of PAAs. The latter concern the relationships maintained by a PAA with the public and private actors of its social environment who are not directly affected by the policy in question.

Context defined by other public policies: homogeneity or heterogeneity

The scope for manoeuvre of the PAA of a policy being analysed largely depends on the context defined by other policies. Depending on the competencies and tasks assumed by the actors who fulfil – exclusive or simultaneous – functions in relation to other policies, this influence may constitute either a support or a handicap for the actors of the PAA. Thus, it is necessary to establish whether the administrative framework, which is characterised by the institutional rules governing administrative organisations (see Section 5.2.3 in Chapter Five) in

Public policy analysis

which the actors of different policies evolve, is heterogeneous or homogeneous (see Figures 8.4 and 8.5).

If the main actors of the PAA belong to several ministries or departments or several units within one and the same ministry (offices or administrative services), the context is then considered as heterogeneous. Conversely, a high level of homogeneity is defined as a situation in which these actors will all belong to one and the same ministry or even a single administrative unit within this ministry. Thus, it is necessary to carry out a positional analysis of the actors of the PAA. This is important because this context often translates into specific traditions prevailing within each ministry, into predominant types of career structures and recruitment, into traditional interaction networks maintained by preference with other ministries or divisions, specific social groups ('clientele') or external advisers who enjoy privileged access to an administrative body ('house scientific expert', quasi-permanent consultant).

Thus, a policy may undergo a change of PAA due to the transfer of (some of) its public actors to a new administrative context, as, for example, policy governing health controls of meat that traditionally benefited from a context closely associated with agricultural circles while involving the competencies of veterinary services and becoming part of a 'public health' context when integrated into policy for the general control of food products.

The most common examples of PAAs with heterogeneous administrative contexts are provided by policies dealing with natural disasters[11] that traditionally unite civil protection, infrastructure and environmental actors.

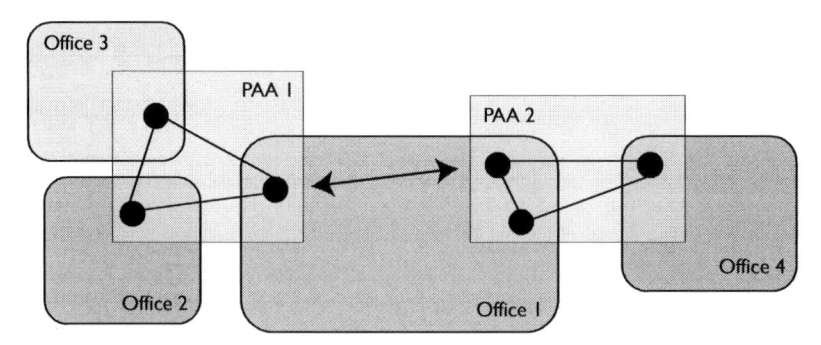

Figure 8.4: Heterogeneous administrative contexts

Note: PAA 1 is composed of three actors each situated in a different office (or ministry). PAA 2 is composed of three actors of which two belong to the same office (or ministry) and the third to another. Interaction between PAAs 1 and 2 is facilitated by the fact that three of the six actors belong to the same office.

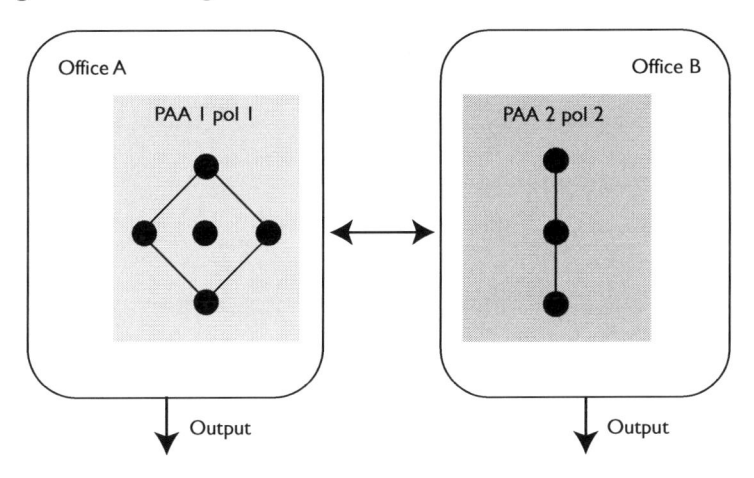

Figure 8.5: Homogeneous administrative contexts

[Figure: Two boxes labeled Office A (containing PAA 1 pol 1 with diamond-shaped network of four nodes around a central node) and Office B (containing PAA 2 pol 2 with three vertically connected nodes), with a double-headed arrow between them and Output arrows below each.]

Note: PAAs 1 and 2 are each composed of actors in the same office (or ministry), who cannot easily facilitate interactions between them.

Defence policies generally have a homogeneous institutional context. Agriculture has also been a similarly homogenous area, but in the UK the decline of the economic importance of agricultural lobby and the rise of environmental and recreational concerns has changed this (see Toke and Marsh, 2003, for an interesting exploration of the genetically modified crops issue examining this point).

Finally, it should be noted that the constitution of PAAs is also governed by the country's general institutional rules, such as, for example, the constitutional state, equality, the governmental system in place, legislative or executive federalism, the guarantee of individual liberties and the roles played by the courts in their protection.

Degree of openness: open or closed PAA

The degree of openness of a PAA measures the intensity of the interaction between the actors of a PAA and the actors that constitute their immediate social environment. What the analyst must do here is to identify the conditions for communication with the public actors of PAAs; these conditions may be more or less selective depending on the nature of the arenas of the given policies (see Section 3.3.2, Chapter Three). Furthermore, some are characterised by a very clear demarcation between public and private actors that makes the establishment of contact between these two groups difficult, while others feature very frequent formal and informal exchanges of communication.

The social environment of PAAs is composed of interest groups and individual actors who generally represent the target groups, end beneficiaries and, possibly also, the third parties (found in the arena of the analysed policy). The interaction between the actors of the PAA and these 'external' actors often remains selective. It is structured by a set of formal procedural rules as well as various habits and customs (informal rules), including the organisational culture of the different administrative services and authorities concerned. Nevertheless, the interaction between the PAA and its environment enables the political administrative actors to achieve a better understanding of the social problems subject to or to be subject to public intervention, and to 'manage' any eventual opposition to the proposed solutions better.

At the level of the empirical analysis of PAAs, a distinction is traditionally made between closed PAAs, partly open PAAs and open PAAs. If a PAA is closed to target groups, beneficiaries and third parties, the products are formulated in a unilateral manner.

Examples of closed PAAs include policies whose products may not be contested by appeal to a court as is often the case with 'technical' or 'sensitive' policies (for example, the infrastructure policies of the 1970s, public security policy and the different military security policies).

The examples of partly open PAAs include the spatial development policies of the 1970s to 1980s whose PAAs were generally open only to target groups (landowners) and remained closed to neighbours, tenants and citizens. In contrast, like infrastructure policy, the spatial development policy of the 1990s appears more open and equipped with procedures described as participative (see Knoepfel, 1977; Linder, 1987; Fourniau, 1996).

8.3 Process: mobilised actors, resources and institutions

The programming of a public policy generally unfolds on the basis of a highly formalised procedure. The legislative process is generally less open than the policy agenda-setting process. The following discussion is primarily concerned with summarising the major stages in the adoption of legal and regulatory basis of a public policy. The actors involved in the programming and their scope for institutional manoeuvre ultimately emerge as strongly dependent on (inter)national regimes. However, the mobilisation of a given resource by different actors united in several coalitions may differ significantly and, as a result, have a major influence on the decision-making process (that is, the products PAP and PAA).

Policy programming

Table 8.1: Actors, resources and institutional rules involved in the decision-making process (programming)

Stage	European	Pre-parliamentary	Parliamentary	Referendum-related (in Switzerland)	Regulatory
Content based on chronological sequence	1. Variable initiative 2. Expert commissions, working groups 3. Pilot study for directive proposed by the Commission 4. Presentation to the Council and Parliament 5. Reformulation 6. Adoption by the Council	7. Pilot project carried out by the administration 8. Expert commission 9. External consultation procedure 10. Reformulation with possible co-reporting procedure 11. Legislative proposal with Federal Council/government memorandum	12. Recommendations by parliamentary commissions (with amendments) 13. Debate (with defence of the project by the government) and vote in the two chambers 14. Eventual conciliation procedure between the chambers 15. Final adoption by the Federal/National Assembly	16. Collection of 50,000 signatures in the case of legislative referendum (optional) 17. Referendum campaign 18. Popular ballot	19. Development of an ordinance/executive decree 20. Possible consultation procedure 21. Adoption of the decree by the government 22. Eventual passing of administrative directives (circular) by department or office/ministry concerned
Principal actors involved	• European Commission • National ministries • Interest groups • Government	• Administrative services • Extra-parliamentary commissions • Government	• Parliamentary commissions • Political parties • Interest groups • Government	• Government • Political parties • Interest groups	• Government • Administrative services • Interest groups

(continued)

Public policy analysis

Table 8.1: Actors, resources and institutional rules involved in the decision-making process (programming) (contd.)

Stage	European	Pre-parliamentary	Parliamentary	Referendum-related (in Switzerland)	Regulatory
Principal mobilisable resources	Information, law, personnel, organisation, consensus, infrastructure, political support, time	Information, law, personnel, organisation, consensus, infrastructure, political support	Law, consensus, political support, time	Money, organisation, infrastructure, time, political support	Law, consensus, political support
Principal institutional rules (general and specific)	Procedural rules for European decision-making procedures	Procedural rules for internal and external consultation procedure, right to be informed and heard, informal pre-consultation and consensus rules (collegiality), freedom of expression etc	Decision-making rules for the functioning of parliamentary assemblies, informal rules of consensus (majority parties), rule of legislative federalism (for Council of States in Switzerland), rule of loyalty to political parties etc	Laws of direct democracy (optional or mandatory referendums), rule of legislative federalism, freedom of expression etc	Principles of administrative law (right to be informed and heard, legality, equality of treatment, proportionality, non-retroactivity etc), procedural roles for internal and external consultation procedures etc

184

At this stage, the analyst should primarily concentrate on the general institutional rules of the political-administrative system within which the public policy in question is formulated (for example, partisan composition of the government and parliament, separation of powers, majority decision versus consensus, extra-parliamentary commissions systems, formal and informal pre-consultation procedure, possible types of referendums and popular initiatives, parliamentary proposals and motions). It should be noted, however, that, in addition to national democratic regimes, it is – increasingly – necessary to consider the European/EU level to adequately take into account the decision-making arenas where public policies are programmed.

This is not the place for a detailed discussion of the legislative process attached to the democratic regimes of specific countries. In Table 8.1, we have limited ourselves to a presentation of the most important actors, resources and institutional rules with respect to the legislative and regulatory processes at federal level in Switzerland and national level in France and the UK. For information on the process of assembly of real PAAs, which are more complex and sometimes extremely informal, consult the chapters on actors (Chapter Three) and institutional rules (Chapter Five) in Part I, and on the research hypothesis (Chapter Eleven, in particular concerning indirect stakes).

Notes

[1] We use the term in a more concrete way that is more directly based on formal documents than is the case in the North American literature (Bobrow and Dryzek, 1987; Dryzek and Ripley, 1988; Linder and Peters, 1988, 1989, 1990, 1991; Schneider and Ingram, 1990).

[2] For a British application see Whitmore (1984).

[3] Article 1 of the Federal Law of 22 June 1979 on Spatial Development (RS 700).

[4] In Switzerland, the 'shopping basket' is still defined in the frame of an order of the Federal Council (government) and in France it is defined in the context of a decree passed by the Cabinet. It has a less formally recognisable character in the UK but is nevertheless important for the uprating of social benefits with legal force where benefits are required to be uprated in line with the movement of prices.

[5] See Lowi (1972); Morand (1991), and in particular the contribution by Freiburghaus (1991) on the modes of state action; the contribution by Knapp

(1991) on information and persuasion; and another by Delley (1991) on action by training; see also König and Dose (1993) and Klöti (1998). On the 'contractual mode', see Gaudin (1996) and Godard (1997). On the 'conventional mode', see Lascoumes and Valuy (1996).

[6] For example, the Swiss Federal Law on Administrative Procedure of 20 December 1968 – RS 172.02.

[7] This is the case with cantonal legislation in Switzerland. At federal level in Switzerland, there is no system for the constitutional control of legislation produced by the federal parliament (rejected by the people in 1999).

[8] See Article 7 of the Federal Ordinance on the Organisation of the Federal Department of Justice and Police of 19 November 1999 (RS 172.213.1). Participation in the preparation of legislative texts is not exclusively limited to questions of legality. The Federal Chancellery (legal and linguistic service) also assumes important transverse work during this internal administrative process.

[9] On this point, see Article 61a of the Federal Law on the Organisation of the Government and the Administration of 21 March 1997 (RS 172.010). Following the new regulation adopted in 1989, authorisation is only necessary if explicitly required by a federal law or a general decree. As a result of this provision and the elimination of submissions for authorisation, the number of authorisations has been significantly reduced.

[10] For more information on this sociological concept, see, for example, Jaeger et al (1998).

[11] See Baroni (1992); Bourrelier (1997); Zimmermann and Knoepfel (1997).

NINE

Policy implementation

The analysis of policy implementation involves the researcher and practitioner in what often constitutes the most complex and rich part of a public policy process. In effect, this phase of the 'policy life cycle' brings about a direct relationship between the public actors of the political-administrative arrangement (PAA), the target groups, the end beneficiaries and third-party groups (positively and negatively affected third parties). In this analysis considerable attention is given to target groups. Where the distinctions between target groups, beneficiary groups and third parties are less clear, or not applicable to the argument, the loose expression 'affected groups' is used to encompass all groups.

The following sections deal, firstly, with the concept of 'implementation' (Section 9.1) from the perspective of classical theory on policy implementation and recent developments in this area (Section 9.2). From the policy analyst's perspective what is involved at this stage is the study of the interaction between these actors so as to reach an understanding of the in situ functioning or failure of a policy.

Secondly, we define the products of this stage of the policy process from an operational perspective, that is, the action plans (APs) (Section 9.3) and administrative products (Section 9.4). By analysing certain types of implementation processes, we then indicate the relationships between the different types of actors involved that need to be subject to a relational analysis so as to facilitate the identification of the factors behind the success and failure of a policy (Section 9.5).

9.1 Definition of policy implementation

It is necessary to start by providing a precise definition of the 'implementation' of a policy as this term is used both widely and selectively in different countries and/or schools of political and administrative science.

Many North American authors use the term *implementation* to designate all activities involving the execution of a piece of legislation. This term, which is also adopted in Germany by the *Forschungsverbund Implementation politischer Programme* (Research Association for the Implementation of Political Programmes) (see Bohnert and Klitzsch,

1980), incorporates into the concept of 'implementation' all of the political-administrative processes that follow on from parliamentary decision making. Thus, this definition includes[1] the development of all the elements of political-administrative programmes (PAPs) contained in governmental decrees that are not subject to separate parliamentary decisions.

In contrast to the above-described approach, the definition of implementation that we use does not include all of the post-parliamentary phase that extends to the end of the decision-making process within the legislative assembly up to the concrete and individual decisions taken by the administrative authorities. Instead, we define policy implementation as the *set of processes after the programming phase that are aimed at the concrete realisation of the objectives of a public policy.* Thus, our definition does not cover the regulatory provision – by government and administrative authorities – of PAPs and PAAs by means of decrees or simple governmental decisions. In our opinion, it is necessary to make an analytical distinction between the 'programming' and 'implementation' stages of a public policy that both take place, in part at least, during the post-parliamentary phase (or 'after a bill becomes a law', as the North Americans say). Despite the partly similar thrust of these two stages of the policy life cycle, the actors actually often pursue different strategies during each (Kaufmann and Rosewitz, 1983, p 32). In fact, the distinct phase of the execution 'in the field' of the legal and regulatory norms that govern state intervention can be found in all public policies, irrespective of the nature of a country's institutional system.

Thus, our definition of implementation is very close to the notions of execution or application that are generally used in the daily language of public administration. However, implementation defined in this way does not only involve the production of all kinds of juxtaposed concrete activities (in particular administrative acts); it equally incorporates all of the planning processes necessary for the organisation of these executive activities or APs that define priorities – in time, in space and vis-à-vis social groups – for the application of the PAP[2]. In effect, having provided structures, resources and coordination procedures between public and private actors, policy effectiveness depends on the establishment of an adequate mechanism of planned production.

In summary, we define implementation as the set of decisions and activities:

Policy implementation

- carried out by the public, para-state and private actors who belong to the PAA;
- framed by a PAP (either by a set of legislative and regulatory rules that are more or less flexible and favourable to the interests of the different actors) governing the specific institutional rules of the policy in question; and
- carried out with the intention of creating, influencing or controlling:
  1. the constitution of a 'policy network' (as defined by Clivaz, 1998), which structures the contacts between the formally competent administration (PAA), other stakeholder administrative services, target groups, end beneficiaries and third-party groups;
  2. the conception of an 'implementation strategy', adopted within *APs* (product no 4 as specified in the introduction to Part III), which take into account updated analyses of the public problem to be resolved, in particular its social (or functional), spatial (or geographic) and temporal distribution. Increasingly, the production of these plans is formally organised by means of codified planning exercises (for example, the plan for the elimination of waste in accordance with the Law of 1992 in France, plans for the conservation of natural areas in accordance with the Habitats Directive in France, 'measurement plans' to reduce atmospheric pollution in accordance with the Swiss Decree on the Protection of the Air of 1985 in Switzerland; plans for health and social services in the UK); and
  3. the (preparatory work for) concrete, general or individual decisions and activities that are directly addressed at target groups (*outputs*: products and/or administrative services; product no 5 as specified in the introduction to Part III), such as, for example, administrative operation permits for industrial installations.

Based on this definition of 'implementation', which is applicable to all policies in all political systems, the three types of activities identified above enable the analysis of the substantive and institutional content of the implementation of a public action. This approach also takes the two following points into account.

Firstly, the implementation process is only completed with the production of decisions and activities that directly address those affected (outputs). Thus, it is always characterised by interactions between public and private actors. These exchanges often take the form of negotiations, with the interests and positions of social actors sometimes being relayed by non-governmental organisations or sectoral pressure groups. Contrary to the programming phase that may unfold (exceptionally) without any direct contribution from (certain) civil society (groups), by definition, all of the stages of policy implementation address the external actors of the political-administrative sub-system. Therefore, the products and administrative services as themselves (outputs) serve as a point of departure for the evaluation of the conformity of implementation with the substantive content of the PAP.

Secondly, no PAP, even the most concrete and well developed, can replace or entirely predetermine implementation by claiming to be 'self-executing'. In explicitly limiting the real import of the PAP to an essential but not exhaustive framing role, the definition proposed here stresses that from the specific perspective of implementation, the legislative and regulatory norms contained in the PAP present themselves as a more or less relevant set of 'rules of the game' that distribute the positions and resources of the different actors involved in the 'implementation game' (expression coined by Bardach, 1977). Even if these rules are clearly established, the game itself always remains to be played. Furthermore, a number of implementation processes depend on the forms taken by interactions between actors of a particular policy who are relatively independent because they are organised on the basis of general institutional rules (applicable to all public policies) and/or other concerns of a regional or local nature. The arrival of a new piece of legislation may modify pre-existing policy networks or PAAs, for example by introducing a new actor excluded by the past or giving this actor more political weight than before. This is the case, in particular, with the introduction of a new actor into the game through the attribution of the right of appeal to environmental protection organisations or consumers. It should always be kept in mind that policies that create completely new activities and policy networks from scratch are rare. If not forging a new path for itself, a recent policy must take account of or integrate itself into the existing organisational structures, procedures and relationships between pre-existing actors (see the notion of 'path dependency' proposed by institutional economics – Section 5.1 in Chapter Five).

9.2 'Classical' implementation theory and recent developments

'Classical' implementation research starts with the observation of 'implementation deficits': these deficits were traditionally demonstrated by comparing the products and real effects of a policy (outputs and impacts or outcomes) and the substantive elements of PAPs that describe the policy objectives and instruments. In this regard, the interest of the researcher is close to that of the political-administrative actors (in particular at federal/central level), who consider such deficits as an expression of a failure at the level of implementation and not as raising questions about the intervention instruments and objectives formulated – in the majority of cases – by these actors during policy programming (PAP).

It should be noted, however, that nowadays the analytical concepts used in implementation research have moved far beyond the mere adoption of the formerly predominant doctrine of legislators and lawyers who considered implementation as a purely executive or technical function. As we know from numerous empirical research projects, this old conception overestimated the capacity of the law to influence and control administration and its action with respect to the development of civil society. In fact, it was actually the rejection of this over-determination by the law, a previously very widely held belief among politicians and civil servants and also among lawyers, which gave rise to the impetus for research on implementation (Knoepfel, 1979, p 23). From the outset, empirical studies were used in an attempt to provide a more nuanced explanation of the quality of policy products and effects. The five following dimensions were generally adopted as explanatory factors in such studies:

- *The 'structure of programmes' to be implemented (or PAP according to our terminology):* the notion of the structure of a programme is not limited to the simple substantive content of policies. On the contrary, the first research projects carried out in this context (Mayntz, 1980; Knoepfel and Weidner, 1982; Weidner and Knoepfel, 1983) endeavoured to characterise the different possibilities for expressing the intention of the legislator (for example, degree of precision, scope for manoeuvre given to federal/centralised or decentralised administrative actors) and the different modes of intervention adopted (for example, obligations or bans, financial incentives, information) or the institutional arrangements predetermined in this legislation (see Section 8.1, Chapter Eight, on the PAP). A related UK debate has been concerned with the arguments for and against rules and discretion in the structuring of legislation (Adler and Asquith, 1981; Baldwin, 1995).

- *The 'implementation administrative system'[3] (or PAA in our terminology):* the recognition of the characteristics of different political authorities and administrative organisations responsible for policy implementation as a factor that explains the quality of state intervention is without doubt the main innovation achieved by the 'classical' research on implementation. Thus, these approaches stressed the necessity of conceiving administrative organisations as groups of actors participating in a network of interactions incorporating a multitude of actors ('interorganisational or intergovernmental networks'). After that it was suggested that in many cases implementation processes are propelled through the management of these policy networks. Thanks, inter alia, to the contributions on the theory of collective action (Olson, 1965) and the sociology of organisations (Crozier, 1963), these analyses have not been limited to public actors but have included the interactions between administrative agents and interested social groups (see Section 8.2, Chapter Eight, on the PAA).
- *The economic, political and social weight of target groups:* the capacity of a subject of the administration to influence a state intervention varies according to the composition of the socioeconomic, political and cultural fabric of which that subject is a part. Thus, this position may be dominant or marginal; it may be supported by other social groups or, conversely, rejected by other public and private actors. Furthermore, the target groups of the instruments of a policy may be members of a pressure group whose cooperation is necessary for the realisation of the policy in question and/or other policies considered as more important. Of course, this situation strengthens their position with respect to the intervention of the policy-executing public administration. From another perspective, the weight of a subject of the administration varies in accordance with the responsibility that public opinion and public actors attribute to that subject in relation to the public problem to be resolved. Finally, this position will also vary according to his/her location: independently of the above-mentioned factors, the capacity for negotiation of a target person will be strengthened if this person is located outside 'high pressure problem zones' and, conversely, it will be reduced if they are situated within a zone considered as highly problematical (for example, an industrial enterprise will find it difficult to negotiate reductions with respect to a clean-up order in the context of atmospheric pollution if it is located in a zone in which pollution levels clearly exceed the admissible values).

- *Related issues about the power of target groups within the public policy delivery system:* there is an issue here about the extent the state is able to influence the behaviour of its own functionaries. In this respect the literature on implementation connects up with a wide literature about control within organisations (see the discussion in Hill, 2005, chapter 10). An important concern within the implementation literature has been about the behaviour of staff at the delivery end of policy systems. Furthermore the 'street-level bureaucracy' literature (the seminal work here was by Lipsky, 1980, but the ideas here are further explored in Hill, 2005, chapter 12 and in Hupe and Hill, 2007) suggests reasons why a measure of autonomy may – and even should – be present at this level, particularly when complex professional services are involved. In this sense the targets of policy changes may be changes of behaviour within the system. The whole issue is made more complex, particularly in the context of New Public Management, by the extent to which tasks are delegated to organisations that are not directly managed by policy makers. Hence, we may see issues about targeting, and about the strategies used to resist targeting in similar terms as those where the target groups are clearly private and external to the system, and issues about the 'weight' of such target groups (note, for example, doctors) as having many similarities.
- The position of target groups vis-à-vis public activity is also influenced by *variables referred to as 'situational'*, which may extend or reduce their room for manoeuvre during negotiations concerning implementation. Such variables are constituted by external events, changes in the economic and social context, disruptions of an economic nature etc that occur independently of the will of the actors involved. For example, the increases in the price of petrol have strengthened the position of public actors implementing energy-saving and rational use policies vis-à-vis the target groups that have shown a certain reticence in regard to such processes. Similarly, in the context of synchronous comparisons in particular, the position of actors will vary in different implementation zones in accordance with *variables referred to as 'structural'*. In effect, research has demonstrated the existence of relatively constant determinants with respect to the relative influence of actors, such as institutional rules governing property relationships or constitutional political rights (for example, excluding foreign populations from the policy arena).

The presentation of these five issues affecting the quality of the services provided by public policies and, in principle, adopted in the approach presented here in a modified frame also demonstrates the comparative nature of the process adopted by classical policy implementation research: in order to evaluate empirically the explanatory contribution of each type of factor, it was necessary to examine the implementation processes carried out by different administrative actors in several locations from the outset of these processes. The choice of these 'empirical sites' took into account either the different quality of services (outputs or variables to be explained) or differences with respect to four types of explanatory variables.

In the 1980s, 'classical' research on implementation was re-examined and accused of overestimating policy at the expense of 'politics', that is, power struggles and the more general characteristics of the development of post-industrial societies[4]. Writers interested in the sociology of law (Treiber, 1984) also formulated several criticisms, for example, highlighting the danger of the blinkered state with respect to the sometimes positive role played by implementation deficits (on law, see Müller, 1971, pp 53, 98). Apart from this external criticism, the teams carrying out research on implementation themselves made two significant changes to their initial conception of the policy implementation.

- *From 'top-down' vision to 'bottom-up' approach:* the majority of authors agree with the criticism initially expressed by Hjern (1978), Hjern and Hull (1983) and also Barrett and Fudge (1981), which claimed that the 'top-down' perspective renders researchers blind with regard to the social or political processes that are not foreseen by PAPs. The latter need to be analysed, and should then not be considered as simple obstacles to effective implementation. In effect, the supporters of a bottom-up approach consider these socio-political processes as the expression of the fact that one and the same PAP may inspire different reactions and strategies based on the interests of the public and private actors involved. It is not always a question of simple non-compliance when a local actor, who is subject to all kinds of social, economic and political-administrative constraints, uses or instrumentalises a programme in a way that was not planned by the legislator[5]. For example, it has been confirmed that Swiss civil protection policy (subsidies for the construction of anti-nuclear shelters) has on occasion been used to fulfil the aims of, for example, local authority sport and cultural policy (construction of multipurpose gyms and entertainment centres).

In its attempt to clarify the behaviour and real motivation of these actors, the 'bottom-up' movement proposes that all research on policy implementation should start from the system of basic actors (see Table 9.1). The analyst must, therefore, concentrate on the real behaviour of the target groups of a public policy and on the real interaction between the latter and the actors actually involved (PAA, end beneficiaries and third-party groups). The definition of the implementation proposed here takes this criticism into account when it speaks of the uniquely framing role of PAPs[6].

- *From the concept of 'implementation' towards that of 'implementation game':* following an analysis of different implementation processes that emphasises their many facets, Bardach (1977) proposed a reorientation of research on the execution of public policies. Anticipating the criticism levelled at the excessively 'governmentalistic' nature of the 'top-down' model, in his work entitled *The implementation game*, he proposes the game metaphor to "attract the attention of researchers to the players, to what the latter consider as stakes, to their strategies and their tactics, their ways of entering into the game, the rules of the game (which stipulate the conditions for winning) and the rules of 'fair-play' (which stipulate the limits beyond which you enter the domain of fraud and illegality)" (p 56). Bardach (1977) also insists on "the characteristics of the interactions between the players and on the degree of uncertainty with respect to the possible result of the game ('outcomes')" (p 56). This metaphorical concept should make it possible, among other things, "to draw the attention of the researcher to those who do not wish to participate in the game, to the motives for their abstention and to those who demand that rules of the game be changed before they will enter it" (Bardach, 1977, p 56).

This conception of implementation indicates that policy actors are involved in a competitive process not only with respect to the distribution of resources placed at the disposal of those responsible for application processes, but also with respect to the actual distribution of the power to define and redefine the *rules of the game* in the course of these processes. The (public or private) actors who succeed in (re)defining the rules of the game and who, as a result, are able to use a policy to serve their own interests possibly in cooperation with other authors, are capable of exerting a significant influence on policy implementation. The main challenge, therefore, consists in occupying

Table 9.1: Differences between the 'top-down' and 'bottom-up' visions of policy implementation

Implementation approaches	'Top-down' vision	'Bottom-up' vision
Starting point of analysis of policy implementation	Decisions taken by political and administrative authorities (PAPs, APs)	Activities of actors of the implementation network at local level (PAA, public action network)
Process for identifying the main actors of the public policy	From the top and public sector down to the bottom and private sector	From the bottom ('street-level') to the top with simultaneous consideration of public and private actors
Criteria for the evaluation of the quality of policy implementation	• Regularity (conformity, legality) of implementation procedure • Efficacy: extent of realisation of the formal objectives of the PAP	• No a priori clearly defined criteria • Eventual level of participation of actors involved • Eventual degree of conflict in implementation
Basic question (for the conduct of public policies)	Which implementation modes (structures and procedures) must be adopted to ensure optimum possible realisation of official objectives?	Which interactions between the public and private actors of a policy network should be considered during implementation so that it will be accepted?

Source: Loose adaptation (with our modifications) of the comparison proposed by Sabatier (1986, p 33)

such a position as the person who defines, interprets and modifies the institutional rules of the game ('fixer of the game').

Thus, this approach, which was adopted in part in our theoretical framework ('indirect games', see Section 6.2, Chapter Six), tends to relativise the 'ideal-type' image of implementation as a process based on the intention of implementing actors, the substantive content of a PAP, to abandon the conceptualisation of programming and implementation as two clearly distinct stages and to subject to re-examination the 'legitimate supremacy' of public actors over private actors – both economic and social.

The definition of implementation proposed here only partly takes the logical consequences of Bardach's approach into account. Despite its unquestionably original nature that draws the analyst's attention to all of the actors (and not just the public actors), this approach seemed too 'American-centrist' to fully encompass the realities of certain European democracies. In effect, the latter's traditions with respect to the primordial role of the public function and content of substantive and institutional decisions taken democratically at the level of policy programming (PAP and PAA) are very deeply rooted. In the US, in contrast, the 'rule-making' process (that is, the production of rules by independent agencies in accordance with a procedure of legal inspiration) is located between the 'law making' (or classical 'programming') and 'implementation' (that is, classical implementation). This last statement must not, however, be considered as an invitation to strictly limit the analysis of implementation processes to this last phase. On the contrary, it is increasingly accepted today that the understanding of implementation processes also incorporates the analysis of the programming phase. From this perspective, we discuss below the APs (product no 4) that constitute a direct link between the PAP and the results of its application (outputs, product no 5).

Although our approach does not limit itself to a simple analysis of policy implementation, it does adopt a considerable part of the traditional concept of 'implementation research' while generalising the elements adopted at the level of the entire policy life cycle and bringing them back to the three basic elements, that is, actors, resources and institutions. When applied to the analysis of the implementation stage of a policy, as a factor explaining services, in our conceptualisation, the programmes of a certain 'structure' to be implemented become the substantive elements of product numbers 2, 3 and 4 (PPA, PAA and APs), which guide the direct game of the actors. The old 'administrative implementation system' covers the institutional elements of these three products that are likely to direct the indirect games of the actors participating in the production of outputs. The third factor considered by the traditional approach as decisive for the results of policy implementation, that is, 'the economic, political and social weight of target groups' corresponds to the explanatory (intermediary) variable in our approach, that is, in the – direct or indirect – games of actors (target groups, end beneficiaries and third parties) and their capacity to mobilise their resources in accordance with institutional rules specific to the policy or institutional rules concerning administrative organisations, or general institutional rules.

This conceptualisation does not neglect the variables referred to as situational or structural because the latter become supplementary or increasingly scarce resources for the actors (for example, political support more important for consumer protection movements after the case of hormones in meat, loss of political support for the same movements in periods of economic crisis due to general decline in consumption), or institutional rules that are more or less favourable to the interests of the actors in question (right of constitutional initiative open only to Swiss citizens, freedom to publish free opinion limited to those with access to the media).

9.3 Action plans (product no 4)

We define APs, which are not necessarily observable as distinct formal elements in all policies, as *the set of planning decisions considered as necessary for the coordinated and targeted production of administrative services (outputs)* and which, in certain circumstances, may already be partially established by the PPA. Thus, APs define priorities for the production of concrete measures and for the allocation of resources necessary to implement administrative decisions and activities. As an intermediate stage in the policy execution process between the PAP and the sometimes unplanned appearance of implementation acts, APs are increasingly being adopted in policy processes as real management instruments.

Thus, many federal laws in Switzerland or national laws in France, and financial interventions by the EU in the area of structural funds, necessitate arrangements set up at infra-national levels such as the cantons, regions or departments that they develop in advance for the granting of subsidies and establishment of programmes or plans. This is the case in the area of economic development (development of a regional development plan by the regions in the frame of European policy of support for the regions), in the area of infrastructure (for example, for the construction of national and cantonal roads and universities) and also (or increasingly) in the area of the environment (for example, in the protection of the air, the efforts to combat noise pollution, water management, waste disposal) and in social policy (to facilitate the coordination of health and social care). This kind of planning approach has a longer tradition in the area of spatial development (for example, structure plans). Finally, it should be noted that the 'service contracts (or mandates)' developed as part of New Public Management processes can be related to APs in the sense that we define them here.

The analysis of these planning exercises on the basis of dimensions adopted from legal analysis (see Table 9.2) makes it possible to distinguish these APs from certain other intermediate implementation acts. According to our approach, the AP should be interpreted as an individual product that makes it possible to establish a link between the general and abstract norms of the PAP and the individual and concrete implementation acts. The same plan may be distinguished from the intermediate implementation acts of certain policies (in particular those concerning land) that are defined as general and concrete products (but sometimes have the same name, such as a land-use plan).

What all of these planning activities, which are traditionally found in the context of infrastructure and management policies, have in common is that they precede the production of final implementation acts. Thus, they aim to define temporal sequences and to answer the two following questions: how is the problem pressure (distributed) and – as a result – to which target groups and end beneficiaries of the state action should priority be given? What is the cost of implementation and, consequently, which political-administrative authorities must dispose which resources? (See Flückiger, 1998.)

This definition of priorities and lesser concerns may be undertaken from a functional (according to the type of activities subject to state intervention), temporal (according to the short, medium or long term), spatial (according to geographical zones) or social (according to the boundaries of socioeconomic groups) perspective. The definition of

Table 9.2: Qualification of the products PAP, AP and formal implementation acts according to the type of legal dimension

Legal dimension	General	Individual
Abstract	Norms of the PAP	AP
Concrete	Intermediary implementation measure (for example, land-use plan)	(Formal) implementation acts (outputs)

priorities, in the case of regulatory policies in particular, is often associated with the decision to accept partial implementation deficits among certain target groups for a certain period. The nature of privileges – and conversely discriminations – that derive from this may depend on political pressure, the accentuation of the problem in certain sectors and regions or the provisions of the PAP itself (see, for example, the empirical research on social discrimination specific to measures for the reduction of traffic in Swiss towns carried out by Terribilini, 1995, 1999).

It should be noted here that APs sometimes remain internal to the public administration. They define certain priorities for action without being legally binding with respect to the conduct of state intervention in civil society. In other words, APs do not create subjective legal rights. Even if the situation of a social group is considered explicitly as a priority in an AP (for example, young and unqualified unemployed people, long-term unemployed), this social group may not take advantage of a law to benefit from public services proposed by the PPA ahead of other social groups (for example, older and qualified unemployed people). In this sense, APs allow public actors to manage the implementation of the policy in question better without, however, legally connecting the plans to the private actors that the policy addresses.

Nevertheless, the tendency to introduce open planning activities to the target groups, end beneficiaries and third parties can currently be observed, in particular in France and the UK. Several public action intervention plans in the area of economic development, environment, spatial development, for example, are now subject to the mandatory consultation of stakeholders in the framework of more or less open procedures. This trend is associated, among other things, with increases in the complexity of the PAAs of the policies concerned and the demand by target groups and end beneficiaries to be allowed to participate in the definition of policy implementation priorities. In this case, the value of these APs sometimes lies in their 'opposability' and they can hence result in the greater or lesser restriction of the production of implementation acts. Thus, the current trend involving the formalisation of implementation activities through planning leads to and/or originates from a desire to (re)define intervention priorities, the affected groups or even the causality hypothesis of the policies in question, in particular on the part of the infra-national levels. This demand is supported in the EU by the increasing mandatory establishment of formalised APs (in case of policies linked to structural funds) so as to compensate for its weaknesses in following up the implementation of its policies.

Policy implementation

Figure 9.1 provides a schematic view of the discriminatory logic of all APs. It shows, in particular, that an AP defines priorities for implementation and, as a result, cannot generally incorporate the entire field of application of the substantive objectives of the PAP and will actually lead to predicted and legitimated implementation deficits. Moreover, the concrete measures produced do not necessarily cover the entire field of implementation as defined in the AP. Thus, it is possible that contrary to the AP, a particular social group and/or geographical zone is not affected by the policy measures (unpredicted deficits) during the defined temporal period. During the empirical study of the boundaries of final implementation acts (outputs), the analyst should identify whether eventual implementation deficits are the result of the targeted discrimination of the AP or its inadequate application.

The APs need to be based on sufficient knowledge of the temporal evolution of implementation activities, thus making it possible to ensure that administrative resources are used efficiently. This is the case if the measures selected and resources allocated make a greater contribution to the resolution of the public problem while taking the willingness of target groups where applicable to change their behaviour into account. The economic consideration of the marginal utility of public action plays a decisive role here. In effect, the question arises as to how

Figure 9.1: Links needed between PAP objectives, planning priorities and outputs (scope for implementation deficits)

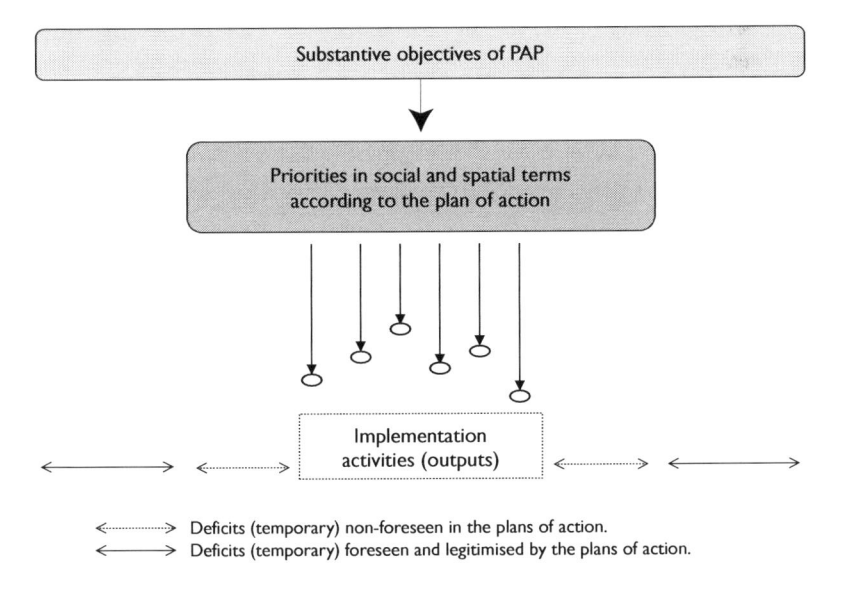

```
           Substantive objectives of PAP
                        │
                        ▼
         Priorities in social and spatial terms
            according to the plan of action
              │   │   │   │   │
              ▼   ▼   ▼   ▼   ▼
              Implementation
              activities (outputs)
```

⇠⋯⋯⋯⋯⇢ Deficits (temporary) non-foreseen in the plans of action.
←——→ Deficits (temporary) foreseen and legitimised by the plans of action.

the state may attain maximum efficiency with respect to the allocation of resources for the resolution of a problem (in the sense of the Pareto optimum or Hicks-Kaldor optimum) by investing the given means. Thus, it is in many cases a question of identifying the target groups whose change in behaviour will contribute in all likelihood to the resolution of the public problem. Secondly, it may be a question of establishing which target groups display the greatest willingness to change behaviour (for example, the sectors in which a new investment cycle unfolds in a way that enables the target groups to support a change in their behaviour economically). Thirdly, it is necessary to identify the potential target groups for which the administrative costs of intervention are the lowest in relation to the expected effects. Thus, the planning of actions also includes the consideration of their effectiveness (relationship between effects and objectives) and their efficiency with respect to allocation (relationship between effects and resources) (see Chapter Ten on policy evaluation criteria).

In practice, experience has shown that the designation of groups that will be discriminated against as opposed to privileged groups is of primary importance. Observation of the execution of national policies by regional authorities have revealed that these policies are often implemented in fits and starts. As a general rule, initial efforts are concentrated on target groups whose change in behaviour makes it possible to anticipate the maximum possible contribution to the resolution of the problem at the lowest possible administrative cost. Thus, in environmental policy, for example, the primary target is major industries while small and medium-sized enterprises are temporarily ignored at the price of an implementation deficit. Similar priorities are also defined in the framework of noise pollution protection policy (according to the size of the population exposed to noise pollution) and public transport policy (depending on the size of new populations linked up). In view of the importance of the sometimes very profound discriminations made by actors in this phase of the policy process, it is important to observe the extent to which these discriminations are made visible and politically debated (note, for example, the way in which this element in the implementation of the Child Support Act in the UK – in which, despite the political rhetoric but for administrative reasons, absent parents who were most willing to pay were targeted – contributed to opposition and ultimately the need for further policy change).

So as to facilitate and systematise the empirical study of an AP, we recommend that the analyst take the five operational elements explained below into account. By way of introduction, we emphasise that these dimensions, which are applicable to all APs, are not exclusive but complementary. In fact, the substantive and institutional content of this product can only be taken into account through their simultaneous analysis.

- *Explicit or implicit APs:* as already indicated, an AP is generally presented in the form of an internal document that does not legally link the political-administrative authorities to the affected groups. Irrespective of this principle, an AP can vary in terms of its degree of explicitness. The fact that it is declared 'official' and is familiar to all of the (public and private) policy actors should positively influence its degree of realisation. Conversely, it can be assumed that an implicit, or (quasi-)secret, AP will only represent a minimal constraint with respect to the different administrative services responsible for its coordinated and targeted application. Nevertheless, it is interesting to note that nowadays it is possible to observe a very real trend involving the formal organisation of these APs as an element for the creation of a consensus during the effective implementation of public policies (production of outputs). The degree of formalisation of the planning activity is, therefore, a relevant criterion for the analysis of these plans.
- *Open or closed APs:* along with the degree of formalisation, the degree of openness of the planning activity requires analysis. The establishment of a priority plan between different areas or social groups may be subject to internal actor activity or, conversely, it may be open to all of the public actors concerned, that is, target groups, end beneficiaries and third parties. As mentioned above, this opening up of the planning process in a way that facilitates political debate is increasingly common.
- *APs that are more or less discriminatory in nature:* by definition, an AP may define priorities and hence be discriminatory in nature. The scope of this discrimination may be large or small and relate to temporal, geographical and social dimensions. Thus, it may clearly establish implementation deadlines or reference periods for the production of implementation acts (for example, annual plans versus ones that run over several years), deadlines that ensure a certain predictability (or pseudo 'acquired rights', for example, in the case of subsidy policies) to the affected groups defined as being in a position of priority. Similarly, the borders of geographical areas designated as priority areas may be more or less clear or fluid, more or less stable or fluctuating. Finally, if the

discrimination operates on the basis of the socioeconomic characteristics of the affected individuals, the criteria for eligibility may also prove very strict or, conversely, leave a significant margin for assessment by the implementing actors. For example, plans for the allocation of subsidies to disadvantaged regions are generally highly discriminatory while plans to provide aid to companies are far less so.

- *APs with extensive or limited (re)structuring of the PAA:* an AP primarily aims to concretise the scope of the substantive content of the PAP of a given policy. To do this, it should also define precisely – as central actors – the actors that participate in the implementation PAA. If the application of the legislative and regulatory programme involves the de facto collaboration between different administrative organisations, para-state organisations, private actors and various public levels (central, regional and local), it is generally necessary to identify the actors who must coordinate their actions for the purpose of targeting implementation, that is, to constitute a special policy network (see Section 9.1, first stage of implementation). Viewed from this institutional perspective, an AP may be interpreted as more or less selective depending on whether it structures the interactions between the responsible actors (for example, in the form of a 'project organisation') – beyond the elements already defined in the initial PAP and PAA – or, conversely, depending on whether it does not define any specific new organisational and procedural rule for the implementation PAA.
- *APs involving a more or less clear allocation of resources:* finally, the development of APs is guided by strategic consideration of the impact and efficiency of the policy in question. Theoretically, it is a question of investing the available or newly allocated administrative resources (for example, a supplementary budget and additional personnel) so the public problem is resolved to the maximum possible extent. This implies that APs clearly establish which resources are at the disposal of which actors for the purposes of policy implementation. This kind of resource allocation process is not so much an exercise in the optimisation of costs as a process of political arbitration between the interests of the different actors (for example, a struggle for resources between administrative services, decision-making levels). Thus, the analyst should examine whether a particular AP formally links the use of a particular resource by a given administration to the implementation of a given measure among a given priority

group or whether, conversely, no explicit link is established between the use of available resources and the fields of action designated as priority areas. Obviously, the AP is considerably less effective in the latter case.

For example, in Switzerland, the planning of anti-noise measures, sections of national roads or cantonal bypass roads (which are subsidised by the Swiss Confederation) specifies priorities and makes financial resources available in accordance with the provisions of the medium-term financial planning. Similarly, in France, the intervention programmes of the water agencies associate temporal, spatial and target group priorities with specific financial sums. On the other hand, many APs contain no link between the planned measures and the allocation of finances (for example, in Switzerland, the cantonal measurement plans to counteract atmospheric pollution merely contain a list of measures and fail to make any statement on the financial resources necessary for their implementation or the sums reserved for this purpose).

In conclusion, it should be noted that an AP is only a real policy management instrument if it is explicitly formulated, makes clear discriminations within a given temporal framework, structures the tasks and competencies assigned to actors in the PAA and links the allocated administrative resources (in a supplementary way) to specific decisions and activities. Needless to say, such APs promote the coherent and targeted management of policy implementation. On the other hand, they tend to make visible to all actors the (temporary) discriminations actually being made. As a result, their formulation presupposes that the responsible political-administrative actors legitimise the targeting of the public action and this involves acceptance of the high political costs while taking into account the imperatives of consensus. In fact, the phase of the development of APs rarely takes place within the legislative assembly, but at the level of the executive authorities, allowing them greater scope for manoeuvre (for example, if the AP remains implicit, a referendum or political control are out of the question).

We would finally like to note that in many European countries, administrative reorganisation has led to the issuing of so-called 'service contracts' or mandates by parliaments, governments and even ministers. These measures, which are concluded between different administrative bodies or between public, para-public and private (or privatised) actors, may be considered as APs to the extent that they operate choices with regard to the desired services (and, more rarely, in practice, undesired ones). They allocate resources, in particular finance, in the form of budgets to implementing actors and stipulate the decision-making mechanisms for the population and the evaluation of services (for Switzerland, see Mastronardi, 1997; Knoepfel and Varone, 1999; for France, see Warin, 1993; Gaudin, 1996; see also Section 12.2.2 in Chapter Twelve). In the UK this is particularly in evidence in the field of the contracting out of services by local government, backed up by the requirement of local authorities to secure 'best value' not only in terms of low-cost services but also customer satisfaction. Criticisms have been expressed, however, with respect to the lack of indicators concerning the effect of the stipulated services.

Another response to the issues explored here is the setting up of monitoring arrangements to deal with situations in which general APs impose broad and complex implementation responsibilities and it may be considered that it is outcomes rather than outputs that really matter – lowered levels of pollution, decreased illiteracy, raised health standards. A characteristic of modern implementation control in the UK has been the extensive use of inspectorates and of the Audit Commission to audit overall performance rather than to ensure exact rule compliance. This has become a key element in central–local government relationships (Power, 1997; Pollitt, 2003).

9.4 Implementation acts (product no 5)

We define the formal implementation acts (outputs[7]) of a policy as the set of end products of the political-administrative processes which, as part of the scope of its implementation, are individually aimed at the members of the defined affected groups. The final acts comprise administrative products directly aimed at the affected groups by the administration and the other (private and para-state) bodies responsible for the execution of public tasks. These products comprise all kinds of decisions or administrative acts[8] (for example, conditional authorisations, individual bans, approvals), the granting of financial resources (for example, subsidies, fiscal exonerations), acts involving the collection of money (for example, indirect taxes, levies, fines), police intervention, direct services (for example, health checks, financial checks, training or treatment services), advisory activities and organisational measures. In reality, these formal acts are accompanied by a large number of informal acts (see below).

The implementation acts are characterised by the fact that they create an individual relationship (in particular in the case of formal acts, even those of a legal nature) between the people that constitute those affected and the competent public bodies responsible for policy implementation. Procedural administrative law then grants the affected groups rights or obligations of participation and cooperation. It is important to remember that, given their limited resources, administrations rarely succeed in (punctually and/or simultaneously) serving or sanctioning all of these groups in relation to the policy in question. In such cases, one refers to temporal and/or regional implementation deficits that arise – at least in part – from the adopted APs (see Section 9.3).

The implementation acts may be understood at different cumulative levels. The lawyers look into some of the individual activities mentioned above and then examine whether and to what extent these take up the provisions of the PAP and the APs (examination of legal conformity). The policy analyst normally relates to more widely encompassing units composed of several outputs; the term 'product groups' has been used to designate this phenomenon. Experience has shown that these product groups are not easy to identify; they generally have to be reconstructed by the analyst, that involves an autonomous and ambitious definition task. It is possible to apply different models of categorisation for this purpose. Despite these difficulties, as a general rule, the conscious definition of implementation acts or products/product groups is particularly relevant in the context of the reorganisation of administrations. In effect, it helps the administrative services to focus their structures and procedures more directly at the quality of the products and the requirements for their production (organisation of the administration on the basis of products rather than laws – refer to the reorganisation of administrations by 'service project'). Furthermore, the identification of these sets of output products may contribute to the reinforcement of the collective identity ('corporate identity') of the administrative service or para-state body concerned. Finally, these definitions make it possible to quantify and justify products better vis-à-vis political instances. Thus, they make it possible to improve the management of policies in accordance with the needs of their own products.

The public bodies play the main role in the formulation of formal implementation acts (outputs) and the fulfilment of the results expected by the policy depends to a large extent on them. The executing bodies can have a significant influence on the concrete application of a policy, depending on the use they make of the margin for interpretation and action that the policy allows them. Thus, it is not surprising that these acts attract the interest of monitoring bodies and that numerous laws

Public policy analysis

require the presentation of activity reports that make it possible to identify the formal implementation acts in both qualitative and quantitative terms. This obligation to inform facilitates the monitoring of policy execution. The reports can act as a basis for the actual monitoring of execution activities. The forms this reporting takes may strongly influence the possibility of benchmarking between administrative units in different regions and, hence, restrict the room for manoeuvre (Knoepfel, 1997b).

The activities of executing bodies also play a key role during the implementation of regulations that address private actors directly and only require subsidiary intervention on the part of the public bodies (for example, monitoring of the respect of a norm and application of sanctions in cases of abuse). In effect, the level of respect for a norm depends essentially on the level of control exerted and eventual sanctions applied to ensure that it is complied with (for example, police control of the observation of speed limits and fines in the case of contravention).

It is generally necessary to collect a large volume of data in the course of the analysis of implementation acts. Depending on the nature of the question being posed, it is usually necessary, for example, to obtain information on the existence, quantity and quality, spatial, temporal and affected group distribution, substantive and institutional content of all administrative acts that are produced during the period being studied. The implementation acts of other public policies must also be documented insofar as they may have an influence on behaviour of the affected groups and the evolution of the problem to be resolved. In cases involving a high frequency in the production of implementation acts, it is recommended that they be represented in graphical form (for example, spatial and/or temporal profiles of outputs based on the extent to which the empirical activities are multifaceted). In order to proceed with the development of implementation output profiles for a specific public policy, the analyst may take the following six dimensions into account:

- *The perimeter of financial implementation acts (= existence):* this dimension establishes a direct link between the priorities defined in the AP and the acts actually produced. In this context, the analyst should establish a correspondence between the temporal and socio-spatial distribution of observable acts (in the form of profiles of all of the outputs produced over time and in space) and the intentions expressed in the AP. By carrying out a comparison of this nature, the analyst will be able to identify the eventual implementation deficits already planned – and legitimised – at planning level (complete implementation even if it does not cover all areas or there is objective problem pressure) from those resulting from incomplete implementation. In the light of the original top-down use of 'deficit', implying fault on the part of implementers, this usage draws a useful distinction between intended and unintended deficits. There is also a possibility lying between these two, that is, differential implementation associated with the need for the exercise of discretion at street-level as highlighted in the work of Lipsky (1980) noted above. In addition to this direct comparison of the perimeter of the planned acts (in the AP) and the real acts, the analyst may put the latter into perspective with the area initially covered by the norms of the PAP and thus discover implementation situations with gaps or distorted perimeters. In other words, the analyst may identify missing acts with the help of a comparison of the profile created for actual implementation with that required under the PAP and the AP.

For example, in Fribourg (Switzerland), traffic reduction measures were initially concentrated in the affluent neighbourhoods, despite the fact that these neighbourhoods were not necessarily exposed to the highest level of disturbance caused by traffic (noise, pollution, accidents) (Terribilini, 1995); this constitutes a distorted output from the level of the AP. In contrast, a consistent output exists in the case of the taxation of all natural people and legal entities within the territory of a given public body. Moreover, cases involving the renunciation of public intervention due to political pressure or lack of resources (personnel, finance and so on) are examples of 'holey' profiles in which specific target groups are omitted. Other examples of this include the dropping of police checks during the carnival period and the failure to pursue the producers of so-called 'soft' drugs.

- *Outputs with a greater or lesser level of institutional content:* just like the PAP or the AP beyond its substantive aspect (how is the problem to be resolved?), the formal implementation act (output) may also contain institutional elements that can be greater or lesser in scope (which actors are supposed to contribute to the resolution of the problem? Which rules of the game do they adopt? Which resources do they use?). In effect, in order to resolve a collective problem sustainably, a growing number of policies are being provided with control and monitoring mechanisms that require the establishment of a network of actors for this monitoring process. Thus, it is possible to observe the establishment of multi-party monitoring commissions, monitoring bodies with strategic committees composed of a multitude of actors representing the public services, target groups and end beneficiaries and the establishment of communications networks for the interpretation of measurement data associated with the effects of a service (for example, verification of the data forecasted and recorded during an environmental impact study on a major infrastructure project when the infrastructure in question is up and running).

Again, and in accordance with the central research hypothesis proposed in this book, these institutional elements will pre-structure the subsequent phase of the policy in question, that is, the eventual formulation of an evaluative statement on the impacts and effects of the policy (see Chapter Ten). For the most part, it is the actors who are fearful of having lost out in terms of the direct game concerning the substantive content of the implementation act who will be interested in obtaining – through an indirect game – a key position within a particular monitoring structure by intervening with regard to the institutional content of the output in question. For example, one of the institutional responses to the LULU phenomenon ('locally unwanted land uses') associated with waste in France was the establishment of a local information and surveillance commission for each waste processing installation (*Commission locale d'information et de surveillance*, CLIS), which is open to the entire implementation PAA, the local populations and environment associations.

- *Formal or informal acts:* once the outputs actually produced have been recorded with the help of profiles, empirical studies can examine the degree of legal formalisation of these administrative activities. This operational dimension is important because it affects the production costs (higher for formal outputs), the forms of negotiation and the institutional content of an act that influences its follow-up. In effect, an administrative decision often includes an appeal clause that opens the final (legal) phase of its production and its follow-up to some or all of the affected groups. It should be noted that for the reasons cited, in many cases, the administration prefers informal acts of implementation (for example, information provided by telephone that is not formally noted and cannot be the object of an appeal given in response to a request as to whether an application for a subsidy or planning

permission has any chance of succeeding in a formal procedure) to heavy-handed formal implementation acts.
- *Intermediate or final acts:* in the above paragraphs, we considered final acts as one of the two products of the implementation stage. However, certain acts are only intermediate in form (acts undertaken within the administration that do not yet address the affected groups: general and concrete acts – for example, draft spatial development plans – requiring further individualisation to render a policy operational). These intermediate acts are sometimes important in helping the analyst to understand the nature of the final acts that directly address the individuals who compose the target groups; however, it is important not to mistake them for final acts.
- *Coherence of the content of a policy's final acts:* the groups affected by a public policy are often subject to several public interventions simultaneously having a combined influence on their behaviour. Thus, it makes sense to analyse the extent to which the different acts produced within one and the same policy appear coherent and capable of mutually reinforcing each other. In effect, a lack of coherence strongly reduces the substantive effect of a policy.

    An elevated level of coherence exists, for example, when the obligation to clean up an industry is accompanied by financial support for the clean-up process, when mandatory health insurance is accompanied by the subsidy of premiums for low-income households or the elimination of locations where drugs are taken openly is accompanied by the establishment of injection centres and programmes for the prescription of methadone or heroin under medical supervision. Conversely, the imposition of a speed limit on the motorways in the absence of the monitoring of violations or the imposition of mandatory sorting of waste without providing individual or collective systems for the collection of sorted waste are indicative of weak coherence.
- *Degree of coordination with the acts produced by other policies:* the question of the coherence of implementation acts is more obvious when these acts involve several policies. Here too, inadequate coordination during the implementation phase, for example, as a result of an excessively closed PAA or AP that does not sufficiently structure activity, is unlikely to succeed in bringing about the desired change in the behaviour of target groups.

    For example, the granting of a subsidy for the updating of energy systems in buildings (energy policy) during a period of economic recession (economic policy based on a programme for the revival of the building sector) is indicative of a significant degree of external coordination, while the parallel payment of subsidies for agricultural production (which encourage the use of natural and/or chemical fertilisers) and introduction of measures to combat water pollution (caused by the spreading of agricultural fertilisers) is indicative of a weak level of coordination.

The collection of exhaustive data on implementation acts presupposes a clear definition of those affected. In accordance with the principles of the rule of law, the affected groups are normally defined in the PAPs as both people (natural and legal) to whom the authorities may grant rights or impose obligations in order to attain policy objectives, or whose behaviour should be influenced by other administrative activities. When analysing implementation profiles, it must always be kept in mind that policies not 'only' produce implementation acts, they also produce effects. Thus, analyses that are limited to formal or informal acts (outputs) and do not take impacts and effects into account are incomplete and run the risk of confusing the services and effects of a policy. For this reason the following chapter will basically deal with the impacts and results (outcomes) of a policy that are normally the object of an evaluation (Chapter Ten). And in anticipation of this fourth stage of the policy life cycle, in the following paragraphs we discuss the interaction between public actors, target groups, end beneficiaries and third-party groups during policy implementation.

9.5 Process: the mobilised actors, resources and institutions

For obvious reasons the policy analyst must take a detailed look at the situation of target groups because, ultimately, the success or failure of a solution proposed for the resolution of a public problem often depends on (the change in) target group behaviour. The methodological approach adopted to identify the interactions between the actors of the PAA, the target groups, end beneficiaries and third-party groups is that of so-called rational analysis. This approach tries to locate each type of actor in the social environment and to identify the political, social and economic forces to which the actor is exposed and, moreover, the intensity of the relationships that develop between the different actors on the basis of their interests and respective resources. Thus, what is involved here is the examination of the interdependencies between actors and the possible coalitions that form between some of

Policy implementation

them. Figure 9.2 presents in very schematic form the main relationships between the actors involved in the implementation of public policy.

In the following paragraphs, we review the main relationships and coalitions that can exist or be formed between the actors (based on the numbering indicated in brackets in Figure 9.2), and examine the potential influence of the latter on the products and effects of the policy in question.

1. *Bilateral relationships between the administration and target groups:* the close relationship between policy-implementing administrations and the target groups arises from the simple fact that the implementation acts are aimed at various natural people and legal entities whose behaviour is intended to be modified by the policy measures in question. In democratic societies legislation governing administrative procedures generally recognises the principle of the right to be heard[9]. Based on this, in practice, numerous processes have been developed for exchange and interaction between the political-administrative authorities and the target groups (exchange of information and resources, negotiations, barter). Thus, the target groups tend to emerge as the privileged negotiating partners of the public actors of a policy. Supported by numerous special rules, this right to be heard has become an important asset at the disposal of target groups in the course of the implementation game.

Figure 9.2: Actors and substantive results of implementation

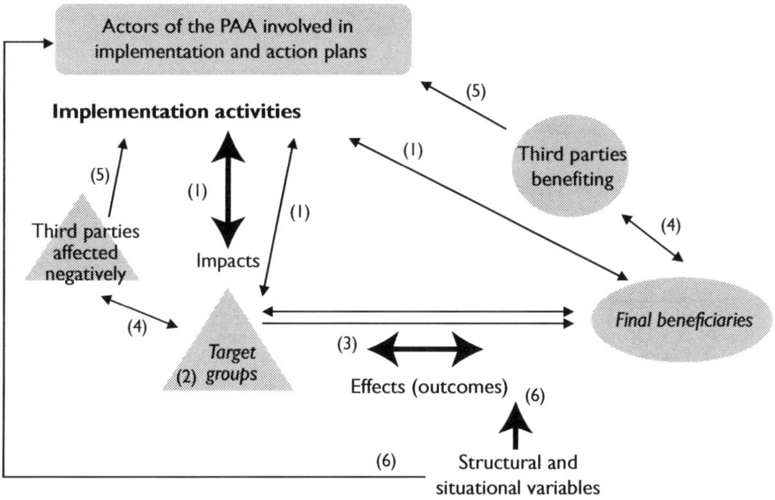

It should be noted that up to the late 1960s[10], the axis between the administration and the target groups formed the essential (and almost exclusive) bridge between implementing actors and social actors. The exclusivity of this exchange was often reinforced through professional confidentiality that guaranteed the 'cosy relationship' between the administration and its 'subjects'. This formula conceals the fact that in many policies these 'subjects' only represent a small proportion of the (potentially) concerned citizens. Thus, the affected group of spatial development is constituted by property owners, that of economic policy by companies likely to benefit from public investments and so on.

This exclusive relationship was re-examined from the early 1970s when the participation movement started knocking at the doors of the closed chambers where negotiations between the administration and target groups were being held. The battle was fought in the context of several specific policy areas (for example, spatial development policy, environmental protection policy, consumer protection policy) and it was increasingly successful in having a legislative impact. 'Third parties' (as the legal expression goes) entered the political-administrative scene: parliaments and the courts started to grant others affected the status of a 'party' in administrative procedures as well as a right of appeal in litigation procedures. This opening resulted in the development of a triangular negotiation structure that can be referred to as the 'basic triangle' between the administration, target groups and end beneficiaries (see Section 3.4, Chapter Three). This triangular arena quickly replaced the old bilateral target group/administration relationship and increasingly infiltrated all policy implementation structures and processes. The emergence of this triangular structure significantly altered the position of target groups vis-à-vis public actors: it was actually weakened, in most cases because the other 'parties' often represented interests contrary to those of the target groups.

2. *The power relationships within the target groups: competition and self-monitoring:* one of the fundamental limits of the systemic, neo-corporatist or neo-Marxist approaches to policy analysis stems from the fact that they often conceive the target groups as a homogenous group whose members are motivated by identical interests. However, social and political reality tends to prove the opposite: in effect power relationships of a competitive nature tend to exist between the target groups of the majority of public policies (for example, between the different companies targeted

by work safety policies, social policy, economic policy or environmental protection policy). If it is true that at the policy programming level these groups join forces to form relatively homogenous associations and interest groups, this solidarity is often replaced by a self-monitoring or competition mechanism at implementation level. In legal terms, this self-monitoring, which is motivated by (economic) rivalry between the different sub-groups of the target groups, has taken the form inter alia of appeals lodged by competitors against decisions targeted at a specific company and, more recently, in the right of appeal in the context of matters of public acquisition (in accordance with the rules of the World Trade Organisation). In cases of this nature, the competitor may cite violation of the principle of the equality of treatment in claiming that the conditions granted to another company are more advantageous than those imposed on it.

Thus, the position of natural people or legal entities belonging to the target group will equally depend on the competitive relationships in the different implementation arenas (see Section 9.2 on classical implementation theory). Monopolistic or oligopolistic structures will be more favourable for them than a nuclear structure. Furthermore, the degree of internal rivalry affects the position of a target group in its entirety vis-à-vis the administration which, in the case of a monopolistic structure, can hardly expect the intervention of these self-monitoring mechanisms.

3. *Conflictual relationships between target groups and end beneficiaries: from state arbitration of conflicts to contractual solutions:* in the majority of policies, the target groups are not identical to the end beneficiaries (note the exceptions to this discussed at the end of Section 3.3.3, Chapter Three). The end beneficiaries are defined on the basis of the public problem that the policy proposes to resolve because it is they who ultimately benefit from the proposed solution.

Thus, the objective of the provisions regarding the classification, size or design of a building, defined in the form of conditions pertaining to planning permission, is not to cause trouble for the owner, but to protect the building's neighbours and to contribute to the harmonious development of a village or town in the interests of all of its inhabitants. Similarly, the issuing of an order to a company to clean up an installation in the interest of work safety or environmental protection primarily aims to protect the workers or those living near the site of the installation in question, or, in the context of certain 'social' policies such as illegal drugs policy, in addition to the target group (that is, illegal drug users) the end beneficiaries of the measures introduced are those who live next to or frequent areas where such drugs are used, and so on. In schematic terms, the typical constellation of the interests at play takes the form of a relationship of indirect proportionality: the more severe the obligations imposed on the target groups, the greater the protection afforded to the beneficiaries. Thus, insofar as a policy is programmed and then executed, it falls to the state and its actors to arbitrate the conflicts of interest between these two types of actors. This kind of interpretation highlights the redistributive effects (between social groups) of all public policies (Knoepfel, 1986).

In numerous cases, the strengthening of the position of end beneficiaries as described above has resulted in the establishment of contractual solutions: the resolution of certain conflicts is directly negotiated between the end beneficiaries and the target groups, even sometimes in cases in which a formal intervention on the part of the public administration is lacking (Weidner, 1997). In fact, the establishment of compensation mechanisms between these two types of actors are becoming increasingly common; these mechanisms are rooted in contracts: for example, those located in the vicinity of nuclear power stations receive danger money, the inconveniences caused by waste treatment installations are compensated by lower prices being charged to the inhabitants of the relevant local authority (Kissling-Näf et al, 1998).

4. *Support of injured parties for target groups and of positively affected third parties for end beneficiaries:* as stated in Chapter Three on policy actors, apart from the target groups where policies aim to alter activities and the end beneficiaries, in a relational analysis it is also necessary to take into account the actors indirectly affected by the implementation of a policy. Without being the primary target of the state intervention, the latter may see their (economic) situation change, either positively (that is, positively affected third parties) or negatively (that is, negatively affected third parties). Depending on the evolution of their new situation and their capacity to organise themselves, the indirectly affected actors will become involved in policy programming and/or implementation by forming coalitions with other social groups who support or oppose the state intervention. Obviously, the 'natural' coalitions form between the target groups and negatively

affected third parties, on the one hand, and the end beneficiaries and positively affected third parties on the other. It should be stressed here that if the indirectly affected actors are very powerful from an economic or political perspective (depending on, for example, their number, financial resources, political support), they may prove more influential than the actors directly targeted by the policy during its conception and execution.

For example, if the target groups of environment policy are polluters, the end beneficiaries are all those whose environment is affected by the many sources of pollution in a region, while the positively affected third parties are those who develop new less polluting technologies that are easier to market among target groups (refer to the sustained development of eco-business – Benninghoff et al, 1997) and the negatively affected third parties are producers who can no longer market their old polluting technologies.

As a result of the entry into the game of groups negatively affected by the acts imposed on target groups, the position of the latter vis-à-vis the administration or the end beneficiaries may also be noticeably strengthened. This constellation arises quite frequently in the area of fiscal measures imposed on producers or traders with the intention that the latter should incorporate them into their prices at the expense of consumers (opposing coalition of traders and consumers). Similar situations are also familiar with licence withdrawal. In such cases, the mobilisation of solidarity between target groups and a more or less wide circle of negatively affected people is quite common. Such situations sometimes give rise to the formation of very unusual coalitions (for example, between traders and consumers, electricity companies and ecologists during the liberalisation of the electricity market). The same thinking applies to the coalitions that arise between the end beneficiaries of a policy and positively affected third parties.

5. *Support of positively affected third parties and opposition of negatively affected third parties for public actors:* the support or opposition of positively and negatively affected third parties is not restricted to social actors. In reality, the latter often make direct contact with the public actors of the PAA and with other political-administrative actors to whom they enjoy greater access and of whom they expect vigorous intervention among the actors of the PAA.

Eco-business companies identified as the positively affected third parties of rigorous environmental standardisation intensify their research activities and invite the state to declare all of their anti-pollution products as 'state of the art' and their use mandatory by all polluting companies in a certain sector, for example.

6. *Opportunities and restrictions prescribed by the situation and structural variables:* as already demonstrated by classical implementation analysis (see Section 9.2), the position of target groups may be perceptibly modified by economic events (or situation variables) that unfold rapidly and are completely beyond the control of the public or private actors involved in the policy implementation process. Thus, in Switzerland the political administrative authority may more readily grant planning permission in a village that has been hit by disaster (for example, flooding, avalanche, fire) and will allow all kinds of exceptions to pass that would never be accepted in normal times. In contrast, events such as technological disasters often result in the tightening of the controls on high-risk operations, even if the disasters in question occur in other countries (for example, 'the Chernobyl effect' on the nuclear sector in energy policy; see Czada, 1991).

Despite the actors' game and the vagaries of situation variables, the position of a target group within a given policy process remains strongly (pre)determined by its political, economic and social power that, in turn, is defined by the structural make-up of civil society in general rather than a single public policy. Thus, for example, large enterprises may be able to frustrate planning controls, particularly when they can threaten that those controls will inhibit the provision of employment opportunities in the area (see, for example, Blowers' study of the brick industry in an English county, 1984). Conversely, an alert raised by the refugee community about the emission of toxic gas from the only factory in the village whose vice-director is the mayor is unlikely to mobilise negotiations between the members of the famous 'basic triangle' described above, even in the case of an obvious contravention of environmental law. While policies and the actors' game undoubtedly aim to resolve public problems it would be mistaken to think that they can eliminate the causes fully and definitively. It should be noted that these situation and structural variables affect not only the position of private actors, but also those of the public actors in the PAA.

Notes

[1] Using the term 'meso-implementation', see Dahme et al (1980, p 158).

[2] Bardach (1977, p 57) defines 'implementation' as a "process of assembling the elements required to produce a particular programmatic outcome".

[3] 'Implementation machine', Bardach (1977), *Implementationsstruktur*, which translates as 'implementation structure', that is, all of the administrative units responsible for implementation (Mayntz, 1980).

[4] See, for example, the papers presented to the congress of the Association of Political Science of the Federal Republic of Germany in October 1984, which were devoted to this debate.

[5] As suggested by the initial work of Sabatier and Mazmanian (1979), which bears the significant title of 'The conditions of effective implementation: a guide to accomplishing policy objectives'.

[6] See also the exploration of this issue in Hill and Hupe (2002).

[7] The terms 'outputs', 'end products', 'administrative implementation activities' and – depending on the circumstances – 'administrative services' are used synonymously in this book.

[8] For Switzerland, in the sense of Article 5 of the Federal Law on Administrative Procedure of 20 December 1968 (RS 172.021). In the case of France, administrative acts are involved here.

[9] For Switzerland, see Article 29 of the Federal Law on Administrative Procedure of 20 December 1968 (RS 172.021): 'The parties have the right to be heard'.

[10] This assumption of the 1960s as a turning point may vary from society to society.

TEN

Evaluating policy effects

A policy aims to resolve a social problem that has been defined as politically relevant to the public arena (see Chapter Seven). Once it has been programmed and implemented (see Chapters Eight and Nine), a policy is – or should be – subject to systematic evaluation. During this final stage of the policy life cycle, the analyst focuses on the effects generated by the state measures. In concrete terms, this means establishing the benefits and costs of policy, including where applicable whether groups have effectively modified their behaviour. In summary, policy evaluation involves the empirical testing of the validity of the causality model on which the policy is based. Thus, the analysis concerns both the relevance of this 'theory of action' and the scope of its practical application.

This chapter deals with 'evaluative statements on policy effects', which is the sixth policy product in our analysis model (see the introduction to Part III). We start by providing operational definitions of the concepts of policy 'impacts', which take account of changes affecting target groups (including changes in their behaviour), and policy 'outcomes', which describe the effects actually generated among the end beneficiaries (Section 10.1). There may be related effects on third parties. Based on these two variables, we present the five criteria that are generally applied when evaluating the effects of a policy: extent of impact, effectiveness, efficiency, relevance and productive economy (Section 10.2). These two preliminary stages then enable us to identify the form and content of the various evaluative statements that can be observed in political-administrative reality (Section 10.3). Finally, we identify the principal actors of the evaluation stage, their direct and indirect games and the resources and institutions mobilised during the process of the production of these evaluative statements (Section 10.4)[1].

10.1 Definition of policy effects

While the concept of the formal implementation act ('output') identifies the final products of political-administrative processes (that is, the *tangible results* of implementation), the 'impacts' and the 'outcomes' concern the *real effects* of a policy in the social arena. Thus, at this level, what is involved is the empirical testing of the relevance of the intervention hypotheses (did the target groups react as anticipated?) and causality hypotheses (do the end beneficiaries see their situation improving?). To facilitate the empirical analysis of these effects, we present below the operational dimensions that make it possible to identify and qualify policy impacts and outcomes.

10.1.1 Impacts (observable among target groups)

We define the impacts of a policy as all of the – desired and undesired – changes in the behaviour of target groups that are directly attributable to the entry into force of the political-administrative programmes (PAPs), political-administrative arrangements (PAAs), action plans (APs) and the formal implementation acts (outputs) that concretise them. Thus, the impacts represent the real effects that policies trigger among the target groups and the key question in this context is whether the implementation of the policy gives rise to the desired (more or less sustainable/lasting) behaviour changes, or the stabilisation of behaviour that would have changed in the absence of the public intervention or the acceptance by these groups of the costs of the intervention. The response to this question indicates whether and to what extent the intervention instrument implemented to realise a policy for a given PAA proves adequate in triggering the anticipated change.

As previously stated the target groups should be defined by the (operational elements of the) PAPs. However, the scale and scope of the observable changes in behaviour only correspond to the expectations and objectives formulated in the legal and regulatory bases in a few cases. The same is true of the objectives defined – more concretely – in the APs and formal implementation acts (outputs).

The analysis of impacts is not restricted to the observation of effective changes in behaviour. It is also interested in the sequence of the causes and effects of a policy, that is, the relationships between its PAP, PAA, APs, implementation acts and the behaviour of the observed target groups. Thus, it does not limit itself to an examination of whether the effective behaviour corresponds to the normative model defined in the PAP and includes an analysis of the causality relationships: we only refer to the impact of a legal norm or implementation act that concretises this norm if the observed change in behaviour corresponds to the normative model and it is truly attributable to the corresponding norm or act. Contrary to the opinion of numerous political-administrative actors, this equation is rarely verified. The changes of behaviour that appear in social reality are more often attributable to factors other than those assumed by public administrations. For example, in the case of environment policies aimed at developing ecological behaviour among private companies, other factors frequently enter into the equation; these include, in particular, the products of other policies (for example, acts associated with energy, agriculture and even fiscal policies), the evolution of market conditions (for example, the development of energy prices) or the social constraints imposed by competitors, consumers and neighbours who directly influence the target groups and have nothing to do with any policy (see Knoepfel, 1997a, for an analysis of the conditions for the success of environment policies).

Since the 1970s, studies have been carried out in numerous countries in the area of road traffic and have led to the analysis of the effects of different intervention instruments on driver behaviour: for example, the limits on drivers' blood alcohol level, mandatory wearing of seat belts and speed limits (DFJP, 1975; Universität Zürich, 1977; Volvo Car Corporation and Swedish Road Safety Office, 1980). This reflects not only the political interest that exists in these topics, but also the fact that they concern relatively simple questions. The relationships between public measures and individual behaviour are easily recorded and quantifiable using an uncomplicated research design (for example, before/after comparisons where suitable data is available or comparisons with – random or non-equivalent – control groups if there is no data available on the situation prior to the introduction of the public measure).

To analyse the impacts of a public measure, the analyst collects information on the real behaviour of target groups before and after the introduction of the measure. Traditionally, this information refers to data on violations, monitoring results, sanctions and unofficial estimations of criminal acts[2]. As already mentioned, the information on changes in behaviour occasionally triggered by measures introduced in connection with other (potentially contradictory) policies, or which are probably not attributable to policy measures (but, for example, evolving social value or economic factors), needs to be taken into account in the study of impacts.

Although the policy acts and impacts are produced by different actors, that is, the political-administrative authorities and members of the target groups, these two categories are very closely linked. State activities (implementation acts, outputs) are almost always necessary to bring about real changes in the behaviour of target groups (impacts): the effective observation of obligations and bans needs to be monitored, services provided, financial contributions allocated, fines collected and information disseminated. Conversely, a number of state measures are only produced when they are requested by private individuals and social groups: investigations are carried out in response to complaints, planning permission is granted in response to applications for the construction or use of buildings, contributions are promised in response to requests for funding, fines are imposed in response to reprehensible behaviour and information is disseminated when a demand for this information is perceived. In these cases, the absence of outputs can be explained not only in terms of the behaviour of public actors. Similarly, the absence of impacts is explained not only in terms of the inactivity of target groups. In numerous situations, these two types of actors act jointly. In cases involving the provision of public services (for example, training, social work, counselling of unemployed people, alcohol and drug rehabilitation, psychiatric clinics), the service providers (public administrations) and clients (the 'administered') interact so closely that the quality of the results often depends on their reciprocal cooperation. However, it is only by making an analytical distinction between the actors of the PAA and the external social actors that the analyst can highlight the efficacy or inefficacy of the modalities of the cooperation between the two groups and distinguish between this cooperation and other observable forms of cooperation, either between service providers within the PAA, or within different target groups.

The systematic study of the complex game of the activities of public administrations (resulting in outputs) and the behaviour of the groups targeted by state measures (impacts) does not (yet) examine the desired effects (outcomes) of a policy. At the same time, this comparison of outputs and impacts – which is in theory restrictive in terms of policy effects – is crucial because the inadequate results of a policy can often be put down to outputs that were not expected or missing or insufficient impacts. It is not rare for analysts to confirm that certain policies fail to produce any implementation acts or sufficient measures due to unsuitable implementation structures and procedures (note the implementation deficits in the strict sense as defined in Chapter Nine). As a result, such policies have only a weak chance of influencing their target groups.

We remind readers that the concept of target group is used throughout the book to encompass not only private actors who may be the direct cause of social problems but also actors, both public and private, who may be able to take action to address those problems regardless of their original causation. In the case of many social services the target groups may be public or quasi-public organisations required to alter the way they operate (with or without attendant costs). In other cases target groups may be required to accept additional costs but not necessarily change their behaviour (this is one of the options allowed for in the use of pollution charges). In some cases there may be no real costs or behaviour changes imposed (as in the case of the English law on access to uncultivated countryside, the 'right to roam'), where while certainly landowners may be seen as a target group in fact all that is required of them is that they tolerate walkers who impose no real costs on them. Sometimes there may simply be no explicit target groups, merely widely dispersed costs (affecting third parties and even perhaps beneficiaries – this is true, for example, of changes to social insurance schemes).

Policies also exist whose political-administrative actors engage in numerous activities but which fail to give rise to any of the expected changes in behaviour (implementation deficits in the wider sense as defined in this chapter). Such 'impact-less' policies result, for example, from a lack of acceptance by target groups of the selected policy instrument or the incorrect estimation of the target groups' capacity to organise themselves and their willingness to cooperate with the proposed measures[3].

As part of the empirical study of the profile of policy impacts, the analyst may reconsider several dimensions that have already been explored in the context of implementation acts (outputs, see Section 9.4, Chapter Nine):

- existing or missing impacts evaluated on the basis of the target groups' reaction or failure to react;
- lasting or fleeting impacts evaluated on the basis of the stabilisation of changes in behaviour or purely temporary adaptation of behaviour;
- the scope of impacts evaluated on the basis of their distribution in time, in space and between the social groups;
- substantive internal coherency between the different impacts triggered among one and the same target group, depending on whether a single message is sent to the target groups by the state or several contradictory messages are circulated by different uncoordinated public policies;
- external coordination of the impacts provoked simultaneously among different target groups, evaluated on the basis of the convergence of changes in the behaviour of the different target groups or the scale of the opposition to their modification.

10.1.2 Outcomes (observable effects among the end beneficiaries)

We define the 'outcomes' of a policy as all of the effects in relation to the public problem to be resolved that are attributable to the policy and triggered in turn by the implementation acts (outputs). The results (outcomes) literally represent that which 'comes out of' the state activity. Thus, the outcomes include all effects – desired and undesired, direct and indirect, primary and secondary, and so on. To identify and quantify the results targeted by a policy, the analyst generally refers to the definitions of objectives and evaluative elements provided by the PAPs and, if necessary, concretised in APs and implementation acts. It should be noted here that these definitions may not be used for this purpose if they are formulated in terms of the (number of) measures to be realised rather than substantive objectives.

The analysis of the effects may show that the existence of optimum outputs and impacts constitutes a necessary but insufficient condition for the achievement of adequate outcomes. Furthermore, the observable changes only contribute to the realisation of objectives if the hypotheses on the causes of the public problem to be resolved (any causal hypothesis that identifies target groups) prove relevant and no counterproductive effects emerge. It should be noted that the cause–effect relationships of a public problem, which a policy tries to influence, are often very complex and, thus, the results are difficult to record and appreciate.

The concept of 'outcomes' is an analytical category. It is only fleshed out by the indicators that provide data on the evolution of the collective problem that the policy aims to resolve. Among this data, it is essential that, in particular, the information on the situation of the social groups affected by the public problem in question – conditions that may have changed over time – be taken into account. These end beneficiaries of a policy may be social groups such as neighbours, tenants, residents or visitors (in the case of spatial development policy), customers (in the case of consumer protection policy) or patients (in the case of health policy). Given that, in most cases, these groups are not clearly identifiable with individual people, the use of aggregate indicators is desirable. However, it is sometimes possible to question the groups affected by certain public policies directly (for example, post office clients, the patients of service X in hospital Y).

However, all of this data concerning the objectives of a policy does not provide any indications on the existence of outcomes. It is not yet possible to conclude the extent to which the policy objectives have been achieved (or not achieved) thanks to the implementation of the policy in question by means of a simple comparison aimed at values and real values (indicators concerning objectives). These changes may also be the outcome of other factors. The results or real effects of a policy, that is, the effects that remain when all other possible influences have been accounted for (for example, economic situation, transformation of social values, personal effort of various social groups involved, collective learning process), may ultimately only be deduced through highly specific research. To this end, it is necessary implicitly or explicitly to compare the situation 'as is' ('policy on') with that which would have prevailed in the absence of the policy being studied ('policy off').

The analyst may use the following four dimensions as a source of guidance when researching empirical data on the effects of public intervention in the context of the public problem to be resolved:

- existing or missing results evaluated on the basis of the evolution of the nature and pressure of the policy;
- scope of effects evaluated on the basis of their distribution in time, in space and between social groups;
- lasting or transient effects evaluated on the basis of the permanent or temporary resolution of the public problem;
- substantive coherence of results in the context of the public problem addressed by the policy and of other social problems based on the resolution of the public problem, its simple displacement or an increase in the scope of another social problem.

Once identified and qualified, the impacts and outcomes must be related to the other elements of the policy (for example, PAP objectives, PAA resources) to enable a true evaluation of its effects. Thus, the criteria that link the different elements are discussed in the following section.

10.2 Policy evaluation criteria

In general, evaluative research makes a distinction between three types of criteria for appreciating the effects of a policy: (1) The *extent of impacts* analyses whether the impacts are triggered as planned by the PAP, APs and outputs produced ('doing something?'). (2) The *effectiveness* relates the observable outcomes to the aimed for objectives ('doing the right thing?'). (3) The *efficiency* compares the outcomes with the applied resources ('doing the thing right?'). In addition to these criteria that examine the policy effects, an evaluation may also analyse the *relevance* of the policy (relationship between the objectives of the PAP and the public problem to be resolved) and the *productive economy* of the administrative processes leading to the formalised acts (relationship between the outputs and resources deployed).

Having presented each of these criteria in detail, we will discuss the links between them while stressing the necessity to consider – from the point of view of policy analysis – the relevance, effectiveness, efficacy and allocative efficiency of a policy before examining its productive efficiency[4].

10.2.1 Impact (testing the intervention hypothesis)

Impact is one of the criteria applied in the evaluation of policy impacts. It measures the suitability of the normative objectives of a policy in terms of the real behaviour of target groups. The examination of the impact of a policy necessitates the systematic comparison of 'the effects as they should be' in accordance with the operational elements of the PAP and any APs that may exist, on the one hand, and the formal implementation acts and changes actually occurring, on the other. Different indicators may be used to measure and assess this impact, depending on the type of intervention instrument being studied, for example, the level of compliance in the case of obligations and bans, the level of use of the financial resources available for measures of a motivational nature or the degree of attention aroused by persuasive measures such as information campaigns.

Thus, the evaluation of impact involves a 'should be' assessment in the sense of the comparison of planned impacts and real impacts. The focus here is on quantitative and qualitative aspects. Quantitative evaluation analyses whether the desired changes can be observed in all instances in which implementation acts have been applied. Qualitative evaluation, on the other hand, is concerned with the (substantive) scope of these impacts. Thus, the criterion of impact includes a strong normative dimension. This is why it is accorded a high level of importance, in highly regulated public policies, for example in France, Germany and – in part also – in Switzerland: in these countries, implementation activities are often defined in a very detailed way at the levels of laws and regulations. The evaluation of impact proves more difficult if the execution is less well defined in legal terms, and if the implementing authorities enjoy greater scope for manoeuvre, for example in the UK. In such contexts, priority is given to evaluations of impact in the sense of the real respect of norms ('compliance') or the relevance of punishable facts ('abuse', 'fraud').

The adoption of a 'causal' perspective enables the analyst to reconstruct the *causal relationships* within public policies. From this perspective, the analysis of impacts is crucial because this policy constitutes a necessary condition for its effectiveness; the deficient effects of a policy may be explained by absent or insufficient impacts. In effect – and as already stated above – policies exist whose outputs do not trigger any of the anticipated changes (bad intervention hypothesis).

Common examples of policies with no impacts include, for example: road traffic regulations that are not observed by drivers such as speed reduction, mandatory seat-belt wearing, bans on drink-driving, and also, in part, fiscal policy (tax evasion) and agricultural policy (continuation of intensive practices despite subsidies paid for the provision of ecological services).

Urban traffic planning is another example of an area where policies without impacts can be found. For example, nowadays, the management of public parking spaces is one of the solutions adopted in order to direct, level off and reduce private motorised transport and, in particular, the volume of traffic arising from commuting. As a new transport policy measure, residents' parking disks are intended to restrict the periods during which non-residents can park in certain city neighbourhoods. The aim of this policy measure is to remove commuter traffic from residential neighbourhoods and to improve the quality of life of local residents and traders. Studies on the contribution made by the residents' parking-disk model to the reduction in the volumes of commuter traffic in the cities of Zurich, Basel and Bern (already quoted; see Section 8.1.2 in Chapter Eight; Schneider et al, 1990, 1995) conclude that this measure remains largely without impacts. Between 70% and 85% of commuters using private means of transport already had private parking spaces prior to the introduction of the disk. A clear majority of the target groups (that is, commuters) have their own private parking spaces or the use of one owned by their employers, thus they do not have to adapt their behaviour (by ensuring their mobility using public transport) (incorrect choice of instruments = bad intervention hypothesis).

These examples from everyday life emphasise once again that, in general, the ultimate aim of public policies is not to produce outputs, but to bring about real changes (which must be triggered by the policy acts) and thus resolve the collective problem that needs to be managed. While the production of formal acts may in itself occupy personnel and consume resources, and thus, in some cases, trigger economic activity, it should not and may not, however, be considered as an end in itself. Although this would appear obvious, the risk of it being forgotten is a very real one in the context of daily bureaucratic practice. Even the recent public management concepts, such as the 'output-oriented' variant of New Public Management, are not immune to this (Knoepfel, 1996, 1997b).

10.2.2 Effectiveness (testing the causal hypothesis)

The criterion of effectiveness is directly connected with the category of effects (outcomes). It refers to the relationship between the anticipated effects of a policy and those that emerge in social reality. The review and evaluation of the effectiveness of a policy are carried out on the basis of a comparison between the objectives defined in the PAP and the effects actually triggered among the policy's end beneficiaries.

In terms of its logical structure (in basing itself on explanations concerning the results), this criterion comprises, on the one hand, a *causal and analytical* reconstruction of the relationship between a policy and social reality. On the other hand, it refers in normative terms to the difference thus identified between the policy objectives and the real resolution of the problem.

The objectives formulated during the political process, however, only rarely respect the complex logical structure required for the application of the criterion of effectiveness. As a rule, the general objectives are defined without specifying the *contribution* that the policy should make to their realisation. Thus, it is entirely possible for the objectives to be fulfilled without any essential contribution being made by the policy. Conversely, it is also possible for a situation to arise whereby the policy objectives were not realised, but without the policy, the problem would have become considerably more serious. In such cases, objectives that have been formulated in absolute terms are of no assistance when it comes to quantifying the extent to which the policy is effective. In this case, it would be necessary when defining the policy objectives to indicate the relative improvement that the policy should make it possible to achieve[5]. The objectives formulated in the PAPs only rarely meet this requirement, however. Furthermore, they are often inexplicit, unclear, unquantified and temporally unstable as they represent the outcome of political compromise (Hellstern and Wollmann, 1983, pp 11-22).

Thus, evaluations may show that in the context of public policies, administrative acts (outputs) are produced and changes in behaviour triggered among target groups (impacts) to the desired extent, but that none of the anticipated results are produced. The reason behind this politically very explosive situation often lies in the incorrect nature of the hypotheses formulated on the contribution of the target groups to the emergence of the collective problem to be resolved (bad causal hypothesis possibly due to false identification of these groups), the aggravation of the problem due to exogenous factors or the incorrect nature of the scientific hypothesis concerning the sequence of the policy effects.

In Switzerland, the policy for the public promotion of the hotel sector is an example of a policy without effects. The economic and financial situation of a number of hotels is worrying in certain tourist regions in Switzerland. Low profits and even losses make it difficult to finance the investments that would be necessary to improve the quality of the hotel services provided. The Swiss Confederation and various cantons provide financial support to the hoteliers with such promotion projects (for example, zero-interest loans, contribution to bank costs). As a result, they aim to improve the international competitiveness of the Swiss hotel industry. An evaluation of the public support of the hotel trade (Hanser et al, 1994) shows that intensive use is made of this public investment support. Three quarters of projects completed could not have been realised without state aid on the planned scale or within the proposed period. Following the realisation of investment projects, the supported hotels obviously show a better financial situation than hotels that do not receive any support. In the medium term, however, no statistical study can show that they have enjoyed a sustained improvement in their profits. Thus, property investments alone are not sufficient to improve the competitiveness of a hotel. Moreover, on a sectoral level, there is a risk of the emergence of indirect or non-desirable effects in terms of the stagnation of hotel system as a whole. Thus, this public support strategy can demonstrate outputs (large volume of investments supported and numbers of projects realised) that have a positive impact; however, it is not effective at the level of the resolution of the problem (that is, it makes no long-term contribution to the competitiveness of the hotel trade).

Such evaluation results are probably more alarming than those relating to ineffective public policies (without impacts). In effect, they generate frustration and a feeling of injustice and prompt accusations of bureaucratic expropriation, particularly among target groups, that can trigger a rejection of all public intervention. Indications of this phenomenon can be observed, for example, when drivers take warnings about smog seriously and reduce their speed in accordance with the regulations and then read in the newspaper that the ozone levels have reached a record high and that official speed limits have had no influence in this context.

Finally, policies also exist whose results correspond to the defined objectives because they produce acts and impacts that are truly capable of improving the problematic situation in the desired way.

An example of an effective policy is that of public support for home ownership in Switzerland. In 1970 an average of 28.1% of households were homeowners. This percentage was very low compared with other European countries. Thus, the Swiss Confederation passed a law supporting residential construction and access to home ownership[6]. This law contained the following measures to reduce the initial costs incurred by future homeowners: a federal guarantee, a reduction in the price of land and non-reimbursable supplementary reductions. The main objective of this policy was to increase residential property ownership in Switzerland. According to an evaluation of this law (Schulz et al, 1993), the federal support of access to home ownership had the desired effect. Up to 1991, some 15,747 construction projects were financially supported by the Confederation (outputs). Access to home ownership with the help of public support was primarily of assistance to young households that, in view of their limited finances, would not otherwise have had an opportunity to become homeowners (impacts). Thanks to this measure the proportion of homeowners increased during the study period (around 15 years) to reach 31.3% (= outcomes in accordance with the objective). Furthermore, the law has had other indirect positive effects. Thus, in a period of recession, the support of access to home ownership constitutes an important support for the economy[7]. This was the case, for example, during 1991, a weak period in the construction sector because 20% of family housing built was supported by federal aid. A similar conclusion could be drawn about the UK legislation on the sale of public rented 'council' houses to their occupiers, a success in terms of the goals of the government of the time (although heavily criticised by those who saw such a measure as undermining local government capacities to respond to the needs of the homeless – but of course exploring that involves the imposition of an evaluation criteria not implicit in the policy goal) (Forrest and Murie, 1988).

10.2.3 Efficiency (outcomes/resources)

The criterion of *efficiency* refers to the relationship between the resources invested in a policy and the effects achieved. Thus, it describes the relationship between the costs and benefits of a policy. The comparison is generally concentrated on the main effects desired by the PAP. In this context, we speak of efficiency in relation to objectives or the effects. Thus, the question arises as to whether the same effects could be achieved using fewer resources or whether fulfilment of the objectives could be even better using the same resources. Two methods are mainly applied in evaluative research to judge the efficiency of policies or some of their measures (see Rossi and Freeman, 1993, pp 363-401). *Cost-benefit analyses* quantify costs and the effects (= benefits), and then compare them. Thus, for example, the costs of clearing the snow on Swiss Alpine passes were compared with the resulting benefits (mainly in the area of tourism). In actual fact the monetisation of utility often poses a very tricky problem for researchers. Thus, the second of these methods, *cost-utility analysis*, is less exacting. Cost-utility analysis compares different measures (for example, speed limits, road widening, mandatory wearing of seat belts on back seats) in terms of the achievement of a specified effect (for example, reduction of the number of road deaths by a defined proportion). Thus, it can facilitate the identification of the most efficient measure for attaining an objective. Central to this comparative procedure is not the absolute values of the cost and benefits of measures, which are difficult to determine, but the relative differences (more expensive/less expensive) between the values of the alternative measures, differences that are easier to establish.

Such reflections on the efficiency of a policy are only relevant if its degree of effectiveness has already been empirically confirmed. In terms of policy analysis, the policies are only efficient from an allocative point of view, firstly, if they are effective and, secondly, if the material and immaterial policy resources are employed in an optimum way.

For example, a policy that displays allocative efficiency is the combination of a tax on household waste bags, separate waste collections and public information campaigns. In Switzerland, since the 1980s, an increasing number of local authorities have moved from a system of all-in taxes on waste (per household or residential unit) to a system of proportional taxes based on the volume of the waste deposited. The majority of these authorities apply various associated measures along with this incentive-based instrument, such as, for example, separate collection (paper, glass, metal etc), public information and motivation campaigns. An evaluative study examined the implementation, principal and secondary effects and relative costs of these three instruments, both individually and in comparison. The effectiveness and efficiency of these local authority waste management policies (at the time considered as alternatives) were evaluated as follows: the tax on waste disposal bags displays the best results when it is combined with a system of separate collection and information measures. It reduces the volume of unsorted waste at a lower cost than could be achieved by significantly increasing the number of waste collection sites and information campaigns. The optimum combination of these three individual measures (allocation tax, sorted collections and information) minimises the cost of the processing of waste, calculated by ton of collected waste. Previous experience demonstrated that one waste collection site for around 2,000-3,000 inhabitants represents an efficient solution. Since then, other studies have been published on the subject that (with a considerably extended database) show comparable results.

In addition to the criteria of effectiveness and efficiency, which make it possible to evaluate policy effects, we discuss briefly below the criteria of relevance and productive economy, which also involve the products of the policy programming (objectives of the PAP; see Chapter Seven, this volume) and implementation (outputs; see Chapter Nine, this volume) stages. They are discussed here because they are an integral part of the 'evaluative statements' produced during the final stage of a policy process.

10.2.4 Relevance (objectives/public problem) and productive economy (outputs/resources)

The criterion of *relevance* examines the link that exists – or should exist – between the objectives defined in the PAP, on the one hand, and the nature and pressure of the public problem to be resolved, on the other. Thus, a policy is described as relevant if the objectives implicitly formulated in the PAP, and sometimes concretised in the APs, are adapted to the nature and temporal and socio-spatial distribution of the problem that the policy is intended to resolve. In fact, the question of the relevance of a policy is the most 'political' and hence most delicate and sensitive dimension that an evaluation may have to examine. For this reason, political-administrative leaders and officials often exclude it from the area of evaluation to be studied by an external expert in the context of a commissioned study.

As the definition of objectives in the PAP (and possibly in the APs) generally involves a political compromise negotiated during the programming phase, the relevance of a policy directly depends on the power relationships between the political–administrative actors. Thus, it cannot be thoroughly examined by means of a simple evaluation. In effect, it is not possible to substitute a rational or technocratic approach, as applied to the definition of public problems to be resolved and policy objectives (for example, according to the Rationalisation of Budgetary Choices and Planning, Programming and Budgeting System models), for the legislative process and the primary legitimation of state actions arising from it. The modification of a public action clearly does not consist in a technical-scientific exercise; instead it involves the democratic arbitration of conflicts of values and interests between the actors who are concerned by a social situation judged as problematic. Nevertheless, the evaluation of relevance may show that the (sometimes implicit) objectives of a policy are not adequately formulated on the basis of the public problem to be resolved. This is the case, for example, if the policy objectives are not very realistic (zero risk in environmental matters) or if they fail to take the institutional data specific to the legislative process (in terms of the political definition of the public problem [PD]) or implementation process into account. A problem that has been given much attention by the UK policy evaluation literature has also been rapid policy succession so that new policies are set up on top of older ones before the latter can be effectively evaluated.

The criterion of *productive economy*, which is rooted in a more managerial rationale, relates the outputs produced to the resources invested. Thus, this criterion makes it possible to evaluate administrative implementation processes. The effects realised in society or in the natural environment are, however, excluded from these calculations because the analyst concentrates solely on administrative acts (outputs) produced by the policy. Furthermore, only the costs or direct resources and materials (for example, cost of the production of a tax form, a fine, planning permission) are considered, and not the costs associated with the material resources. The taking into account of all of the costs incurred in a public action is central, however, when it comes to the benchmarking of processes in different (decentralised) public bodies.

Since the 1980s, several reform programmes have been promoted with the aim of rationalising and increasing the productive economy of administrations. In fact, a high level of internal rationalisation (= high productive economy) and, as a result, low-cost public activity, merely leads to entirely futile bureaucratic activism if it fails to produce no effect or poorly directed effects (= weak efficiency). Thus, from the perspective of policy analysis, attestation of the efficient and rapid

Public policy analysis

processing of administrative procedures could not constitute an end in itself.

10.2.5 Evaluation criteria: overview and application logic

As a summary of the preceding discussion, Figure 10.1 presents the relationships that exist between the constituent elements of a policy and the evaluation criteria, whose purpose it is to assess the capacity of the state to resolve public problems. We stress again here that all evaluations should involve the successive analysis of the criteria of relevance, impact, effectiveness and efficiency, followed by productive economy. In effect, it is a question of finding out first and foremost if the policy enables the effective resolution – or at least partial resolution – of the social problem in question and, secondly only, whether the allocation of resources between the actors of the policy's PAA is optimal.

Having presented the operational dimensions of impacts and the results as well as the evaluation criteria of a policy, we will now set out a typology of these elements in order to distinguish different types of evaluative statements observable in reality.

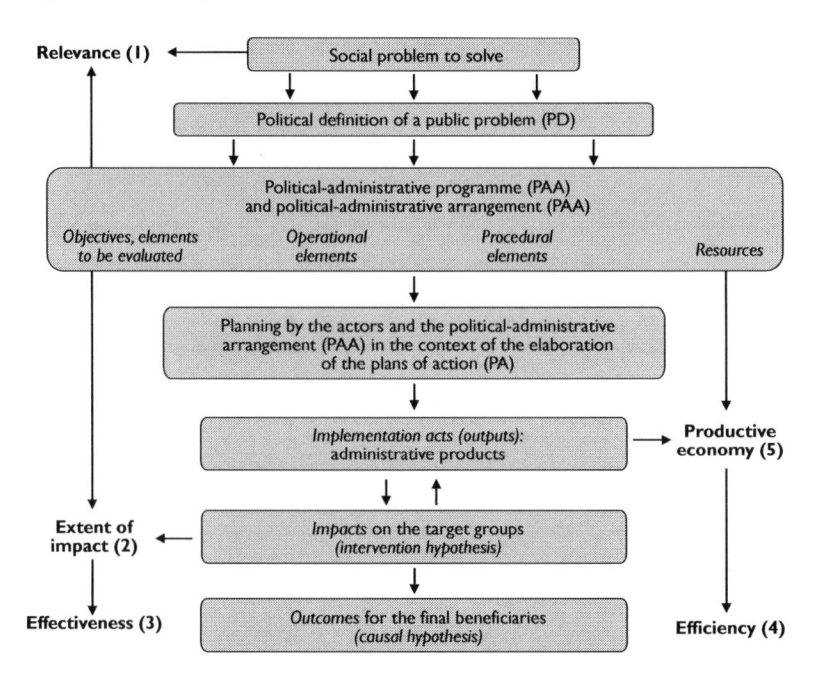

Figure 10.1: Objectives and criteria of evaluation

10.3 Evaluative statements on the effects of a public policy (product no 6)

As a product of the evaluation phase of a policy, 'evaluative statements' may be analytically interpreted on the basis of several dimensions that are connected in terms of their substantive and institutional content. Without making any claim to being exhaustive, we identify below some ideal types of evaluative statements that may guide the analyst in the course of an empirical study of the last stage of a policy cycle. We would also like to stress here that these different dimensions are more complementary than competitive in nature, hence the necessity to consider them simultaneously.

(a) *Reference criteria of statements (relevance, impact, effectiveness, efficiency)*: all evaluative statements can be classified primarily in terms of whether they refer to one or other element of the causal chain of policy effects. In concrete terms, it is a question of identifying whether the formulated assessments deal with the relevance of the objectives of the PAP, impacts and/or outcomes (effectiveness) and whether, with respect to the latter, the end effects reflect the invested resources (efficiency). This first dimension aims to highlight the level at which the policy is actually evaluated and, hence, avoid the confusion that is frequently observed between the results (outputs), intermediate effects (impacts) and end effects (outcomes) of a policy.

(b) *Scientific (causal nature) or political (ideological) statements:* while certain evaluative statements are based on scientific analyses that try to establish causal links between the implemented policy (outputs) and resulting effects (impacts and outcomes) on the basis of reproducible empirical data, other statements are strictly ideological and based on the partisan perceptions of their authors. Such statements do not generally identify the conclusions that may be drawn from a rigorous analysis of the sequence of causes and effects, and the normative recommendations that can be formulated to remedy any deficiencies observed. On the contrary, they are based on the analyst's own opinion, on subjective (hence partial and non-transparent) assessments or on normative arguments. The practical application of this distinction, which is often contested by the initiators of such approaches, is not always easy, however. It may even be contested at the theoretical level by reference to certain theories of a deontological nature (denouncing the distinction as positivistic and contrary to the notion that all evaluations incorporate a political value judgement in the broad sense of the term). The analyst should take these criticisms seriously and be accordingly cautious, in particular when it comes to so-called 'scientific' statements.

(c) *Summary or formative statements:* evaluative readings may also differ on the basis of the actual aims of the evaluation (commissioned by mandate). The latter may try to compile a summary of the previous policy (summary statement) and/or prospectively identify options with respect to the improvement and adaptation of the policy in question and, thus, initiate a learning process (Lascoumes and Setbon, 1996; Kissling-Näf, 1997).

Evaluations of a summary nature are very common in both France and Switzerland. Thus, for example, in Switzerland the evaluation of the Federal Swiss programme entitled 'Energy in the City' produced a summary that was, all things considered, positive with regard to the contribution of this programme to raising the awareness of local authority representatives of energy issues and the placing of energy policy on the agenda at local authority level. This study clearly showed, however, that it is impossible to create a quantitative summary of the results (kWh saved) of this programme (Knoepfel et al, 1999). In France, the majority of evaluations carried out since 1990 under the aegis of the interministerial system were also of a summary nature[8]. Environmental impact studies that must be carried out by all major projects – in both France and Switzerland – are typical examples of prospective type evaluations. In the course of such evaluations, the actors become aware of previously unknown impacts of implementation projects relating to policies of a spatial nature. This information (which was either unavailable or inexplicit prior to the prospective evaluation) may result in the considerable alteration of the actors' positions and lead to the emergence of a consensus with respect to the important future repercussions of evaluative statements (see Kissling-Näf, 1997).

(d) *Ex-ante, concomitant and ex-post readings:* the analyst may also classify the different evaluative readings on the basis of the time at which they were put forward. In effect, the evaluation may unfold before the policy is even implemented (*ex-ante* evaluation), accompany its execution (concomitant evaluation) or be carried out once implementation is completed (*ex-post* evaluation). Evaluations that are carried out at least three to five years after the application of the PAP – and the eventual APs – are the most appropriate in political-administrative practice (a certain gap is generally necessary so that all of the policy effects fully unfold). This empirical review legitimises, therefore, the fact that evaluative statements are defined as the last product to be explained in the analysis of the policy cycle.

The *ex-ante* evaluation process, which is often referred to as 'legislative evaluation', is becoming more and more common as a means of testing variants for new intervention instruments and modifications to the circle of target groups discussed by the expert commissions responsible for the preparation of new legislation. In these cases, methods are adopted that enable the simulated application of several proposed variants in the real context of several implementation regions or zones selected on the basis of their diverging characteristics. An example of this is the application by simulation of a new regulation on hydro-electric power to a number of Swiss factories by the Federal Department of the Environment, Transport, Energy and Communication's 'hydro-electric power' conciliation group (see the evaluation report by Knoepfel et al, 1997). Other examples will be found in the area of family policy, unemployment policy (creation of pilot employment agency schemes in the two Swiss cantons of Soluthurn and Vaud prior to the general establishment of this new regime) and fiscal policy.

On the other hand, concomitant evaluations are implemented for numerous social and economic policies, for which statistical follow-up is organised. This type of evaluation is mandatory in the case of the implementation of the European Commission's structural funds.

(e) *Partial or global readings:* the operational elements of a PAP often comprise several different measures with different aims. Thus, it is necessary to ascertain whether the evaluative statements assess implementation instruments only, all of the measures contained in an AP or the entire policy. Thus, in theory and in practice, a distinction is made – in particular on the basis of national traditions – between evaluations of isolated public measures, programmes ('programme evaluation') and policies ('policy evaluation').

(f) *Formal statements (associated with evaluation clauses) or informal statements (provided by uncomissioned reports):* the weight of an evaluative statement depends, inter alia, on how 'official' it is. In effect, it may be assumed that an evaluation that has been commissioned and financed by public actors (for example, implementing administrations, government or parliament) will enjoy greater credibility and provoke a wider response than a policy assessment that is formulated independently of any institutional frame (for example, by an independent consultancy or uncommissioned academic researcher). A general trend consisting in the inclusion in legislation and formal regulations of 'evaluation clauses', stipulating that these legal provisions must be subject to an (external) scientific evaluation after a specified number of years, should be noted (Bussmann, 1998, p 26). This is the case, in particular, with new social policies whose legitimacy is often questioned (for example, health insurance and humanitarian aid policy in Switzerland, social support policy in France).

(g) *Substantive or institutional statements:* in addition to evaluative statements that are substantive in nature (assessment of concrete observed effects), statements of an institutional nature will also be found in practice. The latter primarily define the conditions or rules to be observed during the process of policy reformulation. Such statements stipulate, for example, that, based on the effects confirmed by the analysis of the policy, "the review commission must take into account the interests of …", "the new legislation must include the concerned milieus …", "the policy must respect the rules of the European Union and the WTO" or again that "the strategy adopted should be located in the international context …".

Several of the empirical evaluation dimensions proposed below depend directly on the political–administrative context of the evaluation, its process and the actors involved in the relevant sequence of events. Thus, the following paragraphs deal with the interaction of actors in the course of policy evaluation. As is the case with the products of the previous policy stages, the (direct and indirect) games of evaluation actors should be interpreted on the basis of their interest in demonstrating whether the policy is effective, whether it should be modified and hence note the resources and institutional rules they mobilise to influence the content of evaluative statements.

10.4 Evaluation process: the actors, resources and institutions mobilised

10.4.1 Institutionalisation of the evaluation

Just like the programming stage, the policy evaluation process and political value of its results (or evaluative statements) depends to a great extent on the institutional rules of the democratic regime in question. The institutionalisation of evaluation in the US through the General Accounting Office (GAO) is very different to the process observable in Switzerland with its *Organe parlementaire de contrôle de l'administration* (OPCA) and in France with its *Conseil national de l'évaluation* (see Bussmann, 1998, pp 13-32 for Switzerland and Monnier, 1992, pp 63-8 for France). In the UK, official evaluation activity is divided between the National Audit Office for much central government activity and the Audit Commission with particular responsibilities for local government and the NHS.

Beyond this institutional data on the place of evaluation in the conduct of public policies, we discuss below the strategic aims of actors with respect to the evaluative process (adopting the arguments of Bussmann et al, 1998, pp 113-17).

10.4.2 Actor constellations and games

Policy evaluation actually represents both a primary policy instrument, that is, information, management and legitimisation (with respect to the subsequent legislative process), and a secondary policy instrument, that is, enabling the validation of the policy by social actors. It makes information available on the relevance, impact, effectiveness and efficiency of the state activity. There can be no question that this kind of information can represent both an end in itself and/or be used in teaching and research when accumulated in the university context. As a general rule, policy evaluations are, however, carried out with a concrete or political objective in mind: for example, to initiate a measure, legitimise a decision, improve implementation, monitor, reduce subsidies. Policy evaluations are intended to prepare the foundations of future decisions and/or legitimise measures already adopted.

Just like individual state measures or entire public policies, evaluations also have desired and undesired, direct and indirect effects that relate to the main objectives and other policy effects. It is impossible to describe in detail all of the objectives aimed at with evaluations as well as their potential effects. Thus, we will restrict ourselves to ideal-type constellations that are known to us from experience. Today, evaluations are part of the repertoire of public activities and, like all other instruments at the disposal of public or private actors, they are human artefacts. Their realisation does not depend on their own nature but on the will of certain people and social groups to attain strategic objectives in specific situations. Thus, any typology of the objectives and potential effects of evaluations remains incomplete because, in practice, the instruments are continually renewed and reformulated.

There are several possible starting points for describing the objectives and effects of evaluations (for example, political domains, historical constitutions). We decided to present the most neutral systematisation possible (that is, independent of historical periods or specific policy domains), which concentrates on (a) the measures and policies to be evaluated, (b) the actors affected by the evaluations and their strategies, and (c) the partisan and general ideologies to which the evaluations refer.

(a) Measures or policies to be evaluated

The objectives or consequences of policy evaluations can involve the reformulation or modification of existing policies, the improvement of their implementation or their consideration. There is broad consensus in the literature on the central uses of evaluations (Chelimsky, 1987; Rist, 1990; Bussmann, 1995, pp 36-45). In practice, however, differences in opinion arise with respect to the temporal dimension of evaluations; the established evaluation types are often only attributed to certain phases of the policy cycle (formulation of measures, improvement of implementation, report). It is assumed, for example, that only prospective evaluations are relevant in terms of the programming of a new policy. As opposed to this, we would like to defend the idea that different types of evaluation may be combined to attain the three main objectives stated above. We will demonstrate this with the help of the following three examples:

- During the *revision or modification of a public action* (prospective dimension), an evaluation of the effectiveness and efficiency of earlier interventions may indicate the sequence of causes and effects, and analyses of the impact may show how the implementation process developed. Finally, syntheses of evaluations may summarise the results of previous evaluations and experience already accumulated in nearby areas or other countries.

- Similarly, different types of evaluation exist that serve in the *accompaniment and improvement of a public action*. Such evaluations primarily involve the collection of monitoring data, which provide information on the nature of the public problem to be resolved (for example, evolution of the environment), or data on impact that define the scope of implementation (what was done?). These data provide an overview of the (causal–analytical) relationships of policy execution. All of this information may then be used to accompany a policy measure and to improve its implementation.
- The *report*, which is the main evaluation instrument, comprises a (retrospective) evaluation of effectiveness and, if necessary, efficiency and productive economy. Evaluations of outputs and of the corresponding monitoring data are often deemed adequate here. The effects that alternative measures would have had are also occasionally considered (hypothetical constructs, econometric simulation models, and so on). In such cases, habitual, retrospective (empirical confirmation of effects) and prospective (hypothetical experiments) are combined.

(b) Evaluations and actors

For the actors, policy evaluations represent a particular form of advice and (social) scientific expertise (see Bussmann, 1989, 1995; Kissling-Näf and Wildi-Ballabio, 1993; and also Linder, 1989; Kessler et al, 1998). Thus, evaluations may be based on different intentions. (1) An evaluation may remain in an exclusive and narrow advisory context, its information and recommendations for action remain solely at the disposal of the actor/actors who commissioned it. (2) In the majority of cases, the information is, however, made available to the public. Its availability may be motivated by the intention of strengthening or undermining the strategic political position of a particular actor. (3) An evaluation may, however, also provide 'neutral' information on the objective facts determined. (4) Furthermore, the perpetuation of an advisory relationship may contribute to the formation of a scientific-administrative coalition whose objective is to protect the competency of all eventual criticism. (5) Finally, advice on policy may be instrumentalised by an actor as a symbolic action to simply win some time.

1. *Creating a direct advantage with regard to information:* when policy evaluations are carried out in the context of a direct consultancy

relationship that is out of the glare of publicity (if not actually confidential) and exclusive to the participating actors, they evade all critical observation by the social science community. Moreover, information about them will not be found either in publications or newspaper articles. It is most probably accessed through confidential knowledge within the administration or during discussions with practitioners about the social scientific advice given. Such consultancy activities are more commonly associated with private consultancies than with university institutes, because for the latter the renunciation of the valuation of results in the form of freely accessible publications is not an attractive condition.

The majority of such expertise involves *advice on matters of organisation and management*. Evaluations in the sense of studies of policy implementation and effects still tend to be uncommon (Zimmermann and Knoepfel, 1997). Such studies create the preconditions for an identification of weaknesses and their correction. Although administrative services ensure they have the right to treat evaluation data in an exclusive manner, they will disseminate it if this involves some kind of gain (improvement of their image, arguments to reinforce their own position). Such knowledge obtained from an evaluation gives its exclusive user a considerable advantage vis-à-vis other public and social actors. Apart from this kind of evaluation based on exclusive advice, technical evaluations also exist whose results are freely accessible (for example, the feasibility of bus routes, evaluation of specific teaching methods), but never make it into the public domain due to the lack of interest accorded to them by the media.

2. *Strengthening one's own strategic position:* many evaluations are commissioned because organisations believe that they will be advantageous. Such evaluations must, therefore, support the commissioning organisation's position or, at least, neutralise those of opposing actors. The four following examples that are typical of this type of evaluation are taken from practice:
   • *Mobilisation of support for a particular project/defined measure:* in 1988, the Swiss Federal Office for Economic Affairs commissioned Dieter Freiburghaus to carry out an evaluation of the Commission for the Promotion of Scientific Research (CERS). In the context of a new credit scheme, the authority wanted an independent assessment of the promotional services provided. In terms of time, the completion of the study was coordinated with the formulation of the government memo to parliament, and the results (Freiburghaus et al, 1990) were

used in this memo as an argument for the continuation of the credit scheme. The improvements recommended in the frame of the evaluation were also taken into account. The same analysis may be applied in the case of the first policies evaluated in the context of the Interministerial Committee for Evaluation in France. In the case of most of the policies proposed for evaluation (policy for the integration of disabled people, policy for the protection of wetlands, and so on) the aim was legitimacy and affirmation of their existence.

- *Mobilisation of opposition to a defined project:* evaluations are also used to block certain projects that place specific actors at a disadvantage. For example, when confronted with increasing costs for the conservation of monuments, the Department of Finance of the Swiss canton of Solothurn commissioned an evaluation of the efficacy of this expenditure. Just before the introduction of a ban on phosphates in washing powders in the mid-1980s, one of the authors found himself involved in a potential attempt to block this initiative. Having seen the warning signs of such a measure in other countries, the major detergent manufacturers became concerned and started to look for arguments to prevent the banning of phosphates in Switzerland. They tried to persuade some of the authors of this book to participate in such a study; the controversial context prevented the acceptance of such a commission and the study was ultimately carried out by a team from a private consultancy. However, they did not allow themselves to be used by the detergent industry either. In the end, it proved impossible to destabilise the proposed ban on phosphates.
- *Mobilisation of support to respond to the needs of a defined policy:* with the expansion of the welfare state from the late 1970s, previously isolated policy areas evolved together. Today, policy does not unfold in clearly delineated arenas, but increasingly in an intersectoral context ('interpolicy' coordination), that is, the area where specific political domains (for example, transport, health, agriculture, water protection) meet and intersect. Various debates now take place on the margins of policy domains: should financial policy be entirely responsible for the organisation of social 'benefits'? Should the environmental and health costs associated with road transport be internalised in the provision of such services? Should agriculture be conceived in a way that is more environmentally friendly? These and many other questions arise along the

boundaries between different public policies, which may be defined differently, depending on the point of view and perspective. Evaluations can and often should provide arguments on how these boundaries should be drawn. The evaluative study on water protection in the context of agriculture, which was initiated in 1987 (Knoepfel and Zimmermann, 1993) at the invitation of the Swiss Agency for the Environment, Forest and Landscape (OFEFP), is an example of this. In its exploration of the protection of water bodies and agriculture, this study clearly demonstrates the relatively weak position of environment policy as compared with agricultural policy. It also formulates proposals for the reinforcement of the environmental perspective, which despite being adopted by agriculture policy actors will, however, only be implemented belatedly and partially.

- *Conduct of 'an evaluation of the political and economic frame conditions':* here too, it is a question of points of view and perspectives, this time, however, not between sectoral public policies but between the social sub-systems (economics, politics, culture, religion, education) and their individual rationales. In fact, economic analyses referred to in German using the term *ordnungspolitische Standortbestimmung* (a kind of inventory of frame conditions) are dominant here. Such analyses are carried out on a number of subjects: for example, lease rights, labour markets, product markets, pension funds, telecommunications. As a general rule, they involve the comparison of theoretical axioms and public regulations, an approach that does not constitute policy analysis in the sense defined in this book. However, the theoretical reflections are also partly complemented by empirical studies, namely effectiveness analyses, so as to substantiate the theoretical propositions (that is, international comparative studies on the relationship between the labour market regulations and the share/number of unemployed people). Seen from this perspective, these studies are evaluative in character. They are often closely associated with the interests of actors in favour of 'deregulation'.

3. *Discovery of the 'truth':* evaluations also exist that are carried out with no intention of creating any advantages for an organisation or institution. Such evaluations follow the more routine channels of research or scientific assessment. This research primarily serves the purposes of the scientific system that tries to supply the

other sub-systems with 'objective' information. Assessments – where possible objective (although controversial from a substantive perspective) with respect to the defined criteria – are increasingly carried out by the major supra-international organisations (for example, OECD, World Bank).

Academic and scientific institutions (for example, university institutes, public or private research centres) produce copious research results, some of which are 'relevant' to specific policies (for example, type of transmission of BSE, greenhouse gas effect and atmosphere) because they demonstrate the opportunities and risks involved in the state activity. Strictly academic research may undoubtedly offer valuable services during the stage of identification of problems by providing information bases that support the state measures. Once the corresponding measures are in place, the studies may also comment on their effects. The research on policy effects/impacts also belongs to this category because it indicates the cost and utility of isolated measures (for example, fiscal effects, cost/benefit of the maintenance of national roads, effects of pension systems) for segments of the population (social stratums, regions, for example). This kind of research on effects is primarily motivated by academic interests; however, the fact that researchers have implicit political preferences or that research results actually exercise an influence on the strategic position of certain actors should not be forgotten. Nevertheless, such research is formally carried out in the context of teaching, publication and well-established research requirements (Swiss National Science Foundation, UK Economic and Social Research Council), thus the primacy of its academic orientation is generally assumed.

In addition to its purpose in the context of academic research, this type of research also increasingly serves the purposes of the evaluative activity of *state monitoring bodies*. In this context it is also finally important to mention the evaluations carried out by countries in the context of international comparisons in accordance with defined requirements. The OECD national studies that are carried out periodically or sporadically in different policy areas (for example, finance, economic, education, agriculture, regional, environment policy) are of particular importance here. One part of these studies presents, in effect, the characteristics of the 'inventories of frame conditions' mentioned above, to the extent that they compare public measures with the models being deduced from all of the accumulated information.

The supranational reviews of this type tend to update their store of experience by including success stories obtained with the help of non-conventional measures (for example, Jänicke and Weidner, 1995).

4. *Formation of coalitions through study commissions:* up to now, we have focused our attention on the objectives and effects of individual studies. However, much of the consultancy, research and evaluative activities take place in well-structured contexts (for example, specialisation of evaluators in defined areas of policy and research). This leads to the emergence of constant expectations (on the part of researchers and the groups they are addressing) and defined types of career (for example, ranging from positions in university research institutes to roles in state or para-public organisations). The task of research and evaluation will be entrusted to a PAA actor who can provide the other public and social actors with a continuous flow of information and arguments, and in this way the researchers obtain a constant stream of commissions. In the long term, evaluations make it possible to guarantee the positions of research communities.

5. *The use of delaying tactics when commissioning studies:* like all state measures, the announcement and conduct of an evaluative study may be used as a symbolic act (Edelman, 1964, 1971; Kinderman, 1988). In this case, the evaluation does not fulfil any of its primary – that is, instrumental, clarifying or legitimising – functions. Instead it is mentioned in conjunction with the vague promise of scientific explanations as a way of reducing the pressure of political demands and winning time. The announcement of the conduct of an evaluation shows that the problem requires a serious explanation and that all measures necessary in this regard should be undertaken. The symbolic function of the evaluation does not exclude, however, the emergence of effects: the announcement of an evaluation may, for example, be a measure that creates confidence (and which may also raise expectations) or a warning against hasty legislative action. Given the solid reputation of scientific work, the request for a scientific analysis or the consideration of these requests with reference to the necessity of such analyses has become relatively common in daily political practice. It is without doubt difficult to provide proof of a purely symbolic function of an evaluation in concrete cases. The analyst would have to demonstrate in effect that any use, including that of legitimisation, was excluded from the outset. Like symbolical legislation (Kindermann, 1988, p 229), the

symbolic function of evaluation is only rarely found in its ideal form, and constitutes instead a continuum that extends up to its efficacious use.

(c) Evaluations and the general political context

At best, evaluations may affirm the relationships between state policy measures and the social effects they give rise to. In fact, their interpretation is generally carried out in a broad political context (see Taylor and Balloch, 2005). Politics is a battle for power. In this context, political concepts and partisan ideologies represent attempts on the part of the competing parties to make sense. Like scientific claims, such concepts are often expressed in terms of an 'if-then' equation (for example, if the state's share is reduced, then the economy will perform better). They consist of guiding lines in the form of causal relationships at a macro-social level. Unlike scientific results, they are, however, based on experiences, suppositions or beliefs. This is why it is possible to assert that it is entirely legitimate for the field of partisan ideologies to take root in cases in which the explanations advanced by scientific-methodological approaches have reached an end.

In general, the empirical results of scientifically based evaluations are only produced for very narrowly defined analysis objects. Thus, the interpretation and (to an even greater extent) the adaptation (generalisation, external validation) of the results of evaluations is normally carried out in reference to such political concepts. For example, if an evaluation concludes that measure A cannot expect the growth envisaged by X per cent of indicator Z (such clearly expressed conclusions are, however, rare), two different conclusions may be drawn: either measure A should either be abandoned or its implementation intensified. Thus, in the majority of cases the use of the results of any evaluation presupposes a political *value judgement*.

In the UK extensive doubts and anxieties have been expressed about both the government's perspective on evaluation and the problems of objectivity in the social sciences (if not all sciences). Solutions to these problems proposed include arguing the case for making evaluative objectives very clear (something implicit in everything in this chapter) but also for adopting a 'critical modernist' stance that recognises multiple and conflicting evaluation criteria, holding "to the importance of the empirical testing of theories and hypotheses, although recognising that this is only one kind of test, and that arguments concerning whether the appropriate conditions for falsification have been met will never cease" (Pollitt and Bouckaert, 2000, p 23).

Notes

[1] A part of this text is adapted from the corresponding chapters in Bussmann et al (1998) (which also contains in-depth historical, conceptual and methodological accounts of policy evaluation that are not included in this chapter).

[2] Such data is difficult to obtain because it is a known fact that the effective degree of social prescription of punishable facts often varies significantly (refer to the research by Killias and Grapendaal, 1997; Killias, 1998).

[3] On the relationship between the characteristics of target groups and the effectiveness/efficacy of policies, see Scharpf (1983) and Windhoff-Héritier (1987).

[4] A wide range of terminology exists for the designation of the different levels of policy evaluation. We adopt the most commonly used here (for example, Monnier, 1992; European Commission, 1999).

[5] Two examples are as follows: programmes for the integration of unemployment data with the aim of reducing the unemployment rate by one per cent; and the new regulation of French scholarships or bursaries aimed at increasing by one third the relative proportion of students originating from underprivileged social classes.

[6] Federal Law of 4 October 1974 (RS 843).

[7] We are unable to judge whether this support should be considered as an implicit objective or an instrumentalisation of the said law in the sense of our statements in Section 4.2.2 of Chapter Four.

[8] Note the evaluation reports on these policies published by French government publications (*Documentation Française*) and concerning, in particular, the prevention of natural hazards, various social and economic policies, mountain policy, and so on.

ELEVEN

Research and working hypotheses

This chapter recapitulates the main analytical dimensions previously identified for the definition of the six products of a public policy found in political-administrative and social reality (see Chapters Seven to Ten). In this context, particular emphasis is placed on the complementary nature of the substantive and institutional content of these products. Based on this synoptic view, we will now present three possible 'access points' for the formulation of working hypotheses to be tested in the course of an empirical analysis of the explanatory factors behind these six policy products. In doing this, we make direct reference to the logic of the analysis model (Chapter Six) and to the basic elements (actors, resources and institutions) on which our public policy approach, which is inspired by actor-centred institutionalism, is based (Chapters Two to Five).

In a nutshell, we will attempt to explain the six products of a public policy as a function of the strategies of public and private actors, the resources that they mobilise to assert their rights and interests and the constraints or opportunities placed on them by institutional rules – both general and specific to the area being studied. Thus, this chapter formulates hypotheses on the (causal) links that potentially exist between the policy products (variables to be explained) and the 'games' played by the actors who compose the basic triangle (explanatory variables).

The proposed analytical model may be applied from different scientific perspectives, that is, to describe, interpret, explain or anticipate the content of a policy. Table 11.1 demonstrates the potential utility of the model in terms of these analytical levels. This chapter concentrates on the formulation of research and working hypotheses that facilitate the development of empirical research based on an explanatory perspective.

Public policy analysis

Table 11.1: Utility of the model on the basis of the level and ambition of the proposed empirical research

	Ambition of the analysis	Utility of the model
Descriptive perspective	• *Describe* (= identify a social phenomenon with the help of concepts and variables)	• Operational elements for systematically describing the six products of a public policy (see Chapters Seven to Ten) • Basic triangle and typologies of resources and institutional rules for describing the main actors and their action strategies (see Chapters Three to Five)
Analytical perspective (knowledge *of* public policy)	• *Understand* (= interpret links between social activities) • *Explain* (= demonstrate the causal relations between social facts) • *Anticipate* (= formulate 'if, then' hypotheses between variables)	• Theories, research and working hypotheses for the development of a research design (comparative, with control variables) and for understanding, explaining and predicting links between actors, resources and institutional rules, on the one hand, and the substantive and institutional content of the policy products, on the other (see Sections 7.3, 8.3, 9.5 and 10.4 in Chapters Seven, Eight, Nine and Ten, respectively)
Prescriptive perspective (knowledge *for* public policy)	• *Advise* (= formulate practical recommendations for the management of public policies)	• Commissioned research to demonstrate the relevance of policy analysis as a measure accompanying public reforms

11.1 Variables to be explained: the substantive and institutional dimensions of policy products

Table 11.2 presents the six products that the analyst can define in the course of a policy cycle as a function of multiple material supports (for example, government programmes, legislation and regulations, annual reports of administrative services, expert evaluations, informal documents produced by the administration and interest groups, syntheses of consultation or negotiation processes, print media, websites).

Beyond the generic definition of these six products, Table 11.2 lists the operational dimensions presented earlier by way of illustration for the detailed study of their constituent elements. We divide these dimensions into two categories, according to whether they are more concerned with the *substantive* content ('how to resolve the public problem') or the *institutional* content of a determined product ('which actors participate in the resolution of the public problem', 'which resources do they use' and 'what are the "rules of the game" that apply'). Once again, we stress that the operational elements listed have all been proven in empirical analysis; at the same time, however, we are not claiming that the list is exhaustive.

Even if the boundary between substantive and institutional elements is at times fluid (or arbitrary), the simultaneous consideration and the examination of these two categories of the content of a product are indispensable in the context of an empirical study. In effect, the quality of a policy depends on the degree of differentiation between its substantive and institutional elements and, to a greater extent, on the coherence – or at least the negative coordination – of the latter. Insofar as a state action aims to achieve a high level of effectiveness (= achievement of stated *substantive* objectives) and a certain level of foreseeable ability and temporal durability (= *institutional* stabilisation of exchange relationships between the actors involved), each of these six products should progressively concretise the causal and intervention hypothesis of its 'causal model' (what needs to be done to resolve the public problem in question) as well as the tasks, competencies and resources of the actors that constitute its 'public action network' (that is, who participates in the resolution of the public policy and according to which of the specific and general rules in force).

As already explained in the introduction to Part III (Chapter Six), as a policy process unfolds, the observer should be able to confirm the concretisation of the actual 'substance' of the policy, the consolidation of the actor network involved, the constitution of real 'institutional

Public policy analysis

Table 11.2: Summary of the operational elements for the analysis of the six products of a public policy

Policy stage	Product to be explained	Generic definition of the product	Operational elements for the analysis of the product — Predominantly substantive content	Operational elements for the analysis of the product — Predominantly institutional content
Agenda setting	Political definition of the public problem (PD)	Mandate formulated for the attention of the political authorities to formulate a policy aimed at resolving the public problem that has been placed on the political agenda (→ request for intervention and start of an initial solution)	• Degree of intensity (severity) • Scope of involvement (audience) • Degree of innovation	• Degree of urgency
Programming	Political-administrative programme (PAP)	All of the legislative norms and regulatory acts that define the substantive and procedural elements of the policy (→ definition of normative content and primary legitimation)	• Concretisation of objectives • Evaluative criteria • Operational elements (or action instruments)	• Administrative authorities and resources • Procedural elements (including judicial)
	Political-administrative arrangement (PAA)	Structured group of public and para-public actors responsible for the implementation of the policy (→ designation of actors' competencies, of intraorganisational and interorganisational management and general allocation of resources)	• Number and type of actors • Context defined by other policies	• Degree of horizontal and vertical coordination • Degree of centrality • Degree of politicisation • Degree of openness

(continued)

Research and working hypotheses

Table 11.2: Summary of the operational elements for the analysis of the six products of a public policy (contd.)

Policy stage	Product to be explained	Generic definition of the product	Operational elements for the analysis of the product — Predominantly substantive content	Operational elements for the analysis of the product — Predominantly institutional content
Implementation	Action plans (APs)	All decisions of a planning nature that define the priorities in time, space and vis-à-vis social groups for the implementation of the policy (→ specific allocation of resources for targeted production of outputs)	• Explicit (formal) versus absent • Degree of discrimination (in time, space and vis-à-vis social groups)	• Degree of structuring for implementing authorities • Associated resources versus non-associated resources • Degree of openness
	Implementation acts (outputs)	All end products of political-administrative processes that address the target groups at whom the policy measures are aimed (→ application, execution)	• Perimeter (complete versus incomplete) • Substantive, internal and external coherency	• Institutional content (for example, creation of a target group) • Intermediary versus final acts • Formal versus informal acts
Evaluation	Evaluative statements on the policy effects (impacts and outcomes)	All value judgements pertaining to the changes in behaviour triggered among the target groups (impacts) and on the improvement of the situation observable among the end beneficiaries (outcomes) (→ secondary legitimation)	• Evaluation criteria applied • Recapitulative versus formative • Partial versus global • Scientific versus ideological	• Ex-ante, concomitant or ex-post • Formal versus informal • Future use of the statement

255

capital' formed by specific rules and the (iterative) exploitation of the entire spectrum of available resources.

This rationale regarding the necessary complementarity of the substantive and institutional elements of a policy is of primary importance for the two following reasons:

- From a *normative* perspective, the so-called primary legitimation (that is, legitimation achieved through democratic decision-making processes, inputs and throughputs) and secondary legitimacy (that is, legitimacy achieved through the quality of public services, implementation acts and effects) of public actions depend on institutional and substantive factors. In effect, these two categories of legitimacy are based on the procedural forms of policy co-production by the social actors (for example, transparent and open consultation processes, delegation of implementation to para-state organisations, equality of treatment of affected groups, publication of evaluative reports) *and* on the real capacity of public actors to resolve concrete problems (for example, political consensus on the collective objectives to be attained, inherent discrimination in the action plans (APs) based on the objective pressure of the problem, adequate measurement of impacts and outcomes). From this point of view, the analyst must pay attention to the substantive and institutional factors that, together, contribute to the dual legitimation of public policies.
- From an *empirical-analytical* perspective, it is accepted that public and private actors generally understand the multiple stakes associated with the substantive and institutional content of a policy very well. Consequently, they develop action strategies that aim to influence the objectives and intervention instruments (for example, direct games relating to the core and internal layers of the PAP) *and* to arrange a strong organisational position for themselves or, at least, minimum room for manoeuvre to influence the subsequent stages of the policy (for example, an indirect game relating to the external layers of the PAP and PAA). At this level, it also proves essential to combine a substantive analysis with an institutional analysis in order to determine the complexity and richness of the actors' games, their interaction and, finally, their influence on the gradual evolution of the policy products.

In adopting an empirical-analytical perspective here, we recommend that the analyst review all of the operational dimensions listed in

Table 11.2 when carrying out an empirical study. This may then serve as a kind of systematic 'check-list'. The application of this analysis grid should, therefore, facilitate the definition and operationalisation of the research variables.

The analyst should then identify the independent variables to explain variations in time and space among the empirical observations made. To this end, we discuss below the different 'games' actors play as a potential means of explaining the substantive and institutional content of a policy's products.

11.2 Explanatory variables: the actors' 'game', the resources and the institutional rules

During the preliminary discussion of policy actors (Chapter Three), we identified a 'basic triangle' composed of the political-administrative authorities (public actors), the target groups and end beneficiaries, to which third-party groups (positively affected versus negatively affected third parties) are often added. According to the general logic of our analysis model, the strategic behaviour of these actors – who in a changing institutional context mobilise different resources to assert their values, interests and rights – make it possible to explain in part the content of the six policy products. In effect, we should recall here that our theoretical approach rests on two postulates (see Chapter Six):

- *Postulate no 1:* the substantive and institutional results of a policy stage (for example, the PAP and PAA) directly influence the results of the following stages (for example, the APs and formal implementation acts).
- *Postulate no 2:* during each stage, the public policy actors resort to (new) institutional rules and (new) combinations of resources to influence the results of the stage in question.

The first postulate indicates that to ensure a certain level of finalisation, continuity and predictability for the policy, the actors formulate products that attempt to restrict the 'field of possibilities' for the subsequent stages of the policy. The substantive and institutional content of a product is directly influenced by the decisions and actions taken during the earlier stages of the same public policy.

However, the second postulate qualifies the first in the sense that certain actors intentionally try to adjust, modify or cancel the measures that have been initiated, predefined or decided by the preceding products. No state action is linear or capable of entirely determining individual and collective behaviour. As a result, the content of a policy product is always influenced by modifications in the institutional frame, resources, constellation and 'games' played by the actors directly affected by the policy stage in question.

Taking these two postulates into account, Figure 11.1 identifies some possible links between the products and the actor strategies. This schematic representation includes the arguments from our earlier discussion of the duality of content that characterises all policy products. In the figure, we have placed each of the six products according to the relative weight (defined on the basis of our previous empirical analyses) of their substantive and institutional elements. Furthermore, this figure suggests that the actors develop different, alternative or complementary games to influence this dual dimension of the products. In concrete terms, what we propose here is the qualification of games affecting the substantive content of a policy product as *direct* and those affecting the institutional content as *indirect* (see Chapter Six). The term 'indirect' indicates both that the strategies of certain actors are not solely concentrated on the product to be defined in the immediate future (that is, the following stage) but, by playing with institutional data, already anticipate the future games that will affect previous products (for example, games affecting procedural elements of the PAP to ensure a right of appeal during the production of formal implementation acts or a privileged position during the evaluation stage).

We make no claim with respect to the exhaustiveness of the actor 'games' identified in Figure 11.1, but attempt instead to demonstrate how these games are integrated into the logic of our analysis model.

Empirical studies of public policies all tend to demonstrate that multiple actor 'games' coexist and have a more or less significant influence on the content of the six products. For reasons of space, it is not possible to list all of the possible 'games' involved here. Instead, we will go beyond a merely descriptive approach by formulating some research hypotheses about these 'games', which are defined here as key explanatory variables with respect to the products of a public policy.

Examples of direct and indirect games

Links between the political definition of the problem (PD) and the political-administrative programme (PAP)

- *Direct game affecting the core and internal layers of the PAP:* in the area of legislation to counteract atmospheric pollution, the end beneficiaries (for example, the neighbours of a polluting factory) try to define clear objectives and evaluative criteria (for example, air quality that prevailed in 1960 to be attained in 1985) as well as restrictive instruments (for example, emission limit values) to ensure the efficacy of the policy.
- *Indirect game affecting the external layers of the PAP:* in the area of military structures (for example, army camp with a firing range), environment groups who are in fact unable to influence the actual definition of national defence objectives at legislative level try to be formally entitled to (potentially) oppose a specific project.

Links between the PAP and the political-administrative arrangements (PAA)

- *Direct game affecting the composition of the PAA:* in the area of direct agricultural payments, the affected groups (farmers) try to have an administrative body with whom they already enjoy privileged relations (for example, agriculture ministry) defined as the only body responsible for the distribution of payments as opposed to an administrative body which, due to its other functions, may be potentially opposed to their particular and short-term interests (for example, environment ministry).
- *Indirect game affecting the structure and procedures of the PAA:* in the area of legislation governing planning permission, the historically dominant service (for example, construction authority) tries to maintain its central position vis-à-vis the other services involved (for example, energy ministry, water protection authority, spatial planning authority) by influencing the forms of internal coordination for the management of a file (for example, exclusive system of consultative notice).

Links between the PAP, PAA and APs

- *Direct game affecting the degree of discrimination of APs:* in the area of legislation to counteract unemployment, if its budget is restricted, the authority responsible for professional training and placement of employment seekers (for example, regional employment offices in Switzerland) will try to reserve priority access to its services at the level of the AP for particular categories of unemployed people (for example, educated young people) over other categories (for example, older untrained people).

Public policy analysis

- *Indirect game affecting the resources linked by APs:* in the area of legislation on economic reflation, the recipients of subsidies (companies that create or maintain employment) try to have a short deadline defined in the AP so that they can quickly profit from the distribution of the budgetary resources intended to stimulate economic growth.

Links between APs and implementation acts (outputs)

- *Direct game affecting the coherence of implementation acts:* in the area of water flow protection, the target groups (for example, hydro-electric production companies), which must observe the minimum flows for certain water courses, try to ensure that the outputs (for example, obligation to reduce the volumes of water withdrawn up to a given date) also contain criteria for financial compensation (for example, assistance for the clean-up of barrages), to reduce the cost of work to be carried out and irredeemable investments (due to reduction in sales of hydroelectric power).
- *Indirect game affecting the controlling clauses of implementation acts:* in the area of the economic promotion of small and medium-sized businesses, as a condition for the granting of tax relief (output), the administrative service (for example, finance ministry) stipulates that that recipients prove that the subsidised posts have been created or maintained at the end of each accounting period.

Links between implementation acts (outputs) and evaluative statements (on impacts and outcomes)

- *Direct game affecting the scope of effects:* in the area of the promotion of energy-saving measures and renewable energy sources, the energy ministry tries to include in the evaluation of the resulting effects not only energy and environmental results (for example, reduction in kWh consumption and polluting emissions), but also the secondary effects in terms of creation or maintenance of employment (for example, employment connected with the eco-industry).
- *Indirect game affecting the participative and formal approach to evaluation:* in the area of the ecological compensation paid to organic farmers, the end beneficiaries (for example, representatives of ecological associations) who are excluded from implementation (for example, no right of appeal against unfounded attribution of subsidy to a non-organic farmer) try to be able to formally participate in the evaluation of the policy results (for example, visible increase in biodiversity on farmland) to express their assessment of the efficacy of the adopted policy.

Research and working hypotheses

Figure 11.1: Direct and indirect games based on the substantive and institutional content of policy products

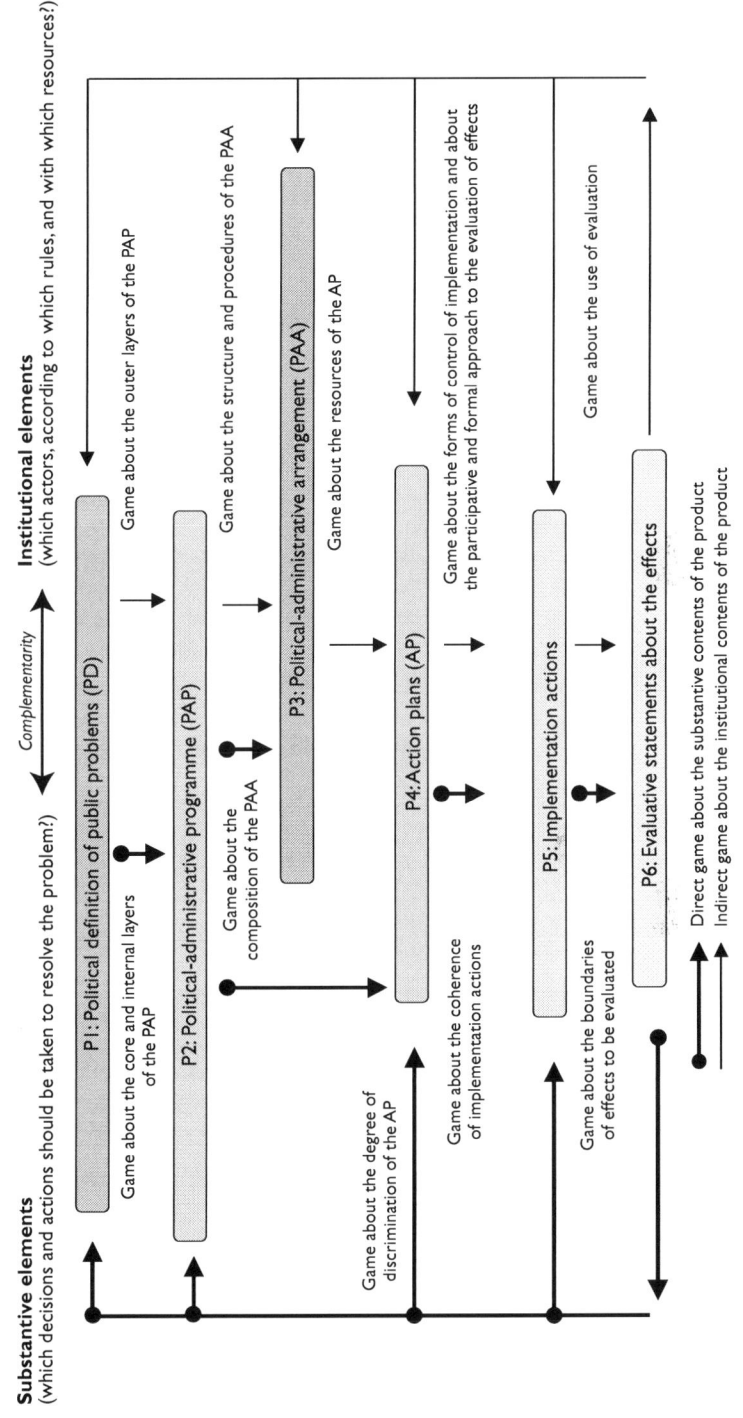

11.3 Hypotheses for an empirical study

In order to formalise the links between the variables to be explained and explanatory variables of the model and, again, to facilitate its application in the context of an empirical study, in the following paragraphs we will explore certain hypotheses. We define three *research hypotheses* (both general and abstract and thus applicable to all policies) and several *working hypotheses* (specific and concrete, thus applicable to a given policy). Thus, an analyst who is embarking on a study in the field may take inspiration from our suggestions when formulating working hypotheses on the basis of the research question and empirical domain involved.

11.3.1 Research hypotheses

The three research hypotheses formalise the potential (causal) links between the content of a particular policy product, the mobilisation of resources and institutional rules by the actors involved and the content of the subsequent policy products. These hypotheses clarify and concretise the two postulates formulated above. At the same time, they also act as a general canvas for the formulation of working hypotheses that will be presented next.

Adopting the epistemological perspective developed by Lakatos (1970), we consider the two postulates and three research hypotheses discussed here as the 'hard core' of our model. The working hypotheses in themselves represent the 'protective belt': their purpose is to make the link between the theory and empirical analysis. As a result, and assuming the analyst accepts this epistemological perspective, he or she is invited to test the working hypotheses proposed below or to formulate more relevant ones without, however, fundamentally reformulating the postulates and research hypotheses. Figure 11.2 summarises the causal chain that underlies the latter.

As indicated in Figure 11.2, with the help of research hypotheses, the three complementary 'access points' make it possible to cover all of the analysis model's causal relationships.

Firstly, we suggest that a quasi-structural (or functional) link exists between the substantive and institutional content of a given product and that of the subsequent policy products. This hypothesis concretises postulate no 1 and extends its scope to the extent that within one and the same stage (for example, implementation), the product X adopted previously (for example, the AP) directly influences the following product Y (for example, the outputs). Formulated in general terms,

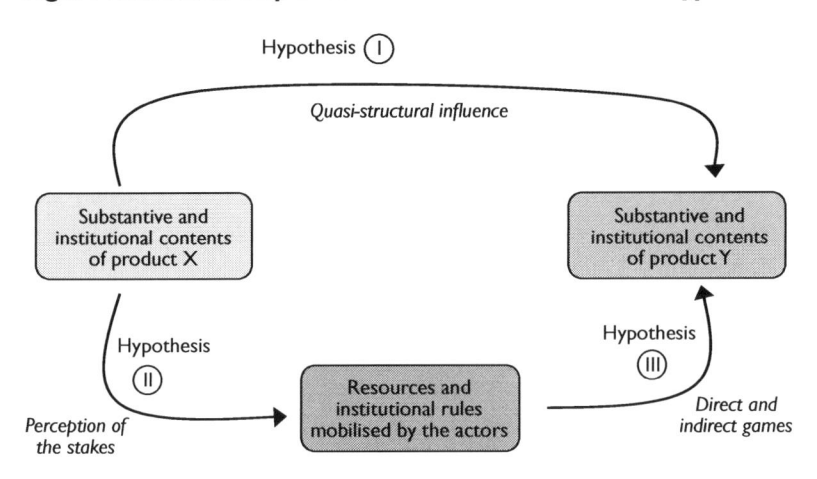

Figure 11.2: Causal sequences formalised in the research hypotheses

```
                            Hypothesis (I)
              ┌─────── Quasi-structural influence ────────┐
              │                                           ▼
    ┌──────────────────┐                        ┌──────────────────┐
    │  Substantive and │                        │  Substantive and │
    │institutional contents│                    │institutional contents│
    │   of product X   │                        │   of product Y   │
    └──────────────────┘                        └──────────────────┘
              │                                           ▲
       Hypothesis                                    Hypothesis
          (II)         ┌─────────────────┐             (III)
                       │   Resources and │
                       │institutional rules│         Direct and
  Perception of  ────▶ │mobilised by the actors│ ──── indirect games
    the stakes         └─────────────────┘
```

research hypothesis I stipulates that *if product X includes such and such substantive and institutional content, the following Y products will displayed, ceteris paribus, this substantive and institutional content* (H_1).

At first sight, this hypothesis would appear mechanical and 'legalistic' because it subtracts any proactive role on the part of the actors from the explanation. In fact, it should instead be understood as predicting the general tendencies of the progressive evolution of policies, which are themselves dependent on the actor constellation and action strategies frequently observed in political-administrative reality.

The criterion *ceteris paribus*, which is included in this hypothesis, means that in specific situations the actors' game does not lead to fundamental shifts between one policy product and the next. On the contrary, it suggests that different policies display several similarities in their development – at least under certain conditions – independent of the actors' game (variations of situation and identical structural variables). If, however, this first research hypothesis is not confirmed, the analyst should take a closer look at the two following hypotheses that themselves concretise postulate no 2 of our model.

Secondly, we suggest that there is a causal link between the substantive and institutional content of product X as perceived by the actors concerned and their resulting (non-)action during the formulation of the following product Y. The fact that actors adopt or do not adopt a (new) action strategy depends on the perception that there are 'stakes' arising from the content of product X that affect them. Depending on how clear and definitive the nature of the substantive direction of the policy arising from product X is and according to the scope of the institutional margin for manoeuvre that this grants to actors, they will be more or less motivated to mobilise (new) resources and institutional rules in the course of the formulation of product Y.

The term 'stakes' refers to that which actors can lose or gain (that is, the safeguarding of their substantive and institutional interests) and that which they must risk (resources and institutional rules mobilised). Formally, *research hypothesis II* assumes that *if the content of product X is perceived by actors as unfavourable to their interests, then they will, ceteris paribus, mobilise certain resources and institutional rules in an effort to redirect the content of product Y (H_{II})*.

As a general rule, it can be assumed that the stakes diminish with the progressive stages of a policy life cycle in that its products successively reduce the substantive options and progressively define the institutional rules specific to the policy in question. Nonetheless, certain (new) actors may sometimes reopen the perspective to a significant extent (for example, by appealing to general institutional rules) and as a result fundamentally redefine the policy stakes.

The *ceteris paribus* condition, which was introduced during the formulation of the second hypothesis, indicates on the one hand that actors mobilise certain resources and institutional rules while considering the others (potentially exploitable also, and by other actors) as constants. On the other hand, the criterion also means that actors develop their action strategies in order to modify a certain substantive or institutional element without necessarily wanting to modify the other elements (hence defined as constants) of a product's content.

Thirdly, we suggest that a link exists between actors' 'games' and the content of the product in question. While the second hypothesis concentrates on the stakes of the public policy (why play?, what are the resources and rules of the game?), *research hypothesis III* deals with types of games, direct and indirect (which game strategy?) and their influence on the substantive and institutional content of the product. Thus its general title is: *If actors play such and such direct and/or indirect games, the product Y will display, ceteris paribus, this substantive and institutional content (H_{III})*.

We have already presented some direct and indirect games affecting different policy products (see Section 11.2). These examples illustrate the range of the third research hypothesis. It should be noted, on the other hand, that the criterion *ceteris paribus* means here that actors concentrate on particular action strategies with the aim of modifying a defined element of the product content: thus they do not necessarily try to combine all of the possible games (in particular due to their high cost in terms of resources) to modify all of the elements of the product. The substantive and/or institutional content of product Y that are not targeted by an actors' games are, thus, considered here as constant.

Theoretically, these three research hypotheses may be applied to identify all of the links that exist between the substantive and institutional content of the six products of a policy, the three main categories of actors that may play directly or indirectly, the 10 types of mobilisable resources and all of the institutional rules, general (relevant to the democratic regime) and specific (relevant to the area studied). Clearly, the systematic intersection of all these variables leads to an uncontrollable set of working hypotheses (see Figure 11.3 on the structure of the possible combinations of variables).

Without specifying all of the possible combinations of variables to be explained and explanatory variables, in the next section we present some working hypotheses that have already been tested in empirical studies. By way of example, we discuss several specific combinations without, however, anticipating their explanatory relevance for all of the products of all public policies.

11.3.2 Working hypotheses

In fact, the working hypotheses discussed in this section each correspond to one of the paths represented in Figure 11.3. They are logically classified on the basis of the three research hypotheses presented above. To avoid excessive redundancy, we will focus on the affected groups in the part dedicated to the causal links between the perception of stakes and resources and the mobilisable institutional rules (hypotheses II, 1ff); in the context of the working hypotheses on direct and indirect games (III, 1ff), we will focus on the public actors. We will then deal with all six policy products. The empirical bases of the hypotheses are provided either by the actors' observations (relatively weak bases) or by systematic studies (indicated).

(a) Working hypotheses on the content of the products (without decisive intervention by actors in accordance with hypothesis I)

- Hypothesis I.1: if the PD displays a high level of complexity (multi-causal PD), the objectives of the PAP will be fluid and the instruments used will need to provide incentives or persuasions. This is the case, for example, in efforts to reduce unemployment (because various individual factors relating to

Public policy analysis

Figure 11.3: Possible combinations of variables for the formulation of working hypotheses

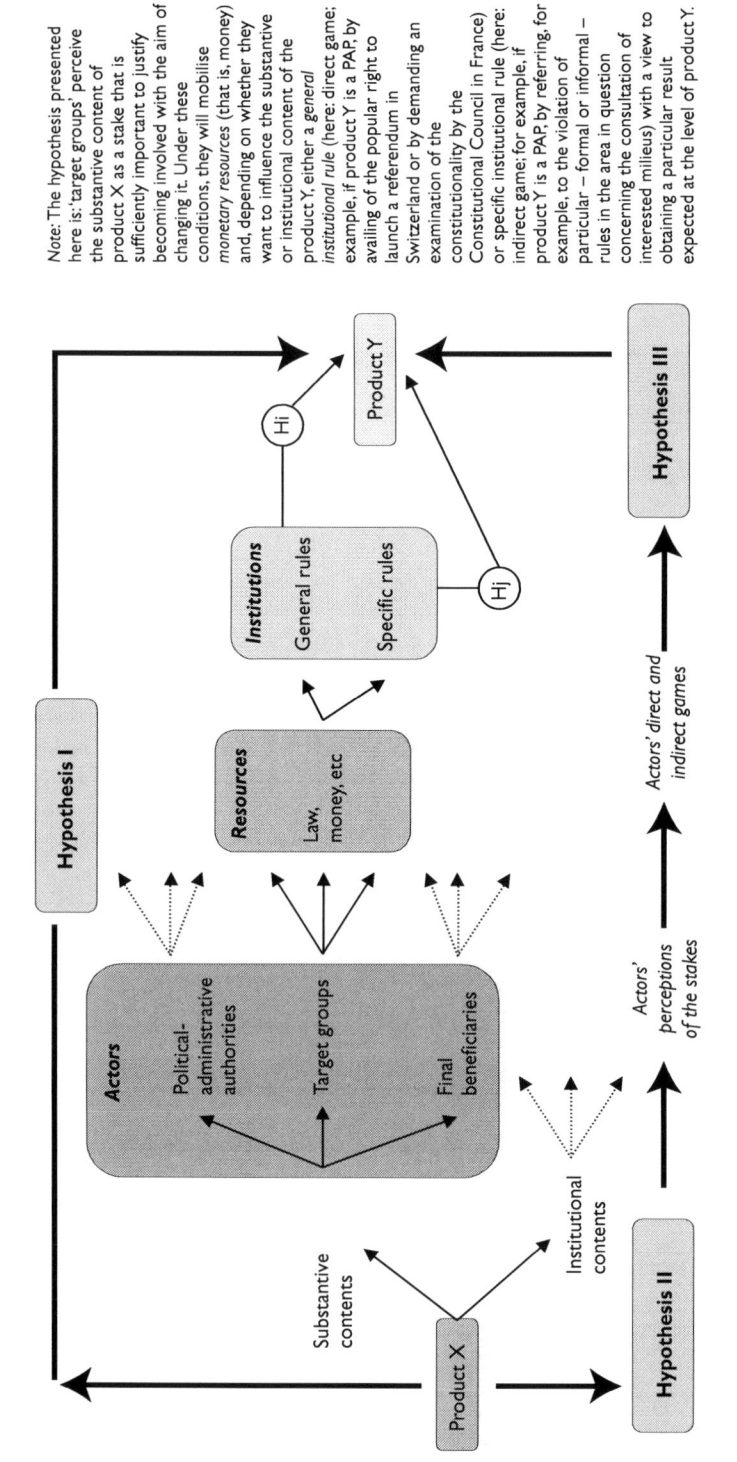

Note: The hypothesis presented here is: 'target groups' perceive the substantive content of product X as a stake that is sufficiently important to justify becoming involved with the aim of changing it. Under these conditions, they will mobilise *monetary resources* (that is, money) and, depending on whether they want to influence the substantive or institutional content of the product Y, either a *general institutional rule* (here: direct game; example, if product Y is a PAP, by availing of the popular right to launch a referendum in Switzerland or by demanding an examination of the constitutionality by the Constitutional Council in France) or *specific institutional rule* (here: indirect game; for example, if product Y is a PAP, by referring, for example, to the violation of particular – formal or informal – rules in the area in question concerning the consultation of interested milieus) with a view to obtaining a particular result expected at the level of product Y.

266

job seekers and macro-economic, economic and structural data play a determining role in the existence of the problem).
- Hypothesis I.2: if the objectives of the PAP are clear and the regulative intervention instruments and the definition of target groups (which also figure in the PAP) precise, the implementation PAA is open (to the affected groups). For example, an inverse empirical proportionality is often observed between the degree of interventionism of the PAP (limitation of rights and liberties of target groups) and the degree of openness of the PAA vis-à-vis target groups (the more severe the planned intervention, the more elevated the procedural involvement of affected groups).
- Hypothesis I.3: if the implementation PAA is highly compartmentalised (high level of fragmentation), the level of discrimination in the AP is high and the scope of implementation acts (outputs) is influenced by the power relations between the opposing local or regional actors. For example, the decentralisation of the implementation of policies with socio-spatial impacts may reinforce the social inequalities in policies to reduce traffic (Terribilini, 1995).
- Hypothesis I.4: if the APs display a high level of discrimination, the implementation acts are formal and comprehensive. This is the case with the central postulate of the service contracts negotiated as part of pilot experiments with New Public Management (more targeted production and easier control of implementation acts based on the priorities defined in the APs).
- Hypothesis I.5: if the outputs are produced without a formal controlling clause, the evaluative statements are informal and ideological. In this case, the evaluative statements have no solid empirical basis, that is, they are formulated without a systematic inventory of implementation acts or real effects (impacts and outcomes). It is possible to observe such a situation in the case of asylum policy in which the debate surrounding the effects of policy measures is dissociated from the real figures on the numbers of requests for asylum, the numbers actually granted asylum and the numbers of criminal acts actually committed by asylum seekers and/or foreigners, for example (Frossard and Hagmann, 2000).
- Hypothesis I.6: if the evaluative statements are official, scientific and precise, the (new) definition of the problem will display a higher level of complexity and a wider perimeter. In general, sectoral public policies have a tendency to become more complex from one cycle to the next, particularly if the commissioned

evaluations clearly demonstrate the need to designate additional new affected groups. Examples here include the way policies like drug policy and water protection policy become progressively more complex.

(b) Working hypotheses on the perception of stakes and resources and the institutional rules mobilised (for example, by the target groups) (hypothesis II)

- Hypothesis II.1: if a social group is designated as exclusively responsible for a PD, it will mobilise, among other things, the resources 'information' and 'political support' as well as the institutional rule 'consultation procedure' to ensure that the intervention instruments adopted in the PAP are not very restrictive and/or also address other target groups. For example, if industries are the only actors designated as air polluters, they try to share the responsibility for the deterioration in air quality with trade, households, drivers and farmers in the hope that the clean-up measures imposed on them will be less restrictive.
- Hypothesis II.2: if a group is targeted by incentive instruments at PAP level, it mobilises, among other things, the resources 'organisation' and 'personal' as well as the institutional rule 'principle of subsidiarity' to ensure a privileged position, for example, as a para-state administration, in the intervention PAA. This phenomenon is observable, inter alia, in agricultural policy whereby farming organisations prefer to take charge of the implementation of milk quotas themselves.
- Hypothesis II.3: if the affected groups are confronted with highly fragmented (vertically) and open PAAs, they mobilise, inter alia, the resources 'information' and 'time' and the institutional rule 'federalism of execution' so that the (discriminations inherent in the) APs take factors specific to the local situation into account. Numerous such examples involving the instrumentalisation of federal (or central) policies by the cantons (or local authorities) can be observed in both Switzerland and France.
- Hypothesis II.4: if an affected group does not belong to the groups designated by the APs as privileged recipients of administrative services, it mobilises, inter alia, the resource 'confidence' and 'law' and the institutional rule 'equality of treatment' to ensure that it also benefits from the more favourable policy outputs. For example, residents near airfields, who are not eligible for state financial aid for the insulation of their windows

(because the noise at their properties does not reach the defined decibel limit values), exert pressure to be allowed to benefit from the public aid.
- Hypothesis II.5: if the affected groups establish that the outputs of several policies are incoherent and lacking in controlling clauses, they will mobilise, inter alia, the resources 'information' and 'money' and the institutional rule 'freedom of expression' to finance an independent evaluation of the efficacy of the policy in question. This is the case, for example, when employers finance a study to show that social security contributions (outputs) have negative effects on the maintenance or creation of employment in a specific region.
- Hypothesis II.6: if a scientific evaluative statement shows that the changes in the behaviour of target groups do not lead to a resolution of the collective problem, the groups will mobilise, inter alia, the resources 'information,' organisation' and 'money' and the institutional rule 'right of initiative' to place a new (causal hypothesis in the) PD on the agenda. For example, if the automobile associations establish no observable improvement in air quality despite the reduction of speed on motorways, they will become involved in efforts to identify other actors (for example, industry) as responsible for the problem (for example, while launching a popular initiative in Switzerland to have the speed limit increased).

(c) Working hypotheses on the direct and indirect games (for example, of the political-administrative authorities) (hypothesis III)

- Hypothesis III.1: if an administrative service almost exclusively appropriates the (substantive) definition of a (new) public problem (direct game), the objectives of the PAP will be defined in accordance with the traditional terms of the policy for which it is already responsible. This phenomenon can be observed in the evolution of drug policy: suppression (by the police), social support (by the social services), medicalisation (by doctors).
- Hypothesis III.2: if a central administrative service devotes itself to reinforcing the substantive impact of a PAP (indirect game), its evaluative elements (technical) will be clearly defined. To avoid political debates on the definition of the objectives of the PAP, an administrative service will try to reinforce the scope of the policy by clearly defining the influence of technical data on the

ultimate evaluation of its effects (for example, X per cent reduction in nitrates in underground water bodies).
- Hypothesis III.3: if a central administrative service wishes to avoid conflicts with local actors – both public and private – (indirect game), the PAA is fragmented (weak vertical coordination) and open. This is the case with the decentralisation of implementation competencies (implementation of environmental regulations), so as to avoid conflicts (predictable during the formulation of the PAP).
- Hypothesis III.4: if an administrative service tries to increase its own margin for discretion and manoeuvre during the application of the PAP (indirect game), the AP will not be very discriminatory and the resources (for example, financial and personnel) not linked. This is the 'traditional' strategy adopted by administrative services when trying to increase their discretionary scope rather than limiting themselves to technically restrictive APs with clear priorities.
- Hypothesis III.5: if an administrative service wishes to ensure the legality and influence of its services (direct game), the implementing actors will be armed with a controlling clause. This is the strategy for controlling the behaviour of groups associated with financial services provided by the state (all kinds of subsidies).
- Hypothesis III.6: if an administrative service tries to revalue its policy and to obtain supplementary resources (indirect game), it will disseminate the evaluative statements of an official report extensively. This is the case when an evaluation is commissioned to demonstrate the policy is going in the right direction (empirical validity of the causality model), but that the administration lacks the resources to improve its efficacy (for example, quantitative evaluation of costs of tobacco addiction to justify an increase in financial resources for the services responsible for its prevention).

In conclusion, we would like to reiterate that these working hypotheses are merely examples. Thus, the analyst is free to refine them or formulate other working hypotheses. Furthermore, for reasons of space, we have not developed working hypotheses from research hypothesis II for the political-administrative authorities and end beneficiaries, or from research hypothesis III for target groups and end beneficiaries. In fact, working hypotheses could (or should) also be proposed in these cases[1].

Note

[1] In summary, for a complex study of a policy cycle, it would be possible to formulate *84 working hypotheses*, that is, two for each of the following 42 theoretical possibilities (institutional/substantive stakes):

- six hypotheses for group I (presented here)
- 18 (= 6 × 3) hypotheses for group II, that is, one for each of the three main actors and six categories of products (here we only present a sample for the six products from the perspective of these target groups)
- 18 (= 6 × 3) hypotheses for group III, that is, one for each of the three main actors and six categories of products (here we only present a sample for the six products from the perspective of these public authorities).

TWELVE

Conclusion

This review of the arguments and cases discussed throughout the book is primarily intended to prompt researchers and practitioners working in the area of policy analysis and management to revisit the arguments presented, develop them further, complement them with other theoretical approaches and apply them in actual analysis situations. Thus, we present some reflections on the strengths (Section 12.1) and weaknesses (Section 12.2) of our theoretical concepts and their application in concrete cases. Finally, we describe two possible future directions for the development of policy analysis (Section 12.3), that is, governance and institutional regimes.

12.1 Strengths of the proposed approach

Based on our experience in teaching and research (both theoretical and applied), we believe that the analysis model presented in this manual has the advantage of not being centred on a single theoretical, and always normative, conceptualisation of the state, but rather offers a balanced approach to the analysis of public policy.

(a) Rejection of a single theory of state

As stated at the beginning of this book (see Chapter One), our analytical model does not propose to develop a new theory on the functioning of the state and its position with respect to civil society in general. To put it in more positive terms, the position on which our conceptual work throughout this book is based stems from our desire to present a model that can be applied in the context of a broad range of conceptualisations and interpretations of the state and its actions. What we have in mind here, for example, are the diverse and often strongly diverging theories on:

- the relationships between public and private actors (for example, neo-Marxist, neo-corporatist and neo-liberal approaches);

- the access to resources available to different categories of actors (for example, the analysis of networks based on the interdependency of resources between actors);
- the role of general or constitutive institutional rules in the context of the effectiveness of public action.

Thus, our analytical model aims to remain open to a number of theoretical trends in the area of the public sector and state action that are inspired by law, politics and economics. However, this openness assumes that the promoters of the various approaches in question will accept the principle of the operationalisation and empirical verification of the concepts and hypotheses on which their theory is based. This dialogue is clearly facilitated if these concepts and hypotheses also concern the actors, resources and institutional rules involved in the public action, even if the involvement is merely partial and based on competing interpretations. Thus, a number of working hypotheses based on different theoretical statements may be formulated and subject to constructive debate and may therefore contribute to the cumulative development of knowledge of the policy process (as in the three main research hypotheses presented in Chapter Eleven).

In order to develop an actual research programme of this nature, it is necessary to combine different research designs that are selected on the basis of the researcher's interests and theoretical perspective. These comprise the following:

- *The comparison of several policies* that affect the areas identified as crucial for the demonstration of the adopted hypotheses should enable the accumulation of sufficient data for the testing of various theories of the state. Based on the logical choice of a sample of policies, the analyst observes one or more of the most significant phases of the policy life cycle. Based, again, on the selected theoretical conceptualisation, the analyst may select other public policies as controls. For example, the research could test hypotheses originating from a neo-corporatist theory of state by carrying out a comparative analysis of the role played by economic associations in the phase of the definition of a problem that different economic policies aim to resolve, and their role in the same phase of policies with minimal economic impacts. Or the research may invalidate or empirically confirm the possibly contradictory theoretical tenets on the influence of federalism or decentralisation on the choices made by local, regional or national actors.

- *The synchronic or diachronic comparison of different phases of one and the same policy* in different countries or regions. For example, in view of the fact that public policies are often implemented by decentralised agencies, the analyst may focus on an empirical test of theories (for example, pluralist versus neo-Marxist) on the capacity of private actors to mobilise themselves to support or change the course of a policy. This second type of research design is highly compatible with the analytical model proposed here, because the model allows the formulation of opposing working hypotheses derived from various theories on the genesis, management and effects of public action. If our model were based on an excessively narrow conceptualisation of the state and its components, it would not be a suitable tool for the testing of competing hypotheses on the role of actors and their resources (for example, neo-Marxism), or on the influence of institutional, general and specific rules (for example, the neo-institutional schools).

This openness of the model to different theoretical currents constitutes one of its main strengths. It is a concrete outcome of its previous practical application by a number of students and researchers with strongly diverging theoretical and ideological perspectives. These applications forced us to adopt a rigorous conceptual procedure that was also guided by a desire for simplicity. Our approach to policy analysis rests on a very simple categorisation of the various products of the political–administrative process – which are widely accepted by lawyers, political scientists and even politicians – and their substantive and institutional elements. Furthermore, the model is based on the analysis of the numerous actors and the institutional rules and resources they mobilise with a view to influencing the substantive or institutional content of these different products. Without aspiring to exhaustiveness, the model proposes several criteria for the measurement, classification and establishment of a typology of these different dimensions.

(b) A balanced approach to policy research

In developing our approach we struck a balance between a number of elements often perceived as in contradiction with each other.

- *Identical analysis instruments regardless of the phase of the public policy being considered:* the proposed approach offers the advantage of applying the same analysis instruments to the processes of policy development, implementation and evaluation. This approach, which aims to be general, accounts in particular for the to-ing and fro-ing between these processes and makes it possible to overcome the differences expressed to a greater or lesser extent by analysts of the policy formulation and implementation phases, each of whom considers that the only phase that ultimately matters is that which they themselves are interested in. The examination of all of these phases under one and the same lens makes it possible to demonstrate the formal and, above all, informal links between the different moments in the decision-making process. It also means that while the policy cycle is accepted as a pragmatic device to structure analysis, attention is given to the interactions between its parts, a key feature many criticisms of that approach have stressed (see Hupe and Hill, 2006). Many researchers tend to concentrate on one phase or another and this inevitably limits the scope of their analysis.

- *Substantive and institutional aspects of policy products:* this distinction, which we initially applied to the political-administrative programme (PAP) only, was later extended to all of the products of the policy cycle. This decision enabled us to stress the direct and indirect games in the policy process that appear to be far more common than generally assumed. It corresponds, at least in part, to what other researchers have also observed in the form of strategic objects and substantive objectives at the level of actor strategy (see, for example, Dente and Fareri, 1998). However, it goes much further in that, within one and the same policy product, it is possible to identify the tangible repercussions of strategic games – in the form of the institutional content of the policy product in question. Furthermore, this conceptualisation makes it possible to demonstrate that the relationship between the substantive and institutional content of a policy product may ultimately lead to either the reinforcement or undermining of the effectiveness of the policy in question.

- *Heuristic and analytical-causal aspects:* the conceptualisation of the policy cycle with the help of six products (which is not in itself particularly original) and the different categories of actors, resources and institutional rules proposed by our model (which are, conversely, innovative in part) merely provides a heuristic framework for the development of a systematic reading of decision-making processes. The introduction of the three basic research hypotheses, two of which concern the games played by the actors, suggests the establishment of causal links between observable products (dependent variables) and actors who mobilise a number of institutional resources. Our concern for prudence in the application of a scheme of intelligibility described as causal is mainly expressed by the fact that the working hypotheses, which are deliberately formulated in an exemplary but incomplete way, also claim to be heuristic as opposed to causal. In fact, instead of observations arising from the application of a particular theory (deductive process), we introduce plausible constellations that we have encountered in our empirical work into these working hypotheses (inductive process). Finally, it should be noted that the three research hypotheses, which are truly causal in nature, only rest on four independent variables (the previous products, the actors, the general and specific institutional rules and mobilisable resources).

- *(Re-)constructivism and positivism:* the dimensions of the empirical analysis proposed here are based on the constructions of social reality created by different policy actors. The task of the analyst is to objectivise these constructions by, for example, explicitly stating the definition of the collective problem to be resolved and the dominant causal hypothesis. However, this reconstructive task is based on data made available for the analysis in the form of documents marking the conclusion of a stage in the decision-making process. This tangible – and hence more easily observed – data includes, for example, the PAP, implementation acts and evaluative statements. The realities described as 'constructed' by actors may be 'objectivised' by the researcher who reconstructs, for example, the substantive, temporal, spatial boundaries of the policy which, in many cases, themselves represent a reality perceived as such by the actors of the policy arena in question. This process involving the (re)construction of social reality on the basis of both the individual and collective constructions made by actors and official documents (even if they are still subject to the interpretation of the analyst reconstructing the 'reality of a public policy') was our guiding principle during the definition of the heuristic categories proposed here. Based on our previous experience in applied research, our approach is located between absolute constructivism and categorical positivism.

12.2 Limits of the approach

In the light of recent publications in the policy analysis literature (the French literature in particular) the limits of our approach can be identified as: (a) in our actual definition of policy, which tends to focus on the role of public actors ('state-centrism'); (b) in our decision to consider that a policy tries to resolve a social problem; (c) the fact that concentrating on the policy as a unit of analysis may restrict our perspective.

(a) Public action: towards an approach through 'the sociology of politics'

Our model actually lends significant although not central weight to the political-administrative actors (refer to the products: PAP, political-administrative arrangements [PAA], action plans [APs]) – although we have repeatedly stressed that the agenda-setting phase is not controlled by the public authorities and that the implementation phase remains an open process with sometimes unpredictable results reflecting the multiple influence of private actors. The theory of the centrality of the state in the conduct of collective actions is questioned, in particular, by Jean-Claude Thoenig who fears that the knowledge generated from this state-centrism is entering a period of diminishing returns.

Hence, Thoenig recommends opting for an analysis of "(organised) public action" (1998, pp 308-9) with a sociological rather than political science bias:

> The separation of problem definition, public agenda setting and evaluation, if not the formulation of solutions, is explicitly abandoned as a sufficiently relevant category in favour of the adoption of a collective activity referred to as transcoding, which mainly takes place between groups of actors capable of adapting according to the specific contexts of a problem. The cognitive processes structure the problems, the actors build themselves up through their capacity to formulate and express a solution, networks and actor communities form and dissolve so nothing institutionalises.

The approach we have adopted clearly involves a bias in favour of the state, "a sin of institutional conformity", according to Thoenig (1998, p 306). We are prepared to relativise the centrality of the state in the conduct of collective actions and the variables proposed in our model leave sufficient space for manoeuvre to this end. However, this is first and foremost an empirical question. Is it really possible to observe a loss of state control in the conduct of all public policies? Or are we merely observing a number of changes in the forms of public intervention? We believe it is essential to respond to these questions before definitively abandoning the term 'public policy' in favour of 'public action'. This is all the more relevant in view of the fact that, today, the actual term 'policy' seems to have been adopted by various administrations and para-public and private bodies. Finally, we note that – if not purely nominal or a simple effect of fashion – this kind of about face proves to be at odds with current (sociological, historical and economic) trends in neo-institutionalism.

We agree with the school of the Max Planck Institute of Cologne (Mayntz and Scharpf, 1995) and remain of the opinion that the recent attack by Thoenig on state-centrism, which strongly resembles that launched by the German sociologist Luhmann (1989) against any state capacity to control society in the late 1980s, merits discussion on the basis of its implicitly prescriptive character, which resembles the recommendations of the neo-liberals: such an approach would legitimise a retreat on the part of public actors (due to their incapacity to control society) and their release from all responsibility by cutting them off from the basis of their democratic legitimation. In terms of the analytical process, this transformation of policies into public actions could result in the abandonment of the distinction between public and private actors. This distinction remains dear to us (see Section 3.3.2 in Chapter Three) because it enables policy analysts to fulfil their most important role, that is, to clearly attribute political responsibility to identifiable actors even if the latter prefer to erase the traces thereof with the help of the – politically easy – formulation of some 'public action' resulting from a sociological rather than political process.

Contrary to Thoenig and other authors whose approach is centred on 'networks of public action' – not as a metaphorical tool for hermeneutic analysis (or as a methodological instrument), but as a normative model that hence legitimises the non-imputability of responsibility to the public actors who participate in these networks – our conceptualisation of decision-making and implementation processes refuses to accept the absence of the process of institutionalisation. Indeed, our model emphasises the role of the institutional components of the different products of the policy cycle in restricting the potential scope that the actors aim to modify by means of their direct and indirect games.

Finally on this point, a related limit of our approach concerns the fact that it ignores the human, personnel, spatial and psychological context of the policy actors and does not place the interactions we analyse in these contexts. This may be a serious limit to an approach claiming to be as explanatory to the extent that ours does. These types of context may play an important role that we deliberately ignore. Being fully aware of this limit, we can make two arguments that will reduce its scope: firstly, as explained in Chapter Three, our approach understands the rationale of actors in relation to their organisational affiliations and in relation to cognitive and perceptual limits. Secondly, we suggest that a more detailed approach to the actors would necessitate the use of other methodological tools that would make the analysis process simply too complex.

(b) Focusing on a substantive public problem

Our analysis model rests on a definition of policy as a response to a problem that has been politically defined as collective. This theory, or its most categorical version, is strongly challenged by several authors who adopt a so-called 'cognitive' approach to policy. These authors include Pierre Muller (2000, pp 194-5) who argues:

> ... that *public policies do not serve (at least exclusively) in the resolution of problems.* Of course, the point of this statement is not to assert that public policies have nothing to do with the resolution of public problems, whose existence is, alas, incontestable. It is a question of being aware that, contrary to what those responsible for policies would like to make us believe and what certain policy analysts would have us think, the relationship between public action and public problems is far more complex than suggested by the common notion to the effect that policies serve in the resolution of problems.[...] Public policies are used in both the construction of interpretations of reality (Why does unemployment continue to exist? How should the changes in the system of international relations be analysed? Is there deterioration in the level of food safety?), and in the definition of normative models for action (work must be made more flexible; the democratisation of the former Eastern countries must be supported; health and safety monitoring must be intensified). This way of making sense of the world involves the production of causal interpretations ('if unemployment increases, it is because our companies are not competitive in the context of globalisation') and normative interpretations ('to increase

the competitiveness of companies, it is "necessary" to increase the flexibility of work').

Thus, the analysis process involves the formulation and application of sectoral frameworks for interpreting the world (sectoral frames of reference) and their relation to the global frame of reference that underlies the interpretation of society as a whole. This approach uses the term 'mediators' to describe key actors within policy processes who implement cognitive and normative functions for interpreting the world and reducing the dissonance that exists between different sectoral frames of reference and the global frame of reference (Jobert and Muller, 1987; Muller, 1995; Muller and Surel, 1998).

In fact, the cognitive analysis of policies includes the global dimension – which is lacking in our approach – to make it possible to understand changes in public policies. It raises the entirely relevant question of the relationship between policies and the construction of a social order. Having contributed to the demystification of the supposed absolute rationality of an omniscient and omnipotent state that transcends the irrationality of individual interests, according to Muller (2000) policy analysis must now turn its attention to the question of the production of political order in our complex, fragmented and globalised societies.

The admission – in agreement with Muller (2000), Sabatier (1987) and a growing number of other authors (see, for example, March and Olsen, 1989; Fischer and Forester, 1993; Nullmeyer, 1993; Kissling-Näf, 1997; Kissling-Näf and Knoepfel, 1998) – that learning processes are unfolding in public policies and influencing both the substantive and institutional content of these policies does not, however, mean that policies must be solely considered as processes of social learning in the context of problems and frames of reference entirely constructed by actors. Furthermore, the deep convictions of the different actor coalitions located within the arena of a public policy, which only change very gradually over time, are generally founded on the recognition of problems deemed 'objective' and as a result shared by all (at least with respect to their public nature), even if it is clear that the actors only partly share the hypotheses on their causes and hence the intervention model on which a policy should be based.

(c) Individual policy as a restrictive unit of analysis

The reality of 21st-century politics represents a serious challenge to the focus of our theoretical model on policies as individual units of analysis. In effect, our process would appear to underestimate the fact that the lives of an administration and a country's citizens amount to more than an incessant passage from one policy to another. In fact, this conceptualisation is increasingly challenged in daily political reality and our analysis runs the risk of being biased due to this focus on one or more isolated policies for at least three reasons.

Firstly, cases whereby administrative units only manage a single policy (single policy administrations) are rare. Our approach takes this undeniable fact into account by (re-)introducing the administrative context as an important institutional dimension of the PAA. However, in specific cases such as that of the crisis of confidence of citizens in their political institutions, this institutional factor would appear to us to be more important than policy analysis would care to admit. Thus, we estimate that the political scandals in France or the crisis concerning 'individual records' in Switzerland have repercussions on several policies despite the fact that these policies have no direct substantive links with the stakes of the aforementioned crises.

There is evidence of a similar situation in the UK in which political action consists rather more in an increasingly desperate attempt to prove to the sceptical public that the government really is in charge rather than careful issue by issue problem solving (this is particularly evident in relation to contentious issues like law and order and immigration control). In such cases, policy analysis instruments prove inappropriate for demonstrating the considerable weight of this political factor. However, from the policy analysis point of view, recognition that there is much symbolic (Edelman, 1964, 1971) political activity occurring as opposed to forms of problem solving prevent analysts from getting sucked into evaluation in situations when rational analysis is of little use. That does not, however, imply that it is never of use.

Secondly, from the point of view of the majority of private actors (associations, economic interest groups, social movements, and so on), individuals, policy target groups and end beneficiaries, public life can hardly be dissected into (clearly identifiable) public policies. For the person in the street, public life presents itself in the form of a fabric of policies that are difficult to dissociate ('policy carpet'; see Knoepfel and Kissling-Näf, 1993). The arenas of these policies are superimposed on each other and in many cases the resulting actions and reactions are inexplicable to actors who focus on the products of a single isolated policy. The choice of policies targeted and singled out for political scrutiny is rarely based exclusively on the quality of the results of the policies in question.

Furthermore, it should not be forgotten that the behaviour of administrations and social actors with respect to a given policy depends largely on the cultural traditions that prevail in the regions and local authority areas. This point is particularly well illustrated in Switzerland – why, for example, do comparisons of the conduct of individual policies in the cantons of Vaud, Geneva and Valais regularly reveal the adoption of similar models at the level of administrative action?

Thirdly, the comparative analysis of policies sometimes proves excessively 'causal' when it comes to researching the explanatory factors behind policy products. It is true that all social scientific studies must define precisely the social phenomena that they propose to analyse and propose, in the form of hypotheses, the factors likely to explain the observed facts. In doing this, however, all such approaches risk quickly taking the wrong turn. Policy analysts, who concentrate on an extremely limited area, which in a great many cases is artificially dissociated from the rest of the world, should interpret their results with even greater care than analysts involved in other social science approaches (for example, the analysis of state measures that makes no claim to be explanatory and only proposes to confirm whether or not a specific measure is accompanied by a change in the real world).

(d) Additional comments on possible limitations

It is appropriate to add here some comments, linking the three points above, which seem particularly relevant to the application of this model to the UK. The emphasis of the model on analysing individual policies with a strong emphasis on problem solving, in a context of (as noted above) increasingly frenetic political action, seems to be at variance with:

- a strong emphasis on the ways in which policies are interconnected (expressed in colloquial terms as a need for 'joined-up' government);
- very rapid policy change, making evaluation very difficult, and suggesting an absence of a clear view of the cause of a problem;
- a tendency of politicians to express justifications of their policies in terms that the public regard with scepticism, something to which any detached policy analysis activity must pay attention.

Exploration of ways to deal with the problems these issues pose for analysis have been expressed at various points throughout the book, although readers who have been concentrating on the main aspects of the model may have disregarded them. They do not provide objections to the model; on the contrary the fact that the model offers an approach to policy analysis that must sometimes be hard to carry through in practice serves to highlight issues about the policy process – particularly issues about power and how it is used – that need attention.

Otherwise, there are clearly questions worthy of further comparative study here about the extent to which problem solving, the careful delineation of problems and the identification of targets and beneficiaries are more readily identifiable in some national institutional and cultural situations than others. There are related questions that have been addressed in the preparation of the English version of this book about the varied applicability of these concepts in different substantive policy areas. Thus problem diagnosis and the identification of target groups for policy (in the sense that particular groups and individuals can be seen as responsible for problems) is probably easier in relation to environmental policy than in many areas of social policy. It is for this reason that the notion of policy target groups is drawn very broadly here to embody actors whose behaviour must change, regardless of whether they can be held responsible for the identified problems in the first place, and to recognise that change by public actors may be as necessary as change by private actors.

12.3 Future developments

Bearing in mind the weaknesses identified above, it is very probable that our policy analysis model will develop further in the direction of (1) the analysis of governance examining the cooperation of several policies in a given functional or territorial unit, and (2) towards the real analysis of institutional regimes which, apart from public policies, would also include property relationships between actors (evolving in the medium and long term). More specifically, what is involved here is the introduction of new heuristic dimensions making it possible to record analytically the links, which in our opinion are still tenuous, between the ideas of governance, 'institutional regimes' and the concept of policy adopted in this book.

12.3.1 'Governance': towards the analysis of a set of policies

The installation of new infrastructure technologies, that is, network technologies (for example, internet, rail and air transport), normally results in the establishment of a large number of interconnected policies. Furthermore, the practical implementation of these policies affects the functioning of a series of already well-established policies (for example, spatial development policies, environmental protection policies, regional economic development policies). Given that they involve a vast number of local, regional, national and sometimes even international actors who produce numerous legislative, executive and evaluative decisions, simultaneously or consecutively and in different places, these policies necessitate a high level of interpolicy coordination (Knoepfel, 1995). Hence, the need for an entire new generation of institutional rules that oblige the actors involved in different policies to observe their obligations with respect to their own competencies and fields of action and also to agree on and exchange their resources, or even pool them (in particular through contractualisation processes). In the context of the new infrastructure networks, this task is made all the more sensitive because these installations often traverse several territories with different jurisdictions and a large number of policy arenas. The need for coordination of the actors of these policies, who are often isolated despite being connected in a network of public action, and the need for institutional innovations providing new forms of management for these 'sets' of policies, is set to increase significantly in the coming years.

Thus, it is imperative that we reflect coherently on new forms of 'governance' for these policies. These 'forms of governance' should be capable of coordinating, by means of legitimate decisions, the forms of cooperation between actors and products that govern the research, development and application of new types of collective infrastructure. What we mean here by 'governance' is a framework of institutional rules that facilitate the integrated management of policies that concern a territory or network of interconnected activities of local, regional, national and international import. These rules will connect and associate the public actors involved, the infrastructure operators and private organisations in the processes of development and implementation of collective choices capable of establishing active and coordinated support between the target groups (operators) and end beneficiaries (users). This framework consisting of rules governing the allocation of resources to the actors, their interaction and the (territorial or functional) boundaries of their actions will reflect the networking of technological systems. It will require rules governing both the internal and external (that is, with respect to other affected policies) functioning of the policies in question. These new regulatory structures for the control of interpolicy coordination must also respond to both the operational needs of each of the policies involved and the requirements dictated by the principles of democracy, the constitutional state, equality of treatment and subsidiarity.

Again, it would appear indispensable to us that tools be made available for analysing the functioning of the governance of such groups of policies that risk being used by political actors to conceal the responsibilities of the public actors involved. The analysis dimensions to be developed will also make it possible to identify the real responsibilities of these actors and to define the contribution made by each actor to the effectiveness or failure of the policies in question.

12.3.2 'Institutional regimes': towards an analysis that includes the property rights of actors

In a number of areas, policy implementation activities consist in the provision of goods (for example, drinking water, electricity) and services (for example, hospital care, education) to citizens. In the past, in France, Switzerland and the UK, these goods and services were produced by public organisations. As part of the ongoing deregulation of these, the production of these goods and services is now being transferred to competing public and/or private companies. We are currently also witnessing a wave of privatisations of former public organisations. This significant trend not only affects traditional public goods and services, it is also resulting in the allocation of new use rights in areas that were previously freely accessible to all. This can be observed, in particular, in the distribution of rights to the use of natural resources such as air, air space, nature and water and in the restriction of rights of access by the state through the levying of fees to public resources, such as roads and public spaces and museums.

In many such cases, what is actually involved are activities controlled by policies that allocate actual use rights to certain goods and services in their attempts to resolve collective problems. These use rights are increasingly characterised by their transferability and their degree of exclusivity. Thus, we qualify this type of public intervention not as the simple management of a policy, but as the creation and maintenance of actual institutional regimes for the production and allocation of goods and services vital to the everyday life of a society.

These institutional regimes are characterised by the creation and (legal) recognition of rights of ownership, disposal and use defined in the constitution (for example, the recognition of private property) and/or in civil law. Certain policies create new rights that modify this general property order or create a property order specific to a given sector. In other cases, this change in the property order arises as a result of the nationalisation or privatisation of public organisations that affects an entire sector of a country's economy. Nonetheless, the 'daily' conduct of these regimes continues to be managed by one or more public policies, and new regulatory bodies may be created to undertake this task (with themselves areas of autonomy that may provide challenges for public policy control).

This particular constellation places new constraints on the choices open to policy actors who must henceforth take the rights of ownership, disposal and use 'acquired' by certain actors into account in their decision making. Thus, to a greater extent than in the past, policies must now observe the institutional rules governing the relationship between actors and also those governing the property relationships between the actors and the relevant goods and services. These rules refer either to one of the policy products provided in the form of a commodity or service or to traditional production factors brought together by new, former public, actors who continue to produce the services to which everyone is entitled, but now as private operators.

It should also be noted that unlike traditional policies, which worked with the simple and enduring property rules laid down in the constitution or law, the policies associated with institutional regimes are increasingly creating institutional rules that will subject the policies themselves to considerably stricter restrictions given that the rights of ownership, disposal and use created attain the status of actual acquired rights. This status is conferred on them either (for the target groups) as a result of the high level of investment necessary for the production of the goods and services in question or (for the end beneficiaries) due to the concern to liberate the administrations and politicians from the burden of making difficult decisions with regard to the allocation of goods and services.

This observation is compatible with our previous argument concerning the creation of an increasing number of specific institutional rules at the level of individual policies. However, it goes considerably further in the sense that we are not dealing with rules of an exclusively decisional (between actors) nature, but with rules that also establish property relationships between an actor and a resource, a particular commodity or service. The creation of such rules contributes to the transformation of policies into components of actual institutional regimes.

Thus, in our opinion, it is now time to extend policy analysis in the direction of the analysis of institutional regimes. In terms of the analysis dimensions, this development necessitates the inclusion of the creation of new property rules because these may considerably strengthen the position of certain (private) actors vis-à-vis other (public) actors in policy arenas. If the existence of such a process were to be confirmed in the future, it would make public actors considerably more dependent on private actors than is currently the case. Thus, it is up to the policy analyst to draw the attention of politicians to such potential consequences of their decisions (in particular in relation to privatisation) and to develop appropriate analysis dimensions to register the emergence and perpetuation of these new institutional regimes.

References

Adler, M. and Asquith, S. (eds) (1981) *Discretion and welfare*, London: Heinemann.

Anderson, C.W. (1978) 'The logic of public problems: evaluation in comparative policy research', in D.E. Ashford (ed) *Comparing public policies: New concepts and methods*, Beverly Hills, CA/London: Sage Publications.

Anderson, J.E. (1984) *Public policy making*, New York, NY: Holt Rinehart and Winston.

Audit Commission (2006) *Annual review 2005-6: Getting better value for public service*, London: Audit Commission.

Bachrach, P. and Baratz, M.S. (1963) 'Decisions and nondecisions: an analytical framework', *American Political Science Review*, vol 57, pp 632-42.

Bachrach, P. and Baratz, M.S. (1970) *Power and poverty: Theory and practice*, New York, NY: Oxford University Press.

Baitsch, C., Knoepfel, P. and Eberle, A. (1996) 'Prinzipien und Instrumente organisationalen Lernens. Dargestellt an einem Fall aus der öffentlichen Verwaltung', *Organisationsentwicklung*, vol 3, pp 4-21.

Baldwin, R. (1995) *Rules and government*, Oxford: Oxford University Press.

Bardach, E. (1977) *The implementation game: What happens after a bill becomes a law*, Cambridge, MA: MIT Press.

Barker, A. and Peters, B.G. (ed) (1993) *The politics of expert advice*, Edinburgh: Edinburgh University Press.

Baroni, D. (1992) *Aperçu sur les politiques cantonales de prévention et de lutte contre les catastrophes naturelles de quelques cantons alpins (Grisons, Tessin, Uri, Valais, Vaud), étude préliminaire*, PNR 31, Berne.

Barrett, S. and Fudge, C. (1981) 'Examining the policy-action relationship' and 'Reconstructing the field of analysis', in S. Barrett and C. Fudge (eds) *Policy and action. Essays on the implementation of public policy*, London: Routledge, pp 3-34 and 249-78.

Bättig, C., Knoepfel, P., Peter, K. and Teuscher, F. (2001) 'Konzept für ein Policy-Monitoring zur Erhaltung der Biodiversität', *Zeitschrift für Umweltpolitik und Umweltrecht*, vol 24, pp 21-59.

Bättig, C., Knoepfel, P., Peter, K. and Teuscher, F. (2002) 'A concept for integrated policy and environment monitoring system', in P. Knoepfel, C. Bättig, K. Peter and F. Teuscher, *Environmental policies 1982-2002*, Bâle: Helbing & Lichtenhahn.

Baumgartner, F.R. and Jones, B.D. (1993) *Agendas and instability in American politics*, Chicago, IL: University of Chicago Press.

Benninghoff, M., Joerchel, B. and Knoepfel, P. (eds) (1997) *L'écobusiness: Enjeux et perspectives pour la politique de l'environnement*, Bâle/Frankfurt am Main: Helbing & Lichtenhahn (série Ecologie & Société, vol 11).

Bernoux, P. (1985) *La sociologie des organisations*, Paris: Seuil.

Berthelot, J.-M. (1990) *L'intelligence du social. Le pluralisme explicatif en sociologie*, Paris: Presses Universitaires de France.

Blowers, A. (1984) *Something in the air: Corporate power and the environment*, London: Harper and Row.

Bobrow, D.J. and Dryzek, J.S. (1987) *Policy analysis by design*, Pittsburgh, PA: University of Pittsburgh Press.

Bohnert, W. and Klitzsch, W. (1980) 'Gesellschaftliche Selbstregulierung und staatliche Steuerung. Steuerungstheoretische Anmerkungen zur Implementation politischer Programme', in R. Mayntz (ed) *Implementation politischer Programme. Empirische Forschungsberichte*, Königstein/Ts: Athenäum, pp 200-15.

Boudon, R. (1979) *La logique du social*, Paris: Hachette.

Boudon, R. and Bourricaud, F. (1990) *Dictionnaire critique de la sociologie*, Paris: Presses Universitaires de France.

Bourrelier, P.H. (1997) *Evaluation de la politique française de prévention des risques naturels*, Rapport de l'instance de la politique publique de prévention des risques naturels, Paris: Commissariat Général au Plan, La Documentation Française.

Bourricaud, F. (1977) *L'individualisme institutionnel: Essai sur la sociologie de Talcott Parsons*, Paris: Presses Universitaires de France.

Bovens, M., 't Hart, P. and Peters, B.G. (eds) (2001) *Success and failure in public governance*, Cheltenham: Edward Elgar.

Brandl, J. (1987) 'On politics and policy analysis as the design and assessment of institutions', *Journal of Policy Analysis and Management*, vol 7, no 3, pp 419-24.

Buchanan, J. and Tullock, G. (1962) *The calculus of consent: Logical foundation of constitutional democracy*, Ann Arbor, MI: University of Michigan Press.

Budge, I. and Farlie, D. (1983) 'Party competition: selective emphasis or direct confrontation? An alternative view with data', in H. Daalder and P. Mair (eds) *Western European party systems*, Beverly Hills, CA: Sage Publications, pp 267-305.

References

Bussmann, W. (1989) 'Von der Doppelbödigkeit des Verhältnisses zwischen Wissenschaft und Politik', *Annuaire Suisse de Science Politique*, vol 29, pp 17-30.

Bussmann, W. (1995) *Accompagner et mettre à profit avec succès les évaluations des mesures étatiques*, Genève: Georg.

Bussmann, W. (1998) 'Les évaluations en Suisse', in W. Bussmann, U. Klöti and P. Knoepfel (eds) *Politiques publiques. Evaluation*, Paris: Economica, pp 13-33.

Bussmann, W., Klöti, U. and Knoepfel, P. (eds) (1998) *Politiques publiques: Evaluation*, Paris: Economica.

Cahill, M. (2002) *The environment and social policy*, London: Routledge.

Callon, M. and Rip, A. (1991) 'Forums hybrides et négociations des normes socio-techniques dans le domaine de l'environnement. La fin des experts et l'irresistible ascension de l'expertise', in J. Theys (ed) *Environnement, science et politiques. Les experts sont formels*, GERMES: Cahier du GERMES, pp 227-38.

Carter, N. (2001) *The politics of the environment*, Cambridge: Cambridge University Press.

Castells, M. and Godard, F. (1974) *Monopolville: Analyse des rapports entre l'entreprise, l'etat et l'urbain à partir d'une enquête sur la croissance industrielle et urbaine de la région de Dunkerque*, Paris: Mouton.

Chelimsky, E. (1987) 'Linking program evaluation to user needs', in D.J. Palumbo (ed) *The politics of program evaluation*, Newbury Park, CA: Sage Publications, pp 72-99.

Chevallier, J. (1981) 'L'analyse institutionnelle', in J. Chevallier et al (eds) *L'institution*, Paris: Presses Universitaires de France, pp 3-61.

Chevallier, J. et al (eds) (1981) *L'institution*, Paris: Presses Universitaires de France.

Clivaz, C. (1998) *Réseaux d'action publique et changement de politique publique*, Cahier de l'IDHEAP 175/1998, Chavannes-près-Renens: IDHEAP.

Clivaz, C. (2001) *Influence des réseaux d'action publique sur le changement politique. Le cas de l'écologisation du tourisme alpin en Suisse et dans le canton du Valais*, Bâle: Helbing & Lichtenhahn (série Ecologie & Société, no 15).

Cobb, R.W. and Elder, C.D. (1983) *Participation in American politics: The dynamics of agenda-building*, Baltimore, MD: Johns Hopkins University Press.

Cobb, R.W., Ross, J.K. and Ross, M.H. (1976) 'Agenda building as a comparative political process', *American Political Science Review*, vol 70, no 1, pp 126-38.

Cook, F.L., Tyler, T.R., Goetz, E.G., Gordon, M.T., Protess, D., Leff, D.R. and Molotch, H.L. (1983) 'Media and agenda setting: effects on the public, interest groups leaders, policy makers and policy', *Public Opinion Quarterly*, vol 47, pp 16-35.

Crenson, M.A. (1971) *The unpolitics of air pollution*, Baltimore, MD: Johns Hopkins University Press.

Crozier, M. (1963) *Le phénomène bureaucratique*, Paris: Seuil [published in English in 1964 as *The bureaucratic phenomenon*, Chicago, IL: University of Chicago Press].

Crozier, M. (1991) *Etat modeste, etat moderne: Stratégie pour un autre changement*, Paris: Fayard.

Crozier, M. and Friedberg, E. (1977) *L'acteur et le système: Les contraintes de l'action collective*, Paris: Seuil.

Crozier, M. and Thoenig, J.C. (1975) 'La régulation des systèmes organisés complexes', *Revue française de sociologie*, vol XVI, no 1, pp 3-32.

Czada, R. (1991) 'Muddling through a "nuclear-political" emergency: multilevel crisis management after radioactive fallout from Chernobyl', *Industrial Crisis Quarterly*, vol 5, pp 293-322.

Dahme, J., Grunow, D. and Hegner, F. (1980) 'Aspekte der Implementation sozialpolitischer Anreizprogramme: Zur Überlappung von Programmentwicklung und Programmimplementation am Beispiel der staatlichen Förderprogramme für Sozialstationen', in R. Mayntz (ed) *Implementation politischer Programme. Empirische Forschungsberichte*, Königstein/Ts: Athenäum, pp 154-75.

Davies, H.T.O., Nutley, S.M. and Smith, P.C. (eds) (2000) *What works? Evidence-based policy and practice in public services*, Bristol: The Policy Press.

Deleau, M., Nioche, J.P., Penz, P. and Poinsard, R. (1986) *Evaluer les politiques publiques: Méthodes, déontologie, organisation*, Paris: Commissariat Général du Plan, La Documentation Française.

DeLeon, P. (1994) 'Reinventing the policy sciences. Three steps back to the future', *Policy Sciences*, vol 27, pp 77-95.

Delley, J.-D. (1991) 'L'action par la formation', in C.-A. Morand (ed) *Les instruments d'action de l'etat*, Bâle/Francfort-sur-le-Main: Helbing & Lichtenhahn, pp 89-112.

Delley, J.-D., Derivaz, R., Mader, L., Morand, C.-A. and Schneider, D. (1982) *Le droit en action. Etude de mise en oeuvre de la loi Furgler*, (Publications du Fonds National Suisse de la Recherche Scientifique dans le Cadre des Programmes Nationaux de Recherche, vol 16), Saint-Saphorin: Georgi.

Denham, A. and Garnett, M. (2004) 'A "hollowed out" tradition? British think tanks in the twenty-first century', in D. Stone and A. Denham (eds) *Think tank traditions: Policy research and the politics of ideas*, Manchester: Manchester University Press.

Dente, B. (1985) *Governare la frammentazione*, Bologna: Il Mulino.

Dente, B. (1989) *Politiche pubbliche e pubblica amministrazione*, Rimini: Maggioli Queste Istituzioni Ricerche.

Dente, B. (ed) (1995) *Environmental policy in search of new instruments*, Dordrecht/Boston, MD: Kluwer Academic Publishers.

Dente, B. and Fareri, P. (1993) *Deciding about waste facilities citing lessons from cases of success in five European countries: Guidelines for case-study analysis*, Milan: Istituto per la Ricerca Sociale.

Dente, B. and Fareri, P. (1998) 'Siting waste facilities: drawing lessons from success stories', in B. Dente, P. Fareri and J. Ligteringen (eds) *The waste and the backyard. The creation of waste facilities: Success stories in six European countries*, Dordrecht/Boston, MD: Kluwer Academic Publishers (series: Environment & Management, vol 8), pp 3-46.

Dery, D. (1984) *Problem definition in policy analysis*, Lawrence, KS: University of Kansas Press.

DFJP (Département Fédéral de Justice et Police) (1975) *Auswirkungen von Tempo 100/130*, Schlussbericht der vom EJPD eingesetzten Arbeitsgruppe "Tempo 100", Bern (mimeo).

Dockès, P. (1997) *La nouvelle économie institutionnelle. L'évolutionnisme et l'histoire*, Cahier No 105 du Centre Auguste et Léon Walras, Lyon: Centre Walras.

Dolowitz, D.P. and Marsh, D. (2000) 'Learning from abroad: the role of policy transfer in contemporary policy making', *Governance*, vol 13, no 1, pp 5-24.

Dolowitz, D.P., Hulme, R., Nellis, M. and O'Neill, F. (2002) *Policy transfer and British social policy: Learning from the USA?*, Buckingham: Open University Press.

Dorey, P. (2005) *Policy making in Britain*, London: Sage Publications.

Downs, A. (1957) *An economic theory of democracy*, New York, NY: Harper and Row.

Downs, A. (1973) 'Up and down with ecology. The issue attention cycle', *Public Interest*, vol 32, pp 38-50.

Drewry, G. (2002) 'The New Public Management', in J. Jowell and D. Oliver (eds) *The changing constitution*, Oxford: Oxford University Press, pp 167-89.

Dryzek, J.S. and Ripley, B. (1988) 'The ambitions of policy design', *Policy Studies Review*, vol 7, pp 705-19.

Dunleavy, P. (1995) 'Policy disasters: explaining the UK's record', *Public Policy and Administration*, vol 10, no 2, pp 52-69.

Duran, P. (1993) 'Les difficultés de la négociation institutionnalisée, le parc national des Pyrénées occidentales', *Annuaire des Collectivités Locales*, 5th series.

Duran, P. and Monnier, E. (1992) 'Le développement de l'évaluation en France: nécessités techniques et exigences politiques', *Revue Française de Science Politique*, vol 42, pp 235-62.

Duran, P. and Thoenig, J.C. (1996) 'L'etat et la gestion publique territoriale', *Revue Française de Sciences Politiques*, vol 46, no 4, pp 580-623.

Duverger, M. (1968) *Institutions politiques et droit constitutionnel*, Paris: Presses Universitaires de France.

Dye, T.R. (1972) *Understanding public policy*, Englewood Cliffs, NJ: Prentice-Hall.

Easton, D. (1965) *A systems analysis of political life*, New York, NY: Wiley.

Edelman, M. (1964) *The symbolic uses of politics*, Urbana, IL: University of Illinois Press.

Edelman, M. (1971) *Politics as symbolic action*, Chicago, IL: Markham Publishing Company.

Edelman, M. (1988) *Constructing the political spectacle*, Urbana, IL: University of Illinois Press.

Emery, Y. (1995) 'Le management de la qualité dans les administrations publiques: une des pierres angulaires du New Public Management', in Y. Emery (ed) *Total quality management und ISO-Zertifizierung in der öffentlichen Verwaltung der Schweiz*, Berne: *Collection Société Suisse des Sciences Administratives*, vol 34, pp 37-83.

Emery, Y. and Gonin, F. (1999) *Dynamiser les ressources humaines. Une approche intégrée pour les services publics et entreprises privées compatible avec les normes de qualité*, Lausanne: Presses Polytechniques et Universitaires Romandes.

European Commission (1999) *Evaluer les programmes socio-économiques*, 6 vol Collection MEANS, Luxembourg: Office des Publications Officielles des Communautées Européennes.

Evans, P.B., Rueschemeyer, D. and Skocpol, T. (eds) (1985) *Bringing the state back in*, Cambridge: Cambridge University Press.

Exworthy, M., Berney, L. and Powell, M. (2002) '"How great expectations in Westminster may be dashed locally": the implementation of national policy on health inequalities', *Policy & Politics*, vol 30, no 1, pp 79-96.

Faber, H. (1974) *Das Organisationsrecht der Planung*, Konstanz: Mskr.

References

Finger, M. (1997) 'Le New Public Management: reflet et initiateur d'un changement de paradigme dans la gestion des affaires publiques', *Nouvelle Gestion Publique*, Genève: Université de Genève/Faculté de Droit, pp 41-60.

Fischer, F. (2003) *Reframing public policy*, Oxford: Oxford University Press.

Fischer, F. and Forester, J. (eds) (1993) *The argumentative turn in policy analysis and planning*, London: UCL Press.

Flückiger, A. (1998) *L'extension du contrôle juridictionnel des activités de l'administration, un examen généralisé des actes matériels sur le modèle allemand?*, Berne: Staempfli.

Forrest, R. and Murie, A. (1988) *Selling the welfare state*, London: Routledge.

Fourniau, J.M. (1996) 'Transparence des décisions et participation des citoyens', *Techniques, Territoires et Sociétés*, no 31, pp 9-90.

Fox, C.J. and Miller, H.T. (1995) *Postmodern public administration: Toward discourse*, Thousand Oaks, CA: Sage Publications.

Freiburghaus, D. (1991) 'Le développement des moyens de l'action étatique', in C-A. Morand (ed), *L'Etat propulsif. Contribution à l'étude des instruments d'action de l'Etat*, Paris: Publisud, pp 49-63.

Freiburghaus, D., Zimmermann, W. and Balthasar, A. (1990) *Evaluation der Förderung praxisorientierter Forschung (KWF)*, Bern: Schriftenreihe des Bundesamts für Konjunkturfragen, Studie Nr 12.

Friedberg, E. (1993) *Le pouvoir et la règle: Dynamiques de l'action organisée*, Paris: Seuil.

Frossard, S. and Hagmann, T. (2000) *La réforme de la politique d'asile suisse à travers les mesures d'urgence – "Le vrai, le faux et le crimine"*, Cahier de l'IDHEAP no 191, Chavannes-près-Renens: IDHEAP.

Garraud, P. (1990) 'Politiques nationales: élaboration de l'agenda', *L'Année Sociologique*, no 40, pp 17-41.

Gaudin, J.-P. (1995) 'Politiques urbaines et négociations territoriales. Quelle légitimité pour les réseaux de politiques publiques?', *Revue Française de Science Politique*, vol 45, no 1, pp 31-56.

Gaudin, J.-P. (ed) (1996) *La négociation des politiques contractuelles*, Paris: L'Harmattan.

Gentile, P. (1995) *Lernprozesse in Verwaltungen. Etude de cas sur trois politiques sanitaires en Suisse*, Cahier de l'IDHEAP no 142, Chavannes-près-Renens: IDHEAP.

Germann, R.E. (1987) 'L'amalgame public-privé: l'administration para-étatique en Suisse', *Revue Politique et Management Public*, vol 5, no 2, pp 91-105.

Germann, R.E. (1991) 'Die Europatauglichkeit der direktdemokratischen Institutionen der Schweiz', *Schweizerisches Jahrbuch für politische Wissenschaft*, vol 3, pp 257-69.

Germann, R.E. (1996) *Administration publique en Suisse*, Berne: Haupt.

Germann, R.E., Roig, C., Urio, P. and Wemegah, M. (1979) *Fédéralisme en action: L'aménagement du territoire. Les mesures urgentes à Genève, en Valais et au Tessin*, Collection Etudes urbaines et régionales, Saint-Saphorin: Georgi.

Gibert, P. (1985) 'Management public, management de la puissance publique', *Politique et Management Public*, vol 4, no 2, pp 1-17.

Glendinning, C., Powell, M. and Rummery, K. (eds) (2002) *Partnerships, New Labour and the governance of welfare*, Bristol: The Policy Press.

Godard, F. (ed) (1997) *Le gouvernement des villes: Territoire et pouvoir*, Paris: Descartes et Cie.

Gomà, R. and Subirats, J. (eds) (1998) *Polìticas pùblicas en España: Contenidos, redes de actores y niveles de gobierno*, Barcelona: Editorial Ariel SA.

Goodin, R.E. (1996) *The theory of institutional design*, Cambridge: Cambridge University Press.

Gormley, W.T. (1975) 'Newspaper agenda and political elites', *Journalism Quarterly*, vol 52, pp 304-8.

Grawitz, M. and Leca, J. (eds) (1985). *Traité de science politique, tome 4: Les politiques publiquers*, Paris: Presses Universitaires de France.

Greer, A. (1999) 'Policy co-ordination and the British administrative system: evidence from the BSE Inquiry', *Parliamentary Affairs*, vol 54, p 4.

Grottian, P. (1974) *Strukturprobleme staatlicher Planung*, Hambourg: Campus.

Gusfield, J.R. (1981) *The culture of public problems: Drinking-driving and the symbolic order*, Chicago, IL: University of Chicago Press.

Habermas, J. (1973) *Legitimationsprobleme im Spätkapitalismus*, Frankfurt: Suhrkamp.

Hablützel, P. (1995) 'New Public Management als Modernisierungschance – Thesen zur Entbürokratisierungsdiskussion', in P. Hablützel, T. Haldemann, K. Schedler and K. Schwaar (eds) *Umbruch in Politik und Verwaltung: Ansichten und Erfahrungen zum New Public Management in der Schweiz*, Bern: Haupt, pp 499-507.

Hall, P.A. (1986) *Governing the economy: The politics of state intervention in Britain and France*, Cambridge: Polity Press.

Hall, P.A. (1993) 'Policy paradigms, social learning and the state: the case of economic policy making in Britain', *Comparative Politics*, vol 25, pp 275-96.

Hall, P.A. and Taylor, R.C.R. (1996) 'Political science and the three new institutionalisms', *Political Studies*, vol 44, no 5, pp 936-57.

Hanser, C., Kuster, J. and Cavelti, G. (1994) *Hotellerieförderung durch Bund und Kantone. Evaluation der Auswirkungen in der Hotellerie*, Berne: Bundesamt für Industrie, Gewerbe und Arbeit, Beiträge zur Tourismuspolitik, Nr 3.

Heclo, H. (1972) 'Policy analysis', *British Journal of Political Science*, vol 2, pp 83-108.

Hellstern, G.-M. and Wollmann, H. (1983) *Evaluierungsforschung: Ansätze und Methoden – dargestellt am Beispiel des Städtebaus*, Bâle: Birkhäuser Verlag.

Hilgartner, S. and Bosk, C. (1988) 'The rise and fall of social problems: a public arenas model', *American Journal of Sociology*, vol 94, no 1, pp 53-78.

Hill, M. (2000) *Local authority social services*, Oxford: Blackwell.

Hill, M. (2005) *The public policy process*, Harlow: Pearson Education.

Hill, M. and Hupe, P. (2002) *Implementing public policy*, London: Sage Publications.

Hill, M. and Hupe, P. (2006) 'Analysing policy processes as multiple governance: accountability in social policy', *Policy & Politics*, vol 34, no 3, pp 557-73.

Hisschemöller, M. and Hoppe, R. (1996) 'Coping with intractable controversies: the case for problem structuring in policy design and analysis', *Knowledge and Policy: The International Journal of Knowledge Transfer and Utilization*, vol 8, no 4, pp 40-61.

Hjern, B. (1978) 'Implementation and network analysis', Paper presented to ECPR workshop on Implementation of Public Policies, Grenoble.

Hjern, B. and Hull, C. (1983) 'Policy analysis in mixed economy. An implementation approach', *Policy & Politics*, vol 11, pp 295-312.

Hofferbert, R. (1974) *The study of public policy*, Indianapolis, IN/New York, NY: Bobbs-Merril.

Hofferbert, R. and Budge, J. (1992) 'The party mandate and Westminster model: election programmes and government spending in Britain, 1948-85', *British Journal of Political Science*, vol 22, pp 151-82.

Hoffmann-Riem, W. (1989) 'Konfliktmittler in Verwaltungsverhandlungen', *Beiträge zu neueren Entwicklungen in der Rechtswissenschaft*, no 22, Heidelberg: C.F. Müller.

Hoffmann-Riem, W. and Schmidt-Assmann, E. (eds) (1990) *Konfliktbewältigung durch Verhandlungen. Konfliktmittlung in Verwaltungsverfahren*, Baden-Baden: Nomos, pp 185-208.

Hood, C. (1986) *The tools of government*, Chatham, NJ: Chatham House.

Hood, C. (1995) 'Contemporary public management: a new global paradigm?', *Public Policy and Administration*, vol 10, no 2, pp 104-17.

Howlett, M. (1991) 'Policy instruments, policy styles and policy implementation: national approaches to theories of instrument choice', *Policy Studies Journal*, vol 19, no 2, pp 1-21.

Howlett, M. and Ramesh, M. (2003) *Studying public policy*, Don Mills, Ontario: Oxford University Press.

Hudson, B. and Henwood, M. (2002) 'The NHS and social care: the final countdown?', *Policy & Politics*, vol 30, no 2, pp 153-66.

Hulley, T. and Clarke, J. (1991) 'Social problems: social construction and social causation', in M. Loney, J. Bocock, J. Clarke, A. Cochrane, P. Graham and M. Wilson (eds) *The state or the market: Politics and welfare in contemporary Britain*, London: Sage Publications.

Hupe, P. and Hill, M. (2006) 'The three action levels of governance: re-framing the policy process beyond the stages model', in B.G. Peters and J. Pierre (eds) *Handbook of public policy*, London: Sage Publications, pp 13-30.

Hupe, P. and Hill, M. (2007) 'Accountability and street-level bureaucracy', *Public Administration*, forthcoming.

Jaeger, C., Beck, A., Bieri, L., Dürrenberger, G. and Rudel, R. (1998) *Klimapolitik: Eine Chance für die Schweiz, das Potential innovativer regionaler Milieus zur Entwicklung praktikabler Strategien angesichts der Risiken einer globalen Klimaveränderung*, Zurich: vdf (Arbeitsbericht NFP 31).

Jänicke, M. and Weidner, H. (eds) (1995) *Successful environmental policy: A critical evaluation of 24 cases*, Berlin: Sigma.

Jenkins, W.I. (1978) *Policy analysis*, Oxford: Martin Robertson.

Jenkins-Smith, H.C. and Sabatier, P.A. (1993) 'The dynamics of policy-oriented learning', in P.A. Sabatier and H.C. Jenkins-Smith (eds) *Policy change and learning: An advocacy coalitions approach*, San Francisco, CA: Westview Press, pp 41-56.

Jobert, B. and Muller, P. (1987) *L'etat en action: Politiques publiques et corporatismes*, Paris: Presses Universitaires de France.

Jones, C.O. (1970) *An introduction to the study of public policy*, Belmont, CA: Duxbury Press.

Jordan, A.G. (1998) 'Private affluence and public squalor: the Europeanisation of British coastal bathing water policy', *Policy & Politics*, vol 26, no 1, pp 33-54.

Jordan, A.G. and Richardson, J. (1982) 'The British policy style or the logic of negotiation', in J. Richardson (ed) *Policy styles in Western Europe*, London: Allen and Unwin.

References

Jordan, A.G. and Richardson, J.J. (1987) *British politics and the policy process*, London: Unwin Hyman.

Jordan, G. (1994) *The British administrative system*, London: Routledge.

Jowell, J. and Oliver, D. (eds) (2002) *The changing constitution*, Oxford: Oxford University Press.

Kaufmann, F.X. and Rosewitz, B. (1983) 'Typisierung und Klassifikation politischer Massnahmen', in R. Mayntz (ed) *Implementation politischer Programme II. Ansätze zur Theoriebildung*, Opladen, pp 25-49.

Keller-Lengen, Ch., Keller, F. and Ledergerber, R. (1998) *Die Gesellschaft im Umgang mit Lawinengefahren. Fallstudie Graubünden*, Zürich: vdf (Arbeitsbericht NFP 31).

Kessler, M.C. et al (1998) *Evaluation des politiques publiques*, Paris: L'Harmattan.

Keynes, J.M. (1936) *The general theory of employment, interest and money*, London: Macmillan.

Killias, M. (1998) 'Consommation de drogue et criminalité parmi les jeunes dans une perspective internationale', *Les délinquants usagers de drogues et le système pénal*, Strasbourg: Edition du Conseil de l'Europe, pp 23-55.

Killias, M. and Grapendaal, M. (1997) 'Entkriminalisierung des Drogenkonsums oder Einschränkung der Strafverfolgungspflicht? Diskussionsvorschlag zur Vermeidung einer sterilen Debatte – unter Berücksichtigung des niederländischen Modells', *Schweizerische Zeitschrift für Strafrecht*, Bern, Bd 115 (1997), H 1, pp 94-109.

Kinderman, H. (1988) 'Symbolische Gesetzgebung', in *Gesetzgebungstheorie und Rechtspolitik*, Jahrbuch für Rechtssoziologie und Rechtstheorie, Band 13, Opladen, pp 222-45.

Kingdon, J.W. (1984) *Agendas, alternatives and public policies*, New York, NY: Harper Collins.

Kingdon, J.W. (1995) *Agendas, alternatives and public policies* (2nd edn), New York, NY: Addison Wesley.

Kiser, L. and Ostrom, E. (1982) 'The three worlds of action', in E. Ostrom (ed) *Strategies of political inquiry*, Beverly Hills, CA: Sage Publications, pp 179-222.

Kissling-Näf, I. (1997) *Lernprozesse und Umweltverträglichkeitsprüfung. Staatliche Steuerung über Verfahren und Netzwerkbildung in der Abfallpolitik*, Bâle: Helbing & Lichtenhahn (série Ecologie & Société, vol 12).

Kissling-Näf, I. and Knoepfel, P. (1998) 'Lernprozesse in öffentlichen Politiken', in H. Albach, M. Dierkes, A. Berthoin Antal and K. Vaillant (eds) *Organisationslernen – institutionelle und kulturelle Dimensionen*, Berlin: Sigma (WZB-Jahrbuch), pp 239-69.

Kissling-Näf, I. and Wildi-Ballabio, E. (1993) 'Kontrollinstrumente zur erfolgreichen Implementation von Politiken: Impulse der Umweltbeobachtung für ein intergriertes Policy-Monitoring', *Annuaire Suisse de Science Politique*, vol 33, pp 277-94.

Kissling-Näf, I., Knoepfel, P. and Bussmann, W. (1998) 'Amorcer un processus d'apprentissage par une évaluation', in W. Bussmann, U. Klöti and P. Knoepfel, *Politiques publiques. Evaluation*, Paris: Economica, pp 247-70.

Kleinnijenhuis, J. and Rietberg, E.M. (1995) 'Parties, media, the public and the economy: patterns of societal agenda-setting', *European Journal of Political Science*, vol 28, no 1, pp 95-108.

Klingeman, H.D. et al (eds) (1994) *Parties, policies and democracy*, Boulder, CO: Westview Press.

Klok, P.J. de (1995) 'A classification of Instruments for Environmental Policy', in B. Dente (ed), *Environmental Policy in Search of New Instruments*, Dordrecht: Kluwer, pp 21-36.

Klöti, U. (1998) 'Les exigences substantielles et méthodologiques de l'évaluation scientifique des politiques publiques', in W. Bussmann, U. Klöti and P. Knoepfel, *Politiques Publiques. Evaluation*, Paris: Economica, pp 37-54.

Knapp, B. (1991) 'Information et persuasion', in C.-A. Morand (ed) *Les instruments d'action de l'etat*, Bâle/Francfort-sur-le Main: Helbing & Lichtenhahn, pp 45-88.

Knight, J. (1992) *Institutions and social conflict*, New York, NY: Cambridge University Press.

Knoepfel, P. (1977) *Demokratisierung der Raumplanung. Grundsätzliche Aspekte und Modell für die Organisation der kommunalen Nutzungsplanung unter besonderer Berücksichtigung der schweizerischen Verhältnisse*, Berlin: Duncker & Humblot.

Knoepfel, P. (1979) *Öffentliches Recht und Vollzugsforschung*, Bern: Haupt.

Knoepfel, P. (1986) 'Distributional issues in regulatory policy implementation – the case of air quality control policies', in A. Schnaiberg, N. Watts and K. Zimmermann (eds) *Distributional conflicts in environmental policy*, Aldershot: Gower, pp 363-79.

Knoepfel, P. (1995) 'New institutional arrangements for a new generation of environmental policy instruments: intra- and interpolicy cooperation', in B. Dente (ed) *Environmental policy in search of new instruments*, European Science Foundation, Dordrecht: Kluwer Academic Publishers, pp 197-233.

Knoepfel, P. (1996) 'Plädoyer für ein tatsächlich wirkungsorientiertes Public Management', *Revue Suisse de Science Politique*, vol 2, no 1, pp 151-64.

References

Knoepfel, P. (1997a) 'Le New Public Management: attentes insatisfaites ou échecs préprogrammés – une critique à la lumière de l'analyse des politiques publiques', in CETEL (Université de Genève), *Nouvelle gestion publique: Chances et limites d'une réforme de l'administration*, Travaux CETEL no 48, Genève: Université de Genève, pp 73-92.

Knoepfel, P. (1997b) *Conditions pour une mise en oeuvre efficace des politiques environnementales*, Cahier de l'IDHEAP no 167, Chavannes-près-Renens: IDHEAP.

Knoepfel, P. (2000) 'Policykiller – Institutionenkiller – ein Triptichon zum Verhältnis zwischen institutionellen und substantiellen öffentlichen Politiken', in P. Knoepfel and W. Linder (eds) *Verwaltung, Regierung und Verfassung im Wandel. Gedächtnisschrift für Raimund E. Germann. Administration, gouvernement et constitution en transformation. Hommage en mémoire de Raimund E. Germann*, Bâle: Helbing & Lichtenhahn, pp 285-300.

Knoepfel, P. and Horber-Papazian, K. (1990) 'Objets de l'évaluation: essai d'identification à l'aide du concept de politiques publiques', in K. Horber-Papazian (ed) *Evaluation des politiques publiques en suisse. Pourquoi? Pour qui? Comment?*, Lausanne: Presses Polytechniques et Universitaires Romandes, pp 27-46. (Cahier de l'IDHEAP no 63, Chavannes-près-Renens: IDHEAP).

Knoepfel, P. and Kissling-Näf, I. (1993) 'Transformation öffentlicher Politiken durch Verräumlichung – Betrachtungen zum gewandelten Verhältnis zwischen Raum und Politik', in A. Héritier, *Policy-Analyse, Kritik und Neuorientierung*, *PVS-Sonderheft*, vol 24, Opladen: Westdeutscher Verlag, pp 267-88.

Knoepfel, P. and Varone, F. (1999) 'Mesurer la performance publique: méfions-nous des terribles simplificateurs', *Politiques et Management Public*, vol 17, no 2, pp 123-45.

Knoepfel, P. and Weidner, H. (1982) 'Formulation and implementation of air quality control programmes: patterns of interest consideration', *Policy & Politics*, vol 10, no 1, pp 85-109.

Knoepfel, P. and Zimmermann, W. (1987) *Oekologisierung von Landwirtschaft. Fünf Geschichten und eine Analyse*, Aarau/Frankfurt-am-Main/Salzburg: Sauerländer.

Knoepfel, P. and Zimmermann, W. (1993) *Gewässerschutz in der Landwirtschaft, Evaluation und Analyse des föderalen Vollzugs*, Bâle: Helbing & Lichtenhahn (série Ecologie & Société, vol 7).

Knoepfel, P., Kissling-Näf, I. and Varone, F. (eds) (2001) *Environmental policies 1982-2000*, Bâle: Helbing & Lichtenhahn.

Knoepfel, P., Varone, F., Imer, J.-M. and Benninghoff, M. (1998) *Evaluation des activités de l'énergie dans la cité*, rapport final, sur mandat de l'Office Fédéral de l'Énergie, Chavannes-près-Renens: IDHEAP.

Knoepfel, P., Bächtiger, C., Bättig, C., Peter, K. and Teuscher, F. (2000) *Politikbeobachtung im Naturschutz: Ein Führungsinstrument für nachhaltige Politik*, Forschungsprojekt im Rahmen des Schwerpunktprogramms Umwelt des Schweizerischen Nationalfonds, Mai.

Knoepfel, P., Eberle, A., Joerchel Anhorn, B., Meyrat, M. and Sager, F. (1999) *Militär und Umwelt im politischen Alltag, Vier Fallstudien für die Ausbildung/Militaire et environnement: La politique au quotidien. Quatre études de cas pour l'enseignement*, sur mandat de l'Office Fédéral du Personnel, Berne: OCFIM, no 614.051, DF 03.99 300.

Knoepfel, P., Enderlin Cavigelli, R., Varone, F., Wälti, S. and Weidner, H. (1997) *Energie 2000: Evaluation der Konfliktlösungsgruppen*, Rapport à l'Office Fédéral de l'Énergie (OFEN), Berne: Office Central Fédéral des Imprimés et du Matériel (OCFIM).

Koelble, T.A. (1995) 'The new institutionalism in political science and sociology', *Comparative Politics*, vol 27, no 2, pp 231-43.

König, K. and Dose, N. (1993) *Instrumente und Formen staatlichen Handelns*, Cologne: Carl Heymanns Verlag KG (Verwaltungswissenschaftliche Abhandlungen, vol 2).

Krasner, S.D. (1984) 'Approaches to the state: alternative conceptions and historical dynamics', *Comparative Politics*, vol 16, no 2, pp 223-46.

Lagroye, J. (1997) *Sociologie politique*, Paris: Presses de la Fondation Nationale des Sciences Politiques and Dalloz.

Lakatos, I. (1970) 'Falsification and the methodology of scientific research programmes', in I. Lakatos and A. Musgrave (eds) *Criticism and the growth of knowledge*, Cambridge: Cambridge University Press, pp 91-196.

Lambeth, E.B. (1978) 'Perceived influence of the press on energy policy making', *Journalism Quarterly*, vol 26, no 2, pp 176-87.

Lane, J.-E. and Ersson, S.O. (2000) *The new institutional politics: Performance and outcomes*, London: Routledge.

Larrue, C. (2000) *Analyser les politiques publiques d'environnement*, Paris: L'Harmattan.

Larrue, C. and Vlassopoulou, C.A. (1999) 'Changing definitions and networks in clean air policies in France', in W. Grant, A. Perl and P. Knoepfel (eds) *The politics of improving urban air quality*, Cheltenham: Edward Elgar, pp 93-106.

Lascoumes, P. (1994) *L'éco-pouvoir*, Paris: La Découverte.

Lascoumes, P. and Setbon, M. (1996) *L'évaluation pluraliste des politiques publiques: Enjeux, pratiques, produits*, Paris: GAPP/Commissariat général du Plan.

Lascoumes, P. and Valuy, J. (1996) 'Les activités publiques conventionnelles (APC): un nouvel instrument de politiques publiques? L'exemple de la protection de l'environnement industriel', *Sociologie du Travail*, vol 4, pp 551-73.

Lasswell, H.D. (1936) *Politics: Who gets what, when, how*, Cleveland, OH: Meridian Books.

Lasswell, H.D. (1951) 'The policy orientation', in D. Lerner and H.D. Laswell (eds) *The policy sciences*, Palo Alto, CA: Stanford University Press.

Lasswell, H.D. and Kaplan, A. (1950) *Power and society: A framework for political inquiry*, New Haven, CT: Yale University Press.

Latour, B. (1991) *Nous n'avons jamais été modernes*, Paris: La Découverte.

Le Galès, P. and Thatcher, M. (1995) *Les réseaux de politique publique. Débat autour des policy networks*, Paris: L'Harmattan.

Le Moigne, J.L. (1990) *La modélisation des systèmes complexes*, Paris: Dunod.

Lehmbruch, G. and Schmitter, P. (eds) (1982) *Patterns of corporatist policy-making*, London: Sage Publications.

Lemieux, V. (1995) *L'étude des politiques publiques: Les acteurs et leur pouvoir*, Sainte-Foy: Les Presses de l'Université Laval.

Lerner, D. and Lasswell, H.D. (eds) (1951) *The policy sciences*, Palo Alto, CA: Stanford University Press.

Lester, P., Bowman, O'M., Goggin, M. and O'Toole, L. (1987) 'Public policy implementation: evolution of the field and agenda for future research', *Policy Studies Review*, vol 7, no 1, pp 200-16.

Levitt, B. and March, J.G. (1988) 'Organizational learning', *Annual Review of Sociology*, vol 14, pp 319-40.

Lijphart, A. (1999) *Patterns of democracy*, New Haven, CT: Yale University Press.

Lindblom, Ch.E. (1959) 'The science of "muddling through"', *Public Administration Review*, vol 39, pp 517-26.

Linder, S.H. and Peters, B.G. (1988) 'The analysis of design or the design of analysis', *Policy Studies Review*, vol 7, no 4, pp 738-50.

Linder, S.H. and Peters, B.G. (1989) 'Instruments of government: perceptions and contexts', *Journal of Public Policy*, vol 9, no 1, pp 35-58.

Linder, S.H. and Peters, B.G. (1990) 'The design of instruments for public policy', in S.S. Nagel (ed) *Policy theory and policy evaluation*, New York, NY: Greenwood Press, pp 103-19.

Linder, S.H. and Peters, B.G. (1991) 'The logic of public policy design: linking policy actors and plausible instruments', *Knowledge and Policy*, vol 4, nos 1-2, pp 125-51.

Linder, W. (1987) *La décision politique en Suisse. Genèse et mise en oeuvre de la législation*, Lausanne: Réalités Sociales.

Linder, W. (1989) 'Wissenschaftliche Beratung der Politk', *Annuaire Suisse de Science Politique*, vol 29, Berne: Haupt.

Linder, W. (1994) *Swiss democracy: Possible solutions to conflicts in multicultural societies*, New York, NY: St Martin's Press.

Lipsky, M. (1980) *Street-level bureaucracy*, New York, NY: Russell Sage.

Lowi, T.J. (1972) 'Four systems of policy, politics, and choice', *Public Administration Review*, vol 32, no 4, pp 298-310.

Lowndes, V. (1996) 'Varieties of new institutionalism. A critical appraisal', *Public Administration*, vol 74, pp 181-97.

Luhmann, N. (1984) *Soziale Systeme. Grundriss einer allgemeinen Theorie*, Frankfurt: Suhrkamp.

Luhmann, N. (1989) 'Politische Steuerung: Ein Diskussionsbeitrag', *Politische Vierteljahresschrift* (PVS), vol 1 (mars), pp 4-9.

Lukes, S. (1974) *Power: A radical view*, London: Macmillan.

Lüthi, R. (1997) *Die Legislativkommissionen der Schweizerischen Bundesversammlung. Institutionnelle Veränderungen und das Verhalten von Parlamentsmitgliedern*, Berner Studien zur Politikwissenschaft, Band 4, Bern: Haupt.

McCombs, M. and Shaw, D.L. (1972) 'The agenda-setting function of mass media', *Public Opinion Quarterly*, vol 36, pp 176-87.

Majone, G. (1996) 'Public policy and administration: ideas, interests and institutions', in R.E. Goodin and H.-D. Klingemann (eds) *A new handbook of political science*, Oxford: Oxford University Press, pp 610-27.

Maloney, W. and Richardson, J. (1994) 'Water policy-making in England: policy communities under pressure?', *Environment Politics*, vol 34, no 4, pp 110-38.

Manfrini, P.-L. (1996) 'Réflexions sur l'objet du recours en droit genevois', *Revue de Droit Administratif et de Droit Fiscal et Revue Genevoise de Droit Public*, Lausanne, Genève, vol 52, nos 3/4, pp 253-64.

March, J.G. and Olsen, J.P. (1984) 'The new institutionalism: organizational factors in political life', *American Political Science Review*, no 78, pp 734-49.

March, J.G. and Olsen, J.P. (1989) *Rediscovering institutions. The organizational basis of politics*, New York, NY: The Free Press.

References

Marsh, D. and Rhodes, R.A.W. (1992) *Policy networks in British government*, Oxford: Oxford University Press.

Mastronardi, P. (1997) 'Aspects juridiques du nouveau management public', CETEL (Université de Genève), *Nouvelle gestion publique. Chances et limites d'une réforme de l'administration*, Travaux CETEL no 48, Genève: Université de Genève, pp 93-103.

Mayntz, R. (1980) 'Einleitung. Die Entwicklung des analytischen Paradigmas der Implementationsforschung', in R. Mayntz, *Implementation politischer Programme. Empirische Forschungsberichte*, Königstein/Ts: Athenäum, pp 1-19.

Mayntz, R. (ed) (1980) *Implementation politischer Programme. Empirische Forschungsberichte*, Königsstein/Ts: Athenäum.

Mayntz, R. (ed) (1983) *Implementation politischer Programme II. Ansätze zur Theoriebildung*, Opladen: Westdeutcher Verlag.

Mayntz, R. and Scharpf, F.W. (1995) 'Der Ansatz des akteurszentrierten Institutionalismus', in R. Mayntz and F.W. Scharpf (eds) *Gesellschaftliche Selbstregelung und politische Steuerung*, Frankfurt am Main: Campus, pp 39-72.

Maystre, L.Y., Pictet, J. and Simos, J. (1994) *Méthodes multicritères ELECTRE: Description, conseils pratiques et cas d'application à la gestion environnementale*, Lausanne: Presses Polytechniques et Universitaires Romandes.

Mény, Y. and Thoenig, J.C. (1989) *Politiques publiques*, coll Thémis Science Politique, Paris: Presses Universitaires de France.

Mény, Y., Muller, P. and Quermone, J.-L. (eds) (1995) *Politiques publiques en Europe*, Paris: L'Harmattan.

Migaud, D. (2000) *Le contrôle de la dépense publique*, Intervention au Colloque de la Société Française d'Évaluation, Rennes, 15-16 juin.

Moe, T.M. (1980) 'A calculus of group membership', *American Journal of Political Science*, vol 24, pp 543-632.

Monnier, E. (1992) *Evaluation de l'action des pouvoirs publics* (2ème édition), Paris: Economica.

Moor, P. (1994) *Droit administratif. Vol. I: Les fondements généraux* (2ème édition), Bern: Stämpfli.

Moor, P. (1997) *Dire le droit: Revue européenne de sciences sociales*, tome XXXV, no 105, Genève et Paris: Droz, pp 33-55.

Morand, C.-A. (ed) (1991) *Les instruments d'action de l'etat*, Bâle: Helbing & Lichtenhahn.

Morand, C.-A. (ed) (1993) *Evaluation législative et loi expérimentale*, Aix-en-Provence: Presses Universitaires d'Aix-en-Provence.

Morand, C.-A. et al (1991a) *L'etat propulsif. Contribution à l'étude des instruments d'action de l'etat*, Paris: Publisud.

Morand, C.-A. et al (1991b) 'Les nouveaux instruments d'action de l'Etat et le droit', in C.-A. Morand (ed) *Les instruments d'action de l'etat*, Bâle: Helbing & Lichtenhahn, pp 237-56.

Morin, E. (1977) *La méthode, tome 1: La nature*, Paris: Seuil.

Morin, E. (1980) *La méthode, tome 2: La vie de la vie*, Paris: Seuil.

Müller, F. (1971) *Theorie der Normativität*, Berlin: Duncker & Humbolt.

Muller, P. (1985) 'Un schéma d'analyse des politiques publiques', *Revue Française de Science Politique*, vol 35, no 2, pp 165-88.

Muller, P. (1990) *Les politiques publiques*, Paris: Presses Universitaires de France.

Muller, P. (1995) 'Les politiques publiques comme construction d'un rapport au monde', in A. Faure, A.G. Pollet and P. Warin (eds) *La construction de sens dans les politiques publiques. Débats autour de la notion de référentiel*, Paris: L'Harmattan, pp 153-79.

Muller, P. (2000) 'L'analyse cognitive des politiques publiques: vers une sociologie de l'action publique', *Revue Française de Science Politique*, vol 50, no 2, pp 189-207.

Muller, P. and Surel, Y. (1998) *L'analyse des politiques publiques*, Paris: Montchrestien.

Muller, P., Thoenig, J-C., Duran, P., Leca, J. (1996) 'Forum: Enjeux, controverses et tendances de l'analyse des politiques publiques', *Revue Française de Science Politique*, vol 46, no 1, pp 96–133.

Müller, U., Zimmermann, W., Neuenschwander, P., Tobler, A., Wyss, S. and Alder, L. (1997) *Katastrophen als Herausforderung für Verwaltung und die Politik. Kontinuitäten und Diskontinuitäten*, Zurich: vdf (Schlussbericht NFP 31).

Musgrave, R.A. (1959) *The theory of public finance*, New York, NY: McGraw-Hill.

Nagel, S.S. (ed) (1990) *Policy theory and policy evaluation*, New York: Greenwood Press.

Newman, J. (2001) *Modernising governance*, London: Sage Publications.

Niskanen, W.A. (1971) *Bureaucracy and representative government*, New York, NY: Aldine-Atherton.

Norgaard, A.S. (1996) 'Rediscovering reasonable rationality in institutional analysis', *European Journal of Political Research*, vol 29, pp 31-57.

North, D.C. (1990) *Institutions, institutional change and economic performance*, Cambridge: Cambridge University Press.

Nullmeyer, F. (1993) 'Wissen und Policy-Forschung. Wissenspolitologie und rhetorisch-dialektisches Handlungsmodell', *PVS Sonderheft*, vol 24, pp 175-96.

References

Odershook, P.C. (1986) *Game theory and political theory*, Cambridge: Cambridge University Press.

Offe, C. (1972) *Strukturprobleme des modernen Staates*, Frankfurt: Suhrkamp.

Olson, M. (1965) *The logic of collective action: Public goods and the theory of groups*, Cambridge: Harvard University Press.

Ostrom, E. (1990) *Governing the commons: The evolution of institutions for collective actions*, Cambridge: Cambridge University Press.

Ostrom, E. et al (1993) *Institutional incentives and sustainable development: Infrastructure policies in perspective*, Boulder, CO: Westview Press.

Padioleau, J.G. (1982) *L'état au concret*, Paris: Presses Universitaires de France.

Pal, L.A. (1992) *Public policy analysis*, Scarborough: Nelson.

Parsons, T. (1951) *The social system*, New York, NY: Free Press.

Parsons, W. (1995) *Public policy: An introduction to the theory and practice of policy analysis*, Aldershot: Edward Elgar.

Perret, B. (1997) 'Les enjeux épistémologiques de l'évaluation', in Conseil Scientifique de l'Evaluation, *L'évaluation en développement*, Paris: La Documentation Française, pp 283-312.

Peters, B.G. (1998) 'The problem of policy problems', Paper presented at the Southern Political Science Association, Atlanta (Georgia).

Pétry, F. (1995) 'The party agenda model: election programmes and government spending in Canada', *Canadian Journal of Political Science*, vol 28, no 1, pp 51-84.

Pierre, J. (ed) (2000) *Debating governance*, Oxford: Oxford University Press.

Plein, C. (1994) 'Agenda setting, problem definition and policy studies', *Policy Studies Journal*, vol 22, no 4, pp 701-4.

Pollitt, C. (2003) *The essential public manager*, Maidenhead: Open University Press.

Pollitt, C. and Bouckaert, G. (2000) *Public management reform: A comparative analysis*, Oxford: Oxford University Press.

Powell, W.W. and Di Maggio, P.J. (eds) (1991) *The new institutionalism in organizational analysis*, Chicago, IL: Chicago University Press.

Power, M. (1997) *The audit society*, Oxford: Oxford University Press.

Pressman, J.L. and Wildavsky, A. (1973) *Implementation*, Berkeley, CA: University of California Press.

Quermonne, J.L. (1985) 'Les politiques institutionnelles. Essai d'interprétation et de typologie', in M. Grawitz and J. Leca, *Les politiques publiques*, 4ème tome du Traité de Science Politique, pp 61-88.

Ranney, A. (1968) *Political science and public policy*, Chicago, IL: Markham Publishing.

Rhodes, R.A.W. (1981) *Control and power in central-local government relations*, Aldershot: Gower.

Richards, D. and Smith, M.J. (2002) *Governance and public policy in the UK*, Oxford: Oxford University Press.

Richardson, J. (ed) (1982) *Policy styles in Western Europe*, London: Allen and Unwin.

Richardson, J. and Jordan, G. (1979) *Governing under pressure*, Oxford: Martin Robertson.

Riker, W.H. (1980) 'Implications from the dis-equilibrium of majority rule for the study of institutions', *American Political Science Review*, vol 74, pp 432-47.

Rist, R. (1990) *Program evaluation and the management of government*, New Brunswick, NJ: Transaction Publishers.

Rochefort, D.A. and Cobb, R.W. (1993) 'Problem definition, agenda access and policy choice', *Policy Studies Journal*, vol 21, no 1, pp 56-69.

Rogers, E.M. et al (1991) *AIDS in the 1980s: The agenda setting process for a public issue*, Austin, TX: Association for Education in Journalism and Mass Communication.

Rose, R. and Davies, P.L. (1994) *Inheritance in public policy: Change without choice in Britain*, New Haven, CT: Yale University Press.

Rossi, P.H. and Freeman, H.E. (1993) *Evaluation: A systematic approach* (5th edn), Newbury Park/London: Sage Publications.

Sabatier, P. (1986) 'Top-down and bottom-up approaches to implementation research: a critical analysis and suggested synthesis', *Journal of Public Policy*, vol 6, no 1, pp 21-48.

Sabatier, P. (1987) 'Knowledge, policy-oriented learning and policy change: an advocacy coalition framework', *Knowledge: Creation, Diffusion, Utilization*, vol 8, no 4, pp 649-92.

Sabatier, P. and Jenkins-Smith, C.H. (eds) (1993) *Policy change and learning: An advocacy coalitions approach*, San Francisco, CA: Westview Press.

Sabatier, P. and Mazmanian, D. (1979) 'The conditions of effective implementation: a guide to accomplishing policy objectives', *Policy Analysis*, vol 5, no 4, pp 481-504.

Salisbury, R.H. (1968) 'The analysis of public policy: a search for theory and rules', in A. Ranney, *Political science and public policy*, Chicago, IL: Markham Publishing, pp 154-72.

References

Scharpf, F. (1983) 'Interessenlage der Adressaten und Spielräume der Implementation bei Anreizprogrammen', in R. Mayntz (ed) *Implementation politischer Programme. Ansätze zur Theoriebildung*, Opladen: Westdeutscher Verlag, pp 89-116.

Scharpf, F.W. (1997) *Games real actors play: Actor-centred institutionalism in policy research*, Boulder, CO: Westview Press.

Schattschneider, E.E. (1960) *The semi-sovereign people*, New York, NY: Holt.

Scheberle, D. (1994) 'Radon and asbestos: a study of agenda setting and causal stories', *Policy Studies Journal*, vol 22, no 1, pp 74-86.

Schneider, A. and Ingram, H. (1990) 'Behavioural assumptions of policy tools', *Journal of Politics*, vol 52, no 2, pp 510-29.

Schneider, A. and Ingram, H. (1993) 'The social construction of target populations: implications for politics and policy', *American Political Science Review*, vol 87, no 2, pp 334-47.

Schneider, A.L. and Ingram, H. (1997) *Policy design for democracy*, Lawrence, KS: University Press of Kansas.

Schneider, S. et al (1990) *Pilotversuch Zürich-Hottingen*, Zürich: Planungsbüro Jud.

Schneider, S. et al (1992) *Parkierungsbeschränkungen mit Blauer Zone und Anwohnerparkkarte: Empfehlungen für die Einführung*, Zürich: Planungsbüro Jud.

Schneider, S., Häberling, D. and Keiser, S. (1995) *Erfolgskontrolle Blaue Zone Bern-Kirchenfeld*, Zürich: Planungsbüro Jud.

Schöneich, P. and Busset-Henchoz, M.-C. (1998) *Les Ormonans et les Leysenouds face aux risques naturels*, Zurich: vdf (rapport final PNR 31).

Schulz, H.-R., Nuggli, C. and Hübschle, J. (1993) *Wohneigentumsförderung durch den Bund. Die Wirksamkeit des Wohnbau- und Eigentumsförderungsgesetzes (WEG)*, Bern: Schriftenreihe Wohnungswesen, Band 55.

Sciarini, P. (1994) *La Suisse face à la Communauté européenne et au GATT: Le cas test de la politique agricole*, Genève: Georg.

Scott, J. (1991) *Social network analysis: A handbook*, London: Sage Publications.

Scott, W.R. and Meyer, J.W. (eds) (1994) *Institutional environments and organizations: Structural complexity and individualism*, Thousand Oaks, CA: Sage Publications.

Segrestin, D. (1985) *Le phénomène corporatiste: Essai sur l'avenir des systèmes professionnels en France*, Paris: Fayard.

Self, P. (1993) *Government by the market: The politics of public choice*, London: Macmillan.

Sharkansky, I. (1970) *Policy analysis in political science*, Chicago, IL: Markham.
Shepsle, K.A. (1979) 'Institutional arrangements and equilibrium in multidimensional voting models', *American Journal of Political Science*, vol 23, pp 27-60.
Shepsle, K.A. (1989) 'Studying institutions. Some lessons from the rational choice approach', *Journal of Theoretical Politics*, vol 1, no 2, pp 131-47.
Simeon, R. (1976) 'Studying public policies', *Canadian Journal of Political Science*, vol 9, no 4, pp 548-80.
Simon, H.A. (1957) *Models of man: Social and rational*, New York, NY: John Wiley.
Skocpol, T. (1985) 'Bringing the sate back in: strategies of analysis in current research', in P.B. Evans, D. Rueschemeyer and T. Skocpol (eds) *Bringing the state back in*, Cambridge: Cambridge University Press.
Smith, B.C. (1976) *Policy making in British government*, London: Martin Robertson.
Smith, M.J. (1993) *Pressure, power and policy*, Hemel Hempstead: Harvester Wheatsheaf.
Spector, M. and Kitsuse, J.I. (1987) *Constructing social problems*, New York, NY: Aldine de Gruyter.
Steinmo, S., Thelen, K. and Longstreth, F. (eds) (1992) *Structuring politics. Historical institutionalism in comparative analysis*, New York, NY: Cambridge University Press.
Stone, D.A. (1989) 'Causal stories and the formation of policy agendas', *Political Science Quarterly*, vol 104, no 2, pp 281-300.
Stone, D.A. (2002) *Policy paradox* (2nd edn), New York, NY: Norton.
Surel, Y. (2000) 'The role of cognitive and normative frames in policy-making', *Journal of European Public Policy*, vol 7, no 4, pp 495-512.
Taylor, D. and Balloch, S. (eds) (2005) *The politics of evaluation*, Bristol: The Policy Press.
Taylor-Gooby, P. (ed) (2004) *New risks, new welfare: The transformation of the European welfare state*, Oxford: Oxford University Press.
Terribilini, S. (1995) *De la distributivité des politiques régulatrices. Discriminations socio-spatiales en matière de modération de trafic. Constat et causes*, Cahier de l'IDHEAP Nr 151, Chavannes-près-Renens: IDHEAP.

Terribilini, S. (1999) 'Fédéralisme et inégalités sociales dans la mise en oeuvre des politiques à incidence spatiale', thèse présentée à l'IDHEAP, fondation associée à l'Université de Lausanne, pour obtenir le grade de docteur en administration publique, Chavannes-près-Renens: IDHEAP.

Theys, J. (ed) (1991) *Environnement, science et politiques: "Les experts sont formels"*, Paris: Cahier du GERMES, 3 volumes.

Thoenig, J.-C. (1985) 'L'analyse des politiques publiques', in M. Grawitz and J. Leca (eds) *Traité de Science Politique*, tome no 4, Paris: Presses Universitaires de France, pp 1-60.

Thoenig, J.-C. (1998) 'Politiques publiques et action publique', *Revue Internationale de Politique Comparée*, vol 5, no 2, pp 295-314.

Toke, D. and Marsh, D. (2003) 'Policy networks and the GM crops issue: assessing the utility of a dialectic model of policy networks', *Public Administration*, vol 81, no 2, pp 229-51.

Touraine, A. (1984) *Le retour de l'acteur: Essai de sociologie*, Paris: Fayard.

Treiber, H. (1984) 'Warum man nicht die Erwartungen hegen kann, beim Blick durch ein Mikroskop den ganzen Elefanten zu sehen', *Programme National de Recherche no 6*, Bulletin no 7, pp 85-109.

Trumbo, C. (1995) *Longitudinal modeling of public issues: An application of the agenda-setting process to the issue of global warming*, Austin, TX: Association for Education in Journalism and Mass Communication.

Universität Zürich, Gerichtlich-medizinisches Institut (1977) *Unfalluntersuchung Rücksitzpassagiere und Kinder*, Im Auftrag des Eidg Justiz und Polizeidepartementes, Von Hansjörg Sprenger und Félix Waltz, Bern: EJPD.

Varone, F. (1998a) 'De l'irrationalité institutionnelle de la Nouvelle Gestion Publique', in M. Hufty (ed) *La pensée comptable. Etat, néolibéralisme, nouvelle gestion publique*, Collection Enjeux, Paris: Presses Universitaires de France, pp 125-39.

Varone, F. (1998b) *Le choix des instruments des politiques publiques*, Bern: Haupt.

Vlassopoulou, C.A. (1999) 'La lutte contre la pollution atmosphérique urbaine en France et en Grèce. Définitions des problèmes publics et changement de politique', thèse de doctorat, Paris: Université Panthéon-ASSAS PARIS II.

Volvo Car Corporation and Swedish Road Safety Office (1980) *Injury-reducing affect of seatbelts and rear passengers*, Göteborg: Volvo AB.

Wade, H.W.R. (1982) *Administration law* (5th edn), Oxford: Oxford University Press.

Walker, J.L. (1977) 'Setting the agenda in the US Senate: a theory of problem selection', *British Journal of Political Science*, vol 7, pp 423-55.

Walker, J.L. (1983) 'The origins and maintenance of interest groups in America', *American Political Science Review*, vol 77, pp 390-406.

Wälti, S. (1999) *Les politiques à incidence spatiale. Vers un mode de gestion médiatif?*, thèse présentée à l'IDHEAP, fondation associée à l'Université de Lausanne, pour obtenir le grade de docteur en administration publique, Chavannes-près-Renens: IDHEAP.

Warin, P. (1993) *Les usagers dans l'évaluation des politiques publiques: Étude des relations de service*, Paris: L'Harmattan.

Weale, A. (1992) *The new politics of pollution*, Manchester: Manchester University Press.

Weaver, R.K. and Rockman, B.A. (eds) (1993) *Do institutions matter? Government capabilities in the United States and abroad*, Washington, DC: Brookings Institution.

Weidner, H. (1993) *La médiation en tant qu'instrument politique permettant de résoudre les conflits sur l'environnement. A l'exemple de l'Allemagne*, Cahiers de l'IDHEAP, no 117, Lausanne: IDHEAP.

Weidner, H. (1997) *Alternative dispute resolution in environmental conflicts: Experiences in twelve countries*, Berlin: Sigma.

Weidner, H. and Knoepfel, P. (1983) 'Innovation durch international vergleichende Politikanalyse dargestellt am Beispiel der Luftreinhaltepolitik', in R. Mayntz (ed) *Implementation politischer Programme II. Ansätze zur Theoriebildung*, Opladen: Westdeutscher Verlag.

Weimer, D.L. (ed) (1995) *Institutional design*, Boston, MA: Kluwer Academic Publishers.

Weir, M. and Skocpol, T. (1985) 'State structure and the possibilities for Keynesian responses to the Great Depression in Sweden, Britain, and the United States', in P.B. Evans, D. Rueschemeyer and T. Skocpol (eds) *Bringing the state back in*, Cambridge: Cambridge University Press.

Weiss, J. (1989) 'The powers of problem definition: the case of government paperwork', *Policy Sciences*, vol 22, pp 97-121.

Whitmore, R. (1984) 'Modelling the policy/implementation distinction', *Policy & Politics*, vol 12, no 3, pp 241-68.

Wildavsky, A. (1979) *Speaking truth to power: The art and craft of policy analysis*, Boston, MA: Little, Brown.

Williamson, O. (1985) *The economic institutions of capitalism*, New York, NY: Free Press.

Windhoff-Héritier, A. (1987) *Policy-Analyse. Eine Einführung*, Frankfurt/New York, NY: Campus.

Wollmann, H. (1980) 'Implementationsforschung – eine Chance für kritische Verwaltungsforschung?', in H. Wollmann (ed) *Politik im Dickicht der Bürokratie*, Opladen: Westdeutscher Verlag.

Wollmann, H. (ed) (1980) *Politik im Dickicht der Bürokratie*, Opladen: Westdeutscher Verlag.

Zimmermann, W. and Knoepfel, P. (1997) 'Evaluation of the Federal Office of Environmental Protection: across two levels of government', in O. Rieper and J. Toulemond, *Politics and practices of intergovernmental evaluation*, New Brunswick, NJ/London: Transaction Publishers.

Index

The concepts of 'actors' (other than public ones when specifically discussed), 'political-administrative programmes', 'political administrative arrangements' and institutions are so central to the analysis that they are not indexed. Some other concepts which are indexed such as 'policy resources', 'institutional rules', 'end beneficiaries', 'target groups' and 'third parties' are indexed where they are given particular attention, but also crop up throughout the book.

A

action plans 19, 188, 198-206, 208-9, 211, 239, 259, 260, 261, 270, 314
administrative inertia 12, 22, 104, 116, 149
advocacy coalitions 46-7
agenda setting 31, 32, 35, 114, 117, 120, Ch 7, 254
audit 10, 206, 241

B

benchmarking 208, 235
beneficiaries, *see* 'end beneficiaries' and 'third parties'
'bottom-up' approach, the 36, 177, 194-6
bounded rationality 7, 96
budgetary tools, see 'money'
bureaucrats 4, 12, 54

C

causal hypothesis/es 57-8, 60, 108, 139, 152, 156-7, 226, 230-2, 236, 237, Ch 11
causal stories 118-9, 136-7, 139
causality model, *see* causal hypothesis
civil servants 8, 43, 63, 67-8, 166, 191, *see also* 'bureaucrats' and 'public actors'
cognitive resources, *see also* 'information' 71-3
comparative analysis 12, 13, 110 (note 4), 123, 171, 174, 246, 274-5, 283-4
comparative politics 13
consensus, as a resource 18, 63, 65, 76-7, 82-6, 122, 145-6, 183-4
constituent elements
 of a political-administrative arrangement 172-3
 of a political-administrative programme 153-63
 of a public policy 25-30
constituent policies 25, 102
constitutional state, the 46, 53, 89 (note 2), 102, 105, 106, 161, 181, 285
cost-benefit analysis 9, 233

D

decentralisation 8, 53, 104, 143, 152, 159-61, 167, 169, 176-7, 267, 270, 274
definitions of public policy 23-5
democracy 11, 46, 53, 63, 76, 105, 107, 130, 143, 161, 279, 285
 direct democracy 99, 102, 141, 143, 146, 184
discretion 42, 168, 191, 209, 270

E

economics 7-8, 19, 35, 43, 92, 93, 101, 155-6, 190, 246, 274
effectiveness 227, 230-2, 236, 237, 241, 242-3, 246
efficiency 98, 115, 202, 204, 221, 227, 228, 233-4, 235, 236, 241, 242-3
electoral competition 60, 142-3
end beneficiaries 18, 45, 53-7, 115, 121, 182, 200, 203-4, 212-17, 221-2, 226-7, 259, 260, 266, 270, 282
European Union, the 9, 141-2, 163, 166, 185, 198
evaluation, *see* 'policy evaluation'

F

federalism 8, 48, 53, 54, 70, 74-5, 106, 152, 159-61, 163-4, 166-7, 169, 170-1, 173, 176, 178, 191, 198, 268
force, as a resource 18, 65, 84

G

game theory 12, 92
globalism, global influences 99, 149
governance 46, 110 (note 6), 284-6

H

horizontal coordination 46, 175-6

I

ideological paradigm shifts 110-1
impacts, *see* 'policy impacts'

315

implementation, *see* 'policy implementation'
implementation deficits 18, 164, 190-1, 201, 209
implementation game(s) 190, 195, 213
implementation strategy 189
incrementalism 7
information, as a resource 18, 59, 65, 71-3, 77, 80, 83, 85, 88, 108, 110 (note 5), 122, 140, 141, 142, 144, 145, 158, 163, 184, 213, 243-4, 247, 268, 269
infrastructure, as a resource 18, 65, 79-81, 87, 146, 184
inspection 76, 206
institutional capital 108, 121
institutional change 97-101
institutional rules 4, 18, 52, 64, Ch 5, 111, 113, 115, 116, 117, 120, 121, 123, 135, 140, 143-4, 147, 159, 161-3, 169, 170, 172, 179, 181, 183-4, 189, 190, 191, 197-8, 209-10, 240, 241, 251, 252, 257-61, 264-5, 286-8
instruments, *see* 'policy instruments'
interest groups 5, 22, 91, 92, 98, 126, 133, 140-2, 144-5, 163, 182, 183, 190, 192, 215, 282
intervention hypothesis/es 57, 59, 60, 152, 156, 165, 228-30, 236, Ch 11, 274-7 285, 287
intervention instruments, *see* 'policy instruments'

L

law, as a resource 18, 63, 64, 65-6, 77, 83, 85, 87, 88, 122, 141, 146, 152, 166-7, 173, 184, 191, 199-200, 207, 212, 266
legitimacy, legitimation 12, 28, 29, 65-6, 76-7, 81-3, 107-8, 152, 173, 235, 254-5, 256, 279
liberal state, the 24-5
local government 53, 68, 70, 160, 167, 206

M

Marxism, *see* neo-Marxism
media, the impact of 22, 32, 82, 131, 139-40, 244
mobilisation of bias, the 13, *see also* non-decisions
mobilising action through evaluation 244-6
money, as a resource 18, 63, 65, 69-71, 77, 85, 87, 88, 143, 184, 161, 209, 266, 269
monitoring 48, 71-2, 88, 105, 162, 167, 206, 208, 215, 243, 247

N

neo-corporatism 4, 13, 214, 273
neo-liberalism 13, 273, 279
neo-managerialism 4, 6
neo-Marxism 4, 12, 13, 22, 214, 273
neo-Weberianism 12, 22
network theory 13
New Public Management 8, 63, 71, 157, 193, 199, 230, 267
non-decisions 29, 130-1, *see also* 'mobilisation of bias'

O

organised groups, *see* 'interest groups'
organisation, as a resource 56, 74-5
outcomes, *see* 'policy outcomes'
outputs, *see* 'policy outputs'
outsourcing 69-70, *see also* 'privatisation'

P

path dependency 190
personnel, as a resource 18, 63, 65, 66-9, 74, 84, 85, 132, 141, 144, 160, 184, 209, 270
Planning, Programming and Budgeting systems (PPBS) 35, 127, 235
pluralism 4
policy communities 5, 46-7
policy cycle, the 30-7, 113-6, 118, 122-3, 127-8, 242, 249-50, 253, 276-7
policy entrepreneurs 134, 143
policy evaluation 9-10, 31, 32-3, 34, 114, 120, 155-6, Ch 10, 255, 283
policy formulation 17, 31, 32-3, Ch 8
policy impacts 210-11, 222-5, 227, 228-30, 236
policy implementation 11, 18, 24-5, 31, 32-5, 87, 88-9, 114, 118, 120, 159-61, 162, 164, Ch 9, 225, 236, 242, 255, 260-1
policy instruments 17, 156-9, 165, *see also* 'policy resources'
policy networks 5, 52, 162 (note 3), 173-4, 178, 189-90, 190, 192
policy outcomes 108-9, 191, 195, 206, 212, 213, 221-2, 224, 226-7, 230, 233-4, 236, 237, 255, 260, 267
policy outputs 11, 28, 33, 34, 51, 76, 88, 114, 115, 120, 151, 164, 172, 174, 189, 190-1, 194, 197-8, 201, 203, 206-12, 221-9, 231, 234-7, 243, 255, 260-2, 267-9
policy programming 18, 34, 75, 113, 114, 116-19, 128, 149, Ch 8, 188, 197, 215, 235, 254
policy resources 12, 18-19, Ch 4, 120, 122, 183-4, 198, 204-5, 236, 257-61, 266, *see also* the listed resources: 'consensus', 'force', 'information', 'infrastructure', 'law', 'money', 'personnel', 'political support', 'property' and 'time'

Index

policy stages, *see* 'policy cycle'
policy transfer 149
political science 3-5, 10, 19, 35, 91, 131, 274, 278
political support, as a resource 18, 63, 65, 81-3, 141-3, 145, 146, 184, 198, 217, 268
politics of evaluation, the 241-9
pressure groups, *see* 'interest groups'
privatisation 50, 79, 81, 100, 132, 142, 205-6, 286, 288
professionals 54, 108
property, as a resource 65, 79-80, 82, 84, 87, 88
public actors 12, 23, 28, 30, 46, 48-53, 54, 65, 70, 73, 75, 76, 78, 79, 80, 84, 87, 102, 103-4, 114, 115, 130, 144-5, 159, 172-3, 176, 180, 192, 197, 217-8, 224-5 256, 265, 278-9, 285-7
public choice theory 4, 12, 56, 92, 97, 100, 109 (note 1), 142
public management 7, 9, 12, 19, 85, 230, *see also* 'New Public Management'
public problems 11, 21-3, 26-8, 32, 35, 125-37, 142, 146, 148-9, 218, 235, 236, 261, 280
punctuated equilibrium 148

R

research hypotheses Ch 11

S

social class 4, 12, 60
social construction, of problems 126-9, 135-6
social movements 22, 131, 140-1, 144, 147, 214, 282
social problems 21-3, 26, 32, 102, 126-30, 132, 135, 147-8, 224, 227
sociology 6, 7, 11, 14 (notes 2 and 5), 19, 35, 63, 64, 85, 93, 131, 192, 194, 278
state theory 3-5, 12-13, 273-5
street-level bureaucracy 193, 209
symbols, manipulation of 59, 83, 93, 94, 136-7, 248

T

target groups 18, 22, 24, 26-7, 33, 45, 53-60, 75-7, 115, 121, 139, 151, 157-8, 164-5, 182, 192, 195, 198, 200, 202, 209, 211, 212-17, 222-5, 228, 231, 236, 255, 267-70, 284
think-tanks 143
third party groups 54-6, 121, 182, 200, 213, 217-18, 257
time, as a resource 18, 65, 78, 81, 83, 85, 87, 140, 146, 184
'top-down' approach, the 36

training of public officials 66-9, 75, 86, 108
triangle of actors, the 18, 45, 56-61, 117, 121, 139, 214, 218, 251-2, 257
types of
 actors 45-56
 institutional rules 108-9
 policy problems 137-8

U

uses of evaluation 241-9

V

vertical coordination 46, 174, 176-82, 254, 270
violence, *see* 'force as a resource'
votes, voting, *see* 'electoral competition'

W

Weberianism, *see* 'neo-Weberianism'

317

Printed in Great Britain
by Amazon